QUEER KINSHIP AFTER WILDE

Queer Kinship after Wilde: Transnational Decadence and the Family
draws on archival materials, including diaries, correspondence,
unpublished manuscripts, and photograph albums, to tell the story
of individuals with ties to late-Victorian Decadence and Oscar Wilde
who rethought and revised kinship, community, and the concept of
the family in the early twentieth century. These post-Victorian
Decadents and Decadent modernists turned to the fin-de-siècle past
for ideas that might allow them to operate outside of the heteronormative boundaries restricting the practice of marriage and the
family, and they engaged in translation, travel, and transnational
collaboration in pursuit of different models of connection that might
facilitate their disentanglement from conventional sexual and gender
ideals. *Queer Kinship after Wilde* attends to the successes and failures
that resulted from these experiments, the new approaches to affiliation inflected by a cosmopolitan or global perspective that occurred
within these networks, and the practices marked by Decadence's
troubling patterns of Orientalism and racial fetishism.

KRISTIN MAHONEY is Associate Professor in the Department of
English and Faculty Fellow in the Center for Gender in a Global
Context at Michigan State University. Her first book, *Literature and
the Politics of Post-Victorian Decadence*, was published by Cambridge
University Press in 2015.

T0384493

QUEER KINSHIP
AFTER WILDE

Transnational Decadence and the Family

KRISTIN MAHONEY

Michigan State University

CAMBRIDGE
UNIVERSITY PRESS

Shaftesbury Road, Cambridge CB2 8EA, United Kingdom

One Liberty Plaza, 20th Floor, New York, NY 10006, USA

477 Williamstown Road, Port Melbourne, VIC 3207, Australia

314–321, 3rd Floor, Plot 3, Splendor Forum, Jasola District Centre, New Delhi – 110025, India

103 Penang Road, #05–06/07, Visioncrest Commercial, Singapore 238467

Cambridge University Press is part of Cambridge University Press & Assessment, a department of the University of Cambridge.

We share the University's mission to contribute to society through the pursuit of education, learning and research at the highest international levels of excellence.

www.cambridge.org
Information on this title: www.cambridge.org/9781009011501

DOI: 10.1017/9781009019682

First published 2022
First paperback edition 2024

A catalogue record for this publication is available from the British Library

Library of Congress Cataloging-in-Publication data
NAMES: Mahoney, Kristin Mary, author.
TITLE: Queer kinship after Wilde : transnational decadence and the family / Kristin Mahoney.
DESCRIPTION: Cambridge ; New York, NY : Cambridge University Press, 2022. | Includes bibliographical references and index.
IDENTIFIERS: LCCN 2022025805 (print) | LCCN 2022025806 (ebook) | ISBN 9781316519912 (hardback) | ISBN 9781009011501 (paperback) | ISBN 9781009019682 (epub)
SUBJECTS: LCSH: Wilde, Oscar, 1854-1900–Influence. | Decadence (Literary movement) | Homosexuality and literature–History–20th century. | Homosexuality and literature–History–19th century. | Families–Philosophy. | Modernism (Literature) | BISAC: LITERARY CRITICISM / European / English, Irish, Scottish, Welsh
CLASSIFICATION: LCC LCC PR5827.I52 M35 2022 (print) | LCC PR5827.I52 (ebook) | DDC 828/.809–dc23/eng/20220609
LC record available at https://lccn.loc.gov/2022025805
LC ebook record available at https://lccn.loc.gov/2022025806

ISBN   978-1-316-51991-2   Hardback
ISBN   978-1-009-01150-1   Paperback

Contents

List of Figures   *page* vii
Acknowledgments   ix

Introduction   1

PART I QUEERING KINSHIP/KINSHIP AS QUEER POLITICS

1   The Son of Oscar Wilde: Cosmopolitanism and Textual
    Kinship   33

2   "Out and Out from the Family to the Community":
    The Housmans and the Politics of Queer Sibling
    Devotion   57

PART II QUEER RETREAT AND COSMOPOLITAN COMMUNITY

3   An Extraordinary Marriage: The Mackenzies
    and the Queer Cosmopolitanism of Capri   95

4   Decadent Bachelordom and Transnational Adoption:
    Harold Acton in China   126

PART III DECADENT MODERNISM AND EROTICIZED
KINSHIP

5   Richard Bruce Nugent's "Geisha Man": Harlem
    Decadence, Multiraciality, and Incest Fantasy   159

v

6 Hallowed Incest: Eric Gill, Indian Aesthetics, and
  Queer Catholicism   186

Notes   217
References   259
Index   276

Figures

I.1 *Extraordinary Women*, photo album, n.d. [1918?]   *page* 1
I.2 *Extraordinary Women*, photo album, n.d. [1918?]   3
I.3 *Extraordinary Women*, photo album, n.d. [1918?]   4
I.4 *Extraordinary Women*, photo album, n.d. [1918?]   5
I.5 *Extraordinary Women*, photo album, n.d. [1918?]   6
2.1 Laurence Housman, illustration for "The Truce of God,"
     from *All-Fellows*, 1896   66
2.2 Laurence Housman, "Sweyn's Finding," illustration
     for Clemence Housman's *The Were-Wolf*, 1896   71
3.1 Compton Mackenzie and Mimi Franchetti (n.d.), from
     scrapbook 11 (formerly cataloged as P25), a photo album
     titled *Photographs, 1914–24, mostly Capri, also some on Herm* 112
3.2 Photograph of Compton Mackenzie, pasted inside Faith
     Compton Mackenzie's "improved" copy of *Vestal Fire*   118
3.3 Photograph of James Ellingham Brooks, pasted inside Faith
     Compton Mackenzie's "improved" copy of *Vestal Fire*   119
3.4 Group photograph including John Ellingham Brooks
     and Norman Douglas, pasted inside Faith Compton
     Mackenzie's "improved" copy of *Vestal Fire*   120
4.1 Kang Tongbi, portrait of Harold Acton, n.d.   128
4.2 Harold Acton in Beijing, 1933   140
4.3 Harold Acton in Beijing in a group of Chinese and European
     poets in his house at Pei Ho Yen, ca. 1933   142
4.4 Harold Acton in Beijing with Anna May Wong in the
     carved moon-gate of the drawing room of his residence
     at 2 Kung Hsien Hutung, ca. 1930s   154
5.1 Richard Bruce Nugent, *Salome before Herod*, n.d.   170
5.2 Richard Bruce Nugent, *Salome: Negrotesque I*, from *Harlem:
     A Forum of Negro Life*, 1928   172
6.1 Eric Gill, *Madonna and Child*, 1912–13   186

6.2 Eric Gill, *Sketch for Sculpture: Acrobat*, ca. 1915   194
6.3 Eric Gill, *Saint Sebastian*, 1920   195
6.4 Eric Gill, *Animals All*, 1916   203
6.5 Eric Gill, *Nuptials of God*, 1922   205
6.6 Eric Gill, *They* (or *Ecstasy*), 1910–11   211

Acknowledgments

This book is the product of the generosity of many friends, collaborators, and mentors. Kathy Psomiades first guided my interest in this area and continues to be an enormous influence (and fantastic writing retreat partner). I feel like I was formed as a thinker and researcher during a 2008 NEH Summer Seminar led by Joseph Bristow at the William Andrews Clark Memorial Library, and my work remains in conversation with him and the community he built for us at the Clark. I carry with me the memory of discussions that summer with Diana Maltz, S. Brooke Cameron, Emily Harrington, Simon Joyce, So Young Park, Julie Wise, Kate Krueger, Megan Becker, Lisa Hager, Marc DiPaolo, Julie Townsend, Tracy Collins, and Kasey Bass, and I see this book as a continuation of those conversations. During a global pandemic, Kate Hext, Alex Murray, and Sarah Parker have managed to be the steadiest of friends and created a supportive writing group that allowed me to compose the final chapters of this project. Rebecca Mitchell talked through almost every part of this book with me and has become one of my favorite people in the world. My thinking will always be informed by Richard Dellamora's, and I remain indebted to the support he provided since the very beginning of my career. Collaborating on projects with Dustin Friedman and Neil Hultgren made work meaningful and fun. I learned to take joy in this period and its personalities from Margaret Stetz and Mark Samuels Lasner. Rachel Hope Cleves made me aware of key material for this project and offered crucial guidance. I feel incredibly lucky to work alongside the community of scholars of aestheticism, Decadence, and the fin de siècle, who are some of the kindest people I know. Dennis Denisoff, Ana Parejo Vadillo, Marion Thain, Stefano Evangelista, Lindsay Wilhelm, Mack Gregg, Ellen Crowell, Kirsten MacLeod, Anna Maria Jones, Lorraine Janzen Kooistra, Gregory Mackie, Michèle Mendelssohn, Vincent Sherry, Jill Ehnenn, Matthew Potolsky, James Diedrick, LeeAnne Richardson, Catherine Maxwell, Regenia Gagnier, Ellis Hanson, Jane Desmarais,

Peter Bailey, Katharina Herold, Alex Bubb, and Richard Kaye make me want to keep returning to this period so I might continue thinking with them. And the broader Victorian studies community, including Nathan Hensley, Carolyn Lesjak, Lana Dalley, Anne Stiles, Tanya Agathocleous, Kellie Holzer, Genie Babb, Julie Codell, Richard Fulton, Lisa Surridge, Mary Elizabeth Leighton, Chris Vanden Bossche, Sara Maurer, Ross Forman, Sukanya Banerjee, Carolyn Williams, Pamela Gilbert, Dan Novak, and Sharon Aronofsky Weltman, have made this field feel at once vital and like home.

I would like to thank Ray Ryan, Edgar Mendez, and the editorial team at Cambridge University Press for being so helpful and efficient throughout this process. Two anonymous readers provided incredibly thoughtful feedback on the manuscript. Thank you to Matthew John Phillips for assistance with indexing and proofreading.

This research began with the support I received at Western Washington University, including the Radke Family Faculty Award for Innovations in the Humanities and the Marjorie and Glenn Hatter Award. The project was also supported by an IAS Vanguard Fellowship from the University of Birmingham, a Harry Ransom Center Research Fellowship in the Humanities, and a William Andrews Clark Memorial Library Short-Term Fellowship. I would not have been able to complete this project without the support of a Humanities and Arts Research Program Grant from Michigan State University.

This entire project relied upon the labor and assistance of generous archivists and librarians. I am grateful to Francesca Baldry, Cristina Bellini, and Alta Macadam at Villa La Pietra; Scott Jacobs at the William Andrews Clark Memorial Library; Pat Tansell at the Bromsgrove Public Library; and the librarians and staff at the Beinecke Library, the Harry Ransom Center, the Amistad Research Center, the British Library, the Women's Library at the London School of Economics, Bryn Mawr's Special Collections Library, I Tatti – The Harvard University Center for Italian Renaissance Studies in Florence, and the Alfred Gillet Trust in Street.

Parts of Chapter 3 appeared in "An Extraordinary Marriage: The Mackenzies, Post-Victorian Decadence, and the Queer Cosmopolitanism of Capri," *Studies in Walter Pater and Aestheticism* 3 (2018): 113–32, reprinted with kind permission from the International Walter Pater Society. Parts of Chapter 6 appeared in "Michael Field's Eric Gill: Radical Kinship, Cosmopolitanism, and Queer Catholicism," in *Michael Field: Decadent Moderns*, edited by Sarah Parker and Ana Parejo Vadillo (Athens, OH: Ohio University Press, 2019), 230–55, reprinted with kind permission of Ohio University Press, www.ohioswallow.com. For permission to reproduce artworks, I would like to thank Dr. Sandra Lo and the Estate of Kang Tongbi; New York University, Villa La Pietra; the Tate; the William Andrews Clark Memorial Library; and the National Galleries of Scotland. For permission to quote unpublished and published material by Vyvyan Holland, I would like to thank Merlin Holland. For permission to quote unpublished copyrighted material, I would like to thank the Estates of Robert Ross, Michael Field, Marc-André Raffalovich, William Rothenstein, Ananda Coomaraswamy, and Harold Acton. I would also like to thank the Biblioteca Berenson, I Tatti – The Harvard University Center for Italian Renaissance Studies for permission to quote from archival materials. Thank you to Catherine Flynn and Marva Jeremiah at Penguin Random House, UK, for their assistance regarding the Laurence Housman estate, and to Sarah Burton at the Society of Authors for her assistance regarding the Mackenzies' estates. Every effort has been made to trace copyright holders and to obtain their permission for the use of copyrighted material. The author apologizes for any errors or omissions and would be grateful if notified of any corrections that should be incorporated in future reprints of this material.

In the middle of writing this book, I left my community at Western Washington University and some of my closest friends, including Theresa Warburton, Josh Cerretti, Lysa Rivera, Katie Vulić, Brenda Miller, Tiana Kahakauwila, Rich Brown, Kendall Dodd, Sarah Zimmerman, and Chuck Lambert. I am grateful that I got to spend a decade with such loving friends and colleagues. Moving to a new institution was extremely challenging, but the community at Michigan State has quickly come to feel like family. Yomaira Figueroa, Tacuma Peters, and Tamara Butler made me feel at home here. They mapped out chapters on napkins, snapped me out of crises, and made life good. Our pandemic outdoor writing workshops with Delia Fernandez and Lyn Goeringer are the reason I could get this project done and laugh during a trying couple of years. I was lucky enough to land in a department with a fantastic Victorian studies colleague, Zarena Aslami, who has become a true friend. I feel lucky every day to work alongside the members of the Department of English at Michigan State University, including Divya Victor, Josh Lam, Ellen McCallum, Josh Yumibe, Juliet Guzzetta, Kinitra Brooks, April Baker-Bell, Tamar Boyadjian, Kathleen Fitzpatrick, Robin Silbergleid, Jeff Wray, Judith Stoddart, Sheila Contreras, Kuhu Tanvir, Jyotsna Singh, Salah Hassan, Julian Chambliss, Emery Petchauer, and Cara Cilano, and with a chair, Justus Nieland, who could not be more supportive. The graduate students in the Department of English give me energy and keep me engaged, and Sarah Potts, in particular, deserves endless thanks for editorial assistance as I completed the manuscript. The broader community at Michigan State, including Lily Woodruff, Yelena Kalinsky, and Johanna Schuster-Craig, already feel like old friends, and their kindness and input are present throughout this project as well.

This is a book about families, and I have been lucky enough to have many families and wide support structures throughout my life. I am grateful to my mother and father, Liz, P. J., Anna, Patrick, and Elsa, and to the Venas for teaching me what can be good and fun about families. I learned to call friends "family" from Zack Larkin, Niki Bhattacharya, Derek Almstead, Rebecca Apland Seeder, and David Gueriera, and they helped me make it through lockdown with weekly check-ins. Jenny Inzerillo and Ryan Brooks are my Thanksgiving family. Tim Fisher and Andy Wentz have become my Lansing family. Brian Whitener and Tara Samat are my kin. And most of all, when I am thinking and writing about affiliation, I am drawing on the happiness I have found in the connection I have with Kaveh Askari.

Introduction

Figure I.1   *Extraordinary Women*, photo album, n.d. [1918?], Box 58, Norman Douglas
Collection, Beinecke Rare Book and Manuscript Library.
Reproduced courtesy of the Beinecke Rare Book and Manuscript Library.

The pictures inside the *Extraordinary Women* album at the Beinecke
Library were taken on Capri in the late 1910s, a moment when the
Italian island had gained an international reputation as a Decadent outpost
and a haven for sexual dissidents.[1] The pictures in the album provide a

1

visual bridge into the complex network of intimacies fostered by this queer Arcadia in the early twentieth century. In a photograph labeled, "Checca – Mimi," for example, the Italian baroness Mimi Franchetti stares brazenly into the camera half-smiling (Figure I.1). She might be about to laugh. She is wearing a masculine suit jacket and tie with a long pleated skirt. Beside her is the wealthy Australian Francesca "Checca" Lloyd in a bold striped coat and a high-waisted polka dot skirt. She gazes archly at her beloved Mimi's profile. During this period, Checca and Mimi lived together at the Hotel Quisisana. According to James Money, "Checca was hopelessly in love with Mimi, but so were other women. . . . There were frequent quarrels – [they were seen] at the Quisisana throwing bottles at each other – and separations, interspersed with reconciliations and rare periods of harmony."[2] One wonders what underwrites Checca's sidelong glance in the photograph. Is this a "period of harmony" or of quarrels? Is she amused with or suspicious of the striking woman standing beside her? Checca appears enamored in this picture but at the same time somewhat haunted and uncertain. On a later page, Mimi poses in a series of pictures beside the much younger and taller "Baby," the daughter of the Russian Principessa Helène Soldatenkov (Figure I.2). Baby was also, according to Money, "conquered by Mimi."[3] Mimi wears her customary suit jacket and tie while Baby wears a girlish white dress. Baby smiles awkwardly in one photo. In another, she gazes down at the ground, her hands thrust into her pockets. Mimi is again mischievous and brazen, close to laughter, teasing the photographer, crouching playfully on the ground. How does the younger Baby feel beside this charismatic figure who seems to own the space within each picture? In another photograph within the same series, Checca has moved into the frame, and Baby appears more solemn.

Each page of the *Extraordinary Women* album moves the viewer into closer contact with the friendships, flirtations, and romances that connected the members of Capri's lesbian community, who are seen posing together on balconies, in restaurants, and on beaches, in swimsuits and Pierrot costumes, wearing bowties with long flowing skirts, in straw hats and bathing caps. The women pose smiling in the sand and beside canoes, in large groups with their arms locked together, staring up into one another's faces or out into the Tyrrhenian Sea (Figures I.3 and I.4). The playful group photographs and the snapshots of amateur performances, beach scenes, and dinners evoke the family vacation album, calling the viewer to, as Marianne Hirsch has described it, feel family, to sense the affective ties between the figures laughing, smiling, and holding on to one

Figure I.2   *Extraordinary Women*, photo album, n.d. [1918?], Box 58, Norman Douglas
Collection, Beinecke Rare Book and Manuscript Library.
Reproduced courtesy of the Beinecke Rare Book and Manuscript Library.

another.[4] The images speak together about the network of love and desire
that brought these women to Capri and into connection with one another,
that made them into a community and at times endangered that
community's stability.

The cosmopolitan crew of women in these photographs are the figures
upon which the popular British writer Compton Mackenzie based the
characters in his satirical novel *Extraordinary Women* (1928). Mackenzie
represents the island as a perpetually shifting terrain of outrageous flirtations. While Compton and his wife Faith lived squarely in the midst of this
community, Compton's novel works to distance the couple from the
complex grid of intimacies on Capri, treating the women under discussion
with a "sarcastic edge" that Jamie James attributes "to the fact that his wife
had a lesbian affair while they were living on Capri."[5] The album,
however, aggressively collapses that distance by also including pictures of

Figure I.3 *Extraordinary Women*, photo album, n.d. [1918?], Box 58, Norman Douglas
Collection, Beinecke Rare Book and Manuscript Library.
Reproduced courtesy of the Beinecke Rare Book and Manuscript Library.

both Faith and Compton, insisting that they too belong within this space
and among the intimacies represented in the album. Faith is, as the album
indicates, one of Capri's extraordinary women, a haunting beauty in a
headscarf with an umbrella resting on her shoulder as she gazes down the
rocky shoreline of Capri (Figure I.4). And Compton seems very much to
belong here as well, amidst the women he sends up in his novel, as he
crouches beside his androgynous twin Mimi, the two wearing matching
bowties with their heads cocked at the same angle (Figure I.5). The
Extraordinary Women album undercuts the arch derision of its companion
novel, highlighting Faith and Compton's kinship with this sexually
dissident circle.

    The acts that brought the album into existence – the posing of individ-
uals and groups for the pictures, the selection and arrangement of images,
the inclusion of pictures of Faith and Compton in the album – are acts

Figure I.4 *Extraordinary Women*, photo album, n.d. [1918?], Box 58, Norman Douglas
Collection, Beinecke Rare Book and Manuscript Library.
Reproduced courtesy of the Beinecke Rare Book and Manuscript Library.

that fostered belonging and connection. This collective labor generated an object that, as Elizabeth Freeman notes in her discussion of group photography and the making visible of queer history, "[sutures] kin relations."[6] It is unclear who first assembled this album, nestling images of Faith and Compton amidst the pictures of Mimi, Checca, and Baby, or who had this copy made, as the album in the Beinecke is a photographic reproduction of an original housed at the Centro Caprense Ignazio Cerio Library. The original is untitled, but someone also made a choice to print the title *Extraordinary Women* on the spine of the reproduction, tying the object explicitly to the novel it subtly contradicts. These are a set of steps that close the space the novel seeks to put between the Mackenzies' marriage and the community on Capri, acknowledging Faith and Compton's kinship with the figures that *Extraordinary Women* lampoons. The novel and the album taken together are a set of artifacts that function

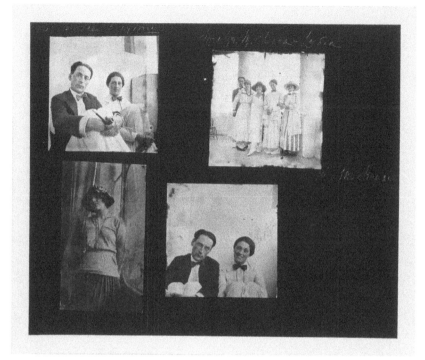

Figure I.5   *Extraordinary Women*, photo album, n.d. [1918?], Box 58, Norman Douglas
             Collection, Beinecke Rare Book and Manuscript Library.
             Reproduced courtesy of the Beinecke Rare Book and Manuscript Library.

as a rich reflection of the Mackenzies' life on Capri in the teens, when they
opened their marriage into the island's queer community, conducting
affairs and flirtations with its members, and remade their union into
something at once more porous and resilient. The individuals that
Compton satirizes in *Extraordinary Women* operated, during the 1910s
and 1920s, as a part of their marriage. They were, for a period of time
and in a sense, their family. As hard as Compton might have worked to
establish a boundary between his own domestic scene and the queer
networks that he represented in his campy, detached novel, the album
razes that boundary, making them members of, rather than simply wit-
nesses to, the complex web of intimate relations on Capri. The album
speaks, in a slightly different register than the novel for which it is named,
to the affective work Faith and Compton conducted on Capri, which had
to do with remaking their marriage so it could incorporate other people

and other intimacies, temporarily absorbing the island's queer coteries into their union. It resembles a family album because it tells us about a form of kinship that we might not be able to see were we to rely solely on public documents like the novel that it illustrates.

The *Extraordinary Women* album also resembles a family album because of the way it was kept and transmitted. Group photographs, Freeman argues, can "function as tangible evidence of queer life for those who privately collect and preserve them" and, in the way that they are "handed down generations or across the boundaries of household," they "[establish] connections similar to the ones they [represent]."[7] Freeman's insights concerning the role that the collecting and transmission of group photographs perform in the construction of queer community should draw our attention to questions of provenance when considering an object like this one. This album is part of a collection at the Beinecke devoted to Norman Douglas, the early twentieth-century travel writer and novelist to whom Compton dedicated *Extraordinary Women* and whose "magic" conversation first sent the Mackenzies to Capri.[8] Douglas was one of Capri's queer refugees, drawn to the island's reputation for sexual permissiveness. (In Paul Fussell's words, he "fled [England] during the war to avoid persecution for kissing a boy."[9] He had been charged with indecent assault after the boy in question complained to the police and spent the remainder of his life, save a brief time in London during World War II, effectively living in exile in Italy and France.) He was an extremely close friend to the Mackenzies and a guiding spirit of queer life on Capri in the early twentieth century. As Rachel Hope Cleves notes in her recent biography of Douglas, while "today almost all of Douglas's sexual encounters with children and youth would be defined as assaults, both in law and in public opinion," during the early twentieth century, Douglas's pagan and hedonistic philosophy "appealed to a lot of sexual nonconformists, not just pederasts," and he "attracted many pathbreaking queer and feminist women who regarded him as a sexual role model."[10] The novel for which the album is named is in many ways a tribute to him, and he and his writing had much to do with the attraction Capri held for the "extraordinary women" within its pages, so it makes sense for these photographs to be located in this collection. But the route the Norman Douglas Collection took to the Beinecke is just as meaningful in terms of illuminating innovative kinship formations among the cosmopolitan network of authors and artists on Capri.

At the end of Norman Douglas's life, he was cared for by a set of queer modernists, an operation funded by the modernist patron Bryher

(Annie Winifred Ellerman, 1894–1983). Bryher was the child of the
multi-millionaire Sir John Ellerman and, as Susan McCabe argues, used
this wealth to play a "'husband' role in curating modernism."[11] While
remembered most often today as the lover of the modernist poet H. D.
(Hilda Doolittle), Bryher was also very close with Faith Mackenzie and
with Douglas. After divorcing the Scottish writer and filmmaker Kenneth
Macpherson, Bryher purchased a home on Capri for him and his partner,
the Welsh photographer Algernon Islay de Courcy Lyons, asking that they
take Douglas into this home until his death in 1952. Bryher constructed
from inherited wealth and intimate connections a resting place for an aging
friend. Upon Douglas's death, Macpherson received a set of Douglas's
papers, and he then left the entirety of his estate, including the Norman
Douglas collection and the *Extraordinary Women* album, to Lyons. Lyons,
in turn, passed the material to Manop Charoensuk, a younger Thai man
who had been Lyons's companion and adopted son at the end of his life,
and Charoensuk then sold the collection to Elysium Press, from which the
Beinecke purchased this material in 2008. The album's movements make
visible an entire chain of queer, Decadent, and modernist connections, and
its survival has relied upon innovative systems of care, kinship, and
property transmission. It is available to consult in the Beinecke Library
because of its queer modernist genealogy and as a result of alternative
modes of intergenerational nursing, community archiving, and inheritance.[12] The *Extraordinary Women* album, which highlights the fascinating
web of affiliations that altered the Mackenzies' marriage, also tells a story
about the queer transgenerational and transnational connections that
persisted on Capri long after their departure. These connections extended
beyond the island that fostered them, forging alternative networks of love,
care, and historical transmission that the survival of the *Extraordinary
Women* album brings to light.

   This album is the archival object with which I want to begin because it
embodies many of the key preoccupations of this project. This is a book
about queer experiments in affiliation as performed by individuals who saw
themselves as part of a Decadent tradition and who operated within
cosmopolitan networks.[13] The queer community on Capri, as I will demonstrate, had much to do with the Decadence of the fin de siècle, and the
cosmopolitan, sexually dissident circle with which Faith and Compton
mingled on the island was drawn there because of Capri's reputation in the
wake of the Wilde trials as a refuge from moral policing, a space apart that
sheltered queer subjects from across the globe. The Decadence of this
community, along with its cosmopolitanism, played crucial roles in its

development of innovative thinking about affiliation. I begin with this album and the novel for which it was named because I am interested in the literary works and artifacts that were produced in concert with the construction of novel ways of enacting kinship and marriage by Decadent figures in the twentieth century. I want to look at the texts, objects, and lives these figures made as they thought through the process of making connection new. In disinterring evidence of the affiliative experiments performed by cosmopolitan individuals with ties to Decadence in the early twentieth century, I have had to turn to an archive of disparate private materials – to diaries and correspondence along with photo albums and unpublished manuscripts, personal libraries, and long-concealed confessional narratives. These, in turn, like the *Extraordinary Women* album, make sense, make meaning, make theories of kinship and connection visible when placed in conversation with the more public-facing projects – novels, banners, speeches, translation projects, sculptures, and engravings – generated by the figures under discussion.

The production and preservation of the *Extraordinary Woman* album was enabled by the very modes of transhistorical queer and aesthetic affiliation with which I am preoccupied in this project. These acts emerged from the contact between post-Victorian Decadents and camp modernists on Capri, which facilitated the handing down of the album through a network of individuals who shared a set of tastes and a commitment to unconventional desires and domestic arrangements. The album, like each of the chapters that follow, reveals literary historical networks that operated across the Victorian/modern divide. *Queer Kinship after Wilde* builds on the work I did in my first book, *Literature and the Politics of Post-Victorian Decadence*, in unearthing further evidence of the persistence of Decadence into the twentieth century. In this case, I contribute to the ongoing effort to render the Victorian/modern divide more porous by demonstrating that theories and practices often conceived of as "Victorian" played a rich and vital role in conversations about affiliation long after the century turned.[14] I perform this work in conversation with the new modernist studies and with Victorian studies scholars whose reach has moved further and further into the modernist period with the hopes that, by attending to the rich interplay between and coexistence of Victorian and modernist aesthetic codes, we may begin to get a richer picture of the long reach of the nineteenth century as well as the aesthetic and political complexity of the early decades of the twentieth century.

The individuals under discussion in *Queer Kinship after Wilde*, like the Mackenzies and the members of their community on Capri, thought and operated within queer, transhistorical networks, and they are all in a sense a part of one larger network, a group of authors and artists who distanced themselves slightly from the modernism of the early twentieth century by linking themselves to the Decadent past. While Oscar Wilde's reputation suffered in the years following his trials for "acts of gross indecency," during the modernist period, a certain subset of individuals interested in radically rethinking kinship and connection turned very purposefully back to his work and the Decadent tradition with which he was associated. The community on Capri is only one example. Wilde's son Vyvyan Holland brought much of his father's thinking into his innovative construction of an alternative family for himself following the death of his parents and brother. The modernist aesthete Harold Acton relied upon the thinking of Vernon Lee as he worked to extricate himself from his biological family and the pressure to marry and reproduce. Eric Gill's sculptures read as modernist, but his vision of eroticized kinship was informed by queer Decadent Catholicism as practiced by Michael Field and the Decadent poet and priest John Gray. For many of the members of this loosely connected group of bohemian aesthetes and Decadent modernists, the turn to the fin de siècle made clear their ties to sexual dissidence as well as their desire to think beyond the masculinist modernism of the period. It placed them slightly out of sync with Eliot and Joyce and Hemingway and Pound and placed them right in rhythm with one another. As Elizabeth Freeman argues, in conversation with Heather Love, "the stubborn linger- ing of pastness . . . is a hallmark of queer affect: a 'revolution' in the old sense of the word, as a turning back."[15] This is the affect that underwrites the network I examine here, a network of "denizens of times out of joint" whose affiliation with the recent past marks them as distinct from more prominent and well-known strains of twentieth-century modernism, such as Bloomsbury.[16] As Christopher Reed has suggested, Bloomsbury could be understood as another locus of innovative ideas about affiliation, intimacy, and home life. However, while Reed stresses Bloomsbury's "alienation from mainstream modernism," the Bloomsbury subculture is much more intimately tied up with high modernist practices and aesthetics than the network upon which I am focusing, a network rooted firmly in the Decadent past.[17] The recurring figures here, surfacing repeatedly in the margins of my chapters and knitting them together, are the Sitwells, Ronald Firbank, Robert Ross, Reggie Turner, Carl Van Vechten – the lingering specters of the Yellow Nineties along with the Decadent mod- ernists of the new century. A shared sense of what Freeman refers to as "temporal drag" weaves a web among this circle of queer and Decadent modernists who operated alongside and often in conversation with high modernism but who thought, wrote, and made community in a slightly different fashion.[18]

As they reached into the fin-de-siècle past for ideas that might allow them to operate outside of the heteronormative boundaries restricting the practice of marriage and the family, these thinkers also engaged with a global set of kinship patterns, and they traveled and read widely, encountering different models of connection and cooperation that helped them to disentangle themselves from conventional sexual and gender ideals. Eric Gill routed his Decadent Catholic vision of eroticized kinship through his study of Indian art history and his engagement with the Ceylonese art historian Ananda Coomaraswamy. Harold Acton insulated himself from his troubled biological family and the pressure to marry by removing himself from Europe in the 1930s and resettling in China, where he collaborated with modern Chinese poets. The Decadent illustrator Laurence Housman came to understand ideal kinship as infinitely expansive through his advocacy work in support of Indian independence. Vyvyan Holland's thinking about affiliation and the family was informed by his work translating queer modernist texts written in French. For the Harlem Renaissance artist Richard Bruce Nugent, engaging with the Orientalism of British Decadence assisted him in theorizing the rupture of Black kinship structures in the United States. Attending to the work of these figures allows us to see how Victorian Decadence's ideas about kinship were revised, reformulated, and inflected with a global sensibility by a network of twentieth-century authors and artists living in China, Harlem, London, and Italy and engaging with Indian, French, and Chinese art and literature.

I begin with the *Extraordinary Women* album because it is representative of the transhistorical and transnational investments shared by the members of the network I want to trace here, but it is also a suitable place to begin because it demonstrates a set of tensions that operate throughout most of this book. What I would also like to stress in my reading of the album and my discussion of the figures included in this project is the extent to which the turn to the Decadent past and to global influence could engender experiments in affinity neither entirely radical and ethical nor fully conservative and exploitative. The Mackenzies, like most of the figures I discuss here, wished to rework conventional models of connection and domesticity, but, significantly, they did not wish to discard these models altogether. Many of the figures I examine in *Queer Kinship after Wilde*, as Elizabeth Freeman puts it, at once "inhabit and exceed the matrix of couplehood and reproduction."[19] The retoolings and revisions of marriage and kinship under discussion here do not amount to "the radical dissolution of the contract, in every sense social and Symbolic, on which the future as putative assurance against the jouissance of the Real depends" described by Lee Edelman.[20] The experiments in connection that these figures conducted were innovative, but they were not so radical that they jettisoned entirely inherited grids of kinship and relationality. The Mackenzies remade their marriage into something more porous and poly so that they might remain married. Their willingness to accommodate other people and desires within their union kept their marriage intact. This is a pattern that reappears throughout this book, a pattern according to which individuals thirsting for new models of connection remain attached to and delimited by traditional structures of feeling. Orphaned adult children find a way to build themselves new fathers. Bachelors fixate on adoption as an antidote to alienation. Fathers working to rupture every taboo governing sexual desire wind up reproducing the abusive logic of the patriarchal family. Queer siblings invoke the rhetoric of Christianity while theorizing a radically open vision of kinship. Without disregarding what is compelling about the work these individuals performed, I also want to acknowledge the more traditional or conservative components of their practices.

This tension between radical desires and conventional tendencies registers similarly in the ways the individuals I examine in *Queer Kinship after Wilde* negotiated cultural differences, a tension to which the *Extraordinary Women* album also testifies. While the women pictured in these albums indicate much about the international openness on the island of Capri in the teens and twenties, which drew individuals from Russia, Australia, America, England, France, and the Italian mainland, the manner in which the Mackenzies related to this community hovered somewhere between the cosmopolitan ideal and an appetitive mode of sex tourism that structurally resembles Orientalism. The couples, siblings, and familial units I discuss in the chapters that follow move similarly between thoughtful and ethical curiosity about the wider world and aggressive appropriation of difference. Travel, translation, and anti-colonial advocacy inform their capacity to practice family and marriage in new and startling ways. However, this interest in otherness leads as often to exoticization and annexation as it does to expansive and ethical modes of cosmopolitan sensitivity.

The members of this twentieth-century Decadent network outlined in *Queer Kinship after Wilde*, with their shared sense of temporal dissonance, sexual dissidence, and cosmopolitan curiosity, engendered modes of living, loving, and connecting that are startling and worthy of our attention. They played with the concept of kin, the structure of the family, and the institution of marriage, and they pierced the national boundaries that continue to delimit work within the fields of Victorian and modernist studies. However, because they are playing with a set of concepts, structures, and institutions that are as much enmeshed in histories of violence and exploitation as in traditions of care and nurturing, the results are not always ethical or just. And, because they are situated within national histories with ties to colonialism and racial trauma, their expansive curiosity is often inflected by imperialist, Orientalist, and exploitative appetites.[21] In delineating the contours of their experiments, I want to keep in mind Kadji Amin's recent call to think in terms of "deidealization" when approaching the history of queer attachments. Amin describes deidealization as the process of "deexceptionaliz[ing] queerness in order to analyze queer possibility as inextricable from relations of power, queer deviance as intertwined with normativity, and queer alternatives as not necessarily just alternatives."[22] This work, Amin argues, acknowledges "the 'complex personhood' of queer, racialized, and subaltern persons too often assigned the psychically flat role of righting the ills of an unjust social order and denied the right to be damaged, psychically complex, or merely otherwise occupied."[23] Amin interrogates the injunction, evident in some strains of queer studies, that demands that "queer collectivities, kinship, coalitions, and counterpublics operate as a utopian model of more just, egalitarian, and caring social forms" and calls for a more "capacious" practice of queer history that "engag[es] *queer's multiple* pasts."[24] Here again the *Extraordinary Women* album operates as a particularly suitable artifact with which to begin this project, as it is named for a novel dedicated to a man who, as much as he operated as a heroic figure for sexual nonconformists, openly indulged his sexual preference for children and would, as Rachel Hope Cleves notes, be understood by "present standards" as a "monster."[25] The history I am mining here is as marked by liberatory impulses as it is by erotic investments driven by power imbalances and exploitation. I should admit that this project began with a desire to disinter evidence of more ethical models of alternative affiliation rooted in Decadence and routed through a global sensibility, and I should also say that, as I conducted my research, I did find some of those things. But I didn't always, and I would like this project and its approach to be capacious enough to acknowledge that. The multiple political directions in which these twentieth-century reimaginings of kinship and connection moved have much to do with the source material upon which this Decadent network drew, the utopian impulses, alternative desires, and ethical failures that marked the aestheticism of the fin de siècle.

Decadent Legacies and Wildean Connection

The subjects of the chapters that follow drew on a broad array of aestheticist influences as they reconceptualized marriage and the family, and they often interwove the earlier and later phrases of aestheticism within their approaches to affiliation, pulling from Walter Pater and Aubrey Beardsley, A. C. Swinburne as well as John Gray. However, it is especially late-Victorian Decadence that operated as the most significant influence on their attempts to reformulate kinship. Their work was certainly informed, for example, by the Pre-Raphaelite Brotherhood's experiments in affiliation or the broader resistance to middle-class morality and Victorian gender ideologies enabled by the "art for art's sake" ethos, but it was what Elaine Showalter has referred to as the "sexual anarchy" of the 1890s, the spectacle of Wilde's fall from grace, the pronounced hedonism, and iconoclasm of the fin de siècle, as opposed to the slightly more muted and less emphatically queer earlier phases of aestheticism that operated as points of inspiration for the figures I discuss here.[26] And it is primarily because of its linkage to sexual dissidence, to a queer ethos, that Decadence is of use. In her work on "queer Dickens," Holly Furneaux notes that she defines "queer as that which demonstrates that marriage and reproduction are not the only, or indeed the dominant or preferred, modes of being, and in doing so, undoes a unhelpfully narrow model of identity as determined by a fixed point of sexual orientation."[27] This is a helpfully elastic way of conceptualizing the manner in which the word "queer" functions here, but that term is inflected throughout this book by its linkage with the purposefully outrageous, taunting, rebellious ethos of late-Victorian Decadence. The term "queer" certainly operates differently in each of the chapters that follow, describing affiliative experiments performed by subjects impacted by homophobic legislation, engaged in queer activism, living in gay and lesbian communities abroad, resisting heteronormative narratives of maturation and affiliation, or reinventing religious faith in conversation with queer communities. However, in each chapter, the figures under discussion come to a new vision of what connection might be, they "queer" kinship, through the framework of their investment in the bold and outrageous aestheticism of the fin de siècle, through Decadence.[28]

Decadence is a term that has proven itself stubbornly resistant to stable definition. As it has been debated and re-envisioned by nineteenth-century thinkers and twentieth- and twenty-first-century critics, Decadence has most frequently been tied to excessive refinement, formalism, detachment, the pursuit of sensation, and a fascination with artificiality and the concept of cultural decline. Many of the authors and artists I examine are certainly drawn to these Decadent stylistic markers and thematic preoccupations. Decadence's dizzying and often perverse beauty, its emphasis on pleasure, resistance to ideologies of the "natural," nihilistic rejection of conventional ideas of progress, and its irony and derision were all highly generative for this network of early twentieth-century sexual dissidents who wished to extricate themselves from the norms governing sexuality and the practice of affiliation. In this, Decadence, despite the term's association with degeneration and decay, was a vitalizing force. As Alex Murray argues, Decadence was "a literature that looked forward," a fact that has been frequently overlooked because of the "retrospective nature of the word itself."[29] But as early as 1913, as Murray notes, Holbrook Jackson was insisting that "much of the genius denounced by Max Nordau as degeneration was a sane and healthy expression of vitality which, as it is not difficult to show, would have been better named regeneration."[30] This is the element of Decadence's legacy that I am highlighting here, its utility in assisting the conceptualization of alternative ways forward, in enabling rebellion, and more specifically modes of queer rebellion.

During the period on which I am focusing, Decadence was, as Kate Hext and Alex Murray put it, taken up as a "badge" meant to advertise the wearer's interest in "challenging the moralizing connotations of the term itself."[31] If Decadence was often condemned for luxuriating in pleasures and practices linked to cultural decline, that condemnation was turned on its head and treated as an emblem of pride for a band of queer subjects invested in generating unorthodox approaches to affiliation. They drew upon Decadence's investment in pleasure, sensation, and the illicit as they insisted upon the possibility of new ways of connecting. They turned, significantly, to the epicureanism of Pater and the hedonism of Wilde rather than to the more earnest and avowedly ethical innovations fostered by other strands of fin-de-siècle radicalism, such as the Fellowship of the New Life. While the Fellowship of the New Life might have enabled similar practices, such as open marriage and "more elastic models of love in community," these practices emerged from a disparate set of moral and political beliefs connected to socialism and an investment in clean and simple living. As Diana Maltz notes, for individuals connected to the FNL, "sexual self-determination" was understood to be a radical commitment and "free union" was seen as "part of an ideological praxis, a way that one might perform one's ethics."[32] For the Decadent modernists upon which I focus, sexual self-determination and a commitment to new forms of kinship provided instead a way to perform one's uniqueness, defiance, and commitment to pleasure. Looking back to the 1890s enabled the kinship innovations of a group of individuals who saw in Decadence "a defiant, vivid assertion of the sexual freedoms promised by a life lived for sensation alone."[33]

And it was Wilde in particular that informed their thinking. This has to do, at least in part, with Wilde's association in the popular imagination of the early twentieth century with sexual resistance and the eschewal of heteronormative traditions. Linking oneself to Wilde became during this period a way to signify one's outsider status as well as sympathy for the causes for which he had suffered. However, the hold he exercised over this group of individuals should also be understood in relation to his own thinking concerning kinship and connection as well as his personal practices. In the "Soul of Man Under Socialism," Oscar Wilde celebrates socialism's "annihilat[ion of] family life," the elimination of marriage that will accompany the abolition of private property, and the eradication of all involuntary associations that might inhibit the development of the individual.[34] Jesus Christ, who stands in this strange essay first and foremost for the cultivation of the self, according to Wilde, "rejected the claims of family life," for "he would allow no claim whatsoever to be made on his personality."[35] As much as Wilde insists in this essay upon the value of self-development uninhibited by kinship ties, he returns again and again in his work to the concepts of affiliation and community, arguing in "The Critic as Artist" that "to know anything about oneself one must know all about others."[36] In his plays, his fiction, and his essays, he considered at length our obligations and attractions to others and the bonds – biological, legal, erotic, and sympathetic – that connect us to offspring, spouses, lovers, and friends, reflecting upon how such bonds might be remade so as to be less destructive and inhibiting. His lived experience similarly showcases his ability to think in broad and imaginative ways about connection. He demonstrated a chameleon-like capacity to move in his personal life between the conventional structures of Victorian domesticity and queer community. He was a theorist and practitioner of innovative modes of intimacy. While the rethinking of connection, kinship, and marriage occurs across Wilde's body of work, for my purposes here, I would like to focus in particular on the role his thinking about

Shakespeare's sonnets played in his theorization of alternative models of familial affiliation.

Wilde's most explicit and extensive theorization of queer parenting and inheritance occurs in "The Portrait of Mr. W. H." (1889). In this short story, the narrator works through a theory concerning the "true secret" of Shakespeare's sonnets, the identity of Mr. W. H., the young man "whose physical beauty was such that it became the very cornerstone of Shakespeare's art."[37] The theory has been relayed to him by his older friend Erskine, who had in turn received the idea from his "effeminate," "languid," and "wonderfully handsome" school friend Cyril Graham.[38] Cyril believed the sonnets were addressed to Willie Hughes, "the boy-actor for whom he created Viola and Imogen, Juliet and Rosalind, Portia and Desdemona, and Cleopatra herself."[39] The narrator finds himself seduced by the theory, since rejected by Erskine, and decides he will not rest until he has established it as true. As he pores over the sonnets, he finds ample proof for Cyril's claims, but a certain element of the poems gives him pause – Shakespeare's insistence that his young friend ought to marry and have children. He puts to rest this "jarring note" of contradiction, however, by concluding that the marriage Shakespeare proposes is "marriage with his Muse" and "the children he begs him to beget are no children of flesh and blood, but more immortal children of undying fame."[40] His beauty will prove "barren" only if he doesn't put it to use upon the stage.[41] Shakespeare, the narrator insists, is simply telling the young man that "you shall people with forms of your own image the imaginary world of the stage. These children that you beget, he continues, will not wither away, as mortal children do, but you shall live in them and in my plays."[42] As James Campbell argues, this reading of the sonnets locates in this body of work the assertion that "the physical production of additional human beings is a pale imitation of the actual creative process, which is thoroughly intellectual, deeply erotic, and exclusively male."[43] The narrator finds in Shakespeare's sonnets, in the manner in which Shakespeare loves young Willie Hughes, an alternative vision of marriage and reproduction that engenders immortal offspring, "eternal lines," made from his love for the boy and the boy's marriage with the Muse, a kind of love that will place them both beyond time and provide them with a much deeper satisfaction than might be produced by any conventional union or genetic descendants.[44]

Following the initial publication of "The Portrait of Mr. W. H." in *Blackwood's Magazine*, Wilde returned to and reworked this story, more than doubling its length, and he paid particular attention to this key moment, when the narrator locates in the sonnets a queer theory of aesthetic marriage and alternative reproduction that at once transcends time and places them both within history, carrying their minds forward into future generations without binding them to the everyday work of family life. In the expanded version of the story, the narrator disinters further evidence from the sonnets of Shakespeare's belief in the immortal quality of Willie Hughes's beauty, which belongs "to all ages and all lands" and "should not pass away without leaving [its] form in Art."[45] It is not enough, however, for the poet to simply describe this beauty: "It is necessary that 'some child of yours,' some artistic creation that embodies you, and to which your imagination gives life, shall present you to the world's wondering eyes."[46] This "child" of the actor's, it seems, would allow the world to continue to wonder at his beauty long after he has passed away. At this point, the sense of what children might be, of what might constitute progeny, multiplies, as the narrator weaves together lines from the sonnets with his own creative glosses, articulating an expansive sense of queer reproduction. According to the narrator, the speaker of the sonnets encouraged the actor to understand "[his] own thoughts" as children, "offspring of sense and spirit": "Give some expression to them, and you shall find – 'Those children nursed, delivered from thy brain.'"[47] The poet, in turn, might be impregnated by the actor: "My thoughts, also, are my 'children.' They are of your begetting and my brain is – 'the womb wherein they grew.' For this great friendship of ours is indeed a marriage, it is the 'marriage of true minds.'"[48] Within the fluid kinship scheme, friendship becomes marriage, brains become wombs, and thoughts become babies. This expanded version of the story was meant to be published by the Bodley Head, which advertised the work as forthcoming in 1893, but it did not appear in book form until 1921, when Mitchell Kennerley produced a limited edition, providing the opportunity for the later generation of Decadent modernists under discussion here to engage with a more fully developed version of Wilde's alternative scheme of queer reproduction.[49]

Even in the earlier and more widely circulated draft of the story, however, Wilde meditates at length on other modes of parenting that respond to what Elizabeth Freeman refers to as "the longing to 'be *long*,' to endure in corporeal form over time, beyond procreation."[50] The love Shakespeare held for Willie Hughes engenders additional offspring within the space of the text, an act of interpretation produced through contact and collaboration between men, an idea made among and passed between what Lawrence Danson has referred to as a "daisy-chain of converts and skeptics": "The sonnets to Willie infect the already-effeminate Cyril Graham, who lures first Erskine and then the narrator into the secret circle; Erskine dies – nominally of consumption – but the book that records it all, 'The Portrait of Mr. W. H.,' carries the pernicious influence into the future."[51] The theory is repeatedly orphaned, abandoned, and adopted by this daisy chain of converts, shared between two friends, given by an older to a younger man, who take turns devoting themselves wholeheartedly to its care. In Campbell's reading, the "entire story is constructed to illustrate [the] procreative concept" that the narrator detected within the sonnets themselves: "new philosophies and new ways of making and critiquing art are produced by masculine inspiration."[52] And, as Danson indicates, future readers might come to further parent and raise this aesthetic child, the Willie Hughes theory, to which they might make their own additions and revisions, allowing the interpretation of the sonnets, like Willie Hughes's beauty, to flourish and persist across history. In this sense, Cyril, Erskine, the narrator, and Wilde are able to participate in what Freeman describes as a temporally expansive mode of belonging, "to 'hold out' a hand across time and touch the dead or those not born yet, to offer oneself beyond one's own time."[53]

Cyril's desperate need for Erskine to believe and care for the theory leads to the production of another "child," a forged portrait of the extraordinarily beautiful and effeminate seventeen-year-old Willie Hughes. When Erskine discovers his deception, finding that the work was produced by a young Victorian painter at Cyril's request, Cyril shoots himself, and his blood, the blood of a martyr/parent willing to die for the love of a faith/ child, splashes itself upon the frame of the orphaned picture. In his suicide letter, Cyril entrusts the theory, presumably along with the portrait, which is in Erskine's possession as the story begins, to his friend. The portrait finds itself as the story concludes in the custody of the narrator, to whom Erskine left the picture on his deathbed. Forged from Cyril's desire to unite Erskine to himself in a shared belief, this vexed work of art, a beautiful painting of a beautiful boy, becomes the narrator's to care for, an illegitimate yet immortal child that brings him to think, when he gazes upon it, that there might be "a great deal to be said for the Willie Hughes theory of Shakespeare's Sonnets."[54] Mentored by the older Erskine, the narrator has learned how to assume the position of caretaker for the orphaned picture, a temporally dislocated image that speaks to the desire for intergenerational connection between sexually dissident men. This story about literary interpretation and literary history is also, at its core, a story about queer fathering, kinship, and care.

This is not, however, the only time that Wilde used Shakespeare's sonnets to theorize queer modes of kinship. According to published accounts of Wilde's trials for "acts of gross indecency" in 1895, the sonnets also figured prominently in his defense of "the love that dare not speak its name." When Wilde was called upon during cross-examination to explain "Two Loves," a poem by Lord Alfred Douglas, which opposes the love between "boy and girl" with "the love that dare not speak its name," he described the latter as the "great affection of an elder for a younger man as there was between David and Jonathan, such as Plato made the very basis of his philosophy, and such as you find in the sonnets of Michelangelo and Shakespeare." According to Wilde, this sort of love "repeatedly exists between an elder and a younger man, when an elder man has intellect, and the younger man has all the joy, hope and glamour of life before him."[55] While, as Leslie J. Moran has argued, published accounts of the trials frequently engaged in acts of "creative fabrication," this speech seems to have "an essential life," surfacing repeatedly (albeit in slightly altered forms) in multiple accounts of Wilde's time on the stand, becoming an essential part of the mythology that surrounded his persecution.[56] According to these published accounts of the trials, which became so central to his story, in defending homoerotic desire, Wilde stressed mentorship, pedagogy, and age differentials, foregrounding the role an elder man might play in the raising of young citizens, as well as the paternal component of such connections. To make "the love that dare not speak its name" beautiful, Wilde made it familial, blurring the boundary between erotic and kinship ties. As Patrick Califia, Kadji Amin, and Alan Sinfield have demonstrated, this tendency to frame pederastic relations as familial continues into the twentieth century, serving as a "means of thinking the age-differentiated pederastic relation as, *in and of itself*, an intergenerational kinship form."[57]

This second stage in Wilde's interpretation of the sonnets is just as central to my understanding of his vision of queer kinship as the earlier theory on display in "The Portrait of Mr. W. H." As Ellis Hanson has recently argued, in our rush to posit Wilde as a queer martyr and icon, we have tended to bracket or elide certain elements of his thinking and his erotic practices.[58] In the decades following his death, posthumous followers of Wilde quickly began to develop what Richard Kaye has referred to as a "sense of Wilde as risk-taking leader of a newly constituted breed of erotically dissident men," and his investment in age-differentiated eroticism was neglected in favor of celebrating the sacrifices he was understood to have made for the cause of sexual freedom.[59] In considering

Wilde's legacy, however, it is worth noting that he was deeply invested in erotic encounters animated by power differentials. His literary works and his biography reflect an attraction to significantly younger men, and this attraction was often compounded by class differences. While he certainly emphasized the centrality of mentorship and pedagogy within cross-generational and cross-class relationships, as Kadji Amin argues, an eroticism that places asymmetrical power relations at its center has the potential to be as damaging as it is nurturing. The unease this causes, however, should not inspire us to avoid or overlook these attachments and the role they have played in queer history. With Amin's call for a more capacious mode of queer history underwritten by what he refers to as deidealization in mind, I want to center Wilde's interest in troubling forms of attachment as much as I highlight his radical and innovative manner of conceptualizing queer belonging and duration, and I would like to remain attentive to the manner in which these multiple political possibilities play out within his early twentieth-century legacy as manifested in post-Victorian Decadent and Decadent modernist practices of queer kinship and connection.

Wilde also served as a crucial model for twentieth-century Decadents in his cosmopolitanism, an ethos that was both for Wilde and his successors significant in terms of conceptualizing both connection and detachment. Matthew Potolsky has argued that Decadence was "fundamentally inter-national in origin and orientation," and that Decadent writing "is a form of cultural production that begins with and recurrently thematizes the act of literary and artistic border crossing."[60] As Michèle Mendelssohn notes, late nineteenth- and early twentieth-century aesthetes and Decadents seemed particularly attuned to the forms of freedom and pleasure engendered by the cosmopolitan stance, the modes of wide-ranging encounter and impar-tiality facilitated by conceptualizing oneself as a citizen of the world. Mendelssohn turns to Baudelaire's reflections on *flânerie* in describing the appeal that this model of sensual impartiality held for those operating within an aestheticist tradition: "To be away from home and yet to feel oneself everywhere at home; to see the world, to be at the centre of the world, and yet to remain hidden from the world – such are a few of the slightest pleasures of those independent, passionate, impartial natures which the tongue can but clumsily define."[61] This is a mode of being and perceiving that meshes seamlessly with the detached hedonism espoused by Pater in his "Conclusion" to *Studies in the History of the Renaissance* (1873), a practice of mobile curiosity that optimizes the pursuit of pleasure and extricates the self from forms of national rootedness and affiliation that might delimit that pursuit.

It has become something of a critical commonplace to posit Wilde as a representative cosmopolite of the fin de siècle due to his explicit celebration of rootlessness and the traversal of national boundaries. (According to Richard Ellmann, while visiting with Henry James during his American lecture tour, he responded to James's remarks about his nostalgia for London, "Really? You care for places? The world is my home."[62]) He also celebrated in his essays and lectures art's capacity to foster cosmopolitan understanding, arguing that "by creating a common intellectual atmosphere between all countries [art] might ... make men such brothers that they would not go out to slay one another for the whim or folly of some king or minister."[63] Wilde's cosmopolitanism is often understood in relation to his complex sense of national identity. As Stefano Evangelista has argued, his epigrammatic description of himself (*"Français de sympathie, je suis Irlandais de race, et les Anglais m'ont condamné à parler le langage de Shakespeare"*) captures his complicated national positioning, condemned by English colonizers, marginalized by his Irishness, and enlivened and liberated from these ties by "a heavily French-accented cosmopolitanism."[64] Evangelista asserts that Wilde remade his marginality as an Irish subject into a source of cultural authority. His Celticism, in his eyes, equipped him "to criticize modern England with a clarity that [was] unavailable to natives."[65] Wilde's Irishness, according to this formulation, allowed him to at once hover above and perceive more keenly the shortcomings of English sensibilities, and this acuity was only sharpened by his French sympathies. His national outsiderism enabled his critical capacity, and his cosmopolitan detachment from and derision for English morality facilitated his sexual dissidence. As Amanda Anderson has argued, Wilde located in detachment the possibilities for both "reflective distance and radical freedom," and the twentieth-century Decadents on which I focus here found this model of aloofness from English morality generative and liberatory.[66] Cosmopolitanism was not, however, for Wilde nor his successors solely about distance and freedom. Wildean cosmopolitanism also emerges from curiosity about otherness, facilitates engagement with place, and motivates expansive reading and travel practices that lead in turn to friendships that traverse national boundaries and knowledges that emerge from transcultural pollination. Wilde's cosmopolitanism, as Jessica Berman puts it, "rests upon deep encounters with each culture that is met."[67] According to Margaret S. Kennedy, Wilde's "life and work set an example of cosmopolitanism that is ... committed to revitalizing culture and fostering ties between people based on tolerance and love."[68] If Wildean cosmopolitanism provided the figures upon which I focus in *Queer Kinship after Wilde* with a template for operating above English morality and laughing down one's nose at provincialisms that might delimit personal freedom, it also informed their nomadic curiosity and deep desire to connect with difference, affective tendencies that took them out of England and into contact with other cultures and kinship schemes.

The Decadent encounter with difference is not, however, as we all know, all benign curiosity and love. Wilde and the Decadents are known as much for their Orientalism as they are for their cosmopolitanism. As Elleke Boehmer notes, the characteristics most fetishized by the Decadents of the fin de siècle, "ornate patterning, strangeness, diversity, languor," "bore stereotypically orientalist ... associations," and for Oscar Wilde in particular, "a devotion to the sensations that beauty aroused was bound up with an excitement about refined and beautiful oriental things."[69] While the Orientalism of Decadence may appear obvious, emerging so clearly in Beardsley's Japonisme or the exoticization of the court in Wilde's *Salome* (1894; first published in French in 1893 as *Salomé*), it is certainly worthy of further discussion, particularly because it is so often imbricated within seemingly contradictory ways of conceptualizing difference emerging from Decadence's tendency to counterculturalism. More recent work by Katharina Herold and Grace Lavery has allowed us to begin thinking in more comprehensive ways about the manner in which Orientalism shaped aestheticism and Decadence while still allowing for the presence of cosmopolitan aspirations within these movements. Herold, for example, has raised questions about whether Wilde's cosmopolitan resistance to nationalist specificity, evident in works like "The Sphinx" (1894), might be understood as Orientalist in light of its disregard for the "political implications of engrossing foreign cultural traits and disconnecting them from their history."[70] Here the cosmopolitanism of Decadence is not placed in opposition to its Orientalism. Wilde's Orientalist tendencies are rather understood as bound up with his cosmopolitan objectives. Lavery's treatment of the Aesthetic Movement's fascination with Japan brings out elements of the aestheticist response to and use of Japanese culture that might be understood as reductive, exoticizing, instrumentalizing, or appropriative – the aestheticist understanding of Japanese objects as "immediately, absolutely, and universally legible as beautiful," an emphasis on "the threatening capacity of Japanese beauty," "trepidation over the narcissistic threat of Japanese culture" – while at the same time teasing out the queer circuits of intimacy in which Japanese objects flowed.[71] In this case, the Aesthetic Movement's response to Japan *is* Orientalism, but it is at the same time other things. This work on aestheticism and Orientalism should be understood in relation to other more recent strands of thinking about the racial politics of Decadence. In her recent work on Wilde's American tour, for example, Michèle Mendelssohn acknowledges the very real forms of oppression Wilde experienced as an Irish subject and the manner in which his Irishness linked him to Blackness in the American cultural imagination. She also, however, brings to light less flattering elements of Wilde's own behavior, such as "playful allusions to Christy minstrelsy and slavery" in his correspondence of the period and comments to the press that objectified Black bodies.[72] In Mendelssohn's account, Wilde is at once the victim and perpetuator of nineteenth-century racism. Imani Perry calls attention to Wilde's sex tourism in Algeria, noting that Wilde's exploits in the company of André Gide and Lord Alfred Douglas allow us to see "how legal persons – and more specifically very elite ones – who were subject to one form of discriminatory discipline were in relationships of domination facilitated by colonialism and Orientalism."[73] The full range of affective encounters with racial and cultural difference that these scholars have located in the Decadence of the fin de siècle is similarly on display within the network I am tracing here, and I would like to operate with this more recent work on the racial and transnational politics of Decadence in mind as I attempt to deidealize the uses to which twentieth-century Decadents put alterity as they endeavored to clear a space for their own experiments in affiliation.

Transnational Decadent Connection in the Twentieth Century

Rather than organizing this book chronologically, I have chosen to organize it thematically grouping together chapters that demonstrate similar affiliative practices and political tendencies. In the first part, "Queering Kinship/Kinship as Queer Politics," which includes chapters on Vyvyan Holland and the Housmans, I focus on ethical revisions of the familial structure as performed by twentieth-century figures with ties to British aestheticism, foregrounding moments when Decadent revisions to conventional kinship structures were informed by transnational contact or operated as a locus for political reform. The second part, "Queer Retreat and Cosmopolitan Community," examines figures, such as the Mackenzies and Harold Acton, whose withdrawals from their home countries into communities abroad facilitated their capacities to radically rethink or deliberately eschew marriage and to reconceptualize familial forms. Here I also pay closer attention to moments when Decadent cosmopolitanism engendered forms of transnational encounter that, while liberatory for queer subjects, resulted in the exoticization and the appetitive consumption, or even exploitation, of cultural difference. In the third part, "Decadent Modernism and Eroticized Kinship," I focus on Decadent modernists Eric Gill and Richard Bruce Nugent, both preoccupied with the concept of incest, and I highlight the political and imaginative work that visions of eroticized kinship performed for these twentieth-century figures working within a Decadent tradition.

Chapter 1, "The Son of Oscar Wilde: Cosmopolitanism and Textual Kinship," argues that Vyvyan Holland forged a textual relationship with his father Oscar Wilde while collaborating with early Wilde scholars in the editing of Wilde's letters and extended his father's practice of importing sexually dissident content from abroad while translating works by the French modernist Julien (or Julian) Green. Following Wilde's trials, his sons were separated from their mother and from one another and shuttled between various boarding schools abroad, an experience Holland described as deeply traumatic and lonely. His existence was devastated by the effects of late-Victorian sexual legislation, which divided him from his family and placed him in exile. But, when he came of age, he found community with a network of men who loved Wilde and loved books, locating himself amidst other forms of relationality and affection. In this chapter, I assert that Holland modeled his own cosmopolitan aesthetic on his father's, remaining similarly detached from and skeptical of English moral sensibilities, and I work to understand how the translation of queer modernist texts allowed him to obliquely continue his father's queer cosmopolitan project. Holland was divided from his father following Wilde's trials for acts of "gross indecency," but he was able to find his way back to him through textual acts, acts of cosmopolitan collaboration and translation, and by generating an alternative familial bond with early Wilde scholars.

Chapter 2, "'Out and Out from the Family to the Community': The Housmans and the Politics of Queer Sibling Devotion," centers on Laurence and Clemence Housman, siblings who spent their entire lives living and working together in a collaborative relationship that more closely resembled a marriage. The two cooperated in the production of suffrage posters and engraved book illustrations, and their early acts of political and aesthetic collaboration informed Laurence's later activism work as he contested war, British imperialism, and the oppression of queer subjects. Laurence and Clemence's radical mode of familial affiliation became the locus for larger forms of political dissidence. Laurence argued that love must always move "out and out" from the family to the

community and into the wider world.[74] He believed that radical politics
might emerge from a radical kinship practice that fostered ethics of service
and care. With this in mind, I tie his early feminist work in collaboration
with his sister to his later anti-colonial work in the Indian independence
movement. In the final part of the chapter, I consider Laurence's handling
of his brother A. E. Housman's posthumous papers, which revealed
Alfred's unrequited love for his friend Moses Jackson. Laurence oscillated
in his feelings on what to do with this material between his role as a family
member, concerned for those with "feelings to be hurt," and his role as an
activist, believing that his brother's letters "may be of some benefit to
society as a corrective to social intolerance."[75] His role as executor of
Alfred's estate placed Laurence in the practical position of weighing his
kinship ties against broader political affiliations. The carefulness and
sympathy with which he carried out his responsibilities to his brother
and to the greater political good, however, reveal how skilled Laurence was
at braiding together kinship ties and wider modes of affiliation. His activist
practices inflected his approach to his brother's papers, but his devotion to
his brother also determined the manner in which he implemented those
papers in his activist project.

Chapter 3, "An Extraordinary Marriage: The Mackenzies and the Queer
Cosmopolitanism of Capri," focuses on Faith and Compton Mackenzie's
choice to rethink their marriage in highly unconventional terms, allowing
one another to conduct affairs with other partners, spending a great deal of
time apart while at the same time remaining committed to an ideal of
loving friendship with one another. They came to this agreement while
living abroad on the Italian island of Capri, described during this period as
"a Geneva or a Moscow of the future internationalism of homosexuality,"
and mingling with the queer expatriate community of Decadent aesthetes
on the island.[76] Faith became intimate with Capri's lesbian modernist
coterie, and the Mackenzies remade their marriage in conversation with
the island's aesthetes, cosmopolites, and "extraordinary women" with
whom they drank and danced and conducted affairs. This chapter relies
on analysis of the Mackenzies' life writing and fiction as well as extensive
work with their diaries, notebooks, and correspondence housed at the
Harry Ransom Center to develop an understanding of the rhythms of
their alternative form of affiliation and the manner in which their porous
bond was influenced by their time on Capri. Faith's diaries in particular
reflect the extent to which the openness of the Mackenzies' union allowed
the community on Capri to operate as a crucial component of their
relationship with one another. Their marriage did not engender isolation

or withdrawal into conventional domesticity. As her diaries indicate, she and Compton rather turned their curiosity and their energy outward, serving one another as allies and collaborators in the interpretation of the company they kept. Throughout this chapter, I consider the role of place in the Mackenzies' experiences, the manner in which the islandness of Capri enabled and sheltered queer experiments in connection, while at the same time attending to the manner in which visitors to Capri extracted pleasure from the island and its inhabitants, approaching the site according to an ethos of "Mediterraneanism" that structurally resembles Orientalism. The positing of Capri as a queer Arcadia in the early twentieth century involved an instrumentalization and exoticization of the island, a projection of a fantasy vision of Capri as a primitive and destabilizing erotic resort.

Chapter 4, "Decadent Bachelordom and Transnational Adoption: Harold Acton in China," focuses on the Decadent modernist Harold Acton's time in China and argues that Acton relies on the concept of kinship as he theorizes cosmopolitanism and transnational contact. Inspired in part by Decadent precursors, such as Vernon Lee, he insists that coming into true communion with other nations requires the eschewal of forms of heteronormative domesticity that might delimit mobility or inhibit openness to foreign experience. However, his work is haunted by anxieties about the slippage between cosmopolitanism and Orientalism, and he turns to kinship metaphors, to the figure of transnational adoption, to think through that slippage. He simultaneously suggests that extrication from conventional familial arrangement facilitates transcultural communion and worries, in his figuring of cultural appropriation as unsuccessful transnational adoption, that true transcultural communion is impossible. In examining the manner in which Acton thinks through and against the concept of kinship while theorizing cosmopolitanism, I highlight the influence on his thinking of women writers and artists, such as Vernon Lee, Nancy Cunard, and Anna May Wong, who shared with Acton a vexed relationship to family and marriage as well as the aspiration to move across national and racial boundaries.

In Chapter 5, "Richard Bruce Nugent's 'Geisha Man': Harlem Decadence, Multiraciality, and Incest Fantasy," I turn to the Harlem Renaissance author and illustrator Richard Bruce Nugent, arguing that his "Geisha Man," which centers on the erotic relationship between a white American father and his mixed-race child, should be understood as emerging from his sustained engagement with Decadence and the Salome story in particular. I position this fascinating manuscript within the framework of Nugent's extensive experimentation with Decadent tropes and Decadent style to argue that the text's Orientalism and its preoccupation with incest should be understood as more than a simple echoing of Decadence's more troubling tendencies. This content rather operates within the text in service to Nugent's efforts to conceptualize mixed-race identity and the rupturing of Black kinship structures within the United States. Salome's story is for Nugent a story about a fetishized performer attempting to enact erotic agency within a system of fractured familial formations, and retooling and revising this story allows Nugent to theorize kinship and multiraciality in relationship to what Hortense Spillers refers to as the "losses" and "confusions" that accompanied the "dispersal of the historic African American domestic unit."[77] This chapter sheds light on the manner in which Orientalist Decadence was transported across the Atlantic to perform different types of service for Black thinkers in Harlem in the early twentieth century.

Chapter 6, "Hallowed Incest: Eric Gill, Indian Aesthetics, and Queer Catholicism," considers the modernist sculptor Eric Gill's highly unconventional family life, his interest in Indian art, and his connections with Decadent queer Catholicism in relationship to his preoccupation with the family as a site of divine eroticism. While Gill is often thought of as a "distinctly heterosexual" figure with a circumscribed and highly provincial vision, during the 1910s he affiliated himself with a group of authors and artists, including Katharine Bradley and Edith Cooper ("Michael Field"), whose nonnormative sexual identities were deeply intertwined with their Catholic religious identity, and he exhibited a tremendous thirst for information about global artistic practices, writing frequently to the Ceylonese art historian Ananda Coomaraswamy and engaging extensively with Indian art.[78] He found in Bradley and Cooper, who converted to Catholicism and wrote religious verse concerning their union, a model for conceiving of incestuous desire in divine terms. In his correspondence with Coomaraswamy concerning the treatment of eroticism in Hindu temple sculpture, he found models for the successful integration of faith and sensuality. This network of influences resulted in one of his most well-known works, *They* (or *Ecstasy*, 1910–11), an attempt to hallow incestuous desire and transform an extreme form of sexual dissidence into an expression of divine love. Gill's sister Gladys and her husband Ernest Laughton were the models for *They*, and Gill's diary, housed at the William Andrews Clark Memorial Library, reveals that he was actively engaged in a sexual relationship with Gladys during this period. This work should be understood as an effort to consecrate his love for his sister, to make incest holy – his first title for the sculpture was "Christ and the Church" – and it mimics the style of Hindu temple sculpture. A representation of radical sexual dissidence informed by Gill's contact with queer Catholic communities and his engagement with Indian art history, *They* reflects Gill's belief in the divinity of incestuous desire. Reading Gill within the context of queer Catholic networks and global art history illuminates his controversial ideas about sexuality, the family, and the representation of the body, revealing the extent to which his treatment of incest was inflected by a cosmopolitan aesthetic vision as well as queer, Decadent approaches to the practices of love and affiliation. Understanding his vision of divine eroticism within the Decadent context from which it emerged also highlights the extent to which the sexually dissident Decadent ethos, which we tend to associate with a more progressive, or even radical, politics, did not always result in what we might think of as just practices, as it seems Gill implemented his ideas about divine eroticism to make sense of his sexual abuse of his daughters. I end the book here to demonstrate that making connection new does not always amount to making connection better and that the undoing of taboos can engender abuse as well as liberation.

These are for the most part authors and artists who have not received significant critical attention. Much of that has to do with their conflicted aesthetic affiliations. They are neither Victorian nor modernist, operating on the borders of the twentieth century with an eye turned to the fin-de-siècle past, and this has made them unwieldy for a discipline that has tended to operate within conventional categories of periodization. In some cases, their critical neglect has to do with forms of difficulty and trouble that are central to their own practices and projects. It is easier, I think, not to talk about the forms of abuse that took place in Eric Gill's household. Richard Bruce Nugent kept much of his work to himself, and many of Laurence Housman's most fascinating formulations of queer affinity occur in works he chose not to publish. The most striking and compelling thinking that these figures did often occurred in private forms – in letters and diaries and albums and collections meant only for certain eyes. What I hope to do here is make more of that thinking visible, to disinter from the archives and bring to light an entire chain of novel thinking about connection that emerged from transhistorical and transnational Decadent networks in the early twentieth century.

PART I

Queering Kinship/Kinship as Queer Politics

CHAPTER I

The Son of Oscar Wilde
Cosmopolitanism and Textual Kinship

On September 27, 1896, Constance Wilde wrote to her nine-year-old son Vyvyan from Switzerland. Following Wilde's trials and the exile of his wife and children from England, the two boys were attending a school in Heidelberg while Constance stayed with family in Bevaix. As he recalls in his memoirs, Vyvyan was "very unhappy" in Germany: "The school was run on austere lines, and a lot of bullying went on as well."[1] Constance wrote to her unhappy son, "Are you learning to be less babyish? I do hope so Darling. You are quite old enough now, & of course what you will really have most difficulty in learning is consideration for other people's feelings & that you are not the centre of everything!"[2] While it is, of course, possible, it seems unlikely that a nine-year-old boy who had just been removed from his home and his family understood himself to be the "centre of everything." Constance's comments nevertheless provide tremendous insight into the nature of Vyvyan Holland's experience in the years immediately following his father's imprisonment. Circumstances demanded that he had to learn quickly to be less "babyish" and see himself as peripheral. He was separated from both his parents. His mother died when he was twelve. His mother's relatives kept him and his brother apart, believing that this would assist in concealing their shameful heritage. They also purposefully isolated Cyril and Vyvyan from Wilde's friends. Severed from his most significant and intimate kinship ties by his mother's relatives, he learned to see biological family as a source of trauma and loneliness.

In the decades that followed, Holland wrestled with the question of how visible he might like to make himself in relationship to his father's legacy. As he records in his autobiography, following Wilde's imprisonment, Vyvyan and Cyril's names were changed in an effort to conceal their identities. Their surname was altered to "Holland," and the spelling of Vyvyan's first name was normalized to "Vivian."[3] Holland spent the rest of

33

his life revisiting and suturing this linguistic severance from his father. His name is nowhere to be found in the editions of Wilde's letters on which he collaborated with Christopher Sclater Millard (1872–1927) in the 1920s, and he refused to sign the copies of the letters, stating that he wished to remain "in the background."[4] He does appear, however, on the title page of the Dulau and Company catalogue of *A Collection of Original Manuscripts Letters and Books of Oscar Wilde* (1928) as "the younger son of Oscar Wilde," a spectral yet unnamed presence amidst his father's textual remains.[5] In 1949, after Lord Alfred Douglas's death, he produced an edition of *De Profundis* accompanied by an introduction to which he appended his name. And, in 1954, he issued *Son of Oscar Wilde* in which his connection to his father becomes the primary signifier of his identity. His follow-up to this work, *Time Remembered after Père Lachaise*, published in 1966, similarly places his father at the center of his life and his persona, opening with the reinterring of Wilde's remains at Père Lachaise cemetery. In this set of memoirs, Holland allows himself to mourn publicly for his father and reinstate the kinship relation that was first severed in 1895. He textually reconstructs the bond that had been broken by the trials, writing himself back into filial connection with Wilde.

In this chapter, I examine the stages by which Holland found his way out of the loneliness and isolation of his childhood and found his way back to his father, the series of nonbiological ties and the set of textual practices that allowed him to generate an alternative model of kinship with Wilde. When he became an adult and was no longer under the control of his guardians, he turned to Wilde's body of friends and formed bonds with the surviving members of his community as a method for generating connections with his father. As Holland negotiated the question of his father's legacy with figures such as Robert Ross and Christopher Millard, he forged unconventional connections with a deceased parent and the men that mourned him, connections that were textually based, that circulated around the appreciation of beautiful books and collaborative editing projects. In writing to these men about his father and cooperating with them in the arrangement of his literary remains, Holland was able to experiment with the possibility of identifying publicly as Wilde's son before composing his later memoirs in which he proudly foregrounds his connections to his father. Connecting with Ross facilitated his entry into the bibliophilic world, a space in which he could begin to reestablish his identity as Wilde's son. Collaborating with Millard to edit his father's letters allowed him to textually suture his connection with his father. Through his connections with figures like Ross and Millard, he was also able to rethink the concept of familial bonds in the wake of the traumatic impact sexual legislation had on his own family and to conceive of new modes of connection and community that operated outside the boundaries of normative heterosexual association. Holland's connections to Wilde's body of friends will serve here as a model of queer kinship that continues the innovative thinking about affiliation performed by his father during the late-Victorian period.

Holland also textually reconstructed the severed kinship bond with his father in his work as a translator. In his translation projects, Holland carried forward the playful, shocking, and transnational aesthetic of Wilde. He brought erotically charged and sexually dissident content into British cultural conversation, and he paid particular attention to work that highlighted the dislocating and liberatory effects of cross-cultural contact. Holland's translation work, like the editing projects in which he engaged with Millard, allowed him to generate an alternative form of connection with his father. Through this work, he entered obliquely into a discussion about sexuality and desire and extended the cosmopolitan project of aestheticism. Holland's inheritance of a Wildean form of cosmopolitanism facilitated his detachment from England's ideals concerning gender, sexuality, and kinship. This, in turn, allowed him to participate in transnational conversations concerning gender and sexuality taking place in the works of authors such as Julien Green and transmit the content of those conversations to the English-speaking public, replicating and echoing his father's own transmission of French Decadence to late-Victorian readers. In choosing to engage in translation, a fundamentally cosmopolitan creative process, Holland highlighted his connections to Wilde and a tradition of late-Victorian cosmopolitanism and continued the sexually dissident work of his father.

Texts, stories, editing, and translation allowed Holland to foster affinity with his father and to build family and affiliation out of what he had been told should only be a source of shame. While Holland himself never seems to have entered into erotic relationships with men, his experience of kinship must be understood as marked by a legacy of queer affiliation and engendered by a circle that placed desire between men at its center. In finding alternative, textual ways to connect with his father and by connecting with nonbiological kin, finding community and emotional subsistence outside of conventional familial networks, Holland entered into a queer approach to kinship, one that violated those heteronormative conventions that had first placed him in isolation.

"No Longer a Pariah": Holland, Ross, and Textual Kinship

Son of Oscar Wilde begins with an account of what Holland refers to as the "happy years" that preceded his father's imprisonment, but most of the text is devoted to detailing the family's "exile" following the trials and the boys' unhappy childhood.[6] The warmth and color of the boys' life at Tite Street is supplanted by the roughness of a German boarding school, the gloom of a Jesuit school in Monaco, and the coldness and formality of Constance's relations. The boys were shuttled around from country to country, which delimited and curtailed any opportunity for rootedness, bonding, or connection. After Constance's death, Cyril and Vyvyan were kept apart from one another by her family with the idea that "it is much easier to keep a secret by oneself than to share it with someone else."[7] Constance's family worked to obliterate the memory of Wilde from his sons' minds and to destroy "all evidence that might conceivably connect [the boys] with the family of Wilde."[8] Cyril and Vyvyan's biological kin sabotaged their sense of familial affiliation with their father and with one another. And they severed the boys, too, from any possibility of connection with Wilde's friends. According to Holland, "The lives of my brother and myself could have been made much happier after our mother's death if we had been allowed to mingle with those friends of our father who had remained loyal to him; this would have enabled us to retain much of the natural self-confidence of youth, which was slowly drained out of us. There were so many people who were willing and even eager to take us to their hearts. They inquired after us and our whereabouts, only to be met with coldness and the statement that we were quite happy where we were and must not be disturbed. The principle was that there should be complete severance of ourselves from anything Wildean."[9] In the wake of the trials, biological family operated for Holland as a source of trauma and isolation, taking him further and further away from his father's memory, his brother's comradeship, and the fellowship of Wilde's friends.

Alternative forms of affiliation, nonbiological kinship ties, however, engendered the possibility for reconnection with his biological father. In the final chapters of *Son of Oscar Wilde*, Holland recounts his return to "happy years" in 1907, when he met Mrs. Helen Carew, who commissioned the monument by Epstein for Wilde's grave at Père Lachaise.[10] Mrs. Carew spoke to him about his father, "saying what a wonderful man she thought him."[11] Holland was moved by this, as it was the first time in twelve years that he had heard his father spoken of with respect. This encounter opened into a new world of connections and meetings as he "found himself, within the space of a few days, no longer the friendless, haunted creature [he] had been for years, but in the midst of well-wishers in the literary and artistic world of London."[12] He was brought back into connection, into affiliation, not by his biological family but by the strong kinship circle that grew up around Wilde and his memory. Mrs. Carew invited him to dine again the following week, and, at this "highly emotional meeting," he mingled with Max Beerbohm, Reginald Turner, one of Wilde's closest friends, and Wilde's truest friend, Robert Ross.[13] These figures, and the admiration they expressed for Wilde, transported him back into community and into contact with his father. As Joshua Weiner and Damon Young argue, "Queer bonds mark the simultaneity of 'the social' and a space of sociability outside, to the side of, or in the interstices of 'the social' – bonds that occur not in spite of but *because* of some force of negation, in which it is precisely negativity that organizes scenes of togetherness."[14] The negation of same-sex desire initiated by the trials produced a set of individuals banded together by their shared position outside of "the social" and their stubborn loyalty to Wilde. The negation of the bonds between the members of the Wilde family by Constance's relations placed Holland in a state of openness to new forms of relationality. When these negated individuals came into contact with one another, their common experience of ostracization placed them in a state of readiness to forge new kinds of community and kinship.

Holland's relationship with Ross became particularly intimate. On August 1, 1907, Robert Ross wrote to Holland enthusiastically and optimistically about the possibility of a growing intimacy between them: "I hope you realise how very fond I am of you simply because you are your Father's son and I am sure I shall become very fond of you on your own account."[15] According to Holland, "from the moment [he] met Robert Ross, [he] knew that [he] had found a true friend of his own, one who would be loyal and true and never betray [him]."[16] Ross wrote to Holland, "I believe that I could have made your childhood happier, and it would have made me happier to know that you realised how fond and devoted I was to you both, because you were the sons of my greatest and most intimate friend, and the most distinguished man of letters in the last years of the last century."[17] While he was unable to remold Holland's childhood into a happier shape, he transformed his present, bringing him into contact with a warm and brilliant circle of post-Victorian dandies. Three months after they met, Ross gave a "magnificent dinner party" for Holland to celebrate his coming-of-age.[18] The guests included Charles Shannon, Charles Ricketts, Reggie Turner, William Rothenstein, and More Adey.

Placing himself in the position of guardian and intermediary, Ross provided the kinds of affection and connection that Holland had been denied since the trials, fostering connections between Wilde's son and Wilde's surviving friends and making Holland a part of literary London. As Holland notes:

> With Robert Ross and my father's old friends I found myself in the middle of a Social and Literary world which was quite new to me. I was no longer a pariah to be sent away from England, to be apologised for and to be concealed. On the contrary, I was a welcome guest at the houses of many of the people who had been my father's friends and were friends of Robert Ross, who was not only my father's most loyal friend, but who now constituted himself my guide and mentor.[19]

The two became increasingly close over the next decade. Ross and Holland traveled together to Paris to reinter Wilde's remains. Ross was the best man at Holland's wedding. When Lord Alfred Douglas stood trial for libel on charges brought by Ross, Holland testified as a character witness and asserted that Ross was like a second father to him.[20] When Holland's wife died, he wandered instinctively to Ross's lodgings in search of comfort, though Ross himself had recently passed away. Ross was, according to Holland, his "greatest friend" and "the dearest man [he had] known."[21]

Texts operated at the center of the intimacy between Ross and Holland. Books, manuscripts, and copyrights supplanted blood ties in this alternative model of kinship. Ross was the executor of Wilde's literary estate. As Holland notes, "From the date of my father's death, Robert Ross laboured to rehabilitate the literary reputation of his friend. His first act was to get himself appointed my father's literary executor. That in itself, in view of the fact that he was not a relative and that the estate was bankrupt, was a real feat."[22] Holland notes that Ross's position as executor seemed somewhat unlikely due to the fact that he was not a relative, but the community formed in the wake of Wilde's trials centered upon forging new forms of relationality and violating traditional ways of conceiving of connection and heritage. By positing himself as the guardian of Wilde's literary legacy, Ross also positioned himself as the appropriate guardian for his biological legacy. In this invented kinship structure, Wilde's writing and his boys became strange siblings overseen by a protective nonbiological guardian. Wilde's truest friend and most loyal ally served in the wake of the trials as a parent to both his literary and biological offspring.

By negotiating so fiercely for the copyright and royalties for Wilde's works, Ross also was able to provide financially for Wilde's children. Prior to his first meeting with Vyvyan, Ross had endeavored to make Cyril and Vyvyan the beneficiaries of any royalties received on Wilde's work, but Adrian Hope, Constance's cousin and the boys' legal guardian, had insisted that the boys should not have "any official benefit from their father's works."[23] As Maureen Borland notes, Hope "was fearful that, as their names had been changed to avoid their being tainted by their father's guilt, any official recognition of them would undo all the good the years of anonymity had achieved."[24] However, following Hope's death in 1904, Ross altered this arrangement. Ross was also the one who returned Wilde's estate to credit, allowing the royalties from his work to generate financial support for his children. Holland states, "He fought like a wildcat against the opposition he encountered everywhere, extracting royalties from reluctant producers of the plays in Germany."[25] He worked tirelessly to acquire copyrights and proceeds from editions and performances. The bankruptcy was finally annulled in 1906, and the estate began to generate income. The severed legal and financial bonds between Wilde and his children were sutured by his friend. Wilde could again support his sons due to the endeavors of his and their nonbiological kin.

As the "happy years" continued and Holland became further integrated into the world of literary London, his connections continued to be textually mediated. These new friendships also served to further solidify his ties to his father and to allow him to grow more accustomed to identifying as his son. After World War I, he became an avid book collector, and this pastime brought him into contact with the bibliophilic sphere. While living in Carlyle Square, he met Edward Heron-Allen, who had been a friend of Wilde's. Heron-Allen was an avid book collector and a member of the Sette of Odd Volumes, a bibliophilic dining club founded in 1878. As Ellen Crowell notes in her recent work on the Sette:

> The group's name derives from bibliophilic parlance: bound volumes not paired with others in their "set" were "odd," and thus less valuable than when united. Members of the Odd Volumes extended this bibliophilic metaphor to the social sphere; each individual member – identified by a distinctive title and cartouche which demarcated that member's unique talent – was "odd" until, at a monthly meeting held at one of London's fashionable restaurants, he and his fellow volumes were "unite[d] to form a perfect sette."[26]

Crowell's work demonstrates that the Sette had strong ties to aestheticism and Decadence. Ernest Dowson, Lionel Johnson, and Arthur Symons were guests of the club in the 1890s, and Wilde himself dined as a guest of the

Sette at least six times between 1885 and 1892. According to Crowell, while the Sette seemed to move away from aestheticism in the aughts and teens, at the time that Heron-Allen proposed Holland as a member, the club was finding its way back to late-Victorian Decadence, inviting the seventy-year-old John Lane to reminisce about the *Yellow Book* days in 1923. When Holland delivered his inaugural lecture, a requirement for all new members, he highlighted his connections to his father by delivering a speech titled "A Few Odd Reflections on Idleness." His selected pseudo-nym, "Idler," and its accompanying cartouche, a sloth, similarly served to link him to a Wildean tradition of eschewing work and responsibility and Wilde's assertion that "to do nothing at all is the most difficult thing in the world, the most difficult and the most intellectual."[27] Holland had begun experimenting with the adoption of Wilde's idle mantle in his earlier correspondence with his father's close friend Ada Leverson, telling her, "I am ... living my philosophical ideal of existence, the absolute negation of energy. I have almost given up smoking, regarding it as too strenuous."[28] Presenting on the topic of idleness to the Sette served to solidify the link between his own public persona and his father's suspicion of smug productivity. His published compilation, *A Few Odd Reflections on Idleness* (1927), which was composed entirely of quotes from other writers such as Samuel Johnson, Robert Louis Stevenson, and Jerome K. Jerome, similarly linked him to his father's contempt for the concept of originality, his argument that "it is only the unimaginative who ever invent," as well as his assertion that selection is "the very spirit of art."[29] In becoming part of this "perfect sette" of "odd volumes," Holland playfully referenced his ties to Wilde, allowing his kinship with his father to organize and underwrite his affiliation with fellow book lovers.

Books and Wilde also played a central role in Holland's friendship with another member of the Sette of Odd Volumes, A. J. A. Symons, author of the experimental biography of the Decadent writer Frederick Rolfe (Baron Corvo), *The Quest for Corvo* (1934). Holland first encountered Symons at his First Edition Club during a period when he was "avidly collecting first editions of books by writers whom [he] knew."[30] As Laura Marcus notes, the book clubs of the 1920s, of which the First Edition Club is a representative example, "were in many cases touched with the aesthetic and aristocratic hedonisms of the late nineteenth century," and for these collectors, "the 1890s and its literary objects [were] the primary focus of bibliophilia, and the figure and image of Wilde [were] central."[31] Symons, in fact, undertook a never-completed biography of Wilde and, according to Holland, went "to endless trouble to interview all the people he [could] find with first hand knowledge of [his] father."[32] For one so fascinated with Wilde and the 1890s, Holland's heritage must have held great appeal. Marcus asserts that the milieu in which Symons moved and for whom he wrote was a homosocial one, and, in this world, books operated as the "traffic between men."[33] Repeatedly in the 1920s and 1930s, Holland's heritage along with a shared affection for books solidified his connections with a network of men fascinated by Wilde and the Decadent 1890s. Textual relations and the admission of his kinship with his father facilitated his entry into an insider world of connoisseurship and epicureanism and this, in turn, brought him into stronger connection with Wilde himself.

In the opening pages of *Son of Oscar Wilde*, Holland recounts a dream he had in which his mother came to him and said, "I want you to tell the story of your childhood and of the loneliness of being Oscar Wilde's son in those far-off days when he was still alive, or only recently dead."[34] The story Holland tells, however, in his first memoir and its follow-up, is only partially one of loneliness. In the immediate aftermath of the trials and while under the care of his biological kin, Holland certainly suffered. However, the kinship ties that Constance's family encouraged him to forget, when recollected and foregrounded, served to place him firmly in the center of a warm and affectionate circle of Wilde's surviving friends and a new generation of admirers. He writes, "I had my father continually as a spectre behind my shoulder. At the same time there was always a slightly conspiratorial feeling at the back of my mind; a question of what *would* people think if they knew the truth about me? Would they ostracise me? Would they be sympathetic?"[35] When Holland began to tell the truth about his identity, he got his answer. Joshua Weiner and Damon Young argue,

> Queer bonds might designate shifting encounters in the borderlands of phobic interpellation, the ephemeral being together of those who find, against the backdrop of a phobic world, themselves and each other in a temporary zone where togetherness seems, for the moment, not *only* scripted by hegemonic forms of power, or *determined* by the resistance to that power. . . . It is on the terrain of a social death that a "we" precipitates into a mobile and precarious assemblage perennially in excess of the negations it survives.[36]

Holland's existence was devastated by the effects of late-Victorian sexual legislation, by the negation of same-sex desire, which divided him from his family and placed him in exile. But on the borders of that negation, amongst a network of men who loved Wilde and loved books, he located himself in other forms of relationality and affection. In this body of friends, a precarious assemblage of men who survived the negation of Decadence in the 1890s, he found sympathy, kinship, and connection.

Assembling Wilde's Corpus: Holland, Millard, and Textual Kinship

On August 5, 1921, Vyvyan Holland wrote to Christopher Millard, the compiler of the first bibliography of Wilde's work, concerning an edition of Wilde's letters on which the two were collaborating.[37] He scolded Millard for reintroducing passages concerning the subject of same-sex desire that Holland had deleted from a previous draft, stating,

> It was very wrong of you to put the Uranian passages in after my very careful deletions. But I forgive you, knowing how earnest you are in your devotion to the subject.... I won't have the letters used as Uranian propaganda. I gave you fair warning that if anything of this sort gets in I will destroy the whole edition sooner than anyone should have a copy. To leave passages like this in brings the book down to the level of Teleny [a pornographic novel frequently associated with Wilde's name].[38]

Holland's response to Millard's editorial decisions is complex and conflicted. He expresses frustration with Millard's desire to define his father's legacy in "Uranian" terms while at the same time acknowledging the earnestness of Millard's devotion to the topic of desire between men, "forgiving" him for the inclusion of Uranian content because of his "devotion to the subject." Their correspondence as a whole is marked by a similar tone. The younger Holland asserts his right to define a modern vision of his father while expressing intimacy with Millard and respect for his opinions concerning their editorial collaborations.

In the 1920s, Holland began to take a more active role in shaping his father's legacy. While negotiating the shape of that legacy with early editors of Wilde such as Millard, he further developed an unconventional mode of kinship with his deceased parent and the men that mourned him. His correspondence with Millard reveals his anxiety about how his father might be remembered as well as a developing sense of intimacy both with Millard and with his father. In his letters to Millard, he refers to Wilde as "Papa" and to those who are sympathetic to Wilde as "Papaists."[39] He demonstrates anxiety about his father's legacy as a "Uranian" writer, but he also engages thoughtfully with Millard's desire to represent Wilde's sexuality honestly. While the two editors might disagree, they remain linked as

Papaists, as members of a fellowship with Wilde's interest at heart. The ring that formed around Wilde's memory in the 1910s and 1920s functioned for Holland as a crucial source of contact with his father, and the bond he established with the Papaists like Millard played an integral role in the definition of Wilde's legacy in the early twentieth century.

The editing project on which Holland collaborated with Millard represents a transitional moment in his development of a form of textual affiliation with his father. The collaboration occurred during a period when he wished his ties to his father to remain invisible to the larger public while nevertheless insisting upon his right to construct and determine Wilde's legacy. Millard also had strong ties with Wilde and his legacy. He had served as the secretary to Robert Ross and had himself been arrested twice, in 1906 and 1918, for acts of gross indecency. His connections with Ross granted him insider knowledge of Wilde's biography, and, as Dan Novak has argued, Millard's subjection to sexual discipline and gender policing would have further linked him to Wilde.[40] Millard also possessed an extensive collection of Wildeiana, translated André Gide's *Oscar Wilde: A Study* (1905), and published a defense of *The Picture of Dorian Gray* (1891), entitled *Oscar Wilde: Art and Morality* (1908), as well as a bibliography of Wilde's works under the pseudonym Stuart Mason. In Millard, Holland would have found one of Wilde's most ardent admirers as well as an impressive breadth of knowledge concerning Wilde's work. As much as Millard was a link to Wilde, however, he also served as a point of contact with the recently deceased Ross. The earliest letter from Holland to Millard in the collection at the Clark is dated July 7, 1920, a little less than two years after Robert Ross's death, and the two collections of Wilde letters on which Millard and Holland collaborated, *After Reading* (1921) and *After Berneval* (1922), were addressed to Ross. If Holland's intimacy with Ross should be understood as an act of substitution and an alternative form of kinship that allowed Holland to forge a literary historical bond with his father, the connection with Millard represents a compounded form of substitution, as Millard facilitated Holland's commemoration of both Ross and Wilde, serving as a conduit to a series of lost kinship ties.

On October 3, 1920, the "239th mensiversary" of Wilde's death, as Holland referred to it, Holland wrote to Millard about the woodcuts to be included in *After Reading*, which was to be published by the Beaumont publishing firm. He asserted his right to participate in discussions concerning the woodcuts, citing his authority as a book collector and as editor, stating:

> You might point out to Beaumont that I am a bibliophile of no mean
> enthusiasm, and that I take a very great interest in this, the first book the
> control of publishing which is in my hands. Furthermore, I do *not* wish the
> name of his obscure artist to appear in the book if this can decently be
> avoided. The whole idea of the book is to be intimate, and for the few. The
> prospective artist is probably one of the many.[41]

Holland relies on aesthetic rhetoric in exercising his authority, establishing
a capacity for taste and selection that is at once part of his heritage and an
outgrowth of his own activities as a book collector, and he adopts a
Wildean tone, distinguishing between the aesthetic elect for whom the
collection is intended and the masses. He also refers specifically to the
sense of intimacy that is to be cultivated by the circulation of the book
among the few, the surviving members of the Wilde's coterie and the
emergent generation of admirers that was developing in the 1910s and
1920s. The work is to function as a form of adhesion between members of
the community composed of Wilde's followers. He also makes proud note
of the control he is to have over this publication. The collection is to be the
work of his hands.

Holland did wish to control and delimit the inclusion of "Uranian"
material in the collections that he and Millard produced. The majority of
the elisions in the two collections that they published with Beaumont,
After Reading and *After Berneval,* are references to Lord Alfred Douglas and
the nature of Wilde's affection for him. For example, in *After Berneval,* the
following passage from an 1897 letter to Ross has been eliminated: "I dare
say that what I have done is fatal, but it had to be done. It was necessary
that Bosie and I should come together again; I saw no other life for
myself."[42] In a 1920 letter to Millard, Holland warned his collaborator
that he would not include any "self-damning uranianisms" in the collection, as the books were "being published neither by Carrington or Liseux,"
distributors of banned works on the continent.[43]

In the same letter, however, Holland made note of another category of
intended elisions, "the grosser insults to his mother."[44] Holland systemat-
ically deleted the evidence of the animosities and difficulties that developed
between his parents following Wilde's release from prison. In fact, one of
the lengthiest passages elided from the *After Berneval* collection mentions
neither Bosie nor Uranianism and focuses instead on a "terrible letter"
Wilde received from his wife in 1897. The letter, according to Wilde,
attempted to forbid him to do certain things and require him to do others.
He scoffs,

> How can she really imagine that she can influence or control my life? She might just as well try to influence and control my art. I could not live such an absurd life – it makes one laugh. . . . I wish to goodness she would leave me alone. I don't meddle with her life. I accept the separation from the children: I acquiesce.[45]

Holland's omissions not only eliminate Lord Alfred Douglas from his father's post-prison life. They eradicate the story of the Wildes' troubled marriage and turn purposefully away from the fact that Wilde abdicated his right to contact with his children in favor of continuing his relationship with Douglas. Holland's editorial practices allow him to rewrite his family narrative, to reimagine and reinforce the ties between his parents and between himself and his father, and to do away with the evidence that Wilde might have preferred another life.

Holland's editorial decisions allow for a re-envisioning of Wilde as a husband and a father, producing a representation of Wilde that must have been deeply disappointing to Millard, who was, as Holland noted, earnestly devoted to the subject of Uranianism. Millard, however, had the opportunity to articulate a rebuttal to Holland in the iconography of Wilde that he drafted and sent to William Andrews Clark in 1927. The iconography, which Millard never completed, was to include a series of photographs, drawings, and caricatures of Wilde. As Dan Novak has argued, Millard "completely erased" Constance and the children from his portrait of Wilde.[46] Not a single image of Constance, Cyril, or Vyvyan was meant to appear in the iconography. Novak effectively demonstrates that Millard's selection of images was intended to articulate an implicit claim about Wilde's identity, to posit him as "simply and only homosexual."[47] Novak argues that images of Wilde's family often operate as signifiers of the closet, and, by omitting these signifiers from his iconography, Millard is able to imagine a "Wildean homosexuality without the closet."[48]

But what if Wilde's family is read as something besides the closet? What if their role in his biography and his afterlife might be allowed to complicate our vision of his desires and his object choices? Holland certainly seemed to see his desire to be reintegrated into his father's life as not entirely at odds with his father's connections to a tradition of Uranianism. While he expressed great anxiety about the inclusion of Uranian content in the collections he edited with Millard, he also actively cultivated deep and abiding friendships with Robert Ross, Christopher Millard, and Proust's translator C. K. Scott Moncrieff, friendships that were founded on a frank acknowledgment of Ross, Millard, and Moncrieff's sexuality as well as the

nature of their admiration for his father.[49] Holland found his way back to
his biological father through his affiliation with his Uranian friends, and
these friendships were rich and intimate and loyal. At the moment Millard
was constructing a Wilde album that carefully elided Wilde's family from
his life, Holland clearly demonstrated his loyalty to Millard by writing to
individuals such as Osbert Burdett to obtain funds for Millard's court costs
in a libel trial. Millard had accused the Methuen and Company publishing
firm of knowingly foisting "on an unsuspecting public" a Wilde forgery
entitled *For Love of the King* (1921), and the firm in turn sued him for
libel.[50] Holland wrote to Burdett:

> We are starting a fund to try to help Mr. C. S. Millard out of his present
> difficulties, and I am venturing to approach you in the hope that you feel
> inclined to subscribe. ... I should be so very grateful if you would help.
> I really think it is a good cause, as unless we can avoid Millard's being sold
> up, he will lose his only means of livelihood.[51]

Millard was being prosecuted, after all, for attempting to preserve the sanctity
of the Wilde canon, for exercising his authority as an expert and editor, as one
who truly knew and thus could accurately identify his work. Holland's
assistance to Millard at this moment testifies to their affiliation, founded on
a shared sense of affection for and responsibility to Wilde, their intimacy, and
their status as members of the aesthetic few as opposed to the many.

   Holland's collaboration and correspondence with Millard speak to the
manner in which Wilde, even after his death, generated rich possibilities
for conceiving of affiliation and friendship. This is not to say that the
alternative forms of kinship inspired by contact with Wilde were always
practiced in an open or proud manner. In a March 1921 letter, Holland
expressed hesitance about signing the editions that he and Millard had
produced. "If I could sign as V.W. it would be right and proper, but I have
an innate loathing of *noms de plume* and still greater loathing of *noms de
camouflage*. To sign as V.W. would be silly unless I meant to adopt the
name."[52] Holland would not be ready to "adopt the name" of Wilde's son
until three decades later. However, the nascent form of affiliation expressed
in this editing project, the manner in which he began to feel his way
toward his father in arranging his textual remains, and, in so doing, created
intimacy with the Papaists, the select community of Wilde's admirers who
were finding their way toward one another in the 1920s, indicates the
extent to which Wilde continued to operate as a generative locus for
innovations in the understanding of kinship and community long after
the century turned.

Exile, Queer Cosmopolitanism, and Kinship: Holland as Translator

Holland continued to textually suture the connection with his father in the translation work that he performed in the 1920s and 1930s. In his work as a translator, Holland displayed an adventurous sensibility, at once cosmopolitan and sexually progressive, that resembled his father's. He was drawn in his translation work to challenging content and to avant-garde writers whose work reflected and investigated the effects of exile, travel, and transnational contact, and he imported to England the work of highly modern and experimental twentieth-century authors from France, America, and Switzerland. In the early 1920s, Holland translated *Ouvert la nuit* (1922) (*Open All Night* [1923]) and *Lewis et Irène* (1924) (*Lewis and Irene* [1925]) by Paul Morand, a French modernist and diplomat with ties to aestheticism whose work also appealed to and was translated by Ezra Pound. As Roxana Verona notes, Morand's works contain a strange blend of cosmopolitanism and xenophobia, high modernism and fascism, and cultural mediation and racism.[53] In the late 1920s, Holland began translating the works of Julian/Julien Green, a Franco-American writer who wrote primarily in French in a style that Dayton Kohler refers to as "modern Gothic."[54] Green's works are preoccupied with queer desire, Catholicism, and the biological family as a source of hostility and discord. Holland produced translations of four of his works, including *Le visionnaire* (*The Dreamer* [1934]) and *Minuit* (*Midnight* [1936]), novels that engage in the frank representation of sexual and gender dissidence, erotic contact, and illicit desire. In 1935, he produced a translation of the French novelist Henri Barbusse's flattering biography of Stalin, *Staline: Un monde nouveau vu à travers un homme* (1935) (*Stalin: A New World Seen Through One Man*). In 1940, he translated the Swiss writer Albert Cohen's *Mangeclous* (1938) (*Nailcruncher*), a work often referred to as "Rabelaisian" that focuses on a Jewish community that has emigrated from France to Greece. George Orwell's review of the translation described the novel as "scatological" and "calculated to make any ordinary person physically sick."[55] While Holland's most interesting work as a translator allowed Anglophone readers to come into contact with innovative and politicized contemporary French literature, he also translated French works from the eighteenth and nineteenth centuries. In selecting texts from earlier periods, he exhibited a similar taste for erotically charged authors and works that think in transnational or cross-cultural terms, such as Pierre Victor, Baron de Besenval's short stories, which depict open marriages and the adventures of Spanish soldiers in Africa, and Jacques-Rochette de La Morlière's

Angola, histoire Indienne (1746) (*Angola: An Eastern Tale* [1926]), an Orientalist fairy tale that satirizes French aristocratic society. He brought to English readers novels by Americans written in French, about French Jews living in Greece, biographies of Russian leaders by French communists, short stories by fascists about cosmopolitan mobility, and Orientalist tales that are allegories about France. He performed the work of cultural mediation in works that themselves reflect on or engage in cultural mediation. And, like his father, he imported challenging and sexually dissident content into England, expressing a cosmopolitan detachment from English sexual morality and pointing to sites abroad as models of progressive sexual politics. He transmitted to Anglophone readers scatological and queer literature written in French, works that dwell on same-sex desire, ephebophilia, and sadomasochism. For Holland, like Wilde, cosmopolitanism and sexual dissidence were intimately bound up with one another, and Holland's work as a translator and cultural mediator should be understood as a continuation of his father's queer cosmopolitanism.

In the memoirs that Holland composed in the 1950s and 1960s, he tends to stress his own cosmopolitanism, and he explicitly links this element of his identity to his experience of exile in the wake of the Wilde trials. He notes that, immediately following the trials, the "hue and cry after the Wilde family" made it seem wise to "go and hide [themselves] abroad" so that they might "live unmolested, . . . lose [their] identity and forget the past."[56] This decision "started an exile that was to last for more than three years."[57] The experience of exile was initially quite traumatic for the boys. Holland notes that he and Cyril were "deeply conscious of going out into the unknown, and aware of the fact that every moment was taking [them] further away from the life [they] knew and from [their] familiar surroundings and possessions."[58] However, as the children were shuttled around the Continent, they became "hardened and experienced travellers."[59] When Holland finally returned to England to attend Hodder Place, the preparatory school attached to Stonyhurst, he seemed altered, transmuted, and transnationalized: "Boys hate other boys to be different from themselves. I was different in that I had been to foreign schools and could speak French, German, and Italian. To the other boys there was something very un-English and rather unsporting about this."[60] In the final chapters of Holland's first memoir, remarks concerning his own un-Englishness become something of a refrain. He states that he "cannot claim to be very English."[61] He argues that his mother's family should have encouraged the boys to acknowledge their heritage "bravely and resolutely," even if that had necessitated their entire education taking place outside of England, as "it was not as though [they] were English anyway."[62] It is unclear at times whether he wants to highlight his Irishness or his cosmopolitanism, but it is nevertheless evident that he wishes to distance himself from "Anglo-Saxon" men, whom he describes as "innately conventional."[63] He implies that his Irish parentage and the exile he experienced as a result of his father's disgrace place him beyond that conventionality, and he argues that his "largely nomadic" life made him permanently "restless and disinclined to settle down to any humdrum form of existence."[64]

In writing about his father, Holland also tends to play up Wilde's cosmopolitanism as well as his global appeal. In his memoirs and critical essays, he stresses that Wilde's works lend themselves to mediation, translation, and global transmission and, by highlighting the appreciation for his oeuvre in other, presumably more sophisticated locations, implicitly critiques English audiences' reluctance to embrace Wilde's writing. He states that when Wilde's works were "totally banned in England," they "were already being used as textbooks of English in Germany."[65] In an essay on his father's fairy tales, he notes with approval that "The Devoted Friend" (1888), which Holland incorrectly and poignantly refers to as "The Deserted Friend," is used by the "Soviet education authorities" to "illustrate the undemocratic attitude demanded of the down-trodden writer under a system of predatory capitalism."[66] He boasts that "more books have been written, in more languages, about Oscar Wilde than about any literary figure who has lived during the past hundred years."[67] While English readers might have been hesitant to come back to Wilde, the larger world never seems to have halted in their appreciation of his work. His transnational appeal as well as his radical politics allowed him to circulate globally even when England had purposefully turned its back upon his work. He accounts for Wilde's global appeal by arguing that the plays "when translated into other languages" or performed abroad "lose practically nothing," an assertion he substantiates with evidence from his experiences of performances of *The Importance of Being Earnest* (1895) in "half a dozen different languages" as well as *Lady Windermere's Fan* (1893) acted by a Black South African cast.[68] Wilde's works seem in Holland's eyes to be innately cosmopolitan, mobile, and open to globalizing effects. Whatever it is that makes him so distasteful to English readers seems to make him more dashing to readers in France, Germany, Russia, and South Africa. He also stresses that his father is, like himself, un-English and thus innately unconventional. He opens his *Oscar Wilde: A Pictorial Biography* (1960) by stating that his father had "the misfortune, or perhaps the fortune, to have been born and to have lived" at a moment when "English Society was encompassed by conventionality: every utterance and every action of the individual were required to conform to rigid rules of behavior and ethics, the slightest deviation from which being regarded as an outrage and as putting the offender 'beyond the pale.'"[69] His father had "made it his mission in life to break down" this "state of affairs," and, according to Holland, "it is a remarkable tribute to the forcefulness of his character that he largely succeeded in doing so, against overwhelming odds."[70] Here Holland pits his father against the very essence of Victorian Englishness and proudly celebrates him as victorious against his highly conventional foes. He similarly describes *The Picture of Dorian Gray* (1891) as an attack on Englishness, arguing that the text "[exposes] the hypocrisy of Victorian Englishmen who, living in one of the most vicious cities in the world, kept priding themselves, sanctimoniously, upon their virtue," and he highlights the xenophobia of the backlash against the text, citing the *Daily Chronicle*'s assertion that the novel "is a tale spawned from the leprous literature of the French *décadents*."[71] Holland also makes much of his father's declaration in a Paris newspaper, following the Lord Chamberlain's refusal to license the performance of *Salomé*, of his intention to "transfer [himself] to another fatherland" and become a Frenchman. He argues that "it is a pity that Oscar did not carry out his threat to adopt French citizenship."[72] While the tone of Holland's pictorial biography is, for the most part, measured and detached, the occasional emotional intrusions in the text posit Wilde as a heroic dissident and opponent of English moralism. He repeatedly stresses Wilde's role as a mediator of French culture, and he celebrates his oppositional relationship to the nation that disciplined and destroyed him.

When Holland began his translation work, then, he foregrounded an element of his identity that was intimately bound up with his father's. His experience of exile and his cosmopolitanism were prominent elements of, or might even be considered results of, his kinship with Wilde, and, in bringing writers like Julien Green to British readers, he replicated his father's transmission of the "leprosy" of French ideas about sexuality to English audiences. In practicing translation, he made concrete his father's more abstract practice of cosmopolitanism. Cosmopolitanism itself might be understood as a process of cultural translation that enables one culture to rethink and alter itself in view of its contact with another, but Holland's work literalized this process, digesting and disseminating contemporary French thinking about sexuality, subtly enlarging and revising English readers' understanding of desire.[73] As Esperança Bielsa notes, recent work in translation studies has emphasized not what is lost but what is gained in the process of translation, on "how translated texts work in their receiving cultures."[74] The texts Holland translated "worked" in a fashion quite similar to the texts his father composed. However, whereas his father aggressively confronted English audiences with an aesthetic inflected by French sexual politics, Holland's intervention in discussions of sex and gender in the twentieth century occurred in a more oblique form, through the selection and transmission of queer or transgressive texts by other writers. Responding to Lawrence Venuti's characterization of translation as a form of ethnocentric violence that involves the "forcible replacement of the linguistic and cultural difference of the foreign text," Bielsa insists that "this violence works in both directions, as cosmopolitan openness to the other leaves the receiving culture exposed to the penetration of foreign elements that subvert it."[75] Holland exposed Anglophone readers to this penetration by foreign elements in curating for them a set of contemporary French and Swiss authors who represented desire and the body in frank and challenging ways, facilitating their encounter with alternative visions of the family and sexuality.

As I have argued, Holland's translations introduced British audiences to a wide range of modern French writing, but I will be focusing here on his translations of the works of Julien Green, works which seem to have resonated with and inflected Holland's understanding of and representation of his own childhood. Green's works seem to have attracted Holland more than any other writer's, as he translated four of his novels. (He only translated multiple works by one other writer, Paul Morand, for whom he produced two translations.) In a chapter devoted to "Translating" in *Time Remembered*, he highlights Green's hybrid national pedigree:

> It may seem strange that a man named Julian Green cannot write his own books in English; but he is the son of an American diplomat and of his French wife. The diplomat had died when Julian was an infant and his mother brought him up in France as a Frenchman; so that, although he speaks perfect English he does not feel competent to write in it.[76]

In light of Holland's interest in cosmopolitanism, Green's hybridity might in part explain the appeal of his works to Holland. However, the content of Green's novels, their stories of orphaned figures, the family as a source of trauma, and erotic temptation, seem just as likely to have been the source of their attraction. Julian Jackson describes Green's entire oeuvre as "a dramatization of the struggle between the flesh and the spirit, homosexuality and Catholicism," and as Kathryn Eberle Wildgen argues, "overtly homosexual characters, male and female, populate his novels."[77] However, the queer valence of these texts arises most clearly in their treatment of conventional familial affiliation as violent and unpleasant, a theme that is echoed and repeated in Holland's own life writing. As Wildgen notes, "Julien Green did not write 'Familles, je vous hais'; but a reading of his novels could lead one to conclude that he shared André Gide's pessimism regarding family relations."[78] Green's novels not only confront readers with representations of same-sex desire. They also perform a critique of conventional kinship structures, representing parental figures as repressive and tyrannical while turning sympathetically to the traumas that a lonely child experiences as a result of parental cruelty and domination. Green's persecuted orphans frequently find a release from familial abuse in illicit erotic connections, but these relations often in turn lead to their demise. Green's novels construct a dark world in which the family inhibits desire and true freedom only comes in death. Holland was drawn to this dark vision of sinister and repressive forces and the forbidden desires that resist them, and the trace of their influence registers in his own work. In their preoccupation with the fates of orphaned children and their treatment of biological family as a source of distress, the novels by Julien Green that Holland translated presage Holland's later life writing and could be understood as informing his own queer treatment of the concept of kinship. Holland published his first translation of a novel by Green, *The Dark Journey* (*Léviathan* [1929]), in 1929, and his second, *The Strange River* (*Épaves* [1932]), in 1932. In each of these novels, familial abuse figures prominently. Mothers take joy in the red marks that their slaps leave upon children's faces.[79] Children are "conceived in a wave of hatred."[80] I will focus here, however, on two later works, *Le visionnaire* (*The Dreamer* [1934]) and *Minuit* (*Midnight* [1936]), in which critical representations of biological kinship intersect with representations of gender fluidity and sexual dissidence.

The Dreamer concerns itself with what Glenn S. Burne refers to as a "familiar [situation] in Green's fiction: an unloved child in a household dominated by a single parent."[81] The fourteen-year-old Maria Teresa suffers under the cold tyranny of her mother who seems to thrive on emotionally abusing her. She is joined in her experience of her mother's cruelty by an older orphaned cousin, Manuel, whom her mother alternately berates and nurtures, throwing Manuel into a state of emotional confusion. Manuel develops a sexual obsession with his cousin, which culminates in him nearly assaulting her, and Maria Teresa confesses the details of the attack to a priest and then to her mother. Manuel denies the story when confronted by the mother, and the mother turns on Maria-Teresa, shaking her so violently she screams, and forces her to abject herself before Manuel and apologize on her knees. The pressure of the situation causes Manuel to fall ill, and he experiences a break with reality, generating for himself a fantasy life in a castle with a cold and cruel Vicomtesse and her sadistic brother Antoine, for whom Manuel seems to feel an erotic, masochistic attraction. Manuel thrills at the sight of Antoine's "powerful arms" while he "rub[s] his tan riding-boot with his riding-whip," and he engages in a strange, intoxicating altercation with him in the woods during which Antoine demands that Manuel throw a stone at him and then strikes him in the face with his whip.[82] Soon after, he has a violent sexual encounter with Antoine's sister that ends in her death. Wildgen argues that Manuel's encounters with the Vicomtesse and her brother in *The Dreamer* constitute an important precursor to Green's later treatment of bisexuality in texts such as *Moïra* (1950).[83] In the novel's conclusion, Manuel emerges from this fantasy, takes a walk with Maria-Teresa, lays his head in her lap, experiencing a moment of peace and satisfaction, and then dies.

Midnight focuses similarly on the fate of an orphaned child in a world filled with unconventional erotic potentialities. The heroine Elizabeth's mother kills herself in the novel's opening chapter after being rejected by her lover Monsieur Edme. Following her mother's death, Elizabeth is exchanged between her "harsh and neurotic" aunts, from whom she finally flees.[84] She is taken in by a kindhearted man and introduced into a "typical Greenian" family that includes "a prematurely aged, tired mother [and] an ugly, ill-tempered older sister who is jealous of [Elizabeth]."[85] While in this household, Elizabeth is the subject of amorous advances from her piano teacher, Mademoiselle Bergère. When the kindly father dies, a mysterious man named Monsieur Agnell arrives to escort her to an enormous and eerie mansion inhabited by her deceased mother's former lover Monsieur Edme. As Wildgen argues, Edme is represented in androgynous terms.[86] Green uses feminine pronouns to refer to him, and Holland's translation notes that "the structure of his face betrayed the almost painful sensitiveness which is usually only seen in women, and it was of a woman, too, that one thought on seeing his bare emaciated hands."[87] Edme has assembled about himself a set of lost souls whom he involves in midnight rituals, preaching to them that night is superior to day and a nocturnal existence is a visionary one. Elizabeth develops an erotic fixation on one of these lost souls, a beautiful boy named Serge, but she is also drawn to Edme. She spies on one of Edme's nocturnal gatherings and hears him declare that he was in love with both Elizabeth and her mother and sought Elizabeth out in the hopes of "rediscover[ing] in [the] child something of the emotions which her mother had aroused in" him.[88] She is lured in by Monsieur Edme's seductive mysticism, but Serge attempts to wrest her away from his influence by taking her away to an upstairs room and ripping her dress from her. Elizabeth "len[ds] herself willingly to his violence because her hands told her that her tormentor had an exquisite body."[89] Following their sexual encounter, the two are set upon immediately by the other occupants of the house. Serge jumps from the window to escape and dies, and Elizabeth follows him, throwing herself to her death.

The trace of Green's novels is visible in the story Holland constructs of his own sad childhood in *Son of Oscar Wilde*. His account of his early years echoes Green's representation of the Gothic terror and shame that Maria-Teresa, Manuel, and Elizabeth experience as children. Green's children are powerless and humiliated and confused, existing in a world governed by tyrannical adults tied to them by blood but lacking altogether in tenderness. Holland's uncle's stern announcement "that in future our names would no longer be Wilde, but would be changed to Holland"; the remarking of their clothes with their new names; his brother's "lethargy of despair" in the wake of this announcement; the "thought that at any moment an indiscreet remark or a chance encounter with someone from our former lives might betray us," which hung like a "sword of Damocles" over the boys' heads – each of these events are relayed so as to communicate the shame and alienation that pervaded Holland's existence in the years when he was in the care of his relatives, before he found his way to Wilde's friends.[90] The queer form of alternative kinship that Holland generated with Wilde's friends should be understood alongside the queer critique of kinship Holland transmitted to England in his translations of Green's works and the manner in which they influenced his own life writing.

These translations also allowed Holland to engage in a textual performance of his kinship with Wilde by continuing his father's queer cosmopolitan project and his transmission of erotically charged French content into England. *The Dreamer* and *Midnight* take place in sinisterly erotic worlds, and Holland's translations relay the reader directly into these worlds with tremendous fidelity to the original text. While Holland might have expressed hesitation about the inclusion of "Uranian" content in his editions of his father's letters, he does not shy away from transmitting to English readers the sexually dissident content in Green's work. He is not, for the most part, excessively literal in his treatment of Green's work, but he is particularly true to the original when translating the most sensational or erotic passages. Mademoiselle Bergère's advances to the young Elizabeth are rendered almost word for word from the French. Manuel's sadomasochistic sexual encounter with the Vicomtesse, during which his "mistress's cold white body closed over [his], like one of those monstrous flowers which are said to imprison insects attracted by the sweetness of their scent" and his "cry of anguish and delight ... was stifled in the heavy coils of her hair" while her limbs moved in a "spasmodic frenzy," similarly follows Green's French closely.[91] His departures from literal translation only serve to reinforce the erotic valence of a given passage, as when he makes *"un affreux délire"* into "frantic rapture" in the passage concerning Manuel's encounter with the Vicomtesse.[92] Although Holland cannot himself take credit for generating these strange stories, in bringing them to Anglophone readers and refusing to censor or diminish their eroticism, he continues obliquely the work his father began at the fin de siècle while relaying the "disease" of French Decadence into England.

Holland's friendship with Ross in the 1910s, his editing of Wilde's letters with Millard in the 1920s, and his translation projects in the 1920s and 1930s represent his initial forays into identifying with his father. As he grew older, he performed this identification more publicly, coming into stronger and more explicit textual kinship with his father in his memoirs and the editions of Wilde's works that he produced in the 1940s and 1950s. Five years before the publication of the memoir that so aggressively foregrounded his connections with Wilde, Holland published "the first complete and accurate version" of *De Profundis* (1949).[93] In his introduction, he indicates how this work might function in the recuperation of his father's reputation: "Through it he hoped that posterity, and even his enemies, might find some sympathy for him. In this tragic document he has, as he himself says, tried to explain his conduct without defending it. Let it rest at that."[94] As Wilde's son, he establishes his right to determine the motives behind his writing and to dictate how readers might interpret it. More importantly, in publishing an "accurate" edition of *De Profundis* with his own name appended, Holland rejects the shame he was taught to feel about his father's sexual identity. A few years after the publication of *Son of Oscar Wilde*, Holland produced a translation of Wilde's *Salomé* (1957), and in his foreword, he continues to highlight his father's global appeal, noting that, in the years since its first performance, the play "has been translated into all the principal European languages, including Czech and Greek, and into many Oriental languages as well. It has also become part of the repertoire of nearly every European stage. It has, in fact, as

Robert Ross remarked, 'made the name of Oscar Wilde a household word wherever the English language is *not* spoken.'"[95] Beneath this defense of his father, articulated via an implicit cosmopolitan critique of English close-mindedness expressed through the ventriloquism of Wilde's closest friend and his own "second father," Holland displays his name prominently.

CHAPTER 2

"Out and Out from the Family to the Community"
The Housmans and the Politics of Queer Sibling Devotion

In an unpublished, undated manuscript for a work entitled "What I Believe", Laurence Housman (1865–1969) articulates his vision of an ever-expanding form of fellow-feeling that emanates from the self to the family to the nation and outward to the globe.[1] He asks his readers to imagine an ideal world and then to consider what stands at the center of that world:

> Is it our own little individual selves, our own prosperity, our own aggrandisement, our importance in the eyes of others? Or is it that larger self which is the true self of man, the social self with no hard and fast limits that say "Thus far and no further" – which does not stop at family, or class, or nation, or race – but is infinitely brotherly and expansive, friendly to all life, embracing all.[2]

He calls his readers to conceive of love as a form of giving that can expand infinitely from the closest and most immediate ties of biological kinship to the wider world:

> It is in the thought of loving as giving, as a willing service, that we can meet the often-raised objection that it is not possible to love others as much as our own family, or, as President Theodore Roosevelt crudely put it, "to love other men's wives as much as your own." But it is quite possible to give willing service, without partiality, out and out from the family to the community, and thence on through the race to the whole of humanity.[3]

According to this formulation, familial love is not set up in opposition to other broader or more inclusive types of sympathy. Kinship does not produce clannishness. Rather, the family operates as the locus for the development of a kind of love that can emanate further and further afield, across boundaries of race, gender, and nation. We can, he insists, love all life as we love our own family.[4]

In this chapter, I consider the centrality of familial affection, and of sibling devotion in particular, to Laurence Housman's work and life, and the manner in which his collaborative relationship with his sister, the author and engraver Clemence Housman (1861–1955), inflected his theorization of fellow-feeling and his political work on the part of the suffrage and the peace movements. Laurence lived with Clemence for ninety years, and their relationship at times more closely resembled a marriage. They addressed one another as "Dearest" and "Dearest Own" in their correspondence, and in a letter to his friend Sarah Clark, Laurence insisted that "*Clem* is the right man for *me* in much the same way as Roger [her husband] is for you."[5] Laurence illustrated Clemence's story *The Were-Wolf* (1896), and Clemence produced wood engravings of Laurence's illustrations for his fairy tales as well as banners for the suffrage movement based on Laurence's designs. Their careers and their domestic lives were thoroughly intertwined, and I argue here that this relationship, based on an ethics of collaboration and equality, fostered Laurence's political sympathies, allowing him to feel across the boundaries of gender and devote himself to feminist activism, an experience that in turn informed the extension of his sympathies across national and racial boundaries in his advocacy for Indian independence and peace. His love for Clemence made her political interests his own, allowing him to identify across gender distinctions in a manner that had an expansive impact on his political sympathies. The capacity to identify, sympathize, and engage politically across boundaries of identity operated as the foundation of his work in support of internationalist causes and allowed him to cultivate a sense of political responsibility that did not "stop at family, or class, or nation, or race." His love for Clemence moved "out and out," from their devotion to one another to his devotion to the cause of women more generally, the alleviation of suffering on the part of colonized people, and the cessation of international political violence.

Laurence's political activism in turn inflected his kinship practices, as his work in the field of sex reform informed his thoughtful treatment of the legacy of his brother, the poet A. E. Housman, who was, like Laurence, attracted primarily to men. Sex reform was, in fact, the cause with which Laurence's activist career began. As he developed his "larger self" in the 1890s, he came to conceive of himself as part of a Uranian community and an advocate for greater understanding of sexual identities. He was a member of the Order of Chaeronea, a society founded by George Ives in the 1890s to support Uranian men, and, as Lorraine Janzen Kooistra has argued, his *All-Fellows: Seven Legends of Lower Redemption with Insets in Verse* (1896), which he sent to Oscar Wilde when he was released from prison, could be understood as "a coded message of solidarity and fellowship to Wilde . . . and an artistic expression of the aims of the Order of

Chaeronea."[6] When the century turned, he became a more outspoken campaigner for sex reform, serving as the chairman for the British Society for the Study of Sex Psychology, which "aimed at a greater openness, and a putting aside of received prejudices, in the discussion of sexual matters, and aspired to greater sexual freedom in society," and he published a pamphlet defending unconventional forms of affinity entitled *The Relation of Fellow-Feeling to Sex* in 1917.[7] His commitment to the cause of sex reform and his kinship ties intertwined and came into conflict with one another during the years following A. E. Housman's death, as Laurence negotiated the complexities of shaping his brother's posthumous reputation. Encountering evidence of his brother's love for a close friend, Moses Jackson, as well as poetry that he understood to be concerned with same-sex desire in his brother's papers, he struggled with the question of whether this material should be made public. Laurence approached his responsibilities to his brother, as well as his responsibilities to the larger queer community, with thoughtfulness and care, releasing material that he felt indicated Alfred's contempt for "social injustice" and his "keen sympathy for those whose problem of life was similar to his own" while at the same time choosing to be subtle and indirect in his discussion of his brother's personal life.[8] The carefulness and thoughtfulness with which he approached this work demonstrate his deep sympathy for his brother despite the fact that, during his lifetime, Alfred often remained quite aloof from his siblings. Laurence's sympathy for Alfred arose, at least in part, from their shared ties to a community to which Laurence had devoted himself as a defender and political advocate. Laurence's political activism began, then, with his own immediate community, with fellow-feeling for Wilde and other Uranian men, and emanated further afield in his suffrage work and internationalism and then turned back upon his kinship practices, underwriting his sympathetic treatment of his brother's sexuality and his careful curation of a vision of his brother as an oblique advocate for sex reform.

For the Housmans, queer kinship practices engendered political activism, and political activism fostered queer kinship practices. I am using the term "queer" to describe the kinship ties between the Housmans not simply because of the erotic object choices of the figures involved. Rather, I use the term to indicate that the Housmans practiced sibling devotion in a manner so excessive and politically radical that they remade a conventional, biological tie into something queer. In choosing to live together for their entire lives, Laurence and Clemence were able to extricate themselves from heteronormative narratives of maturation

involving marriage and reproduction. In privileging the sibling bond so
dramatically, they transformed an ordinary, biological bond into an
extraordinary and oppositional one. In addition, their intense devotion
to one another engendered radical forms of identification across boundaries of gender as well as advocacy for sex reform. The way they cared for
each other produced radical political action, and their political beliefs
informed the way they cared for each other.

   Laurence and Clemence Housman were, as Rodney Engen describes
them, "disciples" of the 1890s.[9] They constructed their aesthetic in relationship to Decadent figures like Wilde, Aubrey Beardsley, and Charles
Ricketts, and they carried the thinking of Wilde and the radicalism of the
fin de siècle into their own familial practice. They allowed the sexual
dissidence of the 1890s to inflect their approach to kinship, and this, in
turn, had larger political consequences, informing Laurence and
Clemence's collaborative suffrage advocacy as well as Laurence's pacifism
and cosmopolitanism. The sibling bond has historically been neglected, as
Leonore Davidoff has argued, by psychoanalytic theory, which emphasizes
the bond between mother, father, and child, as well as by the state, which
does not tend to recognize "relationships that have no obvious outcome in
reproduction."[10] However, Davidoff's *Thicker Than Water* as well as
recent work by Valerie Sanders and Leila Silvana May have encouraged
us to turn our attention to a relationship that is "the longest family
relationship of many people's lives."[11] This work, drawing on G. W.
F. Hegel's representation of the sibling bond as "untainted by the urge
to mastery," has considered the association of fraternal and sororal ties with
egalitarianism and democracy in nineteenth-century literature and culture
as well as the manner in which sibling bonds could shield individuals from
the "perils of exogamy," "the stresses of childbearing," and "the inevitable
inequality of status that legally divided husbands and wives."[12] Victorian
studies scholarship concerning the sibling bond has foregrounded the
manner in which this kinship tie, which rests at the center of the
patriarchal family, can push back against the hierarchical tendencies of
that familial model and operate as alternative to heterosexual marriage
and reproduction. In other words, this work has demonstrated how often
the sibling bond, even at its most conventional, could be understood as at
odds with patriarchal and heteronormative structures. The Housmans
make explicit the queer potentialities of the sibling bond, inflecting their
kinship practices with a Wildean and Decadent ethos that allows their
relationship to operate as the locus of feminist, sex reform, and pacifist
activism. In this chapter, then, I build on the work of Davidoff, Sanders,

and May by considering what becomes of the egalitarian sibling bond when integrated with the sexual radicalism of the 1890s and the further effects these affective experiments had in the twentieth century, during the struggle for suffrage, the campaign for Indian independence, and World War II.

Amativeness, Fellow-Feeling, and the Linking Up of the Human Family: Laurence Housman at the Fin de Siècle

Though Laurence does imply, in later writings such as "What I Believe", that all individuals have the capacity for infinitely expansive fellow-feeling, in a pamphlet published for the British Society for the Study of Sex Psychology in the 1910s, *The Relation of Fellow-Feeling to Sex*, he argues that "certain types of humanity," more "sympathetic natures," are particularly capable of forging unconventional bonds and making unusual connections.[13] He argues that, in childhood, the amative instinct, which has not yet developed into sexual desire, is much less narrowly directed and might more properly be described as "fellow-feeling."[14] This instinct is most powerful, not in those individuals who will go on to desire sex the most intensely but rather "in those natures which are in a special degree sensitive, sympathetic, and imaginative."[15] For these individuals, who often possess more "child-like" or aesthetic temperaments or highly developed "social affections," a tendency to "promiscuous" amativeness or fellow-feeling persists even after the sex functions have become active, allowing them to find pleasure in connections and contact with "both sexes alike," "uncles, aunts, grandmothers," "dogs, cats, fur coats, woolly hearthrugs."[16] Housman argues that this kind of promiscuity in liaisons and attachments, the seeking out of connections that are not utilitarian in character, actually contributes to vitality. "May it not," he asks, "also be a necessary ingredient in the life of social humanity that we should have the capacity and the will to embrace and endear ourselves to objects for which the material ends of sex-function were not designed; and that a latent sex-feeling (not necessarily involving any functional manifestation) may be a real and valuable inducement to the linking up of the human family?"[17] According to Laurence's vision of fellow-feeling, forms of desire that might typically be cast as perverse are, in fact, extremely beneficial, for they open the individual up to new allegiances and sympathies. Strange or unconventional attractions lead one toward innovative affiliations.

In *The Relation of Fellow-Feeling to Sex*, Laurence unapologetically celebrates eroticized forms of affective connection. The pamphlet includes a series of case studies that exemplify the form of expansive amativeness Laurence has described, each of which involves an element of eroticism: a boy who fell in love with one of his father's pupils and drank his bath water; a five-year-old boy who sought to comfort his crying younger brother with embraces "of an amorous character"; a father so devoted to his son that he worships "every motion of his body"; an artist "with homosexual inclinations" whose admiration for splendid living things rouses sexual feelings in him (for example, when he sees a splendid mare, he wishes he "were a stallion"); an artist who had an involuntary emission while watching his friend admire a painting he loved; Aubrey Beardsley, whose fellow-feeling for his body was so intense that, when he drew nudes, he felt that his pen was traveling along his own form; and a man who felt a sexual response when his face was licked by an abused horse to whom he had been kind.[18] Laurence's case studies represent forms of desire that violate taboos and transgress conventional boundaries, such as the incest prohibition, the line between human and nonhuman animals, and the distinction between animate and inanimate objects. He wishes to insist that embodied, highly unconventional types of affinity can be beneficial, for they enlarge the human capacity for fellow-feeling. As he states in his conclusion, "to arrive at the full degree of fellow-feeling which our human nature makes possible," we must understand that those acts and identities we might think of as "aberrations and wayward experiments" in fact operate "in the main for good and for the self-realization of the human race."[19]

The Relation of Fellow-Feeling to Sex focuses on erotically charged modes of affinity that circumvent the "functional manifestation" of eroticism. The relationships that Laurence describes in his case studies are suffused with desire yet obliquely or indirectly sexual. They contain a "latent sex-feeling." These are forms of amativeness that are ongoing, perpetual, and do not conclude in intercourse. They are never truly consummated. The fact that they eschew completion contributes to their generative quality. Perpetual longing and indirect contact inspire a kind of affection that draws individuals closer without culminating in absorption or "the material ends of the sex-function." While each individual described in the case studies is drawn to another, their desire for that other is never truly satisfied, and so they grow increasingly curious about and worshipful of the desired human or nonhuman animal or object. Sex is everywhere and nowhere at the same time in these relationships. It inspires affinity but never comes to fruition.

Laurence began theorizing the connection between unconsummated sexual desire and the "linking up of the human family" in the 1890s, as evidenced by his correspondence with Edward Carpenter. He wrote to Carpenter in 1897 after reading Carpenter's pamphlet *Homogenic Love and Its Place in a Free Society* (1894), expressing "wide agreement and cordial feeling" in relationship to Carpenter's claims.[20] He had reservations, however, about the fact that Carpenter licensed the "strongest sexual embraces" short of the "Venus aversa."[21] Laurence pointed to the restraint of Greek sculpture as his ideal, and he argued that it would be a "great mistake" to insist that "the satisfaction of the love-instinct lies only in the sexual function."[22] In fact, he noted,

> I have found for my own part that the higher and more passionate has been my attachment for a person, the less has it affected the lower parts of my body, while intensifying the desire of embrace in the lips and heart, and above all evoking a passionate wish to be of service, to enter in some way into the other one's life and aspirations.[23]

In his eyes, the most beautiful product of intense desire is not the strong embrace but the inspiration of generosity and empathy. He looked forward to a future when, "as the need for the propagation of the race diminishes," this type of desire might become more prevalent.[24] Freed from "the old imperious desire for self-reproduction," sexual attraction might operate then in the service of "the knitting up and perfecting of the social state and for the prevention of the separating tendencies of a selfish individualism."[25] Though Laurence expressed a certain distaste for "the material ends of the sex function," eroticism, particularly queer or oblique modes of eroticism, played a central role in his vision of community. Desire leads to openness, connection, and comradeship. In his eyes, attraction engenders affiliation. Sex makes fellow-feeling.

Queer forms of desire, according to Laurence's formulation, create a more thoroughly united world, one in which individuals can feel across boundaries and forge unconventional bonds. The fairy tales that Laurence wrote and illustrated during the 1890s are in the main preoccupied with this possibility, with figures who love with a difference and in surprising ways. His fairy tale collections might, in fact, be understood as the space in which he began to theorize the form of expansive amativeness described more explicitly in *The Relation of Fellow-Feeling to Sex*. Audrey Doussot has noted that the stories often deal with "fraternity or marginality" or "the rejection or the acceptance of otherness within . . . relationships," and she argues that Laurence found in the fairy tale "a genre in which he could express his ideals of social tolerance and harmony."[26] Housman is, of course, not alone in turning the genre of the fairy tale to these types of political ends. As Lorraine Janzen Kooistra argues, Wilde's fairy tale collections inspired an entire "coterie of radical writers at the fin de siècle to use the fairy-tale genre to critique existing norms and posit utopian alternatives founded on notions of equality and social justice."[27] She notes in Laurence Housman's fairy tales, nevertheless, a particularly intense preoccupation with "the human capacity for love" and "all the directions love can flow."[28] His fin-de-siècle fairy tales operate as primers in promiscuous fellow-feeling.

Laurence published six collections of fairy tales in the 1890s and 1900s, and these works as a whole cooperate in celebrating queer forms of desire and articulate a queer politics that responds to late-Victorian sexual legislation and the trials of Oscar Wilde. However, as Kooistra has argued, the collection *All-Fellows* should be distinguished among Laurence's fairy tale collections as particularly tied to the emergent sex reform activism inspired by the persecution of Wilde.[29] Laurence states in *Echo de Paris: A Study from Life* (1923), which records his conversations with Wilde, that he had sent the collection to Wilde on his release from prison, "hoping that its title and contents would say something on my behalf."[30] *All-Fellows*'s title and contents express an affinity with Wilde, regret for his fate, as well as reverence for the beauty of bonds between men. The collection is dedicated to "my friend and dear fellow Shadwell Boulderson," whom Laurence described as his "dearest friend" and the object of an unrequited passion in his later (unpublished) sexual autobiography "Outrageous Fortune" (1933).[31] The collection opens with a set of poems that look forward to a future moment when such passions will no longer be condemned and all men will live together in fellowship, when "pleasure can no more be sin / Nor friend want help of friend."[32] And, as Kooistra notes, all of the stories but the first "focus on same-sex desires or on the comradely attachments between an older man and a younger 'son' whom he loves and teaches."[33]

The queer valence of *All-Fellows* does not, however, emerge solely from its preoccupation with Wilde and same-sex desire. The collection's most sophisticated thinking concerning queer affiliation occurs in its representation of the affective labor involved in promiscuous fellow-feeling. "The Truce of God," for example, considers the complexities involved in expansive affiliation, the difficulties that attend the wide extension of kinship bonds, the temptation to privilege certain bonds above others, and the pain involved when one refuses to do so. It is the story of a holy man who goes to live "among the beasts of the forest."[34] The animals accept him because he "is no hunter, but a lover of peace" and allow him to dwell with them "as one of themselves."[35] The beasts become increasingly intimate with the hermit, allowing him to see them at their most vulnerable and heal their wounds. As he tends to the forest creatures, he comes more and more to love them, and his heart grows wiser and wiser. The hermit clearly possesses the "sympathetic nature" and highly developed "social affections" celebrated by Laurence in his later sexological writing. One day, a lion brings to the holy man a human child, and he takes the child to be "his own son," enlisting a female deer to suckle the boy.[36] This is a loving family constituted of cross-species, nonbiological ties, the product of the capacity to care and trust across conventional boundaries. The illustration that accompanies the story stresses the connectedness between the members of this interspecies family and the wider natural world (Figure 2.1). They are not genetically linked, but their lithe, long-limbed bodies nevertheless rhyme with and echo one another, and their home opens out into the forest just as the forest grows into their home.

The story shifts, however, to consider how an individual involved in expansive forms of love and community negotiates competing allegiances. The boy grows older and comes into contact with hunters who teach him how to kill. When he returns from this encounter with the "smell of blood" about him, the hermit becomes "troubled with a divided mind" and a divided set of loyalties.[37] The boy finally shoots a lion, and, when the beast comes to the holy man to be healed, the hermit's "days of . . . peace [are] over: love for his son, and love for the lower kinds could not strive in his heart."[38] He becomes increasingly divided from the animals in the forest, who grow more and more fearful of his foster son. His son is finally killed while hunting a lion, and the hermit is seized with rage. However, when the opportunity to kill the lion that took his son presents itself, he has a vision of his son with his arm encircled around the animal's neck, and he drops the bow and arrow, his grief suddenly evaporating. The next day, the beasts come to him for a blessing, and the hermit and the animals are reunited as friends. The story considers the work involved in forging radical kinship ties and in balancing bonds that conflict with one another. A sense of familial obligation inspires the holy man's thirst for revenge against the animal world, but he is able to repress and control the desire for vengeance and honor his ties to the nonhuman animals that love and trust him. The story articulates a pacifist argument grounded in an ethos of promiscuous amativeness.

Laurence returned to the question of how to negotiate competing allegiances repeatedly throughout his career. The later fairy tale collection

Figure 2.1   Laurence Housman, illustration for "The Truce of God,"
from *All-Fellows*, 1896.
Reproduced courtesy of University of Michigan Special Collections Research Center.

The Cloak of Friendship (1905), for example, includes a story entitled "The
Troubling of the Waters" that similarly details the predicament of an
individual beloved by the animal world who must decide if his ties to a
cruel and abusive brother who engages in horrific acts of violence against

nonhuman animals carry more weight than his "queer fellowship" with the beasts.[39] As Kooistra and Doussot emphasize, Laurence celebrates sympathetic communion with otherness and the crossing of boundaries. However, his works also exhibit a deep attentiveness to the difficulties involved in loving so expansively and balancing sets of obligations. Queer or expansive affiliation, as he acknowledges, frequently involves pain or sacrifice. He is honest and thoughtful about the limitations that inhibit the capacity to transcend one's own pain and feel into the traumas and experiences of others. He opens "Outrageous Fortune", for example, with an anecdote about a moment early in his life when he "passed in a London street a young girl of negro race, followed by a rabble of street-urchins, jeering at her because she was black."[40] He feels deep sympathy for the girl and drives the boys away. However, he notes, "if fellow-feeling then made me kind, it made me angry as well; for the thought came in me afterwards, how little relief from persecuting contempt I should be able to secure for myself, if I carried my colour as openly in my face as did she."[41] Extending himself in sympathy across racial boundaries, he almost simultaneously retracts back into his own suffering, experiencing a moment of resentment and insisting that the persecution of same-sex desire is more severe than racial prejudice. The choice to open his sexual autobiography, a narrative concerning the pain of living a "concealed life," with an anecdote about another's pain is significant. He highlights the connections between persecuted groups while at the same time indicating how difficult it often is for these groups to understand their experiences as similar. His works exhibit a deep investment in the extension of sympathy across boundaries as well as a rich awareness of the affective and intellectual labor this kind of feeling involves. This thinking operated as the foundation for his pacifism, allowing him to consider the sacrifices involved in detaching oneself from nationalist affiliation in order to see oneself as a member of a global community, and he developed and refined this ethos of expansive fellow-feeling in collaboration with his sister Clemence.

"Being a Brother and Sharing House with My Sister": Feminist Activism and the Queer Kinship of Laurence and Clemence Housman

Following the publication of *All-Fellows*, Laurence wrote to Clemence to say that he should have dedicated the collection to her: "It is more yours than the poems [*Green Arras* (1896)], are, and more *mine*; and I am prouder of it."[42] *All-Fellows*'s meditations on expansive amativeness and fellow-feeling emerge as much, he implies, from the radical experiments in kinship and collaboration conducted by the two siblings as they do from the queer activism that arose in the wake of the Wilde trials. Laurence's devotion to his sister was bound up with this desire to "link up the human family," to move further and further outside the limits of his own concerns and into care and work for others, and his ideas about kinship and community were expressed and refined in the fairy tale collections he produced at the turn of the century, many of which included wood engravings by Clemence. The collections' cooperative mode of production echoed and reinforced the consideration of queer kinship and radical affiliation conducted within the stories themselves.[43] Clemence's careful engravings of Laurence's illustrations, which James Guthrie has described as "marvel[s] of sympathy," physically manifest the Housmans' collaborative ethos.[44] They are the product of the intense intimacy between these two siblings who left home together in 1883 and spent the rest of their lives working and thinking together. If the content of the fairy tale collections could be understood as pointing forward to Laurence's internationalist and pacifist thinking during World War II, the manner in which they were made served as a gestation site for Laurence's developing capacity for empathy across gender.

According to Laurence, he and Clemence's intimacy began in childhood, and Clemence from the first served as a defender of and advocate for Laurence: "I suppose it was because I was the most put-upon member of the family . . . that in quite early days Clemence began to take pity on me, and become my protector. . . . It was from this defence of the weak and whiney-piney by the strong, that the special attachment and pairing-off arose, which has lasted throughout life."[45] When Laurence left for London to study art, "Clemence was released from the Victorian bonds of home, for the sole reason that it was considered too risky for [him] to go alone without some one of more stable character to look after [him]."[46] The relationship, then, was beneficial to them both. Laurence received protection, and Clemence was "released from the bonds" of conventional domesticity. Their home life, first in London, then in New Milton, and finally in Street, became the locus for their aesthetic and intellectual labor and operated as an experiment in a new model of queer kinship. In articulating his devotion to Clemence, Laurence often borrowed from the rhetoric of romantic love, referring to his sister as his "nearest and dearest" and "lifelong companion," drawing comparisons between their bond and the marriages of their friends, and writing of his hopes that they might spend their "silver wedding" in the Lake District.[47] According to

Elizabeth Oakley, who has written extensively about the Housmans' unique bond, their nephew Jerry Symons described theirs as a "perfect relationship in which, to his credit, Laurence did his full share of household tasks."[48] Oakley argues that "Laurence seems to have been determined, through his partnership with Clemence, to put into practice his belief in a shake-up of power relations between the sexes."[49] If they remade their kinship tie into something resembling a marriage, they also remade marriage into something more closely resembling a partnership, a queer model of companionship that insulated the two siblings from the labors of heterosexual domesticity and reproduction.

Queer sibling devotion emerges as a central preoccupation in the fiction that both Clemence and Laurence wrote in the 1890s, but they articulate their commitment to the sibling bond in highly disparate ways. Laurence's delight in the ethos of sharing and equality that was so central to their relationship registers very clearly in his fairy tales, particularly those that are dedicated to her, such "The Luck of Roses," which, as Oakley argues, idealizes "male-female companionship" in its representation of a "devoted and utterly contented couple who have no children except the roses which they nurture lovingly."[50] The offspring of the couple, like that of the two siblings, is beauty rather than babies. Many of Laurence's works that celebrate affiliation across gender distinctions also express investment in more expansive, cross-species forms of affiliation, suggesting that for Laurence the two affective practices were intertwined and enabled one another. His interest in gender equality, fostered by his collaborative relationship with his sister, opened out into a broader interest in ethics and sympathy with otherness. Kooistra's reading of "The Luck of Roses," for example, emphasizes that the couple's "children" are "non-human," thus "from an eco-critical point of view, this fairy tale offers a vision of living in relationship with (not dominance of) the vegetable world."[51] The works Clemence composed in the 1890s, on the other hand, often exhibit suspicion of the kinds of figures (feminine, otherworldly, or nonhuman) that would typically be celebrated in Laurence's stories. While her fiction certainly privileges sibling bonds, in every other respect, Clemence's writing seems to stand in direct contradiction to Laurence's vision of gender equality and expansive amativeness.

On first reading, for example, Clemence's *The Were-Wolf* appears to oppose the feminist and queer politics advanced in her brother's fiction. A beautiful huntress in "half masculine" dress named White Fell infiltrates the home of the twin brothers Christian and Sweyn.[52] Sweyn immediately becomes enamored with the mysterious woman, but Christian remains suspicious and shares with his brother his belief that she is a werewolf. Sweyn scoffs at Christian's fears, and Christian is left to nervously police his brother's conduct, spying upon him as he shares a kiss with White Fell and begging him to abandon his dangerous passion for a monster. Christian finally confronts White Fell, chasing her and engaging her in battle. He is mortally wounded, but the blood from his wounds, "the life-blood of a pure heart poured out for another in free willing devotion," acts like holy water and destroys the creature when it touches her flesh.[53] Critics have struggled with the fact that this text, written by an ardent feminist at the fin de siècle, seems to condemn an androgynous woman and express anxiety about the phenomenon of the New Woman.[54] The story certainly appears to vilify threatening forms of femininity as well nonhuman animals and, in addition, make conservative claims for the sanctity of biological ties.

Reading *The Were-Wolf* in relationship to Clemence's larger body of fiction, however, reveals that the story is doing something more peculiar than critiquing transgressive forms of femininity. In this story, as in much of Clemence's fiction, it is sexual desire that is vilified rather than any particular kind of woman. Eroticism, and more specifically heterosexual eroticism, has the capacity to lure siblings away from the sibling bond and into conventional narratives of sexual maturation. It is this that Clemence consistently posits as monstrous. Though *The Were-Wolf* does not preoc-cupy itself with promiscuous amativeness and identification across gender identities in the same manner that Laurence's fairy tales do, it can never-theless be understood as advancing a queer vision of kinship. Again and again in Clemence's work, heterosexual attraction operates as a threat to sibling bonds. Peace can only be restored when the lust that drew the sibling from the home is exorcised. The investment in sibling bonds expressed in Clemence's fiction is so excessive, it renders the relationship between brothers into something queer, something that has the power to redirect love and affection away from heterosexual object choices and back into the fraternal tie.

Laurence's illustrations for John Lane's 1896 edition of *The Were-Wolf* reinforce and extend the story's investment in queer sibling devotion, particularly the final plate, "Sweyn's Finding" (Figure 2.2). When Sweyn finds Christian's body beside the body of a great white wolf, he realizes the enormity of his brother's sacrifice and "dare[s] not touch [his face] with lips that had cursed so lately, with lips fouled by kiss of the horror that had been death."[55] Laurence, however, represents Sweyn embracing Christian's body and bringing his lips to his brother's. It is this kiss, the

Figure 2.2   Laurence Housman, "Sweyn's Finding," illustration for Clemence Housman's
The Were-Wolf, 1896, engraving by Clemence Housman.
Reproduced courtesy of Michigan State University Special Collections.

kiss between brothers, a kiss that the text insists is impossible, rather than the kiss between Sweyn and White Fell witnessed by Christian, that Laurence has chosen to make visible. The expelled threat of heterosexual eroticism, in the form of a wolf, lies dead in the foreground as Sweyn cradles the body of his most true beloved. Lane's edition of *The Were-Wolf* serves, as Oakley has argued, as "a supreme example of [Clemence's] close artistic and literary partnership with Laurence."[56] A story by Clemence with illustrations by Laurence that were in turn engraved by Clemence, it is a material manifestation of as well as a manifesto for queer sibling devotion.

Clemence's *The Unknown Sea* (1898) similarly privileges fraternal and sororal allegiances over heterosexual attraction. In this later novel, Clemence again links the sibling bond with fellowship and self-sacrifice and posits that bond as far nobler than any tie underwritten by erotic desire. The story's hero, Christian, washed ashore as a child and was adopted by Lois, who had recently lost her own daughter to the sea. This daughter had never been baptized, for Lois refused to have dealings with the local priest after her sister, whom he had impregnated, died in childbirth. She understands the appearance of Christian on the beach as an opportunity to atone for her sins against her lost child, and she raises Christian as her own. Lois wishes for Christian to marry Rhoda, her sister's child, whom she has also taken into her home. Christian, however, has become enamored with Diadyomene, a sea witch who lives on the nearby Isle Sinister. At his foster parents' urging, he finally asks for Rhoda's hand, but she declines, knowing he loves another. Christian is overwhelmed with relief: "His face grew radiant; he caught her in his arms suddenly and kissed her, once, twice. 'O my sister!' he cried, 'my dear sister!'"[57] He is free to pursue Diadyomene and continue in his efforts to convert her to Christianity, and Rhoda is remade as a sister figure rather than a potential mate. Thereon, Rhoda and Diadyomene occupy opposing poles of feminine virtue and serve as figures for the beauty of sisterly devotion, on the one hand, and the baseness of lust, on the other.

Like White Fell, Diadyomene is cast as dangerous and deceptive, an alluring and irresistible object of desire. She is consistently cold and cruel to Christian, but his need for her nevertheless grows increasingly overwhelming and embodied. He wrestles with his "base lust" for the sea-witch, which vies with his desire to save her soul:

> The mere thought of contact with Diadyomene, close contact with her, cool, soft, naked there in the cold dark, swept the bright delirium of sea-

magic over him again, stung his blood to a burning fever, set him writhing as pain had never. ... The place of pure love was assaulted and taken by base lust; his desire was most strong, not for the winning of a human soul, but for the wicked winning of a human body.[58]

Christian finally loses his life in the quest for her salvation, however, and his love for her is thus purified. His sacrifice frees Diadyomene from the spell that caused her to forget her origins: "Dawned a vision remote ... the tale of a loved and lost child, long years ago lost to the sea."[59] She is Lois's daughter, who, because she had not been baptized, was vulnerable to the sea spirits that tempted her into the water. Diadyomene is, in essence, Christian's sister. Remembering her mother, remembering her childhood self, she repents and leaves the Isle Sinister to be baptized. Christian has, through his martyrdom, saved his sister's soul, and their bond is remade as something beautiful rather than base. As the novel concludes, Lois is granted a vision of her two children "hand and hand" and recognizes in this "the wonderful ways of God and His mercy."[60] *The Unknown Sea*, like *The Were-Wolf*, banishes the threat of eroticism, but it does so not by simply destroying the monstrous object of lust but by transforming her into a sister. The novel, in fact, repeatedly transmutes potential erotic object choices into sisters, first Christian's cousin Rhoda and finally the sea-witch, exhibiting a wish that all would-be mates might be remade as siblings. In a reversal of conventional narratives of sexual maturation that draw the individual farther away from the kinship ties of childhood, Clemence leads her characters from sexual desire back to sibling devotion, a relationship that she associates with the finest types of kindness and self-sacrifice.

Laurence and Clemence, then, each in their own way, theorized and celebrated queer sibling devotion, and they each in their own way insisted upon the centrality of sacrifice to fellow-feeling. According to their disparate but linked formulations of love, devotion to and sympathy for another constitutes arduous affective labor that involves real work and pain. You must allow the other to occupy you, allow their concerns to take precedence over your own. Clemence's devotion to Laurence, the extent to which he occupied her psyche, manifests itself materially in her careful reworking of his designs into wood. She allowed his vision to guide her work, to physically guide her hand. And Laurence's devotion to Clemence, his deep identification with her and the manner in which concern for her well-being consumed him, is most evident in his feminist activism.

As the century turned, Laurence became increasingly interested in feeling himself into women's experience, in coming to comprehend the types of disempowerment that they experience, and working to address the power structures that enable their subjugation. The foundation for his investment in the suffrage campaign seems to have been his capacity for identification with women, cultivated in his relationship with Clemence as well as in his fiction. In *An Englishwoman's Love Letters* (1900), for example, he carried the sympathy he developed for his sister into a more general sense of connection with women's suffering.[61] The book was sensationally popular, and Laurence himself often dismissed it as his least serious work. However, it offers valuable insight into Laurence's developing interest in gender ideology at the moment immediately preceding his most intense period of feminist activism. It details the sorrows of a woman abandoned by her beloved. Composed entirely of letters written by the heartbroken heroine, the work preoccupies itself first and foremost with abjection, with waiting and passivity and longing. The novel interrogates the affective habits of women in a patriarchal culture, the tendency to romanticize powerlessness and subjugation, and the destructive consequences of the fundamentally "unequal ... love between a man and a woman."[62] Writing of Laurence's role in the suffrage campaign in 1909, Ethel Hill celebrated the work as a "poignantly pathetic analysis of a women's soul," and she asked her readers, "Is it not fitting that [the letters] were written by a man who has so bravely and persistently with voice and pen championed the women in their fight for the means of self-expression in the essentials that affect the destiny of the nation they help to create?"[63] The work, she argues, like most of his writings, exhibits strong traces of "suffragitis."[64]

Laurence placed a great deal of himself into *An Englishwoman's Love Letters*. In *The Unexpected Years* (1936), he notes that two instances in his childhood contributed to his development of a conscience and a sense of sympathy, and these events were reproduced in *An Englishwoman's Love Letters* "exactly as each thing happened."[65] Both events constitute failures in fellow-feeling on Laurence's part. In the first instance, his younger brother asked him to share a piece of cake, and Laurence instead placed the entire remainder of the cake in his mouth. He notes he has never forgiven himself for teaching his brother at that moment a "sudden lesson of the hardness of a human heart."[66] The second anecdote details the young Laurence's attempt to retrieve eggs from a swallow's nest by breaking its floor. The nest was, in fact, filled with nestlings, and when they fell to the ground, all but one died. The parent-birds returned and "shrieked at the horror of it all, and fled away not to return."[67] The final nestling soon died as well, and Laurence states that "the poignancy of [his] regret . . . has never softened," and at times he thinks he might "give [his] life that those swallows in their generations might live again."[68] He refers to these events as "religious experiences," though they have nothing to do with God.[69] They are crucial moments in his development of an intense and generous religion of fellow-feeling, and it seems noteworthy that he deployed these stories while constructing a work whose primary aim was the cultivation of empathy across the boundaries of gender. When writing his own autobiography years later, he simply reproduced these repurposed anecdotes word for word. The intertextual citation of *An Englishwoman's Love Letters* and *The Unexpected Years* indicates the extent to which Laurence had poured himself into his suffering heroine. The composition of *An Englishwoman's Love Letters* represented for Laurence an experiment in the dissolution of the self into another, a linguistic rendering of his affective experiments with his sister and the movement of his sympathy outward from their relationship to a broader sense of connectedness with women.

This foray out of the self and into the concerns of women continued as Laurence devoted himself to the suffrage campaign, a project that consumed him entirely from around 1908 until the outbreak of World War I.[70] His immersion in the cause was so complete, he notes, that his relatives and friends referred to him as a "lost soul."[71] Musing on the origins of his interest in the cause, he states, "being a brother, and sharing house with my sister" probably "had something to do with it."[72] Their domestic situation served as the foundation for his feminism and their cooperative activism. The suffrage campaign was for the Housmans a shared project and one that mimicked structurally their collaboration in the production of the fairy tale collections. The siblings became involved with the Women's Social and Political Union, a militant suffrage organization, in 1908. Soon after, Laurence's studio at their cottage in Kensington became the home for the Suffrage Atelier, which produced banners for the suffrage movement. According to Laurence, he designed "five or six" of these banners while Clemence became the Atelier's "chief worker," cutting, stitching together, and embroidering Laurence's designs.[73] "From Prison to Citizenship," which Stephen Housman has described as the "first and finest" of their banners, was displayed prominently at multiple suffrage marches in the 1900s and 1910s.[74] The Women's Library at the London School of Economics also holds a design for a banner by Laurence, "In This Sign Conquer: To Open the Eyes of the Blind & To Bring the Prisoner Out of Captivity."[75] And the Museum of London holds a banner designed by Laurence and "executed by the Suffrage Atelier, possibly by Clemence Housman," for the Hampstead branch of the Church League for Women's Suffrage, "The Glorious Liberty of the Children of God."[76] Like *The Were-Wolf*, these collaboratively produced banners can be understood as physical evidence of the interpenetration of the Housmans' beliefs and their aesthetics, their capacity to let one another's well-being as well as one another's visions occupy their minds, guide their hands, and determine the direction of their labor.

The Housmans' fellow-feeling served as the locus for broader forms of political affiliation. Tara Morton's recent work on the Suffrage Atelier stresses the role that the Housmans' home and the work that occurred there played in the cultivation of feminist community: "Working cooperatively on banners meant that new relationships could be forged between women based upon a commonality of interests in craft and the suffrage, rather than on normative family relations."[77] In opening their home, itself a site of innovative kinship and cooperation, the Housmans created the possibility for the formation of wider ties between politicized women. Their home was also the site for other forms of civil protest and disobedience. On the night of the 1911 census, for example, four women stayed in the Housmans' home and refused to give their details to government officials "as a protest against their exclusion from the franchise."[78] Undoing the conventional division between public and private, the Housmans remade their home into a haven for political dissidence and a workshop for political propaganda.

The Housmans' feminist activism played a crucial role in Laurence's political development. While, as Oakley notes, "Clemence seemed to prefer a less public role" in the suffrage campaign, Laurence found himself enjoying, and being quite skillful at, political speaking.[79] In his speeches for the suffrage movement, Laurence circulated their shared feminist convictions to a broader and broader community, traveling throughout England to speak in support of the cause. It is at this moment in his career that Laurence's interest in expansive amativeness seems to have translated into an interest in direct political action as he expanded his "willing service" "out and out from the family to the community," identifying increasingly as an activist as much as an author and artist. The theorization of and experiments in expansive amativeness that Laurence conducted in his fiction enlarged his capacity for empathy for women and infected him with "suffragitis." This stage in his activist career in turn operated as a foundation for his later pacifist activism in which he expanded his empathy and his devotion "on through the race to the whole of humanity."

"Yet Greater Unity": Laurence Housman, the Peace Movement, and the Fight for Indian Independence

In the 1910s, Laurence began to understand feminist critique as part of a larger system of political critique that must take into consideration international and racial politics. The suffrage work Laurence conducted in collaboration with Clemence, as Oakley argues, deepened "his awareness of the shortcomings of English society ... and led him towards the pacifism and anti-colonialism which he later espoused."[80] Rodney Engen similarly notes that, behind Laurence's political criticism, "lay his sister's outspoken views against a male-dominated government. Laurence learnt to question and doubt the events of the day from Clemence."[81] The feminism he came to in cooperation with Clemence became the foundation for a more broadly oppositional stance in relationship to existing political structures and institutions. In *Sex-War and Woman's Suffrage* (1912), he links feminism with political clear-sightedness and thoroughgoing dissidence. He argues that suffragists tend in the direction of both skepticism and optimism, being frequently "revolted by present conditions" while at the same time believing that these conditions may be improved, and this skeptical optimism enables their keen perception of the failings of international policy: "They are ashamed that men should find so much to pride themselves on, and so little to be ashamed of in the accepted institutions upon which we base our polity of home administration and of peace and war between nations."[82] Occupying an oppositional stance, which puts feminists in a position to perceive the shortcomings of the state in its treatment of women, allows them to see the flaws in its treatment of other nations just as clearly. He encourages women to attend to the links between patriarchal ideology and white supremacy, asserting that the two are underwritten by a similar drive to subjugate and possess. In "dominant-male States," he argues, an ethos of "physical force" often predominates, and this ethos impacts the women of those states as much as the races of others: "So long as civilized humanity fights murderously to possess itself of wealth and territory and power, without regard for justice and fair-dealing, so long, out of that fever in its blood, will it inevitably tend within its own borders to seek a solution for sex and class problems on lines which have in them some element of war."[83] He calls the women of the suffrage movement to "have it in mind that your fight is indissolubly bound up with the peace of class and the peace of nation, – that the Woman's Cause, so long neglected and set at naught, is the cause of humanity itself, and of the whole world."[84]

Laurence's hopes for cosmopolitan feminism were dashed at the onset of World War I. He notes in his autobiography that prior to that moment the suffrage movement "had been of an international character – a break from Nationalism."[85] "Voteless women, we were told, were not responsible for the mess men had made of things in a man-governed world."[86] After the declaration of war, however, the world "had suddenly become divided up between allied and hostile nations." He recalls attending a meeting in which his entreaties for the considerate treatment of women from enemy countries were denied, and the pleas of a "trembling old woman, born a German, but naturalized by marriage," for a "tolerant spirit toward those who could not help themselves" was met with "stony silence."[87] At this moment, he argued, "the spirit of the Suffrage Movement ... died a sudden death."[88] The spirit of the movement was undone by a spirit of separation, a vision of the world as "divided up between allied and hostile nations."[89] Separation, Laurence would later argue, is the one true sin.[90] In perceiving ourselves as separate from others, we free ourselves to engage in hateful and violent behavior toward those others. During the war years, an ethos of separation became the guiding spirit of the land. The "war-spirit" demanded that all believed "everything evil of the enemy," and "the joy of hatred" was understood to be a "patriotic virtue."[91]

Laurence's thought moved, however, as the war progressed, toward an even greater sense of unity, and internationalism and pacifism became his most cherished causes. He traveled to New York in 1916 to campaign for the establishment of a League of Nations, and throughout the 1920s, he continued to develop his thinking about pacifism in his plays about St. Francis, a figure whose life and thought convinced him that, "if rightly treated, human nature would respond to conciliation and non-violence."[92] He grew increasingly adamant and active in advocating for peace in the 1930s and 1940s, publishing numerous columns in *Peace News* as well as an essay collection entitled *The Preparation of Peace* (1941). He was an active member of the Peace Pledge Union and drew on his experience in the suffrage campaign as he traveled the country delivering pacifist lectures. He ran as a pacifist candidate in the 1938 Glasgow Rectorial Election. In the 1940s, he became the president of the War Resisters' International and the director of the Peace News Ltd. At the end of his life, he took up the cause of nuclear disarmament. If he had lost his soul to the suffrage movement in the initial decades of the twentieth century, he retrieved it and turned it over to pacifism for the remainder of his life.

Laurence's ongoing thinking about and experiments in empathy and affiliation structured his approach to pacifism. The rhetoric he employed in theorizing pacifism borrows directly from the conceptualization of promiscuous fellow-feeling in his sexological writing and his fairy tales. While I do not wish to simply conflate the Laurence of the 1890s with the Laurence of the 1930s and 1940s, I want to emphasize the continuity between the stages in his career, the manner in which the thinking he did in collaboration with his sister on the topic of queer kinship and affiliation informed his interest in peace. The Laurence of the fin de siècle, I am arguing, who so carefully thought through the negotiation of competing allegiances and the eschewal of vengeance in stories such as "The Truce of God" paves the way for the Laurence of World War II, who called the English public to "check the instinct of retaliation."[93] In each stage of his career, he moved further and further afield from the confines of his own self and interests, from queer activism, to suffrage, to internationalist pacifism, insisting always on the fellowship that unites humanity. Reflecting on the most fundamental precepts that governed his thinking in "What I Believe," he defines sin as

> the separation of our own interest from the interests of others; the will to acquire what seems good for ourselves, to the hurt of others; the deprivation of others that we may gain; the refusal of sympathy and understanding; indifference to the harder lot of others; a belief in our own superiority to others; – all these are acts and thoughts of a separating character.[94]

He argues that "prayers for self or family or nation to be favoured above others, are by their very nature imperfect. The true aim of prayer should be so close a unity of interest that a desire for the partial bestowing of benefit can have no part in it."[95] This aversion to separation, this desire for unity underwrites each phase in Laurence's thinking. Like the hermit in "The Truce of God," he asserts, we must understand that we cannot pray for our kin to be favored above the wider world. Like the hero of "The Troubling of the Waters," we must see that our links to our brothers cannot come above our ties to the broader community. He came to this interest in unity through his collaboration with his sister, and their practice of kinship brought Laurence into understanding of his kinship with the globe. Fellowship, he insists, can only be valuable when it expands infinitely. It can begin within the family, the community, or the nation, but its merits are negated if it stops there. "The inequalities of society," he asserts, arise from "indifference to the needs and welfare of others outside our own family," a mode of affiliation that results in "evil."[96] "The indifference of one nation to the welfare of another," he notes, "has produced similar evil results."[97] Clannishness and nationalism lead to violence. Our sense of fellowship must have "no hard and fast limits."[98]

Laurence developed and disseminated his arguments for international fellow-feeling in the pages of *Peace News*, a pacifist paper founded in 1936. The periodical was a highly appropriate forum for his theorization of unity. *Peace News* preoccupied itself with the transnational peace movement, covering events in India, Ceylon, Siam, Samoa, Rhodesia, South Africa, the United States, and the Arab world. It integrated the consideration of pacifism with coverage concerning anti-colonial movements, labor politics, vegetarianism, and communal living, and it featured work by some of the most prominent pacifist authors and artists of the period, including Vera Brittain, Siegfried Sassoon, Eric Gill, Havelock Ellis, and M. K. Gandhi. Laurence's vision of expansive amativeness paired neatly with the cosmopolitan and radical ethos of the paper. He published regularly in its pages, and his lengthy editorials, often appearing in installments, articulated his belief in unity and his disdain for the sin of separation. He braided together a critique of militarism and violence with an interrogation of capitalist ideology and religious hypocrisy. In "The Makings of the War Mind," for example, he argues that a system that "enables its members to separate concern for the welfare and life-conditions of others" has within it "the germs of war."[99] In "Why Man Has Failed," he states, "If then we have not a mind for love and good will beyond the bounds of nationalism, our Christianity is a lie."[100] Repeatedly, in the years leading up to World War II and following England's declaration of war, he forced the British public to confront the contradictions between the religious beliefs that they espoused and the military practices that they condoned. In the face of jingoism and violence, however, he insisted that Britain could evolve "from dominion over others to fellowship with others, from the spirit of strife and division to the spirit of love, unity, and peace."[101]

In his essays for *Peace News*, Laurence also linked pacifism to the dismantling of the imperial project. In this, again, his thinking was in keeping with the spirit of *Peace News*, which regularly featured articles that called colonial ideologies into question, such as "Brutality Under British Rule," "Who Bears the Burden of Empire?" and "We Must Give Up the Colonies." Laurence decried colonial practices in India and Kenya, "where the best of the land is taken from the native for the benefit of the white settler, and where taxes are imposed not to better the condition of the native, but for the sole purpose of extracting from him the forced labour without which the white man's occupation of the country would be impossible."[102] And he condemned the ethos of "racial domination," so fundamentally opposed to "love and good will," that "States and communities which claim to be Christian" employ in their exploitation of colonized peoples.[103] According to Laurence's arguments, racial domination is a manifestation of the sin of separation, a result of "the will to acquire what seems good for ourselves, . . . a belief in our own superiority to others," and practices based in such sin are an offense against Christianity.[104]

Laurence's evolving critique of white supremacy and colonialism emerged from his interest in the Indian independence movement, which seems to have begun in the late 1920s or early 1930s in conversation with his close friend Reginald Reynolds.[105] Reynolds was a Quaker as well as a socialist, a pacifist, and, following a visit Gandhi's ashram in 1929–1930, a committed campaigner for Indian independence in England. Laurence's friendship and correspondence with Reynolds facilitated the development of his thinking on the topics of peace and the imperial project. After returning to England, Reynolds established the Friends of India Society and helped to organize Gandhi's 1931 visit to England to attend the Second Round Table Conference. Laurence was serving at the time as the head of the Friends of India, and he delivered a welcome address to Gandhi at the Friends Meeting House in London. L. C. Webb's account of the speech in the *Press* stresses Laurence's reliance on a rhetoric of community and affiliation in his defense of Indian rights. Webb states that "Housman set himself gladly to the task of intensifying an already heavily charged emotional atmosphere; his rich voice boomed and quavered, his eyes strayed frequently to the ceiling, and the words 'fellowship,' 'love,' 'brotherhood,' and 'peace' seemed to echo constantly about us."[106] Like his pacifist writing, his arguments for Indian independence relied on the language of fellow-feeling that he had developed in his fairy tales and queer activist writing. He seems to have understood advocating for India as the logical extension of the thinking about expansive amativeness that he had begun in the 1890s. He adamantly and aggressively defended India's right to democratic freedom. On November 27, 1930, he spoke at a public meeting sponsored by the Commonwealth of India League on the "Cause of Indian Freedom." He wrote a preface for Verrier Elwin's *The Truth about India: Can We Get It?* (1932), in which he lauded Elwin's "firm belief in [India's] right not merely to self-government but to independence" and decried the Viceroy and Governor-General of India Lord Willingdon's ordinances suppressing free speech and freedom of assembly "with their inevitable products of injustice, concealment, and abuse of power."[107] As Laurence indicated in his correspondence with Carpenter in the 1890s, love was for him intimately bound up with service. In extending fellowship to India, he placed himself in service to the nation, and in the lectures and essays on Indian independence that he delivered and published in the 1930s, he demonstrated his practical devotion to a nation for whom he had expressed affinity.

Laurence's admiration for Gandhi was linked to his commitment to peace, fellowship, and global unity. He saw in Gandhi not only hope for India's liberation but a lesson in the political power of pacifism, which might be of use to other colonized people. In 1939, he contributed to *Mahatma Gandhi: Essays and Reflections on His Life and Work* an essay in which he argued that "Mahatma Gandhi's life is the most valuable in the present day" because "he has demonstrated that pacifism in action can be a force in world-politics," a demonstration that "is a beacon light for the future to all nations and races striving for liberty."[108] In Laurence's eyes, Gandhi's activism possessed value due to its capacity to emanate further and further afield from his own local commitments and interests, to move out and out from India to the globe and serve as a model to oppressed nations in their struggles for independence.

In his peace writing and his writing about India, Laurence maintained a belief in the possibility that fellow-feeling would grow increasingly promiscuous, that affiliation would become more and more expansive. In loving our kin, he argued, we may learn to love our community, and in loving our community, we may come to see the borders of that community as increasingly wide or permeable. He expressed a deep optimism about the evolution of a greater sense of unity amongst all people:

> As you look back into history you see the idea of [Unity of Spirit] emerging. In the family there was some of it – more loving-kindness, more understanding, more co-operation, less competition, than between a family and those outside. In the clan, there was some of it, as compared with the relation of the clan to other clans; in the united nation there was some of it, as compared with the jealousy and cruelty of one nation toward another. And that is where we have stopped at present. And in each case, however partially and imperfectly – there has been as a result a coming-together, and a fore-showing of yet greater unity than seemed practically attainable elsewhere.[109]

We might, he insists, extend our capacity for "loving-kindness" outside the boundaries of our families, our clans, and even our countries and experience a cosmopolitan "coming-together" that will eliminate jealousy and cruelty between nations. Our family ties, our sense of patriotism should be understood not as limits to our love but as "fore-showings" of the "yet greater unity" we might experience if we use those relationships as models for wider modes of affiliation.

The ever-expanding scope of Laurence's own activism, from his defense of Wilde and "homogenic love" in the 1890s, to his suffrage work in the 1910s, and his internationalist thinking in the 1930s and 1940s, reveals him experimenting with a greater and greater sense of unity that took him further afield from his own interests and well-being, inspiring his advocacy for women and his anti-colonial and pacifist service. As I have argued here, his experience of sibling devotion and his collaboration with Clemence operated as the locus for his interest in empathy and equality, which in turn informed his activism. His activism, however, also informed his practice of affiliation with his siblings. Laurence's curation of his brother's posthumous reputation reveals the manner in which his promiscuous fellow-feeling, which moved ever outward into the globe, also turned inward and guided his treatment of his biological kin.

"A Rather Delicate Work of Selection": Laurence and A. E. Housman

On May 4, 1936, Laurence wrote to Clemence from his brother Alfred's rooms in Trinity College, Cambridge. Alfred had died five days earlier, and Laurence was sifting through his belongings and papers. He reported to Clemence, "I've found strange leavings; some rather private; and I wonder was it trust or just carelessness which left me to have the handling of them."[110] These "strange leavings," which revealed his brother's unrequited love for his friend Moses Jackson, remained a source of confusion for Laurence for many years. In 1943, he wrote to Reginald Reynolds concerning his persistent uncertainty about the handling of this material:

> The fact remains that AEH did unashamedly leave these papers for inspection. They were very human, and some of them very touching. And the letters have not been destroyed, and will or some day may be restored to the light of day when there will be no feelings to be hurt, and when perhaps they may be of some benefit to society as a corrective to social intolerance. . . . Sometimes I think that Alfred definitely wished me to make the truth known when he was safely tucked away into the non-existence which he believed to be man's true end.[111]

Seven years after Alfred's death, Laurence asserted that it was not carelessness on his brother's part that left the letters in his hands. He insisted rather that Alfred had "unashamedly" left them for his brother's inspection. Nevertheless, the hesitancy, contradiction, and doubling back in his letter to Reynolds (the material "will" or "some day may" see the light of day; "sometimes" he thinks Alfred "definitely" wished the letters to be shared) indicate that Laurence remained conflicted about what to do with his brother's "strange leavings." He oscillated, in this letter to Reynolds, between his role as a family member, concerned for those with "feelings to be hurt," and his role as an activist, believing that his brother's letters "may be of some benefit to society as a corrective to social intolerance." While Laurence's devotion to Clemence and his feminist activism merged seamlessly, he experienced more trouble integrating his sense of responsibility to his brother with his service to the queer community. Laurence had been thinking through the difficulties in negotiating competing allegiances since the 1890s, but Alfred's death and his role as executor of his estate placed him in the practical position of weighing his kinship ties against broader political affiliations. The carefulness and sympathy with which he carried out his responsibilities to his brother and to the greater political good, however, reveal how skilled Laurence was at braiding together kinship ties and wider modes of affiliation. His activist practices inflected his approach to his brother's papers, but his devotion to his brother also determined the manner in which he implemented those papers in his activist project.

Laurence and Clemence's relationship with their brother Alfred lacked the intimacy of their relationship with one another. Laurence's autobiography indicates that in his early years, Alfred did, however, inspire great reverence in him. Alfred, he states, "was always our leader," and he records that four lines of Ovid's poetry have remained forever in his memory simply because Alfred declared them "excellent" when they were children.[112] Nevertheless, Alfred seems to have held himself somewhat aloof from his younger siblings. In early adulthood, when Laurence and Clemence moved to London, the connection cooled even further. Alfred met them at Paddington on their arrival, but he "asked [them] not to come" to the rooms he shared with Moses Jackson and his brother Adalbert. Their brother, Laurence states, kept them "rigidly ... at a distance," and their relations "remained for some years strained and perfunctory."[113] He notes that when Clemence first read *A Shropshire Lad* (1896), she cried out with surprise, "Alfred has a heart!"[114] Alfred was much more conservative in his politics than his siblings, and he often expressed disapproval of their activism. When he saw a photograph of them in the *Evening Standard* standing in front of the prison gates following Clemence's arrest for tax resistance, he described the image to

Grant Richards as "a lovely portrait of my disreputable relatives."[115] He refused to sign a petition for suffrage that Laurence submitted to him, and in 1911 he wrote to Laurence to inform him, "I am not coming to hear your seditious play," *Pains and Penalties*, a work censored for its representation of marriage difficulties between George IV and Queen Caroline.[116] While there is much teasing in his tone when criticizing his siblings' causes and activities, Alfred often seemed to occupy the opposing side of the political spectrum from his radical brother and sister.

This is not to say, however, that Laurence and Alfred did not share interests or care for one another. Though their relations were not marked by the same ethos of collaboration that underwrote Laurence's bond with Clemence, Alfred sent Laurence critical notes on the poems in *Green Arras*, and Laurence stated years later that he still cherished his "kind and caustic" feedback.[117] Alfred's comments were extremely detailed, making note of metrical errors and inconsistencies and recommending alterations in stanza breaks. Though he did find some of the poems worthy of admiration, he was quite clear about his distaste for others. He described certain works as "clever and striking" while critiquing the "phraseology" in others as "precious cheap."[118] In response to "The House of Birth," he wrote, "This is less indecent than Rossetti and less comical than W. E. Henley, but that is all I can say for it."[119] The last stanza of "The Sleep of the Gods" was described as "one of your triumphs of obscurity," and Alfred wondered what "black inhumanity" inspired its diction.[120] His criticism was a bit severe, but his letters to Laurence concerning the poems in *Green Arras* show him truly engaging with and thinking through the merits of his brother's work. And there was clearly some fun in Alfred's banter with Laurence. Alfred wrote to him of receiving praise for *Green Arras* from a neighbor who had confused the two brothers' works, adding a postscript to say: "I was just licking the envelope when the following envenomed remark occurred to me: I had far far rather have my poems mistaken as yours, than your poems mistaken as mine."[121] He informed Laurence that he possessed a "wet wit."[122] When Laurence invited Alfred to see him perform his own death scene in an epilogue to *St. Francis*, Alfred wrote that, "though [Laurence's] death had attraction for him, he could not face the journey to London."[123] And behind this banter, there does seem to have been some true affection. Following Alfred's death, Laurence found in his brother's library "a more complete collection of [Laurence's] books than [he] had [himself]," and he "learned from friends in Cambridge that [Alfred] said kinder things about [the books] behind [Laurence's] back than he did to [his] face."[124]

The clearest tenderness between the two brothers emerges, however, in the editions of Alfred's poetry and the accounts of his life that Laurence edited and composed in the years following his brother's death. In these works, Laurence delicately balances his sense of responsibility to his brother with his desire to advocate for sex reform. Sex reform was the first political issue to which Laurence had devoted himself. He became a member of the homophile organization the Order of Chaeronea in the 1890s. Though the Order was a secret society, it nevertheless, as Jeffrey Weeks has argued, engaged in activist activities, operating as "a political grouping attempting, by discrete pressure on highly placed people, to change attitudes and the law."[125] He worked more publicly for sex reform in the teens as a member of the British Society for the Study of Sex Psychology. In 1923, he published his recollections of Wilde in *Echo de Paris*, and he concluded the study with a footnote celebrating a new spirit of progressiveness in the understanding of sexuality in the years since Wilde's imprisonment. He became reenergized in relationship to the issue during Radclyffe Hall's obscenity trial in 1928. He wrote to Hall expressing his support, and in his unpublished sexual autobiography "Outrageous Fortune: The Story of a Concealed Life, 1862–1933," he traces the inspiration of the work to Hall's persecution:

> Within the last few years a book has been publicly condemned by process of law, which stated moderately and decently the case, or life history, of a woman invert. The writer of that book put forward . . . a plea for the social toleration and acceptance of homosexuals who live their full life. That plea for full life caused the book to be condemned . . . . The duty to which I now feel called is to give the facts of my life for the sake of others less able to bear the same burden that has been laid on them – to a public which understands so little what that burden is like.[126]

At the moment of his brother's death, then, Laurence had come to feel particularly strongly the responsibility of queer-identified individuals to "give the facts" of their lives in the service of promoting the cause of sex reform. The amount of discretion he exercised in his posthumous representation of his brother should be understood, then, as arising from a willingness, because of his affection for a sibling, to make sacrifices in relationship to a cause about which he felt very strongly.

In 1937, Laurence published *A. E. H.: Some Poems, Some Letters and a Personal Memoir by His Brother*, a work in which he deftly negotiates his competing obligations to the political "duty" to which he felt called and his allegiances to his kin. The "strange leavings" Laurence encountered amidst Alfred's papers made it clear that his brother had shared the burden of living a "concealed life," but, without explicit instructions as to whether Alfred wished him to reveal this information after his death, Laurence was left vexed and confused. He manages in *A. E. H.* to have it both ways, to speak only in oblique terms of his brother's love for his friend Moses Jackson while signaling subtly that Alfred condemned the persecution of Wilde and the sexual legislation that ruined him. He protects Alfred's privacy while enlisting him posthumously in the battle for sex reform.

The memoir delicately and indirectly tells the poignant story of Alfred's love for Moses Jackson. While Laurence decries recent "items of journalistic nonsense" that have sought to "construct a hidden romance" that might explain Alfred's "celibate life," insisting that his brother was simply a "born bachelor," he nevertheless opens the work by alluding to Alfred's "greatest and most lasting friendship."[127] He states that his brother "left no record" of this relationship, which is, of course, not true.[128] Laurence had chosen to conceal these records. However, in composing this memoir, Laurence constructed a new, albeit murkier and less explicit, record of Alfred's love for Jackson. He refers to "the beginning of [Alfred's] great friendship" with Jackson as "one of the most important events of his life," one that remained definitive for him for the rest of his life.[129] Because Alfred so carefully kept his siblings at a distance during the years that he lived with Jackson, Laurence is unable to supply details concerning their life together. Instead, he highlights the lasting emotional effects of their relationship and the significance it held for Alfred until the day he died. He recollects visiting his brother in his rooms at Trinity College, where a portrait of Jackson hung above the fireplace: "One day, looking at the [portrait], I asked Alfred who he was. In a strangely moved voice, he answered, 'That was my friend Jackson, the man who had more influence on my life than anybody else.'"[130] After Alfred's death, Laurence found in his papers "an envelope endorsed, 'Mo's last letter.' The letter had been written faintly in pencil, in the hospital where Jackson died soon after; and above the faint writing, the better to preserve it (keeping the form of each word carefully), Alfred had himself gone over the whole in ink."[131] Laurence never, of course, classifies explicitly the nature of Alfred's affection for Jackson, but he relays with reverence how important this tie was to his brother, the manner in which it moved him, the fact that he so lovingly preserved Jackson's last letter and assigned his portrait pride of place in his living quarters. He closes the work with his brother's natal horoscope, which similarly hints at the sorrows the work as a whole at once reveals and conceals. Alfred was fated, the horoscope notes, to have "many bitter disappointments in connection with friendship and love."[132] While he was "capable of very faithful attachment and waiting a long time," "some kind of secret and irregular union" would be "more likely than an ordinary marriage."[133] Laurence subtly encodes the story of Alfred's love for Jackson within the pages of the volume, scattering clues concerning its significance amidst astrological appendices and asides about his brother's papers.

Laurence's tone is a bit more direct, however, in his discussion of two poems by Alfred, which he encourages readers to understand as expressing his brother's desire for greater tolerance. He records finding a newspaper cutting in his brother's copy of *A Shropshire Lad* alongside the poem concerning a suicide: "Shot? so quick so clean an ending? / Oh that was right, lad, that was brave: / Yours was not an ill for mending, / 'Twas best to take it to the grave." The newspaper cutting quotes the suicide letter of a young cadet who took his own life in order to avoid "offenses" and "disgraces" that would result were he to act on his desires.[134] Laurence's pairing of the cutting with the poem has informed analysis of this work ever since. Veronica Alfano, for example, states that Alfred "deduced that this young man, who killed himself in the same year as the Wilde trials, was gay," and she argues that "this lyric is understatedly dissident in its insistence that the cadet has become a paragon of virtuous masculinity."[135] There has, however, been some disagreement as to how to understand Alfred's position on the cadet's death. Christopher Ricks, for example, asserts that the poem's admiration for the cadet's decision "resists any emancipated or enlightened insistence that there is in homosexuality no dishonour or guilt of which one should yearn to be 'clean.'"[136] But Laurence leads his readers to a more progressive reading by transitioning from a discussion of this poem into a characterization of Alfred's moral positions, in which he asserts that "certain 'laws of God and man,' with their socially imposed sanctions, he disliked heartily."[137] "This is shown clearly," Laurence argues, in a heretofore unpublished poem that he has chosen to include in the volume.[138] Though the poem is "somewhat lacking in literary quality," it is, he insists, "so strong an expression of his feeling against social injustice that I am sure he would have wished it to be known."[139] This poem, "Oh who is that young sinner with the handcuffs on his wrists?" in which a young man is led off to prison because of a "sin" over which he has no control, "the colour of his hair," is now commonly understood as Alfred's response to the Wilde trials.[140] By linking these two poems and asserting that they represent Alfred's dislike for "certain 'laws of God and man,'" Laurence inaugurated a tradition that positioned his brother as a critic of social injustice.

The readings to which Laurence subtly gestured in *A. E. H.* are articulated with greater clarity in the essay, "A. E. Housman's 'De Amicitia,'" that he presented to the British Museum in 1942, along with his brother's diary and fourteen pages that he had extracted from that diary, with instructions that the material was not to be opened for twenty-five years. Laurence makes plain here exactly what kinds of laws and injustices so troubled his brother. Whereas he had chosen to leave the source of the dead cadet's shame unnamed in *A. E. H.*, in this essay, he states that "the letter made it quite plain that his trouble was what it is the fashion to call 'pathological.'"[141] And, though he writes that he is uncertain how far his brother accepted "the denial of what was natural to him," he argues that "Oh who is that young sinner with the handcuffs on his wrists?" makes "abundantly plain" that Alfred considered "the inhibition imposed by society on his fellow-victims both cruel and unjust."[142] According to Laurence, the poem "refers quite evidently to those who inescapably, through no fault of their own, are homosexual – having no more power of choice in the matter than a man has about the colour of his hair."[143] It is a work, he asserts, "expressing contemptuous anger against society's treatment of these unhappy victims of fate, and a sympathy which went so far as to imply no blame."[144] The meaning is so "obvious," he states, that he hesitated to publish the poem in *A. E. H.* as it might cause pain to his living relatives, but he "felt, nevertheless, that the risk must be taken; it was something of a public duty that [he] should make known so strong an expression of feeling against social injustice."[145] Laurence had hesitated to enlist Alfred in the cause of sex reform during his own lifetime, but in this essay, he wrote into existence the posthumous possibility for their collaborative activism. In 1967, upon the opening of the packet, the two brothers would be twinned in their sexual dissidence and their condemnation of intolerance and persecution.

Laurence had struggled for years with the question of what to do with the diaries he found after his brother's death, which record "the parting of [Alfred and Moses's] ways."[146] Laurence asserts that "nobody reading [the diaries] can have any doubt about the emotional nature of [his] brother's love for Jackson; it was deep and lasting, and it caused him great unhappiness."[147] In 1939, he accidentally sent a page from one to Houston Martin, an ardent Housman admirer and collector in the United States. Upon realizing his mistake, Laurence begged Martin to return the page, noting that, in "letting that page of the diary slip through," he had been "untrue to [his] trusteeship."[148] He told Martin he planned to destroy the diaries, despite their power to move: "The short extracts which I took out of the diary before sending it to you, and this one which went to you by oversight, are so extraordinarily pathetic in their reticence that I have still hesitated to destroy them. I know I shall have to do so, but every time I look at them they stir me with affectionate compassion."[149] The diaries created the possibility for a kind of intimacy, an "affectionate compassion," that did not exist between the two brothers while Alfred was still alive. Nevertheless, Laurence seems to have initially thought it would be necessary to keep them from the public eye. At a certain point, however, Laurence came to believe that their power to move and to create sympathy should be implemented in a larger political project.

In "De Amicitia," Laurence frames the diaries as politically potent, and he makes it clear that, while devotion to his brother prevented him from making the material public during his own lifetime, he anticipated a future when Alfred's sorrow along with Laurence's annotations of that sorrow might cooperate in initiating change. He insists, in contradiction to his prior assessments, that Alfred left the diaries behind to "let [Laurence] know the secret of his life, and to give [him] liberty to make it known."[150] He takes up the task for "two reasons, one personal, the other social."[151] The personal reason has to do with his devotion to his brother and his desire to increase the public's understanding of him. He closes the essay by articulating the "social reason":

> Though, in their treatment of the homosexual problem, "the precious balms of the righteous" have broken many heads, and many hearts, and ruined many lives, I have a hope that, twenty-five years hence, their day of evil power will be gone; and that society may, at long last, have acquired sufficient commonsense to treat the problem less unintelligently, less cruelly, more scientifically. And if not, it may help to that end for the world to be given knowledge that one to whom it is deeply in debt for the beauty of his poetry and the eminence of his scholarship, was one of the sufferers whom it has in the past found it so foolishly easy to despise and to condemn.[152]

When John Carter published "De Amicitia" along with the annotated diary entries in *Encounter* in 1967, he stated that Laurence's hope "was fulfilled almost exactly on time. These papers were unsealed on 11 July 1967: the Sexual Offences Act (1967) went on to the Statute Book on 27 July."[153] Carter's assessment seems a bit optimistic. Though "homosexual [acts] in private" were decriminalized in 1967, the righteous's "day of evil power" was far from over. There was still work left to be done, and Laurence's essay and the diary leaves that it accompanied might still work together to invite "less unintelligent, less cruel" treatment of the "sufferers whom [the world] has in the past found it so foolishly easy to despise and to condemn." In 1942, when Laurence submitted this packet to the British Museum, he looked forward to two possible futures – an ideal future, in which queer activism was no longer necessary, and a bleaker future, in which his brother's story might have political work left to perform. In that latter future, the one that came to pass, he and Alfred could collaborate, as he and Clemence once had, in the service of a cause, being brought closer to one another through their advocacy for others.

In *The Unexpected Years*, Laurence recalls Alfred asking, while recalling their childhood, "Was there ever such an interesting family as we were?"[154] The Housmans were without a doubt a family of interesting individuals, but what is much more interesting is the way that they practiced their kinship ties with one another. Laurence in particular approached the practice of kinship as an activity with much wider political and ethical implications. His devotion to both Clemence and Alfred opened out into political activism, and, at the same time, his activist commitments under-wrote the way he cared for his brother and sister. The collaborative relationship into which he entered with Clemence operated as the locus for a more general devotion to the causes of feminism and pacifism, and the fellowship he felt for members of the queer community informed his treatment of Alfred's legacy. Laurence practiced a sibling devotion with a queer politics. He loved his brother and sister in a manner influenced by his queer activism, and he used his love for them as the foundation for his expansive sense of amativeness. Reflecting on his own sexual identity in "Outrageous Fortune", he writes, "I have never been able to regard as being in the nature of sin those tender emotional longings to serve and worship certain of my fellow-men, which are the undoubted outcome of the inversion from which I suffer."[155] In Laurence's cosmology, queer desire generates kindness, devotion, and service. "Sympathetic natures," individuals who are innovative in their affinities, engage in a love "without partiality," a love that takes on the difficulties of negotiating competing allegiances and finds a way to balance sets of obligations. His belief in the political power of this kind of love arose from the affective experiments he performed with his sister, and, in his later years, it determined his approach to loving his deceased brother. Queer sibling devotion served as the center of his utopian political project, allowing him to experiment with a kind of love that had "no hard and fast limits," that moved "out and out" from biological kin to the community, engendering yet greater unity, loving service, and the "linking up of the human family." He accepted the sacrifices associated with loving expansively, the pain and the discipline that the negotiation of competing allegiances demands, and he approached his devotion to his siblings as well as his sense of responsibility to the wider world with a clear sense of the affective labor involved in promiscuous fellow-feeling.

PART II

Queer Retreat and Cosmopolitan Community

An Extraordinary Marriage
The Mackenzies and the Queer Cosmopolitanism of Capri

In his queer Baedeker, *The Third Sex* (1927), "Willy"[1] describes the Italian island of Capri as "a sodomic capital in miniature, the Mecca of inversion, a Geneva or a Moscow of the future internationalism of homosexuality."[2] He argues that this bewitching setting is capable of remaking "normal" couples in its image, noting that he knows of a young husband and wife who made the "deplorable" decision to spend their honeymoon on the island, only to have their union transformed entirely.[3] Initially "scandalized by the revelry of the '*ragazzi*,'" they soon became intrigued, inviting two "ephebes" to drink sparkling chianti in their rooms.[4] The husband became infatuated with "the more seductive of his guests," who was in turn brought with the couple back to Paris, where the wife waited, according to Willy, for her turn to "console herself" with their newly acquired "Ganymede."[5] Willy characterizes Capri as the capital of a cosmopolitan queer community and as a site that might infect and undo conventional bonds. It is a holy site for those who have unmoored themselves from fixed national identities in order to align themselves instead with an international queer subculture, and it is a seductive and potentially dangerous site for its heterosexual visitors, luring them away from conventional marriages and into innovative domestic arrangements.

Willy's comments on Capri speak directly to the experience of writers Compton and Faith Mackenzie, who moved to the island in 1913 and became enmeshed in its queer cosmopolitan community. The island had operated since the Wilde trials as a refuge for sexual exiles from across Europe who retreated from persecution and criminal proceedings into Capri's permissive expatriate society. Capri was understood to be a site in which individuals might extricate themselves from the cultures that condemned them and operate with greater freedom, and it was, throughout the early decades of the twentieth century, a location that continued to be inflected by the Decadent spirit of the 1890s. Lord Alfred Douglas, for example, rented rooms in Capri while Wilde was in prison, and Wilde traveled with Douglas to the island following his release with the intention of placing flowers on Tiberius's tomb.[6] The French Decadent writer Jacques d'Adelswärd-Fersen retreated to Capri following his arrest for "indecent conduct with minors." In addition, an entire coterie of lesser-known dandies and Decadents, friends of Douglas's and Wilde's, made frequent visits or settled there at the fin de siècle. On Capri, the queer Decadence that had been cast from Britain and, in its more extreme manifestations, from the Continent, persisted and thrived. The Mackenzies remade their bond in conversation with the members of this Decadent community with whom they drank and danced and conducted affairs and who became, in a sense, their family, playing key roles in the manner in which their marriage functioned. Occupying this space facilitated their capacity to practice their relationship with one another in a more radical manner.

While the nature of the Mackenzies' bond shifted and transformed for decades, it underwent its most radical transformation at the midpoint of their time on Capri. In 1918, following a particularly intense and tragic affair of Faith's with a younger Italian man, the Swedish physician and psychiatrist Axel Munthe advised the couple to reconstitute their tie and reconceive their relationship as what we might today call an "open marriage." The Mackenzies followed this advice and remained married to one another while at the same time conducting extended relationships with other partners until Faith's death in 1960. This chapter situates their openness to this suggestion in relationship to their contact with the Decadent exiles on Capri in the teens, and it traces the effects of this decision through the work they produced in the 1920s and 1930s, in which they theorized gender, sexuality, and desire.

The Mackenzies' union indicates how marriage might respond to queer influences and foster queer lifestyles. Their life and their writing offer much in this sense to historians of marriage, who have begun more recently to attend to models of marriage that complicate Lawrence Stone's story of the ascendancy and triumph of companionate marriage and the nuclear family. Talia Schaffer, for example, highlights that, throughout the nineteenth century, multiple forms of marriage coexisted and competed with one another. While scholarship within the field of Victorian studies has tended to focus on romantic marriage, Schaffer argues that an older model of marriage that privileged social rather than sexual desires, "familiar marriage," remained attractive to women who saw in this type of union the possibility to retain ties to a broader community or to participate in fulfilling vocations. She asserts that "familiar marriage could well cover (and permit) a range of feeling among its participants beyond a conventional heteronormative orientation."[7] The Mackenzies' marriage could be seen as a twentieth-century extension of this tradition, a form of loving friendship and professional collaboration that valued connectedness to and kinship with a broader literary and artistic community over erotic desires and provided its participants an economic and domestic base from which to engage in other affiliative experiments.

However, as much as the Mackenzies' bond might draw on a long tradition of familiar marriage, their particular model of affiliation was fostered and nourished by a specific place at a specific moment, the queer Capri of the 1910s. I want to insist upon the specificity of the island of Capri as the locale that engendered their particular approach to connection. The Europeanness of Capri, its separation from British mores and sexual ideologies, was certainly significant, but it was Capri's islandness, its separateness from mainland Italy, that was crucial.[8] Located in the Gulf of Naples, requiring travel by ferry or boat to reach its shores, Capri was a community that was out of time and out of the way. Isolated from the mainland, it looked back to and preserved elements of the 1890s while looking ahead to a more modern and permissive future, operating as a refuge from British sexual legislation. Its reputation as a "sybaritic paradise" with a "tolerance of homosexuality" in the wake of the Wilde trials allowed the island to operate as the Geneva of the "future internationalism of homosexuality."[9] Recent work within the field of critical island studies has highlighted the manner in which islands have tended to function in literature as a space marked simultaneously by withdrawal and engagement, providing isolation from the dangers or concerns of the mainland while at the same time placing diverse inhabitants in close proximity. Gillian Beer's characterization of the function of the island in the British cultural imagination foregrounds this tension, noting that while islands could seem secure and withdrawn, and thus might serve as appropriate bases for imperial activities, islands also "concentrate . . . questions" of the "possible and impossible relations between different tribes, species, and individuals."[10] In *Islandology* (2014), Marc Shell similarly highlights the fact that the term island has two meanings, "insulet" (which stresses the "cutting off" of land from water at the coast) and "water-land" (which stresses the malleability of borders by indicating the "mixture of water and land at the limiting, or defining, 'coast'").[11] With this in mind, Shell traces conflicting histories of islands as sites that can both foster isolationism and operate as geopolitical crossroads. The queer cosmopolitan inhabitants of Capri in the 1910s and 1920s took advantage of these seemingly contradictory elements of island existence, cutting themselves off from the threats of moral policing on the mainland while being brought into intimate contact with members of an international community of sexual dissidents. And the island's geographical remove additionally engendered a peculiar temporality, distinct from mainland temporality, in which the nostalgic preservation of the queer Decadence of the 1890s served as the foundation for a sexual vanguard, making Capri a testing site for new kinds of connection and drawing individuals from across the globe to its utopian promise. This space apart, where many turned purposefully backward to the Decadent ethos of the late nineteenth century in their approach to desire, also operated as a generative locus for innovative modes of affiliation, meaning the island at once preserved fin-de-siècle culture and offered a glimpse forward into potential sexual futures.

It needs to be emphasized, however, that expatriate visitors to Capri also fetishized and exoticized the island and its inhabitants, conceiving of the location as mystical, primitive, and destabilizing. As recent work by Robert Aldrich and R. C. Bleys indicates, tourism and exile played a central role in fostering queer self-realization and new forms of sociality.[12] However, the treatment of a foreign space as a queer Arcadia often involved the projection of sexualized fantasies of otherness and excess onto that space. The queer Decadent community on Capri engaged in this type of projection, relying on a logic that structurally resembles Orientalism to cast the island as an erotic resort in which they might engage in affective experiments and pursue pleasure without consequences. In this they drew on the Decadent tradition of which they were a part, articulating their own dissident sexuality, as their Decadent precursors did, by generating fantasies concerning the excessive eroticism and embodiment of lands south and east of England. In their work on "gay tourism," Gordon Waitt and Kevin Markwell note that, within the "homosexual exile" scenario, lands in what Richard Burton referred to as the "Sotadic Zone" were understood to be more permissive in their treatment of "vice."[13] Burton had argued that, within the Sotadic Zone, which includes Arab countries in Africa, eastern countries such as China and Japan, as well as Italy and Greece, climate contributed to the prevalence of "pathological love."[14] The inhabitants of these zones were depersonalized and objectified, and their homes were recast as sources of pleasure for curious expatriates. Orientalist fantasy informed the exoticization of sites in the eastern sections of the "Sotadic Zone," and what Michael Herzfeld refers to as "Mediterraneanism" generated a similar construct of the Mediterranean as bewitching, enchanting, erotic, and of the past.[15] With this in mind, I also wish to interrogate the intermingling of cosmopolitanism and Mediterraneanism in the Mackenzies' treatment of Capri and to consider this element of their relationship to Capri, along with their sexual dissidence, as an element of their Decadent inheritance. The use of the island as a liberatory tool by queer Decadent expatriates might have engendered fascinating affiliative experiments, but it also involved the exoticization and instrumentalization of an entire island and its people, the treatment of foreign space as a location from which pleasure might be mined and a tool to be put to expatriate ends.[16] Attending to the role that Capri played in the Mackenzies' reconceptualization of their marriage provides insight into the complexities and contradictions of cosmopolitanism, its capacity to foster ethical and pleasing forms of sociality as well as more troubling or destructive modes of engaging with foreign space.

This then is a chapter about place as well as a chapter about affiliation. The Mackenzies' relationship was the product of the queer Geneva on which they made their home, and they reflected on that space and its influence on their understanding of gender and sexuality for the remainder of their careers. Reading their oeuvre through the lens of the enormous archive of material in the Compton Mackenzie Collection at the Harry Ransom Center indicates that they expended a great deal of energy digesting and repurposing their experiences on the island. In this chapter, I treat the Mackenzies' novels, short fiction, historical biographies, and life writing alongside their diaries, photograph albums, and correspondence as a body of aesthetic production that reflects the fact that Capri became central to their understanding of themselves and informed the work that they produced for many years after their departure. Toggling between the Mackenzies' public writing and their personal representation of their lived experience, I read this diverse range of texts and images as a collaborative attempt to theorize and practice alternative modes of affiliation and as a project informed by Decadent tradition as well as an at once cosmopolitan and Mediterraneanist engagement with the island of Capri.

"The First Revelation of a New World": The Mackenzies, Decadence, and the Road to Capri

Compton Mackenzie's interest in Decadence predates his time in Capri. He was initiated into the cult of aestheticism during his adolescence, and while at Oxford, these early influences were compounded and reinforced. His memoirs indicate that the attraction the movement had for him had much to do with its association with sexual dissidence. In *My Life and Times*, he notes with pride the interest that members of Wilde's circle took in him when he was sixteen years old and speaks frankly of his curiosity concerning same-sex desire and the queer community in London at the turn of the century. While he insists he "was not at all physically interested in homosexuals," he states that he "found their company amusing and was fascinated by the way they were able to believe they were superior to normal people."[17] He made the acquaintance of Lord Alfred Douglas, who presented him with a copy of his poetry collection *The City of the Soul* (1899), and invited him to dinner, where, Mackenzie notes with amusement, he ordered "Boy's Blood" liqueur.[18] Though Douglas came off as a "petulant spoilt child," he seems to have operated to a certain extent as a mentor to the younger man, providing him with later numbers of the Decadent undergraduate periodical the *Spirit Lamp*, edited by Douglas himself, and describing "life at Magdalen" in such a way that "confirmed [Mackenzie's] determination to go there."[19] His "most intimate friend" during this period, Dick Hewlett, who was at the time in love with another man, accompanied Mackenzie frequently to the artist Adolf Birkenruth's studio, "where there was always a gathering of homosexuals."[20] At Birkenruth's, he came to know the journalist Philip Sergeant, who educated him in "the excitement of the *fin de siècle* decadence which had captivated literary youth in the 'nineties.'"[21] He recalls Sergeant "resembling somehow a small black cat purring by his fireside" as he lent him *Mephistophèla* by Catulle Mendès, "the first book [he] had read of which lesbianism was the subject," and inspiring in him "rapture" and "the first revelation of a new world" with his gift of Théophile Gautier's *Mademoiselle de Maupin*. Soon after, Mackenzie met Wilde's close friend Reggie Turner, who was, Mackenzie notes, referred to by Wilde as the "Boy Snatcher of Clement's Inn," and began a friendship that "would last many years."[22] Turner introduced Mackenzie to Wilde's staunchest defender Robert Ross, whose "devotion to Wilde" Mackenzie found "courageous."[23] In his memoirs, Mackenzie emphasizes his attractiveness to the two older men, relaying Ross's comment, on watching him depart to pursue a young woman, "Alas, dear Reggie, you and I cannot compete with nymphs."[24] He anxiously insists that he was during this period able to "play with fire and yet avoid getting burnt," but he nevertheless highlights his playful relationships with Decadent figures such as Ross and Turner and the revelatory and titillating impact that early contact with Decadent literature had upon him.[25]

At Oxford, he continued his entanglement with the 1890s, cultivating an aesthetic persona and a Decadent domesticity. He shared rooms with Harry Pirie-Gordon, who possessed similarly aesthetic predilections, as evidenced by his later collaboration with the most decadent of Decadents, Baron Corvo (Frederick Rolfe, 1860–1913).[26] Together Mackenzie and Pirie-Gordon hosted "elaborate dinners . . . usually with roast swan, a boar's head or some other medieval dish as a centrepiece."[27] Max Beerbohm was invited to breakfast, where his silence caused the awestruck Mackenzie to worry he was bored by his undergraduate companions. (Beerbohm later confessed that talking to undergraduates made him terribly nervous, and he was simply "frightened to death."[28]) Mackenzie did wrestle at times with the sway aestheticism held over him. When the periodical he edited, the *Oxford Point of View*, was charged by another Oxford paper with attempting to "rekindle *The Spirit Lamp*," he railed against the accusation, insisting that the magazine would show how much "Oxford had changed its point of view since the 1890s."[29] This assertion was, however, undermined by Mackenzie's own contributions to the magazine. "The Undergraduate's Garden," for example, an essay by his own account, "inspired . . . by the prose of Walter Pater," instructs Oxford students to place La Gioconda in a "place of honour . . . on the chimney shelf . . . with two austere pieces of blue or green china of antique shape . . . rest[ing] against a dim green arras figured with fantastic beasts and golden flowers."[30] In *My Life and Times*, Mackenzie indicates that Turner and Ross also remained significant presences during his years at Oxford, and he stresses his close proximity to the ongoing negotiations over Wilde's posthumous reputation, reproducing in full a diary entry from 1905 concerning an altercation between Ross and Douglas after the publication of Wilde's *De Profundis*.

Mackenzie's early (and enormously popular) novel *Sinister Street* (1913–14) reflects this extensive engagement with aestheticism in both form and content. It is, as Diana Maltz argues, an "aesthetic bildungsroman" that represents the development and refinement of Michael Fane, a young man with a highly aesthetic predisposition.[31] Michael flirts with another young man at school (which caused the circulating libraries to refuse initially to purchase the novel) and with Decadence, and throughout his maturation and education he demonstrates a Paterian sensitivity to beauty. The narrator recounts in great detail Michael's fine-tuned perception of the beautiful and displeasing things he encounters, the way his "eye caresse[s]" the trees, the pleasure he takes in the sight of "a Persian cat purring on the hearthrug."[32] As Theodore Erlandson notes, "The chief influences in the formation of Mackenzie's style were, perhaps, George Meredith and, more importantly, the exponents of English and French aestheticism," and these influences are very much on display in his representation of Michael's development.[33] The lush prose, redolent of Pater and James, thrilled fellow aesthetes, such as Max Beerbohm, who insisted the novel "gives you actual Oxford *experience*" and "notes the separate color of each term," and repelled critics with more modern tastes, such as Edmund Wilson, who described Michael as "swamped in the forest of description" and "smothered by creepers and columbine."[34] This was in every way a work that advertised Mackenzie's Decadent heritage and his indebtedness to an aestheticist tradition.

Just as Compton's engagement with Decadence preceded his time on Capri, the Mackenzies' capacity to accommodate unconventional domestic arrangements antedated their arrival on the island. Compton was a close friend of Faith's brother Christopher Stone at Oxford, and, while visiting her brother's room, she had come "under [Compton's] spell."[35] The two were married in a secret ceremony in 1905. According to Faith, she "knew from the first that [she] didn't want a nice conventional marriage, and [she] was justifiably sure that [she] had avoided this."[36] She states that she "was prepared for almost any possibility in [her] marriage; neglect, abandonment, even divorce," but she remained confident that Compton "would always make life amusing."[37] In the early days of their marriage, they brought the Decadent poet and book designer Althea Gyles into their home as a kind of fin-de-siècle foster child. The aging friend of Wilde, Beardsley, and Yeats, "the golden girl of all the poets and painters" of the 1890s, proved herself a nuisance, refusing to help with the housework and strewing flowers about the floor, and was eventually asked to leave.[38] Soon after, Faith became pregnant, but she miscarried the child and swore "never again."[39] Compton states that he "never understood [babies'] attraction for so many people," so Faith's resolution seems to have been acceptable to him, and the Mackenzies never had children.[40] They did, however, continue to welcome third parties into their home. They shared an apartment in London with Harry Pélissier, the producer and chief comedian in the Follies show for which Compton had been enlisted to write lyrics, which caused Faith's father to write cautioning that this arrangement "would look like a *ménage a trois*" and expressing concern that his daughter seemed "smitten by [Pélissier's] social qualities."[41] Faith, however, "had so long abandoned whatever regard [she] had ever had for appearances" that his concerns were disregarded, and she became involved in another *ménage a trois* involving Pélissier, who had fallen in love with Compton's sister Fay and "got into his head that Faith was jealous of her."[42] At the same time, Compton began an affair with Chrissie Maude, one of the actresses in Pélissier's production of Royston Keith's *All Change Here*, a relationship of which Faith, according to Mackenzie's biographer Andro Linklater, was well aware.

The Mackenzies came to Capri then primed and prepared to engage with the island's culture of Decadence and sexual permissiveness. However, in their life writing, they nevertheless represent their arrival on Capri as transformative and revelatory. They had decided to leave England due to Compton's sciatica, which seemed to be exacerbated by the cold and damp, and they had recently become friends with the writer Norman Douglas, whose Mediterraneanist travel book *Siren Land* (1911) and stories of Capri made Italy an alluring destination. They traveled to Sorrento and took what was meant to be a weekend trip to Capri, but, Compton states, "the moment we emerged from the funicular in the Piazza we felt that nothing must prevent our living in Capri."[43] For Faith, it was "falling in love, irrevocably. Its magic sank into my heart."[44] They began their stay at the Pensione Faraglioni, where, as Compton notes, one of their very first conversations indicated that they had entered a zone of cosmopolitan progressiveness: "I recall one of those Germans saying to me how sad it was that the English had been unable to appreciate the genius of Oscar 'Vilda' and for that reason had persecuted him."[45] While Capri seemed to attract progressive visitors, the Mackenzies' representations of the island also indicate that they believed that something endemic to the island fostered more indulgent attitudes about desire. In his memoirs, Compton represents the island as a world apart, an environment that remakes and remolds its inhabitants, selecting for beauty and exoticism: "Round us, in a jingle of bells and laughter and cracking whips, stood so many people, natives and foreigners, who from living in Capri had achieved such a brilliance of effect as butterflies and humming-birds achieve from competing with the light and colour of the tropics."[46] Faith similarly exoticizes Capri and stresses its capacity to unwind and unsettle, arguing that the island is suffused with a history of epicureanism and bacchanals that continues to bewitch its contemporary inhabitants:

> For two thousand years Capri has been dedicated to pleasure, ever since, and possibly before, Tiberius built his twelve villas there and amused himself in his own way. . . . Capri is haunted by ghosts of revelry and amorous sports of all descriptions. . . . With the tumult of bygone festivals, orgies and saturnalia still raging, what hope is there of escape for any one? Capri is decidedly not suitable for a quiet domestic life.[47]

"Northern Minds Seem to Become Fluid Here": The Mackenzies on Capri

The Mackenzies certainly did not attempt to lead a quiet domestic life on the island. They were launched, via letters of introduction from Norman Douglas, directly into Capri's queer community, overseen by the "passionate old American ladies," Kate and Saidee Wolcott-Perry.[48] The distant cousins, whom Robert Aldrich refers to as "two of the most renowned lesbians in Capri," had hyphenated their surnames to indicate their intimacy.[49] Their home, the Villa Torricella, was the epicenter of the cosmopolitan circle of dandies and aesthetes on Capri in the 1910s, a setting marked by an unapologetic Mediterraneanism meant to foster bacchanals and debauchery. As Faith states, the Villa Torricella was, "with its Moorish fantasies and persistent air of 1890," "built for gaiety: salons and loggias blazed with fairy lamps; long pergolas were lit by coloured bunches of grapes among the vines. Till dawn they would speed the dancers, [and] ply the band with wine."[50]

At the Wolcott-Perrys' entertainments that spring, the Mackenzies met the individual who would become the central figure in Compton's *Vestal Fire* (1927), the French Decadent writer Jacques d'Adelswärd-Fersen, or "Count Jack," who had recently returned to the island after being banished from Italy in 1909. Fersen had moved to Capri in 1904 after standing trial for "incitement of minors to debauchery" in France.[51] Like the many exiles who came to Capri following the Wilde trials, he was drawn to the island's reputation for permissiveness and tolerance. When rumors concerning the exact nature of the charges against Fersen began to circulate, however, many members of the expatriate community turned their backs on him.

He was finally expelled from Italy following a festivity he organized to mark his secretary and companion Nino Cesarini's twentieth birthday and calling up for military service. During the Mithraic ceremony, which took place by torchlight in the Matermània grotto and was attended by the Wolcott-Perrys, Fersen's Ceylonese servants delivered twenty lashes to Nino's naked buttocks. According to Will H. L. Ogrinc, "A passer-by gathering herbs could not understand what was happening; she informed her father, who lodged an official complaint of violation of public decency."[52] The Wolcott-Perrys remained steadfastly attached to their old friend. Their decision to hold a dinner in his honor on his return divided the expatriate community on the island. As Compton records, "Those who accepted an invitation remained welcome guests at the Villa Torricella; those who declined were never allowed to enter it again."[53] But Faith and Compton "were too much newcomers to feel that [they] were involved in the split," and they could thus attend the dinner in honor of Fersen without alienating themselves from the wider expatriate community.[54]

The Mackenzies seemed to share a sense that Fersen was, as Faith put it, "socially impossible," but his presence did much to set the Decadent mood that marked their time on Capri.[55] It was as if Dorian Gray himself had taken up residence on the island. Fersen did all he could to link himself imaginatively to the excesses of the fin de siècle. His outsize performance of a Decadent persona bordered on the absurd. He built himself an Art Nouveau Neoclassical home, the Villa Lysis, which, like Villa Torricella, braided together Mediterraneanism, Orientalism, and Decadence. The villa was equipped with an opium den, a dedication to love and sorrow, "AMORI ET DOLORI SACRUM," above the portico, and a nude statue of Nino in the garden. Faith remarks upon the "luxurious couches" and "wonderful collection of pipes" that filled his opium den, noting that "it was open occasionally to the ladies who would sometimes be sick afterwards on his marble staircase outside."[56] His literary output similarly operated to indicate his allegiance to the Decadence of the 1890s. Comparing Fersen to authors such as Proust, who began their careers as nineteenth-century aesthetes yet reinvented themselves to adapt to changing literary tastes, Jeremy Reed argues that Fersen, however, "remained fixed; he wrote backwards in an attempt to recreate the essentially artificial novel that Wilde, inspired by Huysmans's *Against Nature*, had exhausted."[57] It would be generous to refer to his *Messes noires: Lord Lyllian* (1905) as a revision of *The Picture of Dorian Gray*, as it more closely resembles amateurish plagiarism. Fersen integrates Wilde's biography with his fiction, strips the mixture of any archness or humor, and loosely translates his Decadence back into the French from which it came. The titular hero of *Lord Lyllian*, an aristocratic young man, "lets himself be raped like a pretty woman" by the famous author Harold Skilde, the author of *The Portrait of Miriam Green*.[58] An amalgamation of Wilde and Lord Henry, Skilde precipitates the moral destruction of the younger man, "his jaded pleasure-seeker's soul taint[ing] Lord Lyllian," his "paradoxes, which he developed skillfully with his usual loquaciousness, permeat[ing] his mind."[59] When Skilde is arrested, accused of "having corrupted youth, of having soiled children," he writes to his beloved in a passage that presages *De Profundis*, published in expurgated form the very same year: "When I remember our parties and our frenzies, our madness and our promises, . . . it seems, my Lord, that I have a dagger piercing my chest."[60] The novel doggedly reproduces Dorian's transformation into a remorseless monster, his meditation on the portraits of his ancestors, and his attempts at redemption, and, like Dorian, Lord Lyllian dies abruptly after believing he might find reform in his love for a young woman. Fersen's single innovation lies in his hero's descent into actual Satanism. The novel, which Fersen began during his travels in Ceylon and completed on Capri, allowed him to announce how he wished to be perceived during his exile on the island, as an avatar of Dorian Gray and a dangerous reincarnation of Oscar Wilde.

The links between Decadence and the other sexual exiles on the island were much more subtly encoded. Many had come to Capri in the immediate wake of the Wilde trials. The aesthete John Ellingham Brooks, for example, arrived during what Compton refers to as "the emigration of homosexuals at the time of the Wilde case," and he was soon visited by a younger man he had recently seduced and introduced to the Decadent literature of the fin de siècle, William Somerset Maugham.[61] A friend of Lord Alfred Douglas's, the writer E. F. Benson (author of the Mapp and Lucia novels), arrived the same year. These three frequently lived together in Brooks's Villa Cercola, for, as Faith notes, "they had tastes in common besides literature, which made Capri a desirable retreat."[62] Brooks in particular became a close friend of the Mackenzies, who found his aimless, epicurean approach to existence charming. The dandyish Brooks worked perpetually on Greek translations that were never completed and spent a good deal of his time dining at the homes of others. In her late memoir *Always Afternoon* (1943), Faith looks back fondly at his "useless, selfish life," noting, "For many of us he was the essence of Capri, picturesque and lovable, without much shame, and what is far rarer, without sham."[63] Andro Linklater refers to Brooks as the Mackenzies' "most assiduous visitor" and an "especially sure" source of gossip, who drew them immediately into intimate knowledge of the island's many scandals.[64] He, along with Fersen and the Wolcott-Perrys, welcomed the Mackenzies into their Decadent retreat and inflected their initial years on the island with the ethos of the 1890s.

The most significant friendship for Faith, however, was that with the "aesthete, polymath, and omnisexual hedonist" Norman Douglas, a relationship she described as "eternal" and having "influenced [her] whole life."[65] Born in Austria, raised in Scotland, and spending most of his adult life in Italy, Douglas's restlessness and cosmopolitanism were reflected in the travel writings with which he had first made his name. George Woodcock has contrasted his peripatetic lifestyle with Wilde's exile by stressing that Douglas "never showed any sign of acquiescing in society's condemnation. . . . He did not see himself as an outcast, for there was no community to which he felt enough attachment or loyalty for his casting out from it to affect him emotionally. He was indeed perhaps the best example among English-speaking writers of the other kind of literary exile: the expatriate."[66] Douglas's brazenness and his shedding of British mores and a fixed national identity were exemplary for Faith, and the basis for this friendship, she states, was "respectful ribaldry," a term that accurately describes the tone of their correspondence.[67] Douglas wrote frankly to Faith about the "teat-a-teats" he conducted in her home while she was away, ribbed her about the "menagerie" of men she assembled about herself, and congratulated her on a love affair with another woman: "Well, I'm glad you're having a little of the real thing at last."[68] In 1916, she served as a key witness in Douglas's defense when he was charged with indecent behavior with two young men in London. The police claimed that he had been with the boys during the summer and, in particular, on a specific day in July. Faith, however, presented her diary, which indicated that he had been dining with her in Capri on that date, and the charges were dropped. Theirs was a friendship marked by unremitting honesty and acceptance. In her diary, she referred to Douglas as a "fascinating pagan" and herself as "blessed beyond other women in knowing him as he really is & having had such wonderful times with him."[69] Her affection for him was, it seems, bound up in fantasies of sexual and gender dissidence, for she exclaims in the same entry, "If I were only an attractive boy & could travel in such inspiring company!"[70] Douglas's sensibility and his vision of Capri inflected her own experience of the island, and his most well-known work, *South Wind* (1917), which Faith typed for Douglas, is commonly acknowledged as the primary influence on Compton's Capri novels, *Vestal Fire* and *Extraordinary Women*.

South Wind transports the scenario of Dorian Gray to the Mediterranean, where vulnerable naïfs are morally expanded and transformed, not by a book, but by an island. In this, *South Wind* may be understood as one of the central documents of Decadent Mediterraneanism, positing the island of "Nepenthe," which Aldrich describes as "an amalgam of Capri, Ischia, and Procida," as a hedonistic and bewitching paradise that has the capacity to undermine and unravel British moralism.[71] Nepenthe remakes and remolds both the Bishop Thomas Heard, recently arrived at the "ultra-cosmopolitan" island from Africa, and Denis Phipps, "an absurdly good-looking youth" from England.[72] Richard Aldington has argued that Douglas learned hedonism from Wilde, and Nepenthe's resident Lord Henries, Count Caleveglia and Mr. Keith, certainly reflect this, inundating the island's recent arrivals with a "mediterraneanised" Decadence, an ethos of "multiplied sensations" beyond good and evil.[73] Their words along with the island's beauty cooperate in seducing and transmuting the new arrivals. When critics complained that the novel lacked a plot, Douglas retorted that it was "nothing but plot from beginning to end. How to make murder palatable to a bishop: that is the plot. How? You must unconventionalise him, and instil into his mind the seeds of doubt and revolt. You must shatter his old notions of what is right."[74] And this is just what happens to Heard. He finds himself, in the company of Keith and Caleveglia, "expanding," awakened, newly alive to beauty, transformed utterly by the "sudden strange stimulus of Nepenthe – it was driving his thoughts headlong, out of their old grooves."[75] His "up-to-date theory of life" informs his decision, after witnessing a woman murder a man to protect her family, to say nothing to the authorities.[76] Denis, too, is changed by the "relentless paganism" of Nepenthe and the words of his Wildean mentors.[77] His reserve is "unstrung" and his world "expanded" by the Count's "melodious voice" and his descriptions of "Hellenic life."[78] The novel insists that the island undoes fixed selves. As Mr. Keith states, "This coast-line alone – the sheer effrontery of its mineral charm – might affect some natures to such an extent as to dislocate their stability. Northern minds seem to become fluid here, impressionable, unstable, unbalanced – what you please. There is something in the brightness of this spot which decomposes their old particles and arranges them into fresh and unexpected patterns."[79] This is *South Wind*'s Mediterraneanist refrain, the expansive, transformative effects of the "intense, palpitating, dramatic" life on Nepenthe, and the influence of this refrain is evident throughout the Mackenzies' fiction and life writing.[80]

The Mackenzies replicated the Decadent Mediterraneanism of *South Wind* in the late teens, as their marriage underwent just such a decomposition and rearrangement, a transformation that resulted from their own practice of erotic tourism as well as the influence of the queer cosmopolitan community with which they had surrounded themselves. Both Compton and Faith entered into sexual relationships with the island's native inhabitants and with transplants from Russia, mainland Italy, and the United States, and, according to some sources, they each engaged in affairs with both men and women. While Compton and his biographer Andro Linklater insist that he remained a spectator of rather than a participant in the queer subculture that so fascinated him, James Money states, in his *Capri: Island of Pleasure*, that, soon after their arrival on the island, Compton began an affair with Luigi Ruggiero, the brother of a local man who designed and stocked their garden.[81] The relationship that altered the Mackenzies' union entirely, however, began following the onset of World War I, when Compton was away for months at a time working with the British secret service in Greece. During this period, Faith became close with the Anglo-Italian Caracciolo family, befriending the teenage sisters, Isabella and Bianca, and entering into an affair with their brother Nini, who was almost twenty years her junior. When Compton returned to Capri in October 1917, he forbade Faith to see Nini by herself. Nini pined for Faith beside the olive tree where they had frequently met throughout a cold November, fell ill, and died. Compton notes in his memoirs that "Faith was in an emotional collapse and kept on saying 'My fault! All my fault!'"[82] She fell into a depression that lasted for months. In March of the following year, Axel Munthe, a renowned Swedish physician and psychiatrist who had become close friends with Faith, came to Compton and proposed the following: "Why don't you both admit that marriage in the conventional sense is no longer possible? Why don't you give freedom to each to live his or her own life and yet agree to live together in friendship as man and wife?"[83] In the years that followed, the Mackenzies did as Munthe advised, allowing their marriage to open out onto the island around them. According to Money, soon after the meeting with Munthe, Compton bought a cottage on Capri that he used "for private meetings with his boy-friends," and Faith fell in love with the Italian pianist Renata Borgatti, whom she described in her diary as "a young girl, the hockey type, with the face & figure of a woman, the frank eyes of a boy, & the voice of a man."[84] Compton also began an affair with Ann Heiskell, an American whose husband Morgan was with the American army in France, and Faith became involved with Nikolai Nadegin (or Nadezhin), a revolutionary who had escaped captivity in Russia. Linklater states that "Monty [Compton] and Nadegin often played chess together, and they all met regularly as a quartet for meals and drinks at the [Mackenzies'] cliff-side house."[85]

Faith's diaries from this period offer fascinating evidence concerning the affective labor involved in negotiating an open marriage. While the couple's life writing tends to paint a rosy picture of their semi-detached union, Faith's diary entries indicate much about the emotional rhythms of their radical tie, which included moments of impressive generosity and patience as well as frustration, jealousy, and anger. In addition, her diaries reflect the extent to which the openness of their union allowed the community on Capri to operate as a crucial component of their relationship with one another. Their marriage did not engender isolation or withdrawal into conventional domesticity. Faith's diaries indicate that she and Compton rather turned their curiosity and their energy outward, serving one another as allies and collaborators in the interpretation of the company they kept.

In the days and weeks immediately following Nini's death, Faith's entries register an enormous amount of pain, but they do indicate that, from the first, she and Compton entered into open and honest discussions about what had just occurred. She asserts that "Nini is always there. M [Compton, or 'Monty'] feels it too."[86] She notes that "long long discussions" are taking place and that Compton is "so sweet so sweet."[87] As they enter the new year, she continues to be preoccupied with mourning, spending much of her time sculpting a bust of Nini. The spring and early summer of 1918 seem to have been extremely difficult. An entry from May reads, "Screamed most of the night," and two in June, "Sad evening," and "Very tired & unhappy tonight. Both to bed early."[88]

During the summer of 1918, however, Faith and Compton began to spend more time with the developing lesbian community on the island. This coterie of what Faith referred to as "fair ladies" included the afore-mentioned Renata Borgatti, the American painter (and wife of John Ellingham Brooks) Romaine Brooks, the Venetian Mimi Franchetti, "the moving spirit behind lesbian parties in Capri," and the Australian Francesa Lloyd, whose tempestuous relationship with Franchetti involved "flying bottles, furious quarrels, separations, reconciliations and rare periods of harmony."[89] Capri's reputation as a safe refuge for sexual dissidents following the Wilde trials might have attracted these women to the island, but their arrival also marked Capri's transition into a new age, a moment governed by defiantly modern and sexually dissident women rather than fin-de-siècle dandies. The entries in Faith's diary show her becoming captivated by Capri's newest arrivals, their "kaleidoscopic changes of companionship," and their intermingling of the Decadence of the 1890s with a lesbian modernist aesthetic.[90] In her memoirs, she records watching "a girl in a dark-green tailor-made with a pleated skirt, a bow tie, a cane, and no hat on a head of rippling chestnut hair" walk past Morgano's café one spring day.[91] This was Mimi Franchetti, and her diary entry from that day notes that at this meeting she "fell in love ... with Franchetti who offered me a bottle of absinthe. Walked down & met Franchetti at Morgano's with bottle tied in pale green ribbon & went to see [Franchetti and Francesca Lloyd's] rooms at Quisisana. Amazing. Crammed with photos, toy dogs, dolls (futurist), & Beardsley drawings."[92] It is hard to imagine a better representative figure or event when describing the integration of Decadence and modernism performed by the "fair ladies" on Capri. According to Faith, these dandyish women captured the imagination of the expatriate community: "They had but to walk on the Piazza or the Funicular terrace, swinging military capes, or wearing feminine little frocks as the case might be, fingering interminable cigarette-holders, to be immediately the objects of popular interest."[93] Faith's diaries reflect the extent to which they pulled the Mackenzies forward into a new epoch on Capri, which Faith refers to in her memoirs as "the era of wild parties."[94] Their more boisterous and outré model of queer cosmopolitanism drew the couple out of a phase of mourning and into a period of late nights, heavy drinking, and scandal.

Like the queer community that preceded them, this coterie was markedly international, and their constant movement between Paris and Capri only added to their glamour. However, the attraction the Italian women in particular held for Faith had much to do with her reading of them as exotic, excessive, high-strung, and bacchanalian. Their cosmopolitanism, in other words, did not render them immune to her Mediterraneanist gaze. Faith's interest in Borgatti, for example, was linked to the passion with which she performed opera. In her memoirs, she recollects Borgatti coming to her home and playing "Wagner like an orchestra, every now and then singing in her deep, hoarse, masculine voice" during a thunderstorm "of terrific violence, the thunder roaring and echoing among the cliffs."[95] Faith's passion for Borgatti resembles the "'sapphic' diva-worship" described by Terry Castle as a central trope of lesbian desire, a trope that could often take on Mediterraneanist undertones by fetishizing the

Figure 3.1   Compton Mackenzie and Mimi Franchetti (n.d.), from scrapbook 11
(formerly cataloged as P25), a photo album titled *Photographs, 1914–24, mostly Capri, also
some on Herm*. Compton Mackenzie Collection, Harry Ransom Center.
Reproduced courtesy of the Harry Ransom Center.

maenad-like qualities of the Italian opera singer.[96] Faith's entries reveal her
growing increasingly consumed with Borgatti, selecting her seats at performances so as to have a "good view of Renata's face & hands" and noting
with satisfaction that, at a musical performance with Nadegin, "Renata
came & kissed [her] after the first part."[97]

While Compton's treatment of Capri's lesbian community in
Extraordinary Women is arch and somewhat contemptuous, he, too, seems
to have been fascinated by this new company when they first arrived.
A photo album devoted to the Mackenzies' time on Capri includes playful
images of Compton and Franchetti twinned in their androgyny, heads
tilted at just the same angle, wearing identical ties, and posing in identical
precarious positions on the backs of two chairs facing one another
(Figure 3.1). Faith's diaries reflect how frequently Franchetti and
Borgatti were visitors at their home, brought back for cocktails by
Compton or to dine along with John Ellingham Brooks. While
Compton insists in his memoirs that the endless gossip concerning a
burglary at their home, for which Borgatti was the primary suspect, is
what finally drove him from the island, Faith's diaries indicate that he was
absorbed enthusiastically in the titillating speculation concerning the event
and its causes. On March 16, 1919, the Mackenzies and Nadegin returned

home to find that their home had been robbed. The missing items included gold, some of Faith's jewelry, as well as a bottle of absinthe that Franchetti had presented to Faith. Faith notes in her diary that the fact that the bottle of absinthe had been taken "convinced [her] that it wasn't the act of ordinary thieves, but an act of *dispetto* [mischief or spite]. Theories abound but what is the truth?"[98] It was presumed that Borgatti, believing that Faith was attracted to Franchetti, had stolen the bottle of absinthe Franchetti had presented to her. The following night, Compton attended a party at Pensione Faraglioni, and Faith records, "Someone's manner very queer – M convinced. Can it be?"[99] An entry from a couple of weeks later states that Lloyd, Franchetti, and John Ellingham Brooks came to dinner, and "M told them our suspicions."[100] In *My Life and Times*, Compton writes that he encouraged Faith to forget the entire manner, insisting, "I have myself an aversion from building up a situation."[101] Nadegin, he asserts, was responsible for encouraging Faith to perseverate on the matter and to "go on wandering about in his complicated Russian mazes of the mind."[102] Faith's diaries, however, tell a different story, representing the entire household as equally engaged in and titillated by the erotic intrigue the "fair ladies" had introduced to their island and their home. The spinning of theories, the interpretation of glances, the circulation of accusations allowed Faith and Compton (along with Nadegin) to collaborate in their own reading of the community and to produce together a vision of events in which Faith's attractiveness to that community was central.

"You Expanded Morally, That Is You Became More Elastic": The Mackenzies after Capri

By the decade's end, Compton had begun to grow increasingly restless on Capri, discussing a potential trip to the South Seas with D. H. Lawrence and finally, in 1920, acquiring the Channel Islands of Herm and Jethou on a sixty-year lease from the Crown.[103] He first made his home on Herm, amidst a community of around thirty people, before moving to the even more sparsely populated Jethou in 1923. While Faith remained for a time on Capri and made trips back throughout the 1920s, she eventually joined Compton in this markedly different mode of island existence. On the Channel Islands, their lives altered entirely. If the close quarters of Capri had thrust the Mackenzies and an international cast of eccentrics into intimate contact with one another, Herm and Jethou were islands in the "insulet" sense of the term, lonely and quiet spaces allowing for withdrawal and introspection. Compton insisted that this kind of withdrawal in fact sharpened his perception, arguing that it was not the case that "a man who deliberately lived on a small island deprived himself of the right to criticize the facts of existence. I had always supposed that a man's observation was likely to be helped rather than hindered by a position of comparative detachment."[104] This "comparative detachment," however, inflected his fictional treatment of Capri in significant ways. D. J. Dolley has referred to Compton's *Vestal Fire* and *Extraordinary Women* as composed "in the *South Wind* vein," but Compton's Capri novels articulate a much more aloof and skeptical vision of the Decadent Mediterraneanist ethos.[105] If he represents himself in his memoirs as having succumbed momentarily to the moral expansion described by Norman Douglas, as allowing his Northern mind for a moment to become fluid, in the Capri novels, he communicates a somewhat congealed and hardened sensibility. He wrote these novels after withdrawal from the fray that was Capri, after disentangling himself from the dissidence and disruption of that "water-land."

Vestal Fire and *Extraordinary Women* are Firbankian, camp modernist texts that lampoon the bohemianism and sexual dissidence with which the Mackenzies had so earnestly engaged while living on the island. This detached and critical practice of the Decadent aesthetic is, however, what makes these novels so properly Decadent. Like *The Picture of Dorian Gray* or Aubrey Beardsley's illustrations for *Salome*, Compton's Capri novels at once enact and satirize the hedonism and gender play associated with the Decadent aesthetic. They parody the island's queer population from an insider's perspective. Howard J. Booth has described these texts as performing "a strong attack on adult homosexuality," but their relationship to sexual dissidence might be more accurately described as what Dominic Janes has referred to as "fascinated ambivalence."[106] It is the case, however, that Compton seems to have understood the history of the queer community on Capri as divided into two distinct epochs, marked by the fissure of the war. Though he brings satire to bear on both eras, his treatment of the island's earlier, more distinctly Decadent moment is much milder than his representation of the arrival of Capri's extraordinary women.

Vestal Fire caricatures the prewar "cosmopolitan and tolerant society" on Capri, or "Sirene" as it is called in the novel.[107] The narrative centers on the "famous friendship" between Fersen, or "Count Marsac," and the Wolcott-Perrys, here "Virginia" and "Maimie Pepworth-Norton."[108] The text at once highlights and snickers at the studied cosmopolitanism of the expatriate community. The opening chapter states that the island hosts an American translating Goethe, an Englishman translating the sonnets of Hérédia, and another Englishman wrestling with Mallarmé's *L'Après-midi d'un Faune*. . . . There was a Russian at work on a new system of political economy, and a Swede who was elaborating a theory of health. There was a German writing a history of the Saracens, and there was John Scudamore, an American, who was amassing the material for a history of Roman morals.[109]

Similarly, it is noted that, at their Villa Amabile, the two American ladies foster a "symphony" of accents made from "the mixture of nationalities they loved to entertain."[110] The Decadent Mediterraneanist ethos that drew this transnational cast of characters to Sirene is also lampooned. In a passage that satirically mimics *South Wind*'s expansive refrain, the Pepworth-Nortons' home is represented as the epicenter of the moral transformations that occur on Sirene:

> And on that shady terrace you expanded. . . . You expanded aesthetically as you gazed across a Bay of Naples that was behaving as such famous views usually behave only in railway-posters. . . . You looked up to where five hundred feet above you beyond the lemon-gardens and lush young vines the Piazza with its baroque tower and crowd of little people like dragon-flies glittered in the clear afternoon air, and you expanded morally, that is you became more elastic.[111]

Count Marsac's hedonism and his Orientalism are also held up for ridicule, as he hosts "pink dinners" (where he serves salmon, crayfish, bortsch, and roast flamingos), "proclaims himself a devotee of opium," commissions a portrait of his secretary Carlo di Fiore being raped by the fountain nymphs, and issues invitations to a *thé japonais*, for which "Japanese costume was indispensable" and at which he produces a "Cingalese boy" as his *"pièce de resistance."*[112] Once it is revealed that the Count had been charged with indecent conduct with minors in Paris, the novel treats both sides of the ensuing controversy as absurd, representing the island as what D. H. Lawrence referred to as a "Cat-Cranford," a world of endless gossip and limited perspective.[113]

However, if *Vestal Fire* softly ridicules the queer cosmopolitan community on Capri, it levels its sharpest scorn at the moralism of outsiders to and critics of that community. The three English sisters, Mrs. Onslow, Mrs. Gibbs, and Mrs. Rosebotham, who hold themselves apart from the society at Villa Amabile, share a sense that Sirene's bad reputation "was due to the presence of so many cosmopolitans" and that the island's morals might be cured by "a steady injection of well-to-do English residents – nice people with families who played golf": "Mrs. Rosebotham was sure that it was the absence of golf, more than anything else, which made Sirene so bad for people's morals."[114] The English sisters are rivaled in their absurdity by the "great simple-hearted, prairie-souled, heavy-weight" American Aston Duplock, "one of those virile primitives," a "corn-fed husky child of nature," whose rage concerning the Count's sexuality erupts into violence.[115] He is infuriated by the sight of Carlo and the Count eating together at the Hotel Augusto and pledges to "clear this fairy out of Sirene."[116] He repeatedly attempts to trip the Count in an effort to initiate a physical altercation. While the novel has in its previous chapters often scoffed at the Count, here he is granted the privilege of a dandyish victory, as he calls the head-porter to say, "Somebody has left a leg here . . . . I have already had the inconvenience of falling over it once or twice. Please have it put somewhere out of the way."[117] Duplock proceeds to humiliate himself further by attempting to bore a hole in the hotel wall so as to spy on the Count's "orgies and opium and all the rest of it."[118] He instead drills a hole in the wall of the proprietor's wife's room and is summarily ejected from the island. The novel might tease Decadence, but it wholeheartedly condemns moral outrage and homophobia.

Vestal Fire also allows itself to reflect nostalgically on the unique community fostered by turn-of-the-century Sirene, and it is in the end elegiac in its treatment of the island's Decadent phase. The text closes by expressing earnest regret about the loss of the realm of possibility fostered by the Pepworth-Nortons at Villa Amabile, speaking in its final pages from the perspective of Miss Virginia as she mourns the deceased Miss Maimie and looks back to a moment when they were

> surrounded by so many friends, ... leaning over the balustrade of the terrace above the road, leaning over and clapping and waving and showering genista blossom and red rose-petals upon the throng. And now they are alone together in their new loggia, through which the summer *maestrale* blows with such life-giving freshness when the sun has dropped behind Monte Ventoso, whose towering bulk casts a shadow upon the Villa Amabile. "Oh, Maimie doesn't Vesuvius look a great old boy this afternoon? And my! isn't it good to be alive, honey?"[119]

The novel's conclusion looks back fondly to Capri before the war and the kinds of love and happiness that could happen there. The affection the Pepworth-Nortons had for each other and for the cosmopolitan community they fostered within their home is represented as lovely and sweet and generative, and the novel's closing lament for that community tempers the mockery in the preceding pages. As D. J. Dooley argues, there is a strong note of "pathos or sentimentality" in *Vestal Fire*.[120] In his dedication to John Ellingham Brooks, Compton states that the work "holds much of my heart, and for that reason I can inscribe it . . . to the music and scandal we have enjoyed, but perhaps most of all to the laughs we have had, of which I hope you will hear a faint echo as you turn over the pages of this book."[121] This might be the key as to how to read the work, as a loving caricature of Capri's dandies and Decadents developed and articulated by embedded members of that community.

Nevertheless, while Compton insisted that, in writing *Vestal Fire*, he "was not intending to satirize homosexuality," the novel must be understood as complex and conflicted in its treatment of Decadence and same-sex desire.[122] Florence Tamagne has described *Vestal Fire*'s setting as "straight out of a play by Oscar Wilde or an Aubrey Beardsley engraving," but it would be more accurate to say that the text at once enters into and hovers above the Decadence it represents.[123] Contemporary reviewers made note of the novel's ambivalent orientation toward Sirene. Writing for the *Spectator*, Rachel Annand Taylor noted that, though the book suggests comparison with *South Wind*, "Mr. Compton Mackenzie's manner is flightier and more Puckish."[124] However, she states, the "decidedly cruel and glittering mockery" of the novel is humanized by his treatment of figures such as the "two aged American ladies who love their Sirene with such touching naiveté."[125] In the *Nation & Athenaeum*, Edwin Muir described Compton's treatment of the Sirene scene as marked by "happy detachment."[126] The critical assessment of the novel on its publication acknowledged that, while *Vestal Fire* is far from an indictment of the community it represents, the novel does hold itself slightly apart from the world it at once eulogizes and mocks.

Though *Vestal Fire* works to generate a sense of "comparative detachment" from the world with which the Mackenzies had been so intimate in the teens, an artifact within the Compton Mackenzie Collection at the Harry Ransom Center collapses that detachment and remakes the novel into a fond tribute to their kinship with the men and women of Capri. A year after the publication of *Vestal Fire*, Faith noted in her diary that she had begun pasting photographs into her copy of the novel. Inside the book's cover, Faith has included a photograph of Compton on the hills of Capri wearing a white suit (Figure 3.2). Facing the dedication, she pasted an image of John Ellingham Brooks lounging and reading on a boat (Figure 3.3). A photograph of "Count Jack" is captioned "Baron Robert Marsac Lagerström," while an image clipped from the newspaper retains its

Figure 3.2   Photograph of Compton Mackenzie, pasted inside Faith Compton Mackenzie's "improved" copy of *Vestal Fire*. Harry Ransom Center Book Collection. Reproduced courtesy of the Harry Ransom Center.

Figure 3.3   Photograph of James Ellingham Brooks, pasted inside Faith Compton Mackenzie's "improved" copy of *Vestal Fire*. Harry Ransom Center Book Collection. Reproduced courtesy of the Harry Ransom Center.

label, "Fersen."[127] An image of Nino Cesarini wearing a toga and a diadem on the terrace of Villa Lysis is identified as Carlo di Fiore. The caption beneath a group photograph refers to Norman Douglas by his pseudonym in the novel, "Duncan Maxwell," and to John Ellingham Brooks as "J. E. B." (Figure 3.4).[128] Faith has placed Compton and Brooks within the pages of the text, intermingling them with professional photographs and intimate snapshots of the novel's cast of characters. Her captions toggle between references to characters' names and the individuals upon which those characters were based. The line between the Mackenzies' Capri and *Vestal Fire*'s Sirene is blurred and crossed. Faith remade the text into something resembling a family photo album and closed the distance the novel seeks to generate between the Mackenzies and the community they had left behind, acknowledging their indebtedness to the island and their kinship with its queer community.

Extraordinary Women, however, undoes much of the mending work that Faith performed in her creation of that "improved" copy of *Vestal Fire*.[129] In this later novel, the focus is the development of a lesbian community on

Figure 3.4   Group photograph including John Ellingham Brooks and Norman Douglas,
pasted inside Faith Compton Mackenzie's "improved" copy of *Vestal Fire*. Harry Ransom
Center Book Collection.
Reproduced courtesy of the Harry Ransom Center.

"Sirene" after the war, and the "glittering mockery" becomes far more cruel
and caustic.[130] As a review in the *New Statesman* notes, "If the subject [of
lesbianism] was to be regarded before as unpleasant Mr. Mackenzie has
certainly made it a hundred times more unpleasant."[131] The thinly veiled,
Mediterraneanist caricatures of Mimi Franchetti (as "Rosalba Donsante")
and Renata Borgatti (as "Cléo Gazay") involve themselves in endless and
absurd intrigues and behave like rabid, passionate furies. When Cléo
performs Wagner, she is "a valkyrie writhing to be free from the marble
in which she was confined."[132] Rosalba stalks through the island like a
crazed and erratic panther, dividing romances between women and discarding new conquests without thinking. Howard J. Booth has asserted
that the narrative voice makes clear that "homosexuality is inferior because
of an inherent instability."[133] In *Extraordinary Women*, Compton seems to

be turning his back on Sirene and the affiliative experiments performed there, retracting from the lesbian epoch on the island and the manner in which it intruded into his marriage.

For Faith, however, there was far more continuity between what Compton represented as two distinct eras on the island. She enjoyed the circle to which Norman Douglas introduced them as much as the one governed by Mimi Franchetti, and after their departure, she continued to look back fondly to the island and the modes of sexual and gender dissidence it fostered. It was she, rather than Compton, who truly carried the ethos of Capri in the 1910s into the 1920s and 1930s. Following the move to the Channel Islands, Faith describes herself as affected by a "restlessness which jerked [her] from island to island," from Herm and then Jethou back to Capri, from Compton back to "dancing on the terrace at [their old home on Capri] Solitaria till dawn."[134] On Jethou, where "there was nothing to do in the evenings ... except read or write," she wrote "nostalgic short stories about Italy," three of which appeared in the *New Statesman*.[135] As Bashir Abu-Manneh notes, these works, which "tell of meetings and encounters between the international clientele of [an] exclusive resort," evoke "the careless sense of freedom and opportunities offered by bohemian life" on Faith's Sirene, "Spiaggia."[136] In 1931, she published these stories, along with eleven more, in a collection entitled *Mandolinata*. The stories cooperate to evoke the "rosemary-scented air" of the island and the epicurean and amorous company that is drawn there.[137] In the title story, an Eastern European searching for Nirvana announces he would like to "die of beauty – smothered, intoxicated, asphyxiated by it. I would like to die loving some glorious woman or enchanting boy."[138] In "La Bonne Mine," the island is represented as an enchanting and disorienting maze of sensual delights and distractions: "That's how it was in Spiaggia. Something flashed and was gone. Hardly a memory—so uncertain and eventful was life in that little city of pleasure. They went, and forgot, and you stayed – and forgot, because something else always happened so quickly."[139] The collection as a whole, which includes stories of a spinster experiencing a sexual awakening on Spiaggia, of a thinly disguised Nadegin, of an Italian man in an open marriage with an American woman, expresses an earnest nostalgia for the site that so radically altered Faith's thinking and her marriage.

Faith most effectively and more obliquely repurposed her contact with the island's queer community, however, in a work that never mentions Capri. While Compton was composing *Extraordinary Women*, Faith began writing her own treatise on gender dissidence, *The Sibyl of the North*

(1931), a historical biography of Christina of Sweden (1626–89). Christina was rumored upon her birth to have been thought a boy, frequently cross-dressed, and was reputed to have had affairs with both men and women. Her representation of this androgynous ruler, who "came into the world masquerading as a male, and throughout her life ... continued to do so as often as possible," positioned Faith as a feminist writer and one with queer sympathies.[140] She dwells on the queen's desire to avoid marriage and "to evade the horror of providing with her own body an heir to the throne," and she details her admiration "almost beyond the bounds of what is compatible with admiration" for her maid of honor Ebba Sparre, reproducing their passionate letters to one another.[141] She describes Christina as possessing "by nature and inclination" the temperament of a "bachelor," and she relates anecdotes of her cross-dressing and attractiveness to women, revealing that a girl who encountered her in "male attire" on the road to Antwerp fell in love with her.[142] Christina is represented as stunning in her gender dissidence, with "the beauty of the flaming azure eyes and the general air of 'a pretty little boy' that she presented."[143] Her treatment of Christina served as the kernel for the film about Christina starring Greta Garbo that appeared two years later.[144] As Laura Horak argues, *Queen Christina* (1933) "marked a high point in lesbian visibility and the consolidation of female masculinity as a publicly recognizable code for lesbianism."[145] Faith's description of the queen informed one of the film's most well-known scenes in which Christina replies to concerns that she will "die an old maid," "I shall die a bachelor!" The film also made much of Christina's love for Ebba Sparre, depicting Christina kissing her maid of honor on the lips. Faith's biography played a crucial role in shaping one of the most significant and widely disseminated images of gender dissidence in the 1930s. She may have begun her writing career quite late in life, but she emerged immediately as a proponent of queer desires and identities. She dedicated *Sibyl of the North* to Axel Munthe, who collaborated in the remaking of her marriage, making it clear that the effects of Capri lingered within this work, that through Christina she looked back to her time on the island.

In the late 1920s, D. H. Lawrence published two short stories that, taken together, paint a dark picture of the Mackenzies following their departure from Capri. "The Man Who Loved Islands" (1927), which Viktor Link has argued should be understood as a satirical representation of Compton Mackenzie, depicts a man driven from island to island in search of greater isolation and "insulation," retreating from the love of a woman, irritated even by the meowing of his cat, deriving "his single satisfaction from being alone."[146] "Two Blue Birds" (1927), a story that, according to Faith, emerged from a wine-soaked conversation on Capri during which she "gave [Lawrence] some of the secrets of [her] heart," paints an even crueler picture of the post-Capri years.[147] It describes "a woman who loved her husband, but she could not live with him. The husband, on his side, was sincerely attached to his wife, yet he could not live with her."[148] The two are bound by the "most sincere regard for one another, and felt, in some odd way, eternally married to one another. They knew one another more intimately than they knew anybody else, they felt more known to one another than to any other person. Yet they could not live together."[149] The wife's trips to "the south" are represented as sad and unsatisfying, and she is represented as pathetically jealous of her husband's secretary:

> She, as she drank her cocktail on the terrace over the sea, and turned her grey, sardonic eyes on the heavy dark face of her admirer, whom she really liked quite a lot, she was actually preoccupied with the clear-cut features of her handsome young husband, thinking of how he would be asking his secretary to do something for him, asking in that good-natured, confident voice of a man who knows that his request will be only too gladly fulfilled.[150]

When visiting her husband, the wife restlessly stalks "wolf-like" around the property, spying upon him dictating to his secretary, wishing to make an "onslaught" but acknowledging she has little to offer in place of the younger woman's adoration: "Certainly not slavish devotion to him, nor to his flow of words! Certainly not!"[151]

The years on Herm and Jethou did have their difficulties, and Lawrence did capture to a certain degree the isolation and tension the couple experienced in the Channel Islands. According to Linklater, Faith came into conflict with the string of secretaries Compton brought to the islands, feeling "it was bad for [him] to be surrounded by adoring women who never questioned the quality of his work."[152] Chrissie Maude, with whom Compton had conducted an affair in the early days of their marriage, reappeared, and there was ongoing strife concerning his continuing desire for Ann Heiskell. Faith's diary entries from this period remark frequently on the dreariness of the weather, the fact that the storms will prevent the boats from sailing, leaving them isolated from the mainland, closed off and alone. Nevertheless, the Mackenzies' memoirs, along with Faith's diaries, indicate that Lawrence's treatment of the couple and their time on the

Channel Islands might have been excessively cynical. The marriage they had designed on Capri could accommodate much. It could accommodate the frequent presence of Nadegin in the Channel Islands and Faith's visits with Romaine Brooks and Mimi Franchetti in Paris. It could accommodate a strange interlude with Rebecca West, who, perhaps out of jealousy, reported to Morgan Heiskell about Ann and Compton's affair. (Faith intervened in order to protect Compton's reputation, writing him urgent letters that warned him not to bring Ann to the Channel Islands while Morgan's suspicions were aroused.)[153] If they had withdrawn from Capri to smaller islands and a more insulated existence, their history continued to draw visitors to them and into their open tie. And they remained throughout this period one another's confidantes and allies, allowing Axel Munthe's advice to operate for decades as the foundation of an innovative marriage. In 1956, Compton was the subject of *This Is Your Life*, and Faith appeared on the program. When asked about their relationship, she read the following lines from Kahlil Gibran's *The Prophet*: "Give your hearts but not into each other's keeping, / And stand together, yet not too close together, / For all pillars of the temple stand apart / And the oak and the cypress do not grow in each other's shade."[154] This standing together, but not too close together, developing outside of one another's shade, served as an effective strategy for the Mackenzies. It allowed them to practice marriage in radical terms while at the same time engaging actively and openly with individuals outside of their union. This experience in turn enabled them to contribute in significant (though highly disparate) ways to the ongoing conversation about sexual and gender identity in the early twentieth century.

Capri lay at the heart of this. The Mackenzies' time on the island, their cosmopolitanism and their contact with the queer cosmopolitan community on Capri, inflected their approach to affiliation and their representation of gender and desire. Capri's islandness, at once insulated and internationally integrated, allowed it to operate as a queer Geneva in the 1910s and 1920s. It provided a site for sexual exiles to think outside of mainland discourse about the "future internationalism of homosexuality," and the Mackenzies' contact with the radical thinking and practice occurring at this site rendered their marriage more porous, more "elastic." What I have tried to stress here, however, is that the Mackenzies' affiliative experiments and the circle that informed those experiments must be understood as emerging from a relationship to Capri that structurally resembles Orientalism. The Mackenzies mined Capri for the resources with which to remake their marriage. Italian men and women served as set pieces in the dramatic transformation of their tie. They extracted from the island the materials necessary to engage in a radical practice. They are not exceptional in this. The Decadent tradition of radical and liberatory kinship theory and practice was bound up with systems of exploitation. Decadent Mediterraneanism had been modeled to them by Norman Douglas, by Fersen, by the Wolcott-Perrys, and their models had in turn learned from their fin-de-siècle precursors to base their emancipatory project in an exoticized vision of other places and people. Reading the Mackenzies' writing and their marriage alongside one another brings to light the practical effects of the Decadent tradition, the manner in which it simultaneously engendered troubling fantasies about difference and emancipatory personal practices.

CHAPTER 4

Decadent Bachelordom and Transnational Adoption
Harold Acton in China

When the Anglo-Italian dandy Harold Acton published a volume of life writing in 1948, he chose to title the work *Memoirs of an Aesthete*. Half of his friends, he notes in the book's opening paragraph, disapproved the title: "'What! An aesthete? One of those scruffy, long-haired fellows in peculiar garb, lisping about art for art's sake? No, no. You'll prejudice all your readers in advance. Old Oscar screwed the last nail in the aesthete's coffin."[1] Acton immediately indicates that he is well aware that in titling the text in this manner, he links himself to Oscar Wilde's trials for acts of "gross indecency," to lisping fellows in peculiar garb, and to the Decadent aestheticism of the 1890s. This would have been a long-standing association in the public imagination. He was referred to as the "Beardsley of modern English prose," and Peter Quennell recalls Acton at Oxford in the 1920s as "the leader and favourite figure-head of the contemporary Aesthetic Movement."[2] Though he and his fellow Bright Young Person Brian Howard were called a "pair of Oscar Wildes," Acton worked while at Oxford to distinguish himself from those "pressed fern[s] from the pages of the Yellow Book" he perceived as reenacting a stale caricature of Decadence.[3] He clarifies on the following page of his memoirs that he is the member of "no special movement" and expresses a sense of separation from "the late-Victorian movement which parodied and falsified" the meaning of the term "aesthete."[4] Nevertheless, he moves from this clarification straightaway into a delineation of his own mode of aestheticism that is undeniably Paterian in tone, reflecting on art's capacity to expand the intervals of existence, to endow each moment with the highest quality as it passes, and beauty's ability to set the spirit free for a moment: "For me beauty is the vital principle pervading the universe. . . . By contemplating the myriad manifestations of this vital principle we expand into something greater than we were born. Art is the mirror that reflects these expansions, sometimes for a moment, sometimes for perpetuity."[5] He is, he concludes, an aesthete "in the proper sense of that word."[6] This is the approach Acton tends to take when describing his relationship to his Decadent predecessors. While others might faddishly and superficially align themselves with Wilde and the 1890s, Acton insists from his early days at Oxford that he operates with an intimate and authentic understanding of aestheticist principles and should be understood as uniquely positioned to enact those principles in his approach to living.

Acton opens his memoirs by highlighting his aestheticism, and he concludes by stressing his cosmopolitanism. He points the reader to a "remarkable portrait" that he has chosen to include in the illustrations to the text, a painting by the feminist reformer K'ang T'ung-pi (or Kang Tongbi) of Acton "as a candidate for Buddhist Sainthood," completed during the final years of his stay in Beijing from 1932 to 1939 (Figure 4.1).[7] This brush and ink painting, Acton states in the final paragraph of the memoirs, is "the only portrait in which I could contemplate myself with a glimmer of recognition."[8] Other portraits of Acton by John Banting, Thomas Handforth, Cecil Beaton, and Carl Van Vechten, Acton implies, do not effectively capture his essence, the person he wishes and understands himself to be. It is characteristic of Acton, as I hope to demonstrate in the chapter, to posit the thinking of a feminist intellectual as particularly sharp, clear, and generative for him as he endeavors to conceptualize his own approach to cross-cultural encounter. In this painting, this work by a woman artist in which he most clearly recognizes himself, Acton sits upon a hillside smiling into the middle distance while wearing a Chinese robe. He has titled the work in his list of illustrations "Portrait of the author as a Lohan," as one who has achieved nirvana. According to Acton's translation, Kang Tongbi's calligraphic inscription states, "a believer both in Christ and Buddha, you harmonize in yourself their various teachings."[9] Her "intuition" has, in this statement, Acton insists, "penetrated one of [his] cherished ideals." "Towards that harmony," he proclaims in the final line of the memoirs, "I shall continue to strive."[10] Kang Tongbi's painting is given pride of place at the conclusion of his memoirs because it has "penetrated" his particular understanding of true nirvana, the achievement of true cultural hybridity, the incorporation and balancing of disparate national identities within the self. This painting seems to have operated for him as a type of touchstone, gesturing toward the peace, balance, and cultural integration to which he always hoped to arrive.

I am interested in where Acton begins and ends the story of himself. The first and final paragraphs of *Memoirs of an Aesthete* foreground what he perceived to be the most significant elements of his identity, his

Figure 4.1   Kang Tongbi, portrait of Harold Acton, n.d. New York University, The Acton
Photograph Archive, Villa La Pietra, Florence.
© Estate of Kang Tongbi. Reproduced courtesy of New York University.

aestheticism and his cosmopolitanism, two components of his sensibility that are for him intertwined and interdependent. His sensitivity to and acute perception of beauty, he argues in the chapters bookended by these paragraphs, render him more alive to the textures of other places and cultures. His aestheticism, he insists, *makes him* cosmopolitan. At the same time, he remains anxious that it does not. In the novel that emerged from his time in Beijing, *Peonies and Ponies* (1941), Acton produces a satirical representation of aestheticism's cosmopolitan aspirations, which reveals his gnawing concern that his mode of aestheticizing China might in fact amount to fetishism and appropriation. His aestheticism might in fact *make him* Orientalist.[11]

As he theorizes the constellation of aims and anxieties related to his Decadent transnationalism, Acton centers the concept of kinship. When operating in the mode of cosmopolitan optimism, he argues that his linked aesthetic sensitivity and cultural curiosity necessitate his extrication from conventional familial structures. He must be mobile and detached, a rootless bachelor, if he is to enter freely and fully into communion with other places and traditions. When beleaguered by fears about his own potential Orientalism, however, he relies on kinship metaphors, on the figure of unsuccessful and exploitative transnational adoption, to think through what might make true hybridity, that harmony toward which he strives, difficult.[12] In *Peonies and Ponies*, he literalizes his own desire to adopt another culture in his representation of the protagonist's adoption of a Chinese boy actor, an act that is represented as motivated by erotic desire and ineffective in terms of producing transnational understanding. In both his fiction and his life writing, Acton repeatedly contemplates transnational contact through a familial lens. The desire for global connectivity either requires the eschewal of traditional kinship or inspires queer kinship arrangements. What haunts all of these imaginings, however, is the possibility that real connection might not ever happen. Acton seems to believe that true intimacy with another nation necessitates detachment from modes of heteronormative domesticity that delimit mobility or openness to foreign experience. He nevertheless struggles with the possibility that such intimacy might be impossible, representing transnational adoption in *Peonies and Ponies* as a deluded and sinister attempt to build a new kind of international family that only enables the colonization and appropriation of another culture. Over and over, Acton thinks through and against the concept of kinship while considering the possibility of cosmopolitan communion.

It is also noteworthy that Acton begins his memoirs with a nod to a masculine Decadent tradition, to Wilde and Pater, but concludes by asserting that he was most clearly seen and understood by a feminist painter. Acton is somewhat peculiar among Decadent men in his deep and sustained engagement with women writers and artists, and, as I will argue here, this engagement was crucial to the development of his own thinking about cultural hybridity, kinship, and homelessness. Because of the pressures exerted on him by his father to carry forward a familial legacy tied to the art collection he had assembled at their home, Villa La Pietra, Acton found it particularly arduous to extricate himself from heteronormative narratives of marriage and reproduction. He seems to have been drawn to women who critiqued or successfully defied conventional gender ideologies and to women who, like himself, married their pursuit of transcultural understanding to the eschewal of conventional kinship ties. Their evasions of gendered expectations to marry, to reproduce, to settle operated as heroic models to Acton as he endeavored to carve for himself a similarly dissident and culturally mobile path. At the same time, sustained consideration of their lives and work alerted him to the potential hazards along, difficulties of, and threats to such a path. The queer aesthete Vernon Lee was one of the most significant influences on his manner of conceptualizing transnational aestheticism as well as the dangers conventional modes of affiliation might pose to the freedom of the Decadent cosmopolite, and I focus here on two points, early and late, in his career in which he articulates his indebtedness to her thinking. Acton's close friend Nancy Cunard, who publicly vilified her racist mother and devoted her life to antiracist and anti-colonial activism, similarly served as a point of inspiration as he thought through what it might mean to sever oneself from biological family in order to extend the self more fully across national and racial boundaries. Cunard's romanticized exoticization of and identification with the Black subjects for whom she advocated, however, offered Acton a constant reminder of the potential political pitfalls in their linked projects. The Chinese-American actress Anna May Wong, with whom Acton spent time during her visit to Beijing, shared with Acton the experiences of rootlessness and perpetual exile, concomitant symptoms of the pursuit of transnational affiliation. Like Acton, she abstained from conventional modes of affiliation as she lived across national boundaries, insisting she was "wedded to [her] art," and I conclude the chapter by considering resonances between the experiences of these two deeply hybrid and peripatetic subjects who found themselves without a true home, perpetually disconnected as a result of their pursuit of expansive connection.[13] These women structured and informed Acton's thinking on cosmopolitanism and kinship, and I have therefore structured this chapter around them.

Reinventing Oxford Aestheticism

The early chapters of *Memoirs of an Aesthete* narrate a childhood saturated in aestheticism and Decadence. Acton's taste for beauty was developed and fine-tuned within the walls of Villa La Pietra, the Renaissance villa in which he grew up in the hills north of Florence. His Anglo-Italian father, Arthur Acton, an art connoisseur and dealer, drawing upon the wealth of his wife, the Chicago heiress Hortense Mitchell, filled the home with antique furniture, tapestries, and paintings and peppered the restored Tuscan garden with over a hundred statues. In this atmosphere, supplemented by visits to the Florentine galleries, Harold "did not have to look far to discover beauty."[14] This was a queer milieu (Acton notes that "one was continually hearing that certain men in Florence were queer, not that it made much difference to their popularity: on the contrary! the queerer the dearer"), and a milieu in which artworks and personalities of the 1890s remained very much present.[15] Poring over the magazines in his father's studio, he was drawn to Aubrey Beardsley's "cadaverous tall torches of women, dying upright in pools of their own wax, … dry lips parted hungrily to plunge into some forbidden fruit," images "sombre and mysterious" that brought him into an awareness of "perverse beauty."[16] Wilde's close friend Reggie Turner was a frequent visitor to Villa La Pietra, operating as a Wildean medium as "his voice descended to the depths of an imaginary corpulence, his gestures became sculptured and hieratic and his fingers sprouted scarab rings when he repeated Oscar's sayings."[17] At school in England, he continued his Decadent initiation, "devour[ing]" *The Picture of Dorian Gray* "like strawberries" at the age of twelve, branded a "moral leper" by a tutor who confiscated his copy of Wilde's *House of Pomegranates* (1891).[18] The memoirs reveal him moving toward the moral leprosy of Decadence from his very first steps, as does his book collection at Villa La Pietra, which includes a copy of Wilde's *Ballad of Reading Gaol* (1898) marked by the bookplate he used as a child and a copy of Wilde's *Intentions* (1891) presented to him by his fellow aesthete Brian Howard as they left Eton together for Oxford.

At Eton and then at Oxford, the two friends and rivals Harold Acton and Brian Howard developed their Decadent modernist aesthetic and their dandyish personae in conversation with one another. (Evelyn Waugh, who came to know the pair at Oxford, collapsed the two figures into one in *Brideshead Revisited*'s queer aesthete Anthony Blanche.[19]) They collaborated in producing the *Eton Candle* (1922), a precocious periodical "dedicated to the illustrious memory of Algernon Charles Swinburne."[20] With its loud pink cover and its bright yellow endpapers, the *Eton Candle* visually enacts Acton and Howard's desire to integrate the Decadent aesthetic of the *Yellow Book* with the bombadiering modernism of Wyndham Lewis's *BLAST*, and, as Acton notes in his memoirs, "the print was to emulate that of Max Beerbohm's early works," nodding reverentially to the Beardsley period productions of Decadence's foremost surviving dandy.[21] The contents, too, register their Decadent inclinations, including Acton's short story "Hansom Cab No. 213 bis," intended as the first chapter of a planned novel about a wealthy aesthete whose whole life was a "meticulous study of harmonies," described by Shane Leslie as "Beardsley-ish" and by Humphrey Carpenter as a "heavy piece of Nineties pastiche."[22] In addition, the two young men managed to solicit an unpublished poem by Swinburne as well as a set of contributions from the most outspoken camp modernists of the period, the Sitwells. With this single issue, Acton and Howard announced their presence on the contemporary scene as a "pair of Oscar Wildes" with modernist credentials, a performance they would amplify at Oxford.

Upon his arrival at Oxford in 1923, Acton, in conversation with Howard, further developed his energetic and bombastic Decadent modernist persona. Acton read passages from *The Waste Land* through a megaphone on his balcony. Howard placed a poem in Edith Sitwell's final *Wheels* anthology (1921), and Acton published his first collection of poetry, *Aquarium* (1923), which, as Martin Green notes, integrates the influences of T. S. Eliot and Edith Sitwell.[23] A. L. Rowse, who was a student with Acton at Christ Church, recalls Acton as "the most conspicuous and challenging specimen" of the "Aesthetes," a circle involved at the time in an ongoing dispute with the "Hearties." Rowse recollects a confrontation between the two groups in which "a team of rugger-men awaited a bevy of Aesthetes, led in by Harold, smiling and saying, in his inimitable Italian accent: '*They* are so in-no-cent, and we are *so* de-ca-dent.'"[24] Acton's boisterous aestheticism was meant to rival the defanged Decadence currently on display at the university, which read to Acton as inauthentic and exhausted. He writes in the memoirs that he was introduced soon after his arrival to a "sickly" "pressed fern from the pages of the Yellow Book," whose "long hair and ... ebony cane only stressed his lack of personality." He made up his mind that "if that eunuch represented

Oxford aestheticism something would have to be done about it soon. Now that the war was over, those who loved beauty had a mission .... We should combat ugliness; we should create clarity where there was confusion; we should overcome mass indifference; and we should exterminate false prophets."[25] To outdo and displace the Decadent pretenders, he began fetishizing "the Early Victorian Era," advertising himself as drawn to "Dawns, not Twilights."[26] While he performed at this moment a break with the fin de siècle, his memoirs, his fiction, and the material evidence in his home (including a study and library littered with the works of Beerbohm, Wilde, and Vernon Lee), delineate a Decadent genealogy for the larger-than-life dandyish persona he enacted at Oxford and into his years in China, indicating that late-Victorian aestheticism remained a guiding force for Acton throughout his career. Rather than abandoning aestheticism, he remade it so it might continue to operate as a viable aesthetic during the modernist moment.

In remaking and revising aestheticism, Acton was working to generate an alternative to what he referred to as the "vaunted virility" of the more masculinist modernisms prevalent during the period.[27] If the sickly, impotent Decadence Acton encountered at Oxford threatened to render aestheticism outmoded and unable to engage in true combat with ugliness, the machismo and brutish Englishness and Americanness of the high modernists engendered an aesthetic mode unable to engage with difference. Speaking disparagingly of the Anglo-American "Broncho Bill" modernists he encountered in Paris, Acton notes "how little they assimilated from their sojourn in France! They seldom penetrated French life beyond the apéritif stage." According to Acton, Ernest Hemingway, Ezra Pound, and Ford Madox Ford in their "tweeds and stetsons, ... pugilistic sweaters and ponderous pipes," "simulate[d] the cowboy" and made "a cult of the hair upon [their] chests" in order to "camouflage their timorous souls."[28] In contrast to these timorous Broncho Bills whose bravado masked their inability to penetrate (or be penetrated by) other cultures, Acton's new aestheticism would facilitate vulnerability to and engagement with the wider world.

In the pages of the *Cherwell*, an Oxford undergraduate periodical, Acton clarified his relationship to aestheticism, distinguishing himself from his peers faddishly reenacting a defunct version of the late-Victorian past while at the same time positioning himself as an authority on the Decadent tradition. He wrote frequent book reviews, demonstrating his knowledge of emergent writers (Alduous Huxley, Osbert Sitwell, Ronald Firbank, Norman Douglas) as well as of the fin de siècle, reviewing new editions of

The Picture of Dorian Gray and Osbert Burdett's *The Beardsley Period* (1925). In reviewing *The Beardsley Period*, he exhibits his typical attitude toward the fetishizing of Decadence so prevalent at the time. While "the nineties have never come to a definite end," particularly at Oxford, the "wisest of us realize ... we need not crawl into the Beardsley Period ... for consolation and escape. We remember Miss Gertrude Stein."[29] He advertises his position as a true modern, conversant in the most experimental forms of avant-gardism, including the works of Stein, whom he invited to deliver the lecture "Composition as Explanation" at Oxford in 1926. His response to Burdett's treatment of the 1890s nevertheless insists upon his own status as a *true* expert on the period. He finds the volume superior to other recent texts on the fin de siècle by Bernard Muddiman and Holbrook Jackson, but he bemoans tremendous gaps in Burdett's coverage. Where, he asks, is Arthur Machen? Baron Corvo? *The Hobby Horse*? *The Green Carnation*? This is typical Acton at this stage in his career – at once over Decadence and insistent upon his own superior Decadent expertise.

Aesthetes Above All: Acton, Vernon Lee, and Decadent Cosmopolitanism

It is in Acton's *Cherwell* review of Vernon Lee's *The Golden Keys* (1925), however, that the utility of late-Victorian aestheticism to Acton's larger project becomes most clear. As he generates a Decadent alternative to the "vaunted virility" of hypermasculine modernism, an aesthetic less timorous and more open to penetration by other cultures, the queer and cosmopolitan Lee serves as a crucial model. Reading this early review alongside Acton's later writing about Lee indicates that she, more so than any other Decadent precursor, provided an example in both her travel writing and her lived existence as to how to detach oneself from delimiting nationalist and heteronormative perspectives. Acton's *Cherwell* review emphasizes the complexity of Lee's gender identity as enacted both in her writing and through her public persona. The review opens with a quotation from another sexually dissident woman for whom Acton felt deep admiration, Edith Sitwell: "This world is sick, but men make the better doctors; women should lull the sick world with music like a summer-wind, honeyed as the bee-winged warm lights of afternoon."[30] As he interweaves Sitwell's aphorism with his sense of Lee's significance, he reinscribes and then undoes the gender essentialism of Sitwell's notion of dichotomized duties, pointing to the possibility that the lulling of the sick world with music like a summer wind might be a weightier vocation than medicine. Lee's prose, he notes, is "delicate, facile, picturesque, suggestive, exquisite, serene, and above all, charming," an insight he immediately follows with the statement that she is a "master, we cannot say 'mistress,' of the lighter forms of literature," subtly signaling Lee's female masculinity.[31] When Lee writes in these slight forms, "the essay, the dialogue, the polite story," they "achieve an importance comparable, let us say, to Brabazon's as a painter, or Callot's as a draughtsman."[32] "Her mind," he insists, "is distinguished," and in the final lines of the review, he highlights his belief that she exceeds traditional notions of feminine duty or identity by thanking "that admirable lady who signs herself 'Vernon Lee'" whose writing "shake[s]" its readers, reminding audiences of her adoption of a masculine pseudonym and the strong corporeal effects of her distinguished, important, and masterful prose.[33] What he finds so pleasing and so challenging in her work has much to do with her evocation of the *genius loci*, which, he notes, quoting Lee, constitutes "that portion of nations and civilizations which, while it speaks aloud in their philosophy and poetry and music, and is written clearly in the shapes of their buildings, addresses itself to the initiate mind in their humbler habits, kindly and gracious, sometimes childish and funny."[34] Signaling that he himself is one of those initiate minds to whom the spirit of place addresses itself, Lee's twin in sensitivity to sensuous detail, he celebrates the tremendous effect her writing on place has on its readers, a "tremor irreducible to language, intensely felt by the artist."[35] And he foregrounds that this sensitivity has an ethical valence, citing the notes of despair and dejection interwoven within her charming descriptions of landscapes and cities, as exemplified in her sketch of "a melancholy caravan of Dalmatian tramps," "tattered, fever-stricken, wearily footsore," that she encountered on the Old Bologna road and the "poignant emotion" and "stab of . . . misery" their plight evoked in her.[36] While Anatole France insisted that we are perpetually locked within the prison of the self, Vernon Lee, Acton asserts "has escaped."[37] She moves, through her sensitivity to place, outside the confines of her subjectivity and in turn moves her readers, shakes them, into contact with the world and with alterity.

Acton mourns in this review that "since the war the *Genius Loci* [has] almost disappeared," indicating that Lee's mode of ethical and sensitive cosmopolitanism has been threatened by twentieth-century jingoism and nationalism, which blunt the capacity for openness to alterity that underwrites her mode of perception.[38] Lee's aestheticism, her acute sensitivity to the beauty of all places, is in Acton's eyes intimately bound up with her cosmopolitanism, much as he, twenty years later, linked his own cosmopolitanism to his aestheticism in the opening pages of his memoirs, in which he describes himself as a "[citizen] of the world," the guardian of a "culture which war has interrupted."[39] "Peace on earth and goodwill toward men will only be brought about by individuals like myself," he argues, individuals who, with their focus on beauty and "ideas without national boundaries" might expand beyond their nations to foster contact, exchange, and communication.[40] When he spoke on Lee another three decades later at the *Inghilterra e Italia nel '900 Bagni de Lucca* conference (1972), convened by the British Institute of Florence, he returned to these two key elements of her identity and her appeal, noting that she belonged "to the old guard of cosmopolitan intellectualism" and that she was "above all an aesthete."[41] With this, he makes clear that he and Lee are fundamentally akin to one another, positing her first and foremost as a member of the same tribe to which he assigned himself in titling both his first and second volumes of life writing "memoirs of an aesthete." She is, he insists, like him, a citizen of the world who saw beauty beyond national boundaries and refused the perpetual prison of the national self.

If he binds himself to her in this lecture through their shared cosmopolitanism and aestheticism, he also makes much clearer in this later work the affinity he felt for her as a fellow sexual dissident, as an outsider to conventional forms of kinship and traditional narratives of maturation. He begins his 1972 lecture by reprimanding the conference participants, noting that he is the only presenter to "speak of a woman," suggesting that his speech is meant as a feminist intervention within a primarily masculinist conversation about Italy's history.[42] Lee was, he states, during his youth "the most eminent" of the "English spinsters of intellectual cast" with which the city was teeming, women whose "dress and gestures were not notably feminine," who were "pioneers in the women's movement" and "held the male sex in disdain," acknowledging Florence's queer and feminist history, the manner in which it fostered sexually dissident expatriate communities at the turn of the century.[43] He delineates what made her life unique and, for him, a model. Like Acton, who had a troubled relationship with his father, Lee struggled within a family life that threatened to restrict and confine. Her mother, he states, "was as despotic as she was affectionate."[44] Her brother was "an invalid for 20 years," and both Lee and her mother were forced into the position of nurse. However, Acton notes approvingly, Lee "took refuge in an intellectual life that was filled with feminine friendships on a high platonic level."[45] Queer community and homosocial friendship operated as retreats from the troubles of biological kin. Like Acton, she never married, and he quotes her withering assessment of that highly conventional institution: "I avert my eyes from the matrimonial adventures of my women friends. ... There's something primitive in it!"[46] She might have easily, he notes, "been drained by the vampire of family obligations" like "so many other Victorian women," but she resisted these pressures and maintained a different kind of life at her home, Il Palmerino, near Maiano, two miles from Villa La Pietra.[47] He concludes the lecture by meditating on her eschewal of conventional ties: "Her villa at Maiano could be called a refuge – from unbridled materialism, from sex, and from the passions of this world. ... Today her life seems sad to us because its adventures were intellectual ones, and because the realities of the past were far more important to her than those of the present."[48] Thinking, and more specifically historical and aesthetic thinking, allowed her to evade familial burdens. He acknowledges the solitariness and withdrawal necessitated by this particular kind of freedom: "She described herself as hard and cold: 'I cannot love at the price of being flayed,' she said. 'People do not matter to me. I prefer to do without them.'"[49] He ends by wondering, "would marriage possibly have changed her?" and decides, "It is very doubtful. The wretched experience of the 20 years passed at the side of a brother so difficult and demanding had given her a very poor opinion of men."[50] The demands of Eugene, in Acton's eyes, awakened her to the threat posed by the "vampire of family obligations."[51]

Acton was tremendously indebted to the Decadent tradition, to Pater, to Wilde, to Beerbohm, but, as these two responses to Lee from early and late in his career indicate, her work and her life operated as significant influences on his detached and mobile mode of cosmopolitan bachelordom.[52] In an interview with Naim Attallah in 1990, Acton stated that his father would have "preferred me to marry and have children, but I never had that desire. I never had a feeling for children and family."[53] Acton repeatedly notes in his correspondence that he was a disappointment to his father, and much of that disappointment seems to have arisen from his refusal to reproduce. His father hoped, it seems, for his son to carry forward the legacy he had established at Villa La Pietra, which he is purported to have conceptualized as "a lasting bastion of classic Florentine vision and grace."[54] As Martin Green recounts in his discussion of the dandy-aesthetes of the early twentieth century, "Harold Acton had been oppressed by his father, ... just as Brian Howard had been oppressed by his father – in both cases *because* the sons were dandies."[55] Green stresses that Howard and Acton's mode of dandyism relied upon resistance to conventional narratives of maturation and the eschewal of traditional domesticity and family life. According to Green's account of the new dandies of the 1920s, the dandy "rebels against both the fathers and the mothers of his culture," and "marriage and the home are values as dubious to [the dandy] as are responsibility and business success."[56] In reading Acton's memoirs, one gets the feeling that the pressure from his father to settle and succeed had become particularly acute following his departure from Oxford. He was given, he notes, three years to "make good."[57] His Decadent novel *Humdrum* (1928), written during this period, which treats heteronormativity and natalism as parochial and vulgar, indicates his escalating exasperation with the expectations being placed upon him as well as his equation of family life with provincialism and small-mindedness.[58] To stay in Europe, to give way to reproductive futurism, would be to remain delimited, to never escape. His queer mentors, such as his uncle Guy Mitchell and Norman Douglas, advised him to evade this heteronormative narrative. Douglas encouraged him to "get out of Europe and go to the Far East."[59] Mitchell, who, in Acton's words, "sympathized with [his] wanderlust," offered the necessary financial assistance, and, in 1932, he departed Europe, not to return until 1939, save for one brief interval.[60]

Detached Bachelordom and Transnational Collaboration: Acton in China

When Acton arrived in China, "an immense calm descended on [him]. . . . [He] felt strangely at home."[61] This sense of calm in and connectedness with China depended upon his extrication from home, from family, from all conventional modes of affiliation. In his memoirs, he indicates that he came increasingly to believe that his capacity to truly see and experience China, to encounter the space and the culture in aestheticist terms and perceive his surroundings with "the finest senses," depended upon his eschewal of companionship. He notes that he began to heed to advice of the Buddhist sutra: "Let one who would obtain freedom from desire and follow his own will, wander alone like a rhinoceros."[62] He had, he asserts, "entered upon the way to perfection. The pleasures of companionship diminish our powers of observing and delighting in what we see."[63] To enter into true aesthetic communion with China, to, as Pater put it, "pass most swiftly from point to point, and be present always at the focus where the greatest number of vital forces unite in their purest energy," one must wander alone.[64] Aestheticist integration with China demanded solitude.

He "resolved to keep aloof from Europeans who did not share my enthusiasm for China, which at that time meant the majority."[65] As his integration with his surroundings proceeded, he came to be viewed by his fellow Europeans as "another regrettable case of a 'chap going native,'" which further reinforced the boundary between himself and the expatriate community in Beijing.[66] And, as he turned his Decadent eyes upon China, China in turn transformed him. He grew increasingly keen and lucid in his perception.[67] As he "savour[ed] the symmetrical calm of [his] courtyard" where "everything was perfectly proportioned," his European past came to appear "thinly frivolous":

> At last I had ceased reaching outwards, ever outwards, in an effort to express myself. My real adventures flowed inwards, smooth and fecundating. . . . Veil after veil which had blurred the light was withdrawn. . . . I had never been so powerfully lucid. All deceptive mirages melted before my visionary eyes. Not that I saw things merely as they were. . . . I saw them as they had been and as they were becoming.[68]

This is the Paterian climax of the memoirs, Acton alone in his courtyard in Beijing, achieving an apex of aestheticist perception, withdrawing entirely into himself and thereby seeing with the greatest acuity the Heraclitean flux that surrounds him.

There is, however, more to this story. Acton stresses that he withdrew from the expatriate community, but he developed real intimacies with the students he encountered while serving as a lecturer on English literature at Peking National University. Acton thrilled at the emergent Chinese modernism percolating at the university and within Beijing during this period. As Patricia Ondek Laurence discusses in *Lily Briscoe's Chinese Eyes*, the late 1920s and early 1930s were a high point of cross-cultural modernism in China, as evidenced in the transnational contact between cosmopolitan Chinese literary societies, such as the Crescent Moon Group, and visiting Britons with ties to the Bloomsbury Group, such as Julian Bell.[69] Acton seems to have been electrified by the sense of aesthetic innovation prevalent in Beijing. "China's new generation was," he states, "in revolt against deadening rhetoric, irrelevant descriptions of nature, and ossified poetical diction."[70] He was brought into immediate contact with this new generation's aesthetic revolt at Peking National University, which had, in the late 1910s and 1920s under the leadership of Chancellor Cai Yuanpei, "become the cradle of the Pai Hua movement to promote a new literature in the spoken language, by virtue of which it had gained a position of leadership in the eyes of Chinese youth."[71] Acton's students were stimulated by the possibility of cross-pollination between their efforts and the

Figure 4.2   Harold Acton in Beijing, 1933. New York University, The Acton Photograph
Archive, Villa La Pietra, Florence.
Reproduced courtesy of New York University.

poetry of T. S. Eliot. In a letter to Roy Harrod, he writes that the students "crowded my lectures on Modern English Poetry, and their own compositions in English are so exquisite and amusing that I am trying to publish them."[72] He positioned himself as a conduit and contact point, funneling contemporary English literature to his Chinese students while endeavoring to bring modern Chinese literature to Anglophone readers. He succeeded, for example, in placing translations of modern Chinese vernacular poetry, accompanied by an essay on "Contemporary Chinese Poetry," in a special "Chinese Number" (1935) of the Chicago modernist periodical *Poetry*. Acton exhibited during this period a true commitment to disseminating Chinese modernism to Anglo-American audiences and to developing sustained mentorship relationships with his students. As much as he worked to isolate himself from Beijing's expatriate networks, he plunged himself into the circulation of new aesthetic ideals within and from Beijing. He includes in his memoirs a photograph of a group of students who attended his birthday party ca. 1933 (Figure 4.3), and he notes that this night in particular, when his students presented him with an engraved shield and one student with whom he developed a particularly close relationship, Ch'ên Shih-Hsiang (or Chen Shixiang), played the flute in the garden, was the moment when he "realized in every fibre of [his] being that [he] was in the China of all [his] reveries, as a passionate Hellenist might realize he was in Greece. It was one of the enchanted moments of my existence."[73] This climax, arising from transnational contact and comradeship, operates as a highly social counterpoint to Acton's epiphanic moment alone in his courtyard. However, these two peaks of cosmopolitan pleasure are not opposed or entirely disconnected from one another. This "enchanted moment" of reverie was, in his eyes, enabled by his withdrawal from the expatriate community and conventional domesticity, his turn to his students and to the modern literature of China.

While Chen Shixiang was a junior at the university, he and Acton collaborated in the production of *Modern Chinese Poetry* (1936), which, according to Dominic Cheung, "remains the most representative early anthology of modern Chinese poems in the 1930s."[74] Acton was at the time receiving instruction in Mandarin, but he could not read Chinese. Cheung speculates that Chen "did the initial selection and prepared the first draft of necessary literal translations before handing them over to Acton for reworking and polishing."[75] The collection places contemporary Chinese poetry within a modernist framework, arguing in a fascinating introduction that, while "Chinese poetry had long been wilting in a rococo cage," the modern poets of China wish to "emancipate themselves from

Figure 4.3   Harold Acton in Beijing in a group of Chinese and European poets in his house at Pei Ho Yen, annotated on the verso by Acton: "Birthday group at Pei Yo Hen. Desmond Parsons left, Laurence Sickman right. In the foreground Lee Yi-hsieh, Ch'en Shih-hsiang, Pien Chih-lin, Alan Priest, Lin King, Li Kuang-t'ien and other Pei Ta (or Bei Da) students," ca. 1933. New York University, The Acton Photograph Archive, Villa La Pietra, Florence.
Reproduced courtesy of New York University.

tradition."[76] This is an anthology that highlights the avant-gardism of modern Chinese poetry, describing the poetry of Kuo Mo-jo (or Guo Moruo) as the expression of "force, agitation, speed, the twentieth century, and Cubism," celebrating the concentration of Chinese work that produces a "total effect ... to which only a few of our imagists have approximated in English."[77] And it also foregrounds the extent to which the successes of these poets emerge from transnational forms of cross-pollination. In their introduction and their short biographies of the poets, Chen and Acton center the influence of Symbolism and Decadence on modern Chinese poetry, the fruitfulness of these poets' contact with Baudelaire, Mallarmé, and Arthur Symons. *Modern Chinese Poetry*, an anthology emerging from cosmopolitan intimacy, highlights the value of cultural contact across national boundaries.

The collaboration between Acton and Chen Shixiang seems to have been the product of a friendship marked by deep mutual admiration and affection. According to Cyril Birch, "among all the vital young men before whom [Acton] lectured in Peking, Chen was the closest friend. And indeed there can have been few men with such a genius for initiating others, even foreigners, into that companionship of the mind which the classical Chinese poets delighted to celebrate."[78] Acton notes in his memoirs that he was "sustained" as a teacher by the "silent sympathy" Chen expressed in the classroom, and he devotes great attention to Chen's attractive physical appearance, "his full lips, friendly brown eyes under strongly marked eyebrows curved upward," his expression "full of candour and mobility."[79] When he discovered Chen was "financially embarrassed," he invited him to stay with him, an invitation Acton notes was "courageously accepted."[80] The correspondence between Chen and Acton at the Beinecke Library bears similar markers of intimacy and indicates that their affection for one another continued after Acton's return from Beijing. In a February 1940 letter, for example, Chen narrates his deep longing for contact with his absent teacher:

> I have been desperate to know your whereabouts. Yes, *desperate* is the word. Five letters I wrote to Peiping, Kung-Hsien-Hu-Túng, all missed. Two years thus elapsed while I was disappointed, wondering, despairing. Last summer I saw Mr. Wen Youan Ning in Hong Kong and was told that you were still in Peiping. I confessed a pleasant surprise, but did not write at once, thinking what with the Japanese censors, what with other inconveniences, there might be difficulties for my letter to reach you. Three years absence, a dreadful long time! During this I have been teaching in this nomadic university, and have learnt nothing but to suffer. Now when I write feeling somehow sure that you may receive the letter, I don't know how to begin and how to end it. All thoughts have been so long dammed up and words fail. How I long to see you now, on this fine Feb. morning to let this heavy lump leap out of my throat![81]

The two did eventually find their way back to one another after Chen took up a post as a professor at the University of California, Berkeley. In his correspondence with the connoisseur Bernard Berenson, who lived near Villa La Petra at Villa I Tatti, Acton notes that following his return from China he felt "completely uprooted."[82] In 1948, he writes to say that he is "en route for California, where I shall stay with my former pupil Ch'ên Shi-hsiang, now teaching at Berkeley. His wife has gone mad, so I hope to console him as best I may and inspire him to produce a new work on the Chinese poets."[83] Following his arrival, he informs Berenson, "My host keeps me busy: we are translating *T'ao Hua Shan* or 'The Peach-Blossom Fan,' one of the finest Chinese classical dramas dealing with the collapse of the Ming dynasty."[84] In his preface to the work, Acton notes that the collaboration allowed him "a spiritual return to China when I had no chance of returning there in the flesh," and the translation was a task to which the pair "devoted delightful hours."[85] The manuscript, however, was not finished when Chen died of a heart attack in 1971. It was finally completed by Chen's colleague Cyril Birch. This edition, which was published by University of California Press in 1976 and remains in print with New York Review Books, should be understood, according to D. E. Mungello, as "Acton's most lasting contribution to Chinese studies."[86]

Though Acton appears to have been truly committed to furthering the transnational circulation of Chinese literature and to the mentoring of his Chinese students, his intimacies with China do not seem to have operated solely on an intellectual plane. Acton scoffs in the memoirs at the "lurid stories" of his "arcane activities" that circulated in Beijing.[87] However, according to his friend James Lord, he was during his time in China "ecstatic to experience the willing and eager embraces of Peking's innumerable young boys, to whom he evidently appeared a thrilling and exotic embodiment of desire. . . . Here he was able to lead an openly homosexual life unthinkable in Europe."[88] He notes in a 1935 letter to Roy Harrod that China "rejuvenated" him, leaving him feeling "full, if not of beans, of spermatozoa all of them alive."[89] This is not to say that the relationship with Chen was necessarily a romantic friendship. Mungello asserts that, while Acton was "physically attracted to Chinese young men" and "some of his friendships with them were sexual," others, including his friendship with Chen, were "more intellectual."[90] It is clear, however, that the lure of China had for Acton an erotic component. He chafed, however, at any public acknowledgment of his attractions. He begins his second volume of life writing, *More Memoirs of an Aesthete* (1970), with an indignant "Explanatory and Apologetic" that relates rumors that circulated during his time in Beijing that he, "an Oxford aesthete of ephemeral fame," had "settled in China for the purpose of wallowing in vice."[91] These rumors of his "moral decline" and his reputation as a "scandalous debauchee" inhibited his capacity to serve during World War II, when, as a result of a report concerning his erotic activities written by an embassy official, he was "detained at Barrackpore in a lowly secretarial capacity," rather than being sent to Chongqing, where he felt his linguistic qualifications might have made him more useful.[92] In the angry retort to these accusations that begins the later volume of memoirs, Acton insists on the mutuality of affection and respect that existed between himself and the people he encountered in China: "My Chinese friends trusted me. They paid me the compliment of treating me as one of themselves and our affection was mutual."[93] Here he maintains that he entered into true cosmopolitan communion with Beijing, that there could be nothing exploitative or misguided about his manner of encountering difference. In his fictional representation of his time in China, however, he offers a more careful and self-aware counterpoint to these overconfident assertions.

Transracial Intimacies: Acton and Nancy Cunard

Acton's somewhat caustic fictional treatment of intimacy across national boundaries should be understood in relation to his friendship with the antiracist activist, writer, and great-granddaughter of the founder of the Cunard shipping line fortune, Nancy Cunard. Acton deeply admired Cunard. In his memoirs, he recollects fondly Cunard's "electro-magnetic self," noting that she was understood at the time as the "Gioconda of the Age" and "inspired half the poets and novelists of the 'twenties.'"[94] (Cunard was involved in affairs with Wyndham Lewis, Tristan Tzara, Louis Aragorn, and Ezra Pound, among others.) Cunard was, of course, much more than a muse. She wrote multiple volumes of modernist poetry, including *Parallax* (Hogarth Press, 1925), and operated the successful though short-lived Hours Press (1928–31), which published works by Pound, Beckett, Aragon, Norman Douglas, Brian Howard, as well as Acton's own poetry collection *This Chaos* (1930). She is remembered primarily today, however, for her antiracist advocacy and her work as the editor of the 800-page *Negro: An Anthology* (1934), which included works by Zora Neale Hurston, Langston Hughes, and Alain Locke and endeavored to speak to Black experience across the diaspora.[95] According to Acton, "she felt passionately about injustice" and was a "romantic rebel" who "would not let [the miseries of the world] rest."[96] Over the course of their friendship, he watched her transform from "a popular society girl" into a "militant propagandist for miscellaneous prickly causes." Like many who knew her, Acton seems to have found her zeal at times overwhelming. He notes that she felt "indifferent to calumny" and "smil[ed] at risks" while pursuing the righting of wrongs.[97] "Her austerity," he argues, "was voluptuous," implying that she found in her political devotion a form of pleasure verging on ecstasy. "In the middle ages," Acton states, "she would have become a mystic."[98] Acton and Cunard were in close contact in the years immediately prior to his departure for China, when Cunard was first finding her way to antiracist advocacy, and the points of resonance between their approaches to transnational and transracial communion cannot have escaped Acton. With this in mind, I would like to consider Acton's own pursuit of cosmopolitan connection (as well as his fears about the potential Orientalist pitfalls of his project) in light of Cunard's enthusiasm for Blackness and her tendency toward appropriation and fetishization. The note of self-criticism within Acton's fiction might be understood as an anxious acknowledgment of the similarities between his own mode of transnational engagement and Cunard's voluptuous mode of political bonding.

Like Acton, Cunard felt it was necessary to sever herself from her wealthy family in order to pursue her desire for connection across racial boundaries, and the two were engaged in their struggles away from biological kin and toward the adoption of another culture at the same moment. While Acton was resisting pressure from his father to "make good" and planning his departure for China, Cunard was, as Laura Winkiel puts it, seeking "to escape the privileged claustrophobia of her background through an identification with black diasporic and African cultures."[99] Her very public separation from her family followed upon her commencement in 1928 of a relationship with Henry Crowder, a Black jazz musician from the United States. Taunted with news of the affair at a luncheon, her mother, Lady Emerald Cunard, expressed disapproval, phoning "half of social London" to inquire, "Is it *true* my daughter knows a Negro?"[100] The battle between mother and daughter escalated, with Emerald restricting Nancy's access to the family wealth and Nancy finally publishing a pamphlet, *Black Man and White Ladyship: An Anniversary* (1931), in which she denounced her mother as both racist and classist.[101] As Jane Marcus argues, Nancy's political development was founded upon the rejection of national and biological kinship: "By writing and publishing *Black Man, White Ladyship* [sic] (1931), she repudiated England as mother country and denounced her American-born mother as a racist, mingling matriphobia with the idea of the struggle for black power."[102] Acton, who was close with both Emerald and Nancy, was intimately bound up in their struggle with one another and frequently shared with Nancy the comments Emerald made about their quarrel. In an April 1931 letter, for example, he informs Nancy that he has heard from another friend Michael Rosse that Emerald makes "frequent references to [her] at the lunches and dinners of Grosvenor Square" and recently remarked "that she could not be 'chic' if she lived in Paris because all of the 'chic' Parisians live nowadays with negroes."[103] This latter comment found its way almost word-for-word into Nancy's matriphobic pamphlet. Acton was very much at the center of this public dispute and operated as a confidante and ally during Nancy's struggle to free herself from her delimiting family.

Extricated from familial connection, Cunard endeavored to cultivate a new kinship network for herself, a system of "cross-racial brother-and-sisterhood," and devoted herself enthusiastically to the development of the *Negro* anthology.[104] Acton expressed real interest and admiration for the project in his correspondence with her, stating that he believed the finished project would be "wonderful" and informing her of his contact with Black journalists and actors, presumably recruiting potential contributors for the volume.[105] He himself contributed an essay on "Pushkin and Peter the Great's Negro" to the *Negro* anthology as well as a poem, "From Tiresias,"[106] to a collection of poetry set to music by Henry Crowder, *Henry-Music* (1930), which she published at the Hours Press. However, as much as Acton was, as Anne Chisholm puts it, "in sympathy with her on racism," his contributions to both collections seem to operate in a very different emotional register than Cunard's.[107] His ventriloquism of Tiresias in the *Henry-Music* collection, for example, is marked in its detachment and restraint in comparison to the angry condemnation of the "son o' bitch U.S.A." in "Equatorial Way," a poem in which Cunard imagines herself into the subjectivity of a Black man planning to "tear the crackers limb from limb," appropriates Black vernacular, and wildly deploys racial slurs.[108] This tendency to go too far in her adoption of Black identity and experience is the element of Cunard's project that has come under the most criticism in recent years. Critics make frequent note, for example, of Barbara Ker-Seymer's photograph of Cunard with ropes of beads looped around her neck, solarized so Cunard's skin appears to be black, an image Jane Marcus refers to as a "mimicry of lynching" and a "visual parable of her desire for a black body of her own."[109] Maureen Moynagh has described Cunard as "an outsider striving for insider status [who] continually remakes her identity at the expense of the other she seeks to represent."[110] Acton was not, apparently, blind to the fetishistic and overzealous tendencies in Cunard's romanticized consumption of Blackness. He reported overhearing her say to Crowder one evening, "Be more *African*, be more *African*," to which Crowder replied, "But I *ain't* African. I'm *American*."[111] The fact that Acton recollected and retold this story indicates a certain degree of discomfort with Cunard's approach to racialized difference. Witnessing Cunard's voluptuous form of political bonding provided Acton with an opportunity to reflect on those troubling forms of exoticization and excessive identification that so often mark white attempts to engage with alterity.

Transnational Adoption and the Limits
of Decadent Cosmopolitanism

In his novel *Peonies and Ponies*, Acton turns a critical eye on aestheticist cosmopolitanism and acknowledges the political and ethical shortcomings of the Decadent model of approaching difference. The novel's aesthete protagonist, Philip Flower, could be understood as a composite satire of what Anne-Marie Brady refers to as the "Peking-based aesthetes," a group of British and American men drawn to the city's reputation as a "cultural centre" during this period, described by the Sinologist C. P. Fitzgerald as floating "between the culture of the West and the civilization of China . . . cultured, but unproductive."[112] Flower bears some resemblance, for example, to George N. Kates, an American aesthete, connoisseur, and collector living in Beijing at the same time as Acton who, in the words of Karl E. Meyer and Shareen Blair Brysac, "might have been invented by Noël Coward."[113] Philip has often been read, however, as Acton's "literary double," and I would argue that the character is made as much from Acton as it is from the larger circle of Anglo-American aesthetes with whom he mingled in Beijing. In lampooning the "Peking-based aesthetes" and their attempts to adopt Chinese culture, he, by extension, lampoons himself, representing his adventures in Beijing as somewhat ridiculous and guided by the same types of fetishism and exoticization that marked Cunard's project.[114]

Peonies and Ponies theorizes and interrogates the processes of withdrawal and cosmopolitan integration Acton himself underwent in China and attempts to parse the distinction between Orientalism and cosmopolitan curiosity. Philip's retreat into an aestheticist reverie in China does allow him to distinguish himself from the vulgar Orientalism of his peers, but the novel raises real questions about whether his Decadent mode of appreciation for the beauty of Chinese culture truly brings him into closer contact with the city of Beijing. As Kun Xi has argued, while Philip "strives to understand the nuances of Chinese culture," Acton "seems to suggest that this kind of attempt cannot be always that successful."[115] The most startling element of the text is its representation of an erotically charged transnational adoption. Philip attempts to integrate himself more thoroughly with China by adopting a young Chinese actor to whom he is sexually attracted and from whom he expects to receive access to Chinese culture. In choosing to represent a cosmopolitan aesthete engaging in a highly predatory form of Orientalist exploitation, Acton raises questions about his own attempts to consume difference in Beijing. While the

"Explanatory and Apologetic" in his second set of memoirs speaks righteously and indignantly of his spotless behavior while abroad, *Peonies and Ponies* registers anxieties about his interactions with Chinese youth and Chinese culture, expressing concerns about attempts at transnational communion and mentorship that lapse into extraction and appropriation.

Philip is not by a length, the novel makes clear, the *most* vulgar sort of Orientalist. Acton discriminates Philip's aestheticist cosmopolitanism from the superficial Orientalism practiced by the majority of Peking's expatriate community. "Peking's such loads of fun," asserts the curio dealer Mrs. Mascot in the novel's opening lines, "There's always a delicious spice of the unexpected."[116] Philip sneers in derision at her incurious idiocy and barbarity and thinks, in contrast of all "the city had meant to him," of the manner in which everything about him continues to appear "supernatural" and "brought grist for pantheistic reverie and wonder."[117] "What were the feelings, so copiously aired, of a Mrs. Mascot, in comparison with his? What right had she here? She and her polypus type were profaning all his sanctuaries. Had he not seen her with a party of tourists, who had motored, actually hooting their horns, up to the very Temple of Heaven!"[118] He juxtaposes this vulgar form of tourism with the "ecstasy" he experienced within "the spiritual isolation of those walled precincts," foregrounding his capacity, as a detached, solitary, and refined aesthete, to perceive clearly the beauty of China.[119] Departing Mrs. Mascot and her "jabbering circle of Europeans," he muses to himself that he feels "as if he were married to Peking, and this marriage was to be an inexhaustible adventure."[120] Philip, the text signals immediately, believes he has been brought into a more authentic intimacy with his surroundings by eschewing conventional modes of affiliation so he may be closer married to the city. The novel highlights the fact that Philip understands himself to be engaging the city through an aestheticist framework. He moves around Beijing in a Paterian manner, maintaining ecstasy and forever courting new impressions, reading the landscape through a Wildean lens. Gazing upon a goldfish, for example, in the city's Central Park, he asks, "Is it not like Salome dancing the dance of the seven veils?" and calls his companions to see "Salome is dancing for us. Admire the variety and originality of costume displayed by that chorus, the mannequin with crimson corsage and silvery train, and this one in moiré silk, which in certain lights becomes a mantle of diapered gauze."[121] Philip links his aestheticism and detachment to his capacity for acute perception, which renders him alive to the city's beauty, perpetually readied for ecstatic encounters and the composition of Decadent lyric responses to Beijing's wonders.

As much as Philip insists upon the acuity of his aestheticist perception, he remains frustrated in his attempts to integrate fully with China, and this produces a gnawing sense of isolation and disconnection. In a chapter entitled "A Solitary Flower," Philip reflects on the peculiar hybrid identity and isolation engendered by his enthusiastic veneration of China. He is "too Chinese for the foreign community," but his Britishness nevertheless "separates [him] from the Chinese."[122] This leads to a certain degree of loneliness. "He love[s] the city to distraction," so why, he wonders, "did he suffer from these bouts of solitude?"[123] During these bouts, he longs for connection and intimacy: "He wanted to meet the Chinese on their own ground and be accepted as one of them. He would have liked nothing better than to be adopted by a Chinese family."[124] Philip understands his bachelor status as crucial to his capacity to connect more fully with the city, but he nevertheless pines for a kind of integration that kinship connections with Chinese people might provide.

In an attempt to be brought into truer intimacy with China, Philip turns to the construction of an alternative transnational familial structure. While wandering the streets alone, he ducks into a theater, and, in a scene that mimics Dorian Gray's encounter with Sybil Vane, he is "stirred by an intense curiosity" at the sight of an actor whose "timid little steps mimicked the gait of a girl whose feet had been pinched into the tiniest of slippers" and whose "eyes were animated by a hard flame of lasciviousness that was scarcely feminine."[125] Acton expressed a deep fascination with *nandan*, the young men who performed *dan* roles on the Chinese stage, celebrating them in his memoirs for their Decadent capacity to triumph over nature through artifice: "Paradoxically, the role of heroine was best interpreted by males who created an illusion of ultra-femininity, whereas women on the stage were apt to rely on their intrinsic charm. This was a genuine triumph of art over nature."[126] This fascination is similarly reflected in photographs of Mei Langfang "making up" and of "Six Famous Female Impersonators in the Role of P'An Chin-Lien" (or Pan Jinlian) in his *Famous Chinese Plays* and in the photographs of actors in *dan* roles taken on the porch of Acton's Beijing residence in the archives at Villa La Pietra.[127] In *Peonies and Ponies*, contact with the figure of the *nandan* operates as the potential antidote to the loneliness and longing for integration with China that beleaguers Philip Flower. He sends the young actor Yang Pao-ch'in (or Yang Baoquin) his card and requests an interview. As he awaits the actor's visit, he generates a queer kinship scheme that might counteract his isolation: "The thought struck him, why not adopt a son? He would need a companion in his old age."[128] In his first interview with Yang, he endeavors to demonstrate his cultural links with Yang and his need for companionship. He stresses his connectedness with China, stating, "My body is foreign but my soul is Chinese," and highlights his isolation, insisting, "I have no family. I am alone in the windy dusty world."[129] Philip operates at this moment, in his yearning for Chineseness as well as his insistence upon his cultural expertise, as an exaggerated caricature of the cosmopolitan bachelor persona Acton cultivated in his memoirs.

The novel represents Philip's fascination with Yang as motivated by erotic desire. During the initial interview, Yang sings for Philip, and "sparks [flicker] before his eyes; his ears [are] on fire; his insides [melt] away."[130] Following the actor's departure, he contemplates the photograph Yang left behind, relying on Wildean and Paterian tropes of bewildering and enigmatic feminine beauty to delineate the dizzying impact of Yang's gender dissidence on his consciousness: "He examined Yang's photograph: it was as baffling as the Sphinx, as the smile of Mona Lisa. The stocky youth with close-cropped hair was hard to reconcile with the delicate beauty he had become, full of strange feminine ardour."[131] Filled with longing for this mystifying figure, Philip schemes to bring Yang into his home, but these attempts are rebuffed by Yang's "teacher" Mr. An, an opium addict to whom Yang had been sold by his grandmother. When An is arrested while trying to purchase opium, Philip sees an opportunity, agreeing to bribe the teacher out of prison "on one condition, that Philip should have custody of Yang in future."[132] An is instead executed, and Philip is finally able to achieve his greatest desire and take the grieving and vulnerable Yang into his home.

The new domestic arrangement appears at first to be all for which Philip has longed. When Yang begs to perform his "filial obeisance" to his new father, Philip's heart begins beating "almost audibly," and he goes "a little wobbly at the knees."[133] The arrangement does not, however, live up to Philip's aesthetic and erotic expectations. Yang's grandmother reappears on the scene, demanding to cohabitate with the "father and son," and Yang declines to self-exoticize to Philip's satisfaction and instead exhibits signs of an "Occidental mania," refusing to don the Chinese gown in claret silk Philip presents to him in favor of a Western suit and decorating his room with a photograph of the Empire State Building.[134] (Here one seems to hear Philip whispering, in an echo of Cunard's exhortation to Crowder, "Be more *Chinese*, be more *Chinese*.") In his increasing desperation, Philip slides even further into excessive cultural appropriation, endeavoring to convince Yang of China's aesthetic appeal by mirroring it back to him: "A double transformation thus took place: while his Chinese protégé was striving to Westernize himself, Philip was gradually turning into an extinct type of Oriental .... He grew a moustache which he trained to straggle downwards with a special comb, and he let his nails develop into scholarly talons."[135] Philip's attempts to model the appeal of Chinese culture are not successful, and he grows increasingly disappointed by his attempts to integrate with China via his connections with Yang. This connection is further endangered by Yang's grandmother's insistence that the boy must marry. Philip inquires of Yang if this is his wish, and the boy's response, that first he would like to be taken abroad by Philip, renews Philip's hope in their bond. Yang "clasp[s] Philip's hand and sh[akes] it with all his might. 'I love my Daddy,' he intone[s] in English," eliciting tears in Philip as he muses, "This was the most wonderful thing that had ever happened to him, the moment he had waited for all his life."[136] This ecstasy is fleeting, however, as Philip comes increasingly to realize that Yang's Occidental fetish cannot be overcome. As the text concludes, the Japanese occupy the city, and Philip retreats into the study of Buddhist scripture, while Yang "cease[s] to worry him," moving into "a pleasant niche in the background of his consciousness."[137] In the novel's final passage, Philip returns to withdrawal, isolation, and detachment, leaving the "'burning house' of this world" and becoming a "confirmed recluse."[138] As he chants in Sanskrit, Yang's grandmother shouts at the servants, and the radio of his adopted son "whistle[s] and bray[s]."[139] But "Philip, 'transfused with the mellow light of imperishable truth,' [does] not hear."[140]

Peonies and Ponies is deeply pessimistic in its treatment of transnational engagement. While it is certainly the vulgar expatriate community that the novel subjects to the most ridicule, the text also expresses skepticism concerning Philip's belief that he, in his aestheticism and cosmopolitanism, has somehow managed to truly commune with Beijing. His queer kinship scheme similarly fails to bring him into direct contact with Chinese culture, as Yang refuses to enact the kind of cultural purity that Philip demands. The text's campiest and most outrageous scenes emerge from Philip's adoption project, as he nearly faints when Yang calls him "Daddy," and from his excessive adoption of anachronistic Chinese costume. With this caricature, Acton raises larger questions about the consumption of Chinese culture by the "Peking-based aesthetes," and he also makes himself, his careful study of Chinese literature, his mentorship of Chinese young men, ridiculous. The novel's conclusion, which echoes the Paterian climax of the memoirs, finds Philip withdrawing back into himself, perhaps reaching nirvana, but more likely operating according to another Orientalist delusion. This is turn raises questions about the representation of that key moment of integration in the memoirs, gesturing toward the possibility that Acton finally came to doubt the effectiveness of his practice of detached and solitary aestheticist cosmopolitanism. Across the text, he subjects Philip's behavior in China to a rigorous interrogation, insisting that though Philip might be slightly less absurd than Mrs. Mascot, he is nevertheless, in his desperate attempts to adopt another culture, an Orientalist and a racial fetishist. Acton expressed slight discomfort with Nancy Cunard's exoticization of Henry Crowder, but he absolutely condemned the "Peking-based aesthetes" and their approach to engaging difference in the highly cynical *Peonies and Ponies*.

Transnational Personae and Cultural Exile: Harold Acton and Anna May Wong

If we are meant in *Peonies and Ponies* to laugh at Philip's adoption plan and his belief that he has attained nirvana, the novel does seem to express a certain sympathy for his loneliness, which results from his resolute inbetweenness, his concomitant exile from the expatriate community and his frustrated "quest for a Chinese friend."[141] There is for a figure like Philip, with desires like Philip's, no real home. To conclude, I would like to turn to an image in the photograph archive at Villa La Pietra that registers a similar sort of melancholy about the cultural exile that often accompanies cultural hybridity. This is a photograph of Harold Acton and Anna May Wong in the carved moon-gate of the drawing room of his home in Beijing (Figure 4.4).

Chinese-American actor Anna May Wong, known for her roles in *The Toll of the Sea* (1922), *The Thief of Baghdad* (1924), and *Shanghai Express* (1932), made her first and only visit to China in 1936, hoping to study Chinese theater and learn more about her own heritage. Wong, who remained unmarried throughout her life, lived a life, like Acton's, of international mobility, working for extended periods in Germany and Britain, perpetually willing to relocate from the United States for work opportunities. As Shirley Jennifer Lim notes, she was "a truly cosmopolitan and global actress," but she nevertheless did not travel to China until she was thirty-one years old.[142] She went with the hope of engaging her ancestral past, but she also carried with her a deep ambivalence about these aspirations. Before her departure, she stated, "I am going to a strange country, yet, in a way, I am going home."[143] But she also wondered if, on

Figure 4.4   Harold Acton in Beijing with Anna May Wong in the carved moon-gate of
the drawing room of his residence at 2 Kung Hsien Hutung, ca. 1930s. New York
University, The Acton Photograph Archive, Villa La Pietra, Florence.
Reproduced courtesy of New York University.

her arrival, she might "feel like an outsider."[144] As recent accounts of her
Chinese travels by Anthony B. Chan, Graham Russell Gao Hodges, and
Shirley Jennifer Lim indicate, Wong's sense of homecoming was complicated by the reception she received during her visit. Prior to her trip,
"numerous [Chinese] magazines openly questioned whether she would be
welcomed at all" and charged her with "disgracing China" in her portrayal
of Chinese women.[145] Attention was perpetually drawn, as she com-
menced her travels about the country, to her status as an outsider. At a
party in Shanghai, she met "one of the ladies (who) spoke my dialect and
so I began to chatter away merrily in Cantonese. After a few minutes, she
said, 'Miss Wong, do you mind going back to English? You speak Chinese
charmingly, but you have such a marked American accent.'"[146] In a
documentary concerning her travels, "My China Film," Wong notes that,
"Wherever I went in China, I heard Chinese remarking, who is that
foreign-looking or Chinese-looking lady, I should say, in a foreign
dress.... Well, I thought I ought to do something about that so
Mrs. Wong took me to the leading silk shop, Lau Kai Fouks in

Shanghai, where I chose materials for my first Chinese dresses."[147] As Shirley Lim notes, Wong chose to change her costume so that she might play the role of a Chinese woman. Abandoning this costume led to awkward encounters. According to Hodges, when she first attempted to visit her ancestral village of Chang On, "villagers threw rocks at her as she approached."[148] In an introduction to the televised broadcast of "My China Film," Wong states that during this aborted visit, "I was dressed in a white dress and the children all ran to the mothers and said oh here comes the white devil."[149] When Wong returned, she made the strategic decision to don "one of her dark, not white, 'native' costumes, presumably one of the cheongsams she had made for her in Shanghai."[169] In a highly sentimental finale to her China film, she stands with her father looking over the fields and the village, coming into communion with her familial and national past. What is elided from the film, however, is the fact that, in order to return "home," Wong was forced to adopt a disguise.

In the photograph of Acton and Wong together, they may both be understood as costumed, as in disguise. Wong wears a patterned gown, presumably one of her newly acquired Chinese dresses, and holds a fan. In the words of Kun Xi, Acton has "modelled himself after a Manchurian nobleman," and he has, in addition, "deliberately created an atmosphere" in his selection of the moon gate as frame and the "traditional Chinese painting with mythological aura" in the background.[150] Acton and Wong have together staged themselves in a manner that allows them to perform a sense of embeddedness within a culture from which they both felt, in the end, disconnected. There are numerous images of Anna May Wong in Villa La Pietra's photograph archives, Wong in Acton's garden in front of the lotus pond, outside his study, posing in a larger group and alone wearing a fur coat. However, this image, in particular, I would argue, speaks to their shared experiences as culturally hybrid cosmopolites, out-fitting themselves in Chinese costume, endeavoring to adopt Chinese personae, working to integrate themselves into a culture from which they felt perpetually separated, staging a scene that insists upon their connect-edness to China. On her return, Wong stated, "It's a pretty sad situation to be rejected by the Chinese because I am too American."[151] However, as Shirley Lim has recently argued, Wong was haunted throughout her career by "Western fantasies of the oriental . . . and racial segregation" that denied her "an opportunity to become an A-list Hollywood actress in major studio productions."[152] Her transnational identity, too American for the Chinese, too Chinese for Hollywood, meant there could finally be no place for her to call home.

In the final chapter of *Peonies and Ponies*, Philip Flower, who felt similarly homeless, similarly suspended between two national cultures, is suddenly struck by the sense that "he stood before China as Walter Pater had stood before Mona Lisa."[153] This could mean all types of things. Flower could be understood as bringing to bear upon the experience of China all the perceptive acuity with which Pater approached La Gioconda, enacting a queer and refined Decadent sensibility that frees the subject from delimiting heteronormative attachments and enables true communion with beauty. It could also mean staring at an innocent painting of a woman smiling and deciding it portrays a vampire, a Borgia, Greek animalism, and lustful Rome. It could mean delusion and misapprehension. In his memoirs and fiction concerning his time in China, Acton oscillates between these two possibilities, insisting that he, through aestheticist methods, entered into true communion with Beijing while nevertheless acknowledging that he might have only been a fundamentally ridiculous and deluded European man, adopting Chinese costume, exploiting Chinese youth, playacting at transcultural comprehension, standing before China fanciful, confused, and incorrect.

PART III

Decadent Modernism and Eroticized Kinship

CHAPTER 5

Richard Bruce Nugent's "Geisha Man"
Harlem Decadence, Multiraciality, and Incest Fantasy

Wallace Thurman concludes his chronicle of the Harlem Renaissance's second generation, *Infants of the Spring* (1932), with the spectacular suicide of the novel's most alluring character, the dandy Paul Arbian. Before taking his life, Arbian costumes himself in a set of "Eastern" signifiers. He "don[s] a crimson mandarin robe, wrap[s] his head in a batik scarf," places joss-sticks around the room, and carpets the floor with the manuscript pages of his novel *Wu Sing: The Geisha Man*.[1] Arbian then climbs into the tub, turns on the water, and slits his wrists with a "highly ornamented Chinese dirk."[2] The novel's protagonist, Raymond Taylor, speculates that Arbian arranged this scene as a form of "delightful publicity to precede the posthumous publication of his novel."[3] Arbian had not, however, foreseen that the pages would become saturated with water as the tub ran over, that the pencil transcriptions would be rendered illegible. The novel is destroyed. Only the title page along with the dedication remain:

> Wu Sing: The Geisha Man
> To
> Huysmans' Des Esseintes and Oscar Wilde's Oscar Wilde
> Ecstatic Spirits with whom I Cohabit
> And whose golden spores of decadent pollen
> I shall broadcast and fertilize
> It is written
>
> > Paul Arbian.[4]

Arbian departs the world with an Orientalist, fin-de-siècle bang, creating a "gruesome yet fascinating spectacle," a careful arrangement of textiles and curios that gesture toward Arbian's highly Decadent fetishization of "the East" along with a titillating lost Orientalist masterwork that promised to carry forward the pollen of French and British Decadence into twentieth-century Harlem.[5]

What is this Orientalist text, written in the spirit of Wilde and Huysmans, that was worth dying for, that, had it survived, might have broadcast and fertilized Decadent spores across the United States? Thurman modeled Arbian on the Harlem Renaissance author and illustrator Richard Bruce Nugent (RBN), whose illustrations were featured on the cover of *Opportunity* and in the pages of *Ebony and Topaz* and whose Decadent modernist short story of bisexual desire, "Smoke, Lilies and Jade," caused enormous controversy when it was published in *Fire!!* Nugent did not, however, commit suicide nor destroy his masterpiece. He lived until 1987, and multiple manuscripts of his "Geisha Man" are preserved within the Bruce Nugent Papers at the Beinecke Library.[6] Portions of "Geisha Man" were published in Thomas Wirth's *Gay Rebel of the Harlem Renaissance* (2002), and as scholarship on Nugent proliferates, critics have turned repeatedly to this text, which promises to reveal so much about the manner in which Nugent conceptualized race, identity, and desire.[7] "Geisha Man" centers on a gender-fluid, mixed-race protagonist, the child of a Japanese mother and a white American father, who engages in a sexual relationship with their father and moves restlessly across the globe experiencing "various spatial and racial dislocations as a Japanese [sex worker], immigrant to the United States, and queer black man reveling in Manhattan's polysexual, multiracial ball scene."[8] Nugent planned for "Geisha Man" to be published in an excessive, near impossible format, as a stunning art book in which each page was to be a different color printed with ink of a different color. His elaborate publication plans for this manuscript, along with the fact that Thurman imagined it as the work his friend would die for, suggests that it was particularly meaningful for Nugent. However, this dizzying text, which centers incest, racial ambiguity, and gender dissidence, has proven itself highly difficult to decipher.

With the emergence of queer of color critique and heightened attentiveness to Decadent modernism, Nugent's work has grown increasingly appealing. This is in part because Nugent is so direct in his discussion of queer identities and desires. A. B. Christa Schwarz, for example, celebrates Nugent as a figure whose "gay voice represents an alternative" to the more oblique expressions of sexual dissidence in many works of the Harlem Renaissance.[9] Recent criticism has also highlighted his innovative repurposing of Decadent aesthetics, his remaking of fin-de-siècle modes to Black modernist ends. Michèle Mendelssohn, for example, argues that "more than any other member of the Harlem Renaissance, Nugent mixed nineteenth-century decadent and aesthetic sources" as he generated a formula for "black queer modernity."[10] He also features prominently in Elisa Glick's discussion of the "transformative appropriation of decadence" by Harlem Renaissance dandies as they engaged in a "critique of authenticity and primitivism."[11] It is clear we have come to feel that Nugent's work has much to offer as we write the history of Decadence, of modernism, of queer identity formations, and of the Harlem Renaissance. But what do we do with "Geisha Man," a privileged but only partially and posthumously published text that Thurman nevertheless posited as Nugent's most highly significant work, that Nugent rewrote multiple times, that he envisioned circulating in a wildly ornate, incredibly luxurious and colorful format? A story of sex between a father and child, of a protagonist who is at times Japanese and at others Black, that is formally strange and was meant to be materially even stranger, it seems to at once demand and exceed analysis. It is also a text that appears to replicate and reinscribe some of Decadence's most outrageous tendencies, including its Orientalism and its desperate efforts to shock readers with indulgent modes of taboo eroticism.

In this chapter, I argue that "Geisha Man" emerges as particularly meaningful when read in constellation with a broader set of Decadent modernist texts and drawings by Nugent and that reading the text within this framework allows its central concerns, kinship and multiraciality, to emerge with greater clarity. Positioning this work within the framework of Nugent's extensive experimentation with Decadent tropes and styles materializes its claims and allows for the incest and the Orientalism to become legible as methods for conceptualizing mixed-race identity. Fiona I. B. Ngô is certainly correct in arguing that Nugent mobilizes "images and styles of the Orient, inherited from the European decadent queer canon" as he fashions "a semantic, visual, and mobile vocabulary for queer black aesthetic practices," but this refashioning engenders something more nuanced than a purposely offensive reinscription of some of Decadence's most troubling tendencies.[12] The utility of Orientalist and incest tropes to Nugent as he theorizes kinship and multiraciality only becomes apparent, however, when "Geisha Man" is placed alongside the Decadent texts that were the testing ground for the ideas Nugent developed more fully in this longer work.

Tracing Nugent's implementation of Decadence across a set of texts from the 1920s and 1930s indicates how generative Decadence was for him as he endeavored to rethink race, identity, and affiliation. The story of

Salome in particular was crucial to Nugent's thinking as he wrestled with questions about the spectacularization of difference and the fragmentation of kinship structures in the United States. "Geisha Man," I argue here, is in essence Nugent's most accomplished and thorough revision of Oscar Wilde's *Salome*, in which he retools the Orientalism and incestuous desire so central to Salome's story in a narrative that similarly focuses on a fetishized performer attempting to enact erotic agency within a system of fractured familial formations. "Geisha Man" is built from the raw materials of his Salome obsession, and the series of Decadent stories, drawings, and Salome revisions Nugent produced in the 1920s and 1930s illuminate this strange manuscript's sophisticated and challenging treatment of multiraciality and kinship.

"Smoke, Lilies and Jade": Resisting Maturation, Rethinking Connection

Nugent is most well-known, particularly to scholars of Decadence, for his Decadent modernist short story "Smoke, Lilies and Jade," first published in *Fire!!* in 1926, in which a blasé, bisexual dandy, Alex, smokes a cigarette from an "ivory holder inlaid with red jade and green" and contemplates Oscar Wilde, sexual desire, and his own disinclination to work.[13] Nugent takes up questions of blood ties more directly in later works such as "Geisha Man," but it is clear within this text that Decadent style and Decadent tropes were useful to Nugent, from the earliest points in his career, as he theorized connection and resisted heteronormative ideologies of affiliation. Within this story, Decadent modes of feeling and thinking serve the protagonist as he attempts to imagine himself out of the delimited perspectives thrust upon him by kinship ties and ideologies of the family. Nugent positions Decadence as the antidote to the coercive pressures that dictate life trajectories and restrict the reimagination of association. The focus in particular on extrication from kinship ties as liberatory and enabling forms an important foundation for the later thinking that he performs in "Geisha Man." Attending to Nugent's engagement with Decadence in "Smoke, Lilies and Jade" provides insight into how Decadence served him more broadly in his attempt to resist and contest conventional modes of conceptualizing family and desire.

"Smoke, Lilies and Jade" advances a vision of detachment from kinship ties as the foundation for creative self-fashioning, an idea to which Nugent returns at much greater length in "Geisha Man." The story opens with Alex recollecting the death of his father coolly while appreciating the beauty of his own cigarette smoke "climb[ing] up [a] ray of sunlight" as well as his own "differen[ce] from other people."[14] At his father's funeral, Alex recalls, a woman had insisted he was like his father, but Alex asserted this wasn't the case: "he *wasn't* like his father."[15] Even at this moment of loss, the story indicates, Alex endeavored to extricate himself from imbrication within traditional narratives of kinship, biological likeness, and filial repetition. As Joseph Allen Boone argues, the death of the father frees Alex's psyche, and it is this "break from parental interdiction" that produces the "contentment" Alex is experiencing as the story begins.[16] Reclining and smoking, Alex remembers his aesthetically inflected response to the sight of his father's corpse:

> when they had taken his father from the vault three weeks later ... he had grown beautiful ... his nose had become perfect and clear ... his hair had turned jet black and glossy and silky ... and his skin was a transparent green ... like the sea only not so deep ... and where it was drawn over the cheek bones a pale beautiful red appeared ... like a blush ... why hadn't his father looked like that always ... [...] ... maybe it was wrong to think thoughts like these ... but they were nice and pleasant and comfortable ... when one was smoking a cigarette thru an ivory holder ... inlaid with red jade and green ....[17]

His thoughts turn immediately from this Decadent reverie upon his own father's dead body, a perverse retooling of familial feeling that remakes mourning into an opportunity for discriminating strange colors and courting new impressions, to his artistic vocation and his rejection of conventional notions of productivity and success. While "his mother and all his relatives" decry his dissipation, he is "content to lay and smoke and meet friends at night ... to argue and read Wilde ... Freud ... Boccacio."[18] Alex's turn to Decadence, to sinister forms of beauty and exquisite passions, constitutes a turn away from familial expectations and standard storylines of maturation, allowing him to fashion an alternative narrative of personal success and fulfillment. His biological family, however, derides the narrative he has crafted for himself. Though Alex has managed to integrate himself into Harlem's artistic circles and become intimate with the finest minds of his generation, with Langston Hughes and Jean Toomer, Countee Cullen and Carl Van Vechten, his kin greet his bohemianism with disdain. His mother in particular treats him as a failure:

> if he went to see mother she would ask ... how do you feel Alex with nothing in your pockets ... I don't see how you can be satisfied ... Really you're a mystery to me ... and who you take after ... I'm sure I don't

know ... none of my brothers were lazy and shiftless ... [...] you won't do anything to make money ... wake up Alex ... I don't know what will become of you ....

it was hard to believe in one's self after that ... did Wilde's parents or Shelley's or Goya's talk to them like that ...[19]

His mother's incredulity, her exasperated "who you take after ... I'm sure I don't know," only further enables Alex's extrication of himself from family ties. As Boone asserts, "psychologically this denial of family resemblance completes Alex's separation from his birth family and the bourgeois world it represents."[20] In response to his mother's insistence that he represents a biological aberration, a departure from a genealogy marked by financial stability and a strong work ethic, Alex makes the choice to link himself imaginatively to a set of iconoclasts, sexual dissidents, and geniuses whose aesthetic capacities must have, in Alex's mind, insulated them from this type of familial coercion. Boone notes that Alex actively wants "to be repudiated by the claims of blood in order to realize a fantasy of exile" and "be admitted to a substitutive kinship structure" composed of the authors and artists of Harlem, who accept his bohemian persona.[21] "In figurative terms," Boone states, "Alex undergoes an act of self-orphaning that becomes an act of self-authorization," a set of processes Nugent centers again in "Geisha Man."[22] After contemplating for a moment the "naïve" appeal of suburban New Bedford, with its "snug little houses set complacently behind protecting lawns," where presumably he might enter into the forms of domestic and reproductive life that would meet with his mother's approval, Alex decides that New York's sophistication and modes of community appeal more strongly.[23] He leaves his apartment to "wander in the night," where he concludes that "it was fine to be young and hungry and an artist ... to blow blue smoke from an ivory holder."[24]

Severing himself from the disapproving surveillance of his biological family, Alex is able to move on to imagining new types of affiliation. Having reached the conclusion that his resistant, rebellious, self-authorized path is fine and good, he is able to turn more forcefully into the search for beauty, and he walks the city streets "think[ing] and wonder[ing]."[25] Alex's Decadent mode of *flânerie* brings him into contact with a beautiful young man, Adrian (or "Beauty"), who like Alex wanders the boulevards, "walk[ing] music."[26] They spend the night together, and afterward Alex dreams of a field filled with Decadent signifiers, black poppies and red calla lilies, in which he encounters "the strong torso and broad deep chest" of Beauty as well as the "fragile firm breasts" and "graceful slender throat" of his girlfriend Melva.[27] Resisting the pressure to choose between these two modes of attraction, Alex continues to search on his hands and knees in the field of poppies until, "exhultant," he finds "an ivory holder ... inlaid with red jade ... and green."[28] Once again his aesthetic inclinations operate as an antidote or alternative to the coercive force of conventional ideologies of affiliation. Rather than settling upon any one particular form of desire, he settles on the ivory cigarette holder, the object that has come within the story to stand for reverie, openness, and the aesthetic posture, at once mobile, detached, and enraptured by all the beauty that surrounds. He awakens from the dream and contemplates Beauty's beauty through a Decadent lens: "Alex wondered why he always thought of that passage from Wilde's Salome ... when he looked at Beauty's lips ... I would kiss your lips ... he *would* like to kiss Beauty's lips."[29] Salome, who becomes so central to Nugent's later modes of theorizing kinship, operates here as a model of expansive and mobile desire, allowing him to get to a new place in his thinking about sexual identity. It is fine to long for Beauty, Alex concludes, much as being an artist and being young and hungry are fine. Nevertheless, it is also fine to love Melva, the text argues, delineating in loving detail the kisses the two share: "their tongues touched ... up ... seventh heaven ... the sea had swallowed the sun ... up and out ... her breath was perfumed."[30] In the story's final paragraph, Alex comes into an epiphanic understanding of the fact that "one *can* love two at the same time ... [...] one *can*."[31] Electing to dwell in a kinetic, agile, Paterian space of perpetually mobile desire, a posture Nugent elsewhere referred to as "duosexuality," Alex refuses to succumb, not only to the pressures from his kin to settle, mature, and enter the workforce, but to the ideological pressures that led him to conceive of his attraction to both Beauty and Melva as a predicament that must conclude with a choice.[32]

"Smoke, Lilies and Jade" demonstrates the utility of Decadence to Nugent as he endeavored to think away from the heteronormative narratives and kinship structures that entrap and delimit desire and identity. Stylistically the story resembles the cigarette smoke to which it so often refers, emanating from the ivory holder inlaid with red jade and green that metonymizes Paterian openness, reverie, constant observation, and the refusal of facile orthodoxy. Reclining and smoking, like *flânerie*, engender and facilitate meditative discrimination, and the story's ellipses, its refusal to conclude a sentence, its perpetual movement from thought to thought, each question and possibility winding and careening like smoke, formally enact the quickened, multiplied Decadent consciousness celebrated by Pater. As Alex thinks and rethinks, continuously questioning and retooling his vision of fulfillment, desire, and affiliation, he is led further and further from any "facile orthodoxy" that previously curtailed his imagination.[33] He comes to see that being an artist is fine, that the substitutive kinship structure of Harlem offers more satisfaction than the approval of his biological kin, that one *can* love two at the same time. He is able to extricate himself from the boundaries imposed by his disapproving family and by dichotomous definitions of sexuality, to shed the limitations enacted upon his subjectivity by conventional ideologies that govern the operations of desire and the capacity to love and connect.

Nugent's Salomes: Color, Kin, and Exoticism

Salome is clearly an enabling and generative figure within "Smoke, Lilies and Jade," serving as a reference point for Alex as he reconceptualizes love and desire and the concept of connection. She is also a guiding force for Nugent in the 1920s and 1930s, as he represents her in his fiction and drawings, using the repetition of her story and her image, each time with a difference, to work toward a broader understanding of kin, connection, and racialized difference. Nugent returned over and over again to the figure of Salome. He drew her repeatedly; he reimagined her erotic life; he littered his stories with the echoes of her insistent desire; and he restaged her Dance of the Seven Veils, coming back again and again to the figure of the exoticized dancing girl as the locus for troubling forms of attraction and desire. As David Krasner and Margaux Poueymirou have demonstrated in their discussion of performances of Salome by Aida Overton Walker (1908, 1912), the Ethiopian Art Players (1923), and Hemsley Winfield (1929), the figure of Salome held significant appeal for Black artists and performers in the early twentieth-century United States, who found in these performances avenues to broader recognition and a rich venue for the expression of gender dissidence.[34] Nugent was operating, then, in a cultural milieu in which the Salome story and the Decadent aesthetic operated as tools for propagating Black modernity and aesthetic agency. However, the figure of Salome performed very specific roles for Nugent as he approached the spectacularization of racialized difference and the fragmentation of kinship relations within the context of US history.

Salome is for Nugent useful in terms of theorizing racialized difference and familial dynamics because of central elements within her story along with the way she was understood and received in the early twentieth century. She is during this period a figure linked to the visual consumption of eroticized difference as spectacle, and returning to her Dance of the

Seven Veils enables Nugent's consideration of the experience of being subjected to the gaze and rendered "exotic," an experience he later described as essentially "tiresome."[35] While Yeeyon Im reads Wilde's play as practicing "disorientalism," a form of "disidentification with Orientalism," the vast array of performances and representations of Wilde's tale at the turn of the century and into the 1920s often stimulated Orientalist desire.[36] Performances by, for example, Maud Allan as the dancing girl from "the East" provided opportunities for audiences to participate in, rather than think critically about, scopophilia and the spectacularization of difference, and Salome thus became a figure linked inextricably with the fetishization of racialized bodies.[37] Her name became shorthand in the early twentieth century for the consumption of racialized alterity, and she is helpful to Nugent, therefore, as he thinks about the experience of being looked at, placed, and categorized. He engages with the Orientalism with which her story has become associated, not simply reproducing that Orientalism, but as one who has sympathy for the process of being exoticized.

The story of Salome is also, significantly (and Decadently), an incest story.[38] Jokanaan's condemnation of Salome hinges upon her mother's transgressive and politically ambitious marriage to her husband's half-brother, who is also her uncle ("daughter of an incestuous mother, be thou accursed!"), and Salome dances at the behest of Herod, whose troubling desire for his stepdaughter (and niece) is one of the key preoccupations of Wilde's play.[39] The familial structures within the play are represented as fractured by larger political structures that have confused and disordered kinship formations, and this disorder engenders repeated violations of the incest taboo. Salome turns to her own eroticism in an effort to resist the troublesome power dynamics that govern her experience and the political operations that have distorted her family. Her efforts, however, are represented by Wilde as at once highly effective and entirely futile. She is able to demand the death of a man who condemned her, and she in turn must die. The Salome story allows for the consideration of what happens when the concept of kin is shattered or transformed by political operations beyond the individual's control, an element of the story that Nugent links in his interpretation to processes of enslavement and the fracturing of Black familial structures within the United States.

Nugent's Salome story, "Slender Length of Beauty," serves as a particularly useful key for decoding the manner in which Salome functioned in Nugent's imagination in this period. "Slender Length of Beauty" was meant to appear in an unpublished collection of Biblical stories, "Saffron

and Calamous," that Nugent was writing in the late 1920s and into the
early 1930s.[40] Christopher Vitale notes that the stories in the planned
collection "interpolate between the lines of biblical text, describing what
happened 'off scene,' episodes between those described in the gospels, or
intertwined with bits thereof."[41] Nugent's additions and revisions remake
Biblical characters into erotic, epicurean agents, pursuing illicit pleasures
and affinities. His move to eroticize Biblical tales, to rewrite these narratives in a lush and evocative style and center sensuous experience and
sexual desire, is, of course, a highly Decadent, Wildean project. Vitale
argues that in these stories, which detail the affections and attractions
between biblical figures such as Jesus and Judas, "Nugent produces a
symphony of bodies, desires, fantasies, and desires, crossing race and time,
probing yet further into the nucleus of erotico-political questions which
his works have struggled to bring to articulation from the start of his work
in the mid 20s."[42] "Slender Length of Beauty" certainly operates in this
vein, illuminating much about the appeal the figure of Salome held for
Nugent as he theorized racialization and the undoing of Black kinship
structures. The interpolated material he integrates into her narrative compounds and reinforces the Decadent preoccupation with vivid color in
Wilde's play in order to consider desire for and consumption of alterity.
His additions to the story also reinscribe the biblical story's concern with
the fracturing of familial connections by political forces. "Slender Length
of Beauty" reveals how crucial working with the Salome story was to
Nugent as he developed the ideas to which he turns with greater attention
in "Geisha Man."

"Slender Length of Beauty" exhibits a marked concern with tints and
shades, with color as both a source of pleasure and a form of trouble.
Wilde's lush play, awash in the rich and varied color of bodies, pale skin
and amber eyes and red blood, attracted Nugent as a writer working
through the pleasures of desire across and for difference. The story opens
with a flirtatious exchange between Salome and her lover, the shepherd
Narcissus, that centers subtle distinctions between colors, a consistent
thematic in the bible stories, which, as A. B. Christa Schwarz argues,
"focus on the sexual attraction of color contrasts, thereby presenting the
sensitive topic of miscegenation without addressing it as a contested
issue."[43] Salome notes that Narcissus's eyes are "soft and gray" while his
lashes are "as black as kohl," and Narcissus replies that her lashes "cast a
lacy, blue shadow to match the blue lights of thy hair."[44] Salome teases out
the slight differences in their skin tones, undoing any sense of whiteness as
a fixed category, "stretch[ing] her ivory leg out next to his white one,"

calling Narcissus to "see how rosy-white thou art," and he in turn tells her, "Thy color is like the heart of the golden roses in thy father's garden."[45] The two lovers revel in their subtle differences from one another and the manner in which those differences bring out their distinct, individual attractions. "Are my lips as comely against thy skin, Narcissus, as thine are on mine?" Salome asks her beloved, and he replies that her lips "are like two rubies for color and like unto sun-warmed persimmons to my flesh."[46] Gradations of variation and the specificity of pigments inspire in the two lovers a greater awareness of possible pleasures and an increasingly acute understanding of the fine distinctions between their types of beauty. The manner in which Nugent revels in tints and contact between colors here illuminates his intended future for "Geisha Man," a work that was meant to materially enact this sense of an infinite range of hues brought into finer beauty through their differences from one another.

When it is time for Salome to dance for Herod, however, color operates as a more vexed locus of attraction, allowing Nugent to interrogate more insidious ways of conceptualizing alterity. Nugent's Salome wrestles with the pain of being subjected to an appetitive, exoticizing gaze, as she makes herself more colorful, more pleasurable to look at, and then suffers as a result. She is, for Nugent, a figure who is useful for theorizing the pleasures of difference as well as the manner in which concepts of difference make certain individuals vulnerable to sinister modes of desire. Nugent notes that Salome's toilet for the night upon which she is to dance for Herod must be particularly "elaborate."[47] As she prepares for her performance, she paints her eyelids blue and stains her nipples and her nails crimson. She weights her lashes with gold paint and dusts her body with pale purple powder. She covers herself in veils of blood-red and vermillion and palest yellow along with a brilliant orange scarf and a plaited silver cord, and over the entire arrangement, she drapes "a vaporous scarf of whitest white, through which all the other scarves [show] their separate and aggregate glamour."[48] While the subtle color contrasts with which the story opened inspired languorous desire on the part of Salome and Narcissus, this riot of startling hues makes Salome the center of a rougher form of attention. As cymbals crash, she commences her Dance of the Seven Veils, discarding a rainbow of materials into the laps of the men who occupy Herod's court. Her movements grow "more acrobatic and more sexual" as she tosses into "Herod's rapt and incestuous face ... the vermillion stuff that covered her breasts."[49] The vivid tints here render Salome more vulnerable to scopophilia and the troubling, incestuous desire of her mother's husband. Nugent's revision of Salome thus integrates two of the key preoccupations

Figure 5.1   Richard Bruce Nugent, *Salome before Herod*, n.d.
Reproduced courtesy of the Amistad Research Center.

of his Salome obsession, the manner in which her story allows for a consideration of the pleasures associated with desire across difference as well as the vulnerabilities experienced by racialized subjects as they are spectacularized, fetishized, and Orientalized.

Nugent's Salome drawings may seem to participate in the very sorts of Orientalism he subjects to critique in "Slender Length of Beauty." His *Salome before Herod* (Figure 5.1), for example, links East Asia with excessive eroticism, lavishing attention onto hardened nipples and gauzy fabrics draped over naked flesh, remaking "the East" into an exotic and arousing texture. Nugent's relationship to the concept of the "exotic," however, indicates that drawing and re-drawing Salome was for him a process that allowed him to meditate on the points of continuity between the consumption of the "East" and the consumption of Blackness in the United States. In a recording housed at the Beinecke, Nugent notes that "the Black man in America is an exotic," adding that it is "tiresome" to be an exotic, and "that's a polite phrase."[50] Nugent's use of this terminology to describe the experience of Blackness in the United States might inflect our understanding of the mutability of race in a text like "Geisha Man," in which the half-Japanese protagonist Kondo might come to Harlem and suddenly be read as Black. Moving through the United States, Kondo becomes subject to American forces of understanding difference that collapse Black and Japanese individuals into the category of the "exotic," making clear the structural similarities that underwrite Orientalism and the apprehension of Blackness in America and, as Fiona I. B. Ngô argues, speaking to "modes of racialization that do not discriminate between bodies of color."[51] This sense of continuity between modes of racialization registers more clearly in his *Salome: Negrotesque I* (Figure 5.2), first published in *Harlem: A Forum of Negro Life* in 1928. Like Kondo, Salome seems to be in Nugent's imagination able to move between forms of racial identification, and these transitions speak to a potential sense of alliance with or likeness to Salome that makes the Orientalist gaze evident in the later *Salome before Herod* image slightly more complicated, for it is a gaze that turns upon Blackness as well, that turns back on Nugent as a fellow exotic. The slippage between Salomes in his work makes the Orientalism in his writing and his illustrations mean differently, placing him within that gaze at the same time that he levels it outward at the dancing girl. Playing with and reproducing Orientalism is never for Nugent a straightforward process, and it engenders new ways of conceptualizing how identity distinctions are understood and misunderstood in the country to which he has transplanted and for which he has translated Decadent Orientalism. He Orientalizes Salome, but he also identifies with her, knowing full well how tiresome it is to be that exotic dancing girl.[52] This, in turn, allows the Orientalism of "Geisha Man" to be read in a different register and allows Kondo to emerge as a figure for whose troubles Nugent feels a great deal of empathetic identification.

Nugent is, of course, not unique in positing Salome as a useful figure for thinking through the operations of Orientalism, but his emphasis in "Slender Length of Beauty" on Salome as a story about families is somewhat distinct. Nugent compounds the biblical story's preoccupation with disordered familial networks in the additions he makes to her narrative concerning her beloved Narcissus, and these interpolations make clear why Nugent, as a Black American writer, might have been so drawn to this narrative's attentiveness to ruptured kinship structures. During the extended flirtation with which the story opens, Narcissus tells Salome that he is a twin who has been divided from his brother: "As a twin, I am incomplete. Only together can we be one. And over all the world am I searching."[53] Narcissus emphasizes that though the brothers have been separated, they are psychically bound. Salome inquires, "How wilt thou know when thou hast found him?" and Narcissus responds, "I shall know."[54] Salome begs Narcissus to tell her what he knows of his twin,

Figure 5.2   Richard Bruce Nugent, *Salome: Negrotesque I*, from *Harlem: A Forum of Negro Life*, 1928.
Reproduced courtesy of the Beinecke Rare Book and Manuscript Library.

and Narcissus relates the story of his family, making it clear that his twin is in fact Iokanaan. His father, he states, was Zachariah, and his mother Elizabeth. Elizabeth delivered the first of her sons two months early, and the pair named the child "John." Elizabeth was later separated from Zachariah in the desert and delivered her second son, who was then sent with a cousin into Greece for safety. They were captured, and he was sold into slavery. Narcissus's family is ruptured by the processes of enslavement, and he is haunted by the sense of loss caused by this disruption, eternally hoping to locate his kin so as to make himself whole again. Hortense Spillers argues that within the institution of slavery, "'kinship' loses meaning, *since it can be invaded at any given and arbitrary moment by the property relations.*"[55] Narcissus had been remade from a twin and a son into a form of property, but he nevertheless insists upon his persistent feelings of connectedness to the family from which he has been wrested. He tells Salome, "We are twins, so neither is complete without the other. Perhaps he feels the warmth of love for thee in his heart likewise – for 'tis said, 'that which pierceth the heart of one twin is felt in the heart of the other. And when one heart does cease to beat, the other does likewise."[56] Despite the invasion of his familial bonds by property relations, Narcissus retains an indissoluble link with his elusive brother and insists that their fates remain connected and their desires intertwined.

Narcissus and Salome exist within a world in which kinship ties have been wholly upended, and this complex web of fragmented familial relations cannot be righted within the space of the story. Their distorted families instead intersect and engender more destruction. Narcissus is correct that he and his twin are bound together in their fate and their feeling. Iokanaan is, like Narcissus, fascinated by Salome, but his interest in her travels in a more patriarchal and condemnatory direction. When Iokanaan first arrives on the scene in Nugent's story, it is as a disembodied voice shouting about Salome and her connections to a politically ambitious matriarch: "O Daughter of an adulteress, repent!"[57] And when Iokanaan's heart ceases beating, as Narcissus predicted, his twin's does as well. Salome comes to an understanding of the brothers' relation at the climax of her dance, when she throws to the prophet her blood-red veil and then stands "shamed and still, for now she recognized Iokanaan."[58] Herodias demands the head of Iokanaan, and Salome runs from the banquet hall to find Narcissus, pleading with him to kiss her lips, drawing him to her, and seeing finally that "Narcissus was dead."[59] Salome, a daughter whose mother's politically opportune remarriage has thrust her under the lustful gaze of Herod, has caused the death of her lover by responding to

Herod's desire. Iokanaan's execution extinguishes the life of the brother from whom he has been estranged by the processes of enslavement. Both Narcissus and Salome, in Nugent's revision to the biblical story, suffer as a result of the distortions that politics and property relations have effected upon kinship structures.

Nugent's interpolations serve to reinforce the Biblical story's preoccupation with familial disorder and the impact of forms of greed and acquisitiveness that undo and distort affiliation. He departs from tradition in allowing Salome access to a world outside of Herod's court, but this world is, like the court she seeks to escape, permeated by political forces that unmake kinship structures. The fact that he chose to make Salome's orphaned lover, alienated from his kin, the victim of enslavement indicates much about why he was drawn to the Salome narrative and its representation of upended families and how this preoccupation is connected to his larger concern with race and kinship. The explicit connection he draws between the detachment from kin and enslavement in "Slender Length of Beauty" should be understood as an important context for understanding the representation of division from familial structures in "Geisha Man."

Reading "Slender Length of Beauty" alongside Nugent's Salome drawings illuminates the utility of this Decadent story to Nugent as he theorized the consumption of Blackness and the upending of Black kinship structures in the United States. Salome is for him about the pleasure of color, about racial fetishism, about fractured families, about modes of negotiating distorted forms of affiliation, and "Geisha Man" is a manuscript made from these pieces.

"Geisha Man": Multiraciality and Incest Fantasy

"Geisha Man" emerges from the same period as "Slender Length of Beauty" and focuses similarly on difference and attraction and divided kin. With its emphasis on taboo forms of desire, its Orientalist content, its lavish color, and its projected future as an excessively beautiful art book, it is Nugent's most Decadent endeavor, and it operates in conversation with his many Salomes as well as the larger body of Decadent fiction and artwork he produced in the 1920s and 1930s. Here he centers a mixed-race protagonist who longs for reconnection with the family from whom he has been divided, who, like Narcissus has been impacted by the fragmentation of kinship structures. At the same time, Nugent returns in this work to the idea developed in "Smoke, Lilies and Jade" that detachment from kinship ties might be generative and liberatory. He also compounds and makes more explicit the interest in incestuous desire present in *Salome*, reworking the story of a fetishized performer attempting to enact agency within a system of fractured kinship structures, to speak more directly to the questions around multiraciality with which he is so preoccupied during this period.

Incest drives the plot of "Geisha Man," and it is my hope that placing the story within the context of Nugent's larger body of work allows its treatment of incest to emerge as a meaningful mode for thinking through kinship and race. The manuscript tells the story of Kondo Gale Matzuika, the son of a married Japanese woman, Yetsin Matzuika, and a white American, Gale Barrows, with whom she had an affair.[60] While working as a geisha in Japan, Kondo inadvertently sleeps with their father, finds that they are "in love with [their] mothers [sic] lover," and spends the rest of the novel moving through Paris and then New York to find their way back to their father.[61] As the novel concludes, they encounter Gale Barrows once more at a costume ball, where Gale confesses that he too cannot forget their night together and invites Kondo into his home as his wife. As Tyler Schmidt has suggested, this text, focusing on a child who is "the outcome of a secret transcultural, interracial affair, ... defined by paternal absence, and forced to reconstitute notions of family and community," seems ripe for reading through the lens of Hortense Spillers's theories concerning the incest plot and its relation to slavery's rupture of familial structures.[62] Placing the manuscript alongside "Slender Length of Beauty" as well as Nugent's Salome drawings, which express his sympathy with Orientalized subjects, reinforces this potential reading, allowing its narrative to emerge as something more than sensational, Orientalist erotica. Kondo is a figure impacted by a white American's repeated moves to extract pleasure from Orientalized subjects, and his father's behavior, which emerges as both violent and irresponsible, can be understood as a figure for American modes of colonialist exploitation. The text feels into Kondo's experience, much as "Slender Length of Beauty" felt itself into the experience of Narcissus. It is part of a series of texts in which Nugent explores the impact of Western modes of cultural extraction and dehumanization on racialized subjects.

The focus on incest in "Geisha Man" also emerges as meaningful, rather than simply shocking, when understood as part of Nugent's larger attempt to theorize multiraciality. Nugent composed during this period multiple works that focus on mixed-race protagonists, such as "Geisha Man," *Gentleman Jigger*, and "Half High," and these texts tend to represent their protagonists as detached from their biological kin. This experience can be liberatory, freeing up the subject to engage in marvelous acts of redefinition and self-fashioning. In his reading of "Geisha Man," Tyler Schmidt foregrounds this emphasis on freedom and individual agency, arguing that "Spillers's consideration of bodies in flight, their origins disrupted by enslavement, is refigured in Nugent as the roaming body, contently uprooted and undifferentiated."[63] Nugent, Schmidt, asserts, "is revising the idea of community, showing transient, sexually progressive people unconnected to familial origins."[64] While Nugent does certainly seem drawn to the kinds of freedom with which he associates detachment from family origins, I would argue that "Geisha Man" also highlights the forms of alienation that radical detachment from kin might engender, the feelings of isolation and longing for community and connection. In "Geisha Man," Nugent uses the representation of incestuous desire as he theorizes the mixed-race subject's desire for a sense of connectedness with kin. Nugent's mixed-race protagonists are frequently so divided from their biological kin that they encounter family members as strangers for whom they, at the same time, feel a profound form of desire. The incest fantasy in "Geisha Man," I argue, emerges from this vexed and conflicted response to the concept of kin. For Nugent's mixed-race subjects, biological kindred are at once distant and intimate, and fantasies of sexual union with one's family members emerge from this contradictory sense of sameness and difference and a nagging desire for complete union with kin.

In "Geisha Man," Nugent also wrestles with the anti-Blackness of multiracial discourse, focusing on a mixed-race protagonist haunted by and inexorably drawn to whiteness who finally turns away from this troubling attraction. As Cedric Essi notes, contemporary discourses concerning multiraciality often link "the mixed race subject and the interracial family ... with a vague but euphoric promise of closing historical racial divides."[65] However, critics of this discourse have stressed its privileging of a political horizon that constitutes the elimination of Blackness. Hortense Spillers, for example, argues that many strands of multiracialism reinscribe white supremacy by privileging differentiation and distancing from Blackness, and Brigitte Fielder notes that racial mixedness as a form of racial identification could be understood as a "refusal of oppressed identities in favor of this newly created, third category, of 'mixed' or 'multiracial' identity."[66] Kondo's pursuit of union with his father's whiteness could be read in this vein, as an attempt to move away from his racialized subject position and come into union with their white kin. "Geisha Man" concludes, however, with Kondo's rejection of the white father who cannot provide true satisfaction. This rejection of whiteness was to be reinforced on a material level by the publication format of the text, which was meant to center the profusion of color and the proliferation of difference, the manner in which an infinite gradation of hues brought into contact with one another might produce a greater range of possible beauties and pleasures. Tavia Nyong'o argues that discourses of hybridity often link the concept of reproductive futurity with the transcendence of racialized difference, relying on a "teleology that is forever reducing the many to the one" as racial amalgamation eliminates racial distinctions.[67] Rather than celebrating the *elimination* of difference, Nugent's projected publication plans for the manuscript would celebrate the *proliferation* of color and contrast, the production of ever-more unique modes of being. Nevertheless, as much as Nugent endeavors to theorize a form of multiraciality divorced from post-racial aspiration, the perpetual privileging in his work of mixed-race subjects as more free, detached, and mobile must be understood as marked by the very modes of anti-Blackness that his celebration of profuse and divergent color attempts to contradict.

Kondo moves throughout the narrative between racial and gender identities and across the globe, and their multiraciality at once necessitates and enables their peripatetic and malleable existence. In the opening pages of "Geisha Man," Kondo indicates that they felt, from their earliest days, disconnected from their home and family due to their mixed-race heritage: "My mother was Japanese . . . and her husband was a samurai. . . . I couldn't know why he disliked me----my eyes were slant and my skin was white. . . . my fathers [sic] name I once knew--his face I never saw."[68] While Kondo does not provide much detail about their childhood, it is clear that they longed for the sight of their father's face and that their mother's husband exhibited disdain for the light skin that father bestowed upon them. These conditions make Kondo unhappy enough to run away and become an actor in Osaka. This decision is thrust upon Kondo, but once they have departed home, they begin to enact control over their fate and their self-presentation, remaking themself according to their own pleasures and desires. In escaping home and the policing of racial purity, they are also able to liberate themselves from gender fixity. While Kondo refers to themself as a "son" in the opening pages of the manuscript, they choose to perform in Osaka as a "maiden" and soon begin engaging in erotic encounters with men while dressed as a woman.[69] Kondo is at once highly effective and highly vulnerable in their performance as a maiden:

many men had bid for me for I was the loveliest maid of all--but--they
never stayed after they found I was--a man--many kisses--on the eyelids lips
and throat until they saw that I was--God--and they were shamed--would
tell no one--and that was good--were shamed--and that was right--one
should be ashamed before God.[70]

As Kondo relates the successes and traumas involved in these encounters,
their loveliness as a maid and the men's anger, they also insist upon their
own status as a "god," a rhetoric upon which Kondo relies repeatedly to
highlight their capacity to make and remake themself. The men Kondo
encounters treat their gender expression as a shameful mode of deception,
but Kondo retains a godlike sense of power due to their capacity for self-
fashioning, asserting that it is, in fact, these men who should feel ashamed
as they come up against the enormous creative faculties of a deity.

Despite this emerging sense of power, Kondo remains haunted by lack,
by the desire to "meet Gods [sic] father . . . [their] mothers [sic] lover."[71]
This emerges as the central rhythm of the narrative, as Kondo celebrates
the manner in which their detachment from family enables radical forms
of freedom and self-determination yet nevertheless pines for contact with
their biological kin, for a sense of rootedness and connection. They come
into contact with their father for the first time during their time in Osaka.
One evening, amidst the lanterns and shrill music and the bustle of the
crowd, a man with "strongly chiseled" features and "shapely" legs saunters
toward Kondo, and Kondo solicits the stranger: "my price is--I touched
the brass tag behind me--and stepped inside."[72] While Kondo remains at
this point unaware that this stranger is their father, the attraction they feel
toward this chiseled, shapely figure is profound and arresting. As the two
undress and get in bed together, the sense of who exactly is the god within
this encounter shifts and changes: "I sighed--his teeth hurt--pressed hard
on my lips and . . . I could feel the tenseness of him against me--and could
imagine the little hollow it caused in his buttocks--the thinned waist and
raised chest—the white muscles of his leg--prominent--God and I."[73]
Even prior to the realization of their biological kinship, Kondo's attraction
to Gale takes on a religious fervor, threating to overwhelm Kondo's sense
of their own power and sovereignty as self-fashioner. This stranger has, at
least for this moment, become the divinity. Kondo interrupts the exchange
by informing the fascinating and alluring stranger that they are "a man,"
causing the stranger to pause, place a purse on the table, and prepare to
depart.[74] Kondo asks for "a kiss to remember," and the scene suddenly
erupts in violence: "he called me vile names--raged--and was greater than
I than God or I---and slapped me--with the palm with the knuckles and
left--the taste of blood--of salt and iron."[75] In this moment of abjection,

Kondo places the violent stranger above themself and God, momentarily abandoning any sense of power or control. Kondo then examines the purse and finds a great deal of American money and the name of their father, "Gale Barrows." This is a scenario that emerges repeatedly in Nugent's fiction from this period – a mixed-race subject, divided from kin, encounters an estranged family member and is irresistibly drawn to this unknown relation.[76] This father or brother is at once so separate from the protagonist as to be unrecognizable, yet the parent or sibling nevertheless exercises a magnetic attraction. In "Geisha Man," this moment emerges as the central event for the protagonist, seeding a desire for a type of fulfillment that propels the rest of the story, a longing for union with their white father that perpetually undercuts Kondo's sense of godlike power.

Immediately following this encounter, Kondo departs from Osaka for Paris, and their restless nomadism seems to emerge directly from their newly stimulated desire for connection with their absent kin: "Walk a thousand times to and back and say one thousand prayers for I am in love with my mothers [sic] lover. I am the water weed drifting—finding no place of attachment."[77] Once Kondo leaves Japan, their mixed-race identity operates as a source of both pleasure and vulnerability. In Paris, they are subjected to the same modes of exoticization and fetishization Nugent scrutinized in his Salome fiction and drawings, and it is their multiraciality, in particular, that attracts the gaze of the men they encounter. An English lad, for example, likes "the slant of [Kondo's] grey eyes in a white skin."[78] Kondo, however, soon tires of this liaison and turns the exoticizing gaze to which they have been subjected outward, bringing into their house "a lad of very dark olive skin and dark brown hair."[79] Nothing satisfies, however: "For I am in love with my mothers lover. And Gale is a beautiful name."[80] Kondo, searching desperately for some form of fulfillment, spirals into insatiable, Decadent acquisition, filling their home with "vermilion lacquered chairs" upholstered in "black satin worked with designs of dragons," covering the walls in "lacquered silver and ... a tired overlay of gold" and the floors with "Japan copper tiles ... and rugs of ermine dyed vermilion or black."[81] They acquire countless books, Van Vechten, Huysmans, Beerbohm, Yeats, Verlaine, Rossetti, Pater, Goncourt, Wilde, and Baudelaire. But still nothing, not the Decadent interiors, the Decadent library, nor the Decadent, Orientalist sexual encounters satisfy: "For Gale is a beautiful name. Even when a very dark olive body tenses against mine—, Gale is a beautiful name."[82] Wrestling with this lack and the destabilization of their sovereignty, as longing for the white father threatens to overtake them entirely, they decide to "create a *new* God," whom they christen "Pulcredo," with the head of a man, the body of a horse, and hooves of blue porcelain.[83] Yet another chance encounter with Gale on the streets of Paris reveals that this new God threatens perpetually to collapse into Gale, into the longing for the white father that has been guiding Kondo's existence thus far: "It was under a lamp that I first saw him—Gale in Paris. My knees became weak. I approached him. What could I say to him. I must be careful of the porcelain hoofs. I tried to speak to him but my throat was filled with fears."[84] So overcome with desire for their father, Kondo is unable to speak, and the reunion is aborted.

The eternally restless and perpetually mobile Kondo then departs for New York, where they are again able to remake and remold their identity, and they begin to identify once more as a deity: "In my veins runs the blood of a city. Truly I am God."[85] Kondo notes that they continue to be spectacularized as racially other, and this treatment leads them to align themselves with the members of the Harlem Renaissance: "Because I was looked upon strangely when dining or otherwise I became friendly with . . . many Negroes. . . . I became a 'New Negro.'"[86] In Harlem, they are able to present effortlessly as a Black man (one of Kondo's suitors refers to them as a "colored boy"), drawing again upon their immense powers for self-fashioning to become "part and parcel" of the New Negro movement.[87] Kondo has numerous affairs, with men and women, and experiences tremendous success as one of "the most outstanding exponents of 'Negro Art,'" but they remain haunted by the spectre of the father: "I have seen perfection. Gale is a beautiful name. . . . I love Gale. I love Gale."[88] "Only Gale," they insist, "can calm the whirlpool."[89] The persistent memory of and desire for Gale constantly threatens to arrest from Kondo the position of deity, despite the remarkable control and self-possession they exhibit as they move freely across lines of race and gender.

When Kondo's much longed-for reunion with Gale finally occurs, Kondo has again refashioned themself, in this case for a masked ball, wearing a dress of silver poppies, transparent silver hose, silver slippers, and a skirt that "trailed in a silver moon a yard behind [them]."[90] Even at this apex of creative, godlike performance, Kondo's thoughts return to their father, to desire for acceptance and love from their white parent: "If only I had been born a woman! To dress in flowing silks and silver and colors always [. . .]. Maybe Gale would have loved me then."[91] At the party, Kondo dances, intoxicated by the beauty of the ball, until they turn and "coming toward us was Gale. [. . .] This, the man for whom I had created a God. This, the man whose face had remained an empty ache for a year."[92] The two dance, and Gale confesses that he has been living a

similarly nomadic existence, similarly haunted by the memory of their
night together: "I haven't been able to forget you ... even through
Marseilles. Paris. Budapest. Vienna ... Monte Carlo ... Cairo ... and
the rest."⁹³ Gale, who is "very drunk," asks Kondo to come live with him,
and they depart the party together.⁹⁴ Kondo seems to know almost
immediately that this union with the white father for whom they have
so longed cannot be entirely simple or satisfying: "My one instinct was
proud—to scorn this pseudo-love visited on me in a moment of pique. My
other instinct was to accept this gift, however false, with intense gratitude
and profound humility—to accept this semblance of my strongest
desire."⁹⁵ Kondo understands this communion with their father from
the first as a "semblance" and a form of "pseudo-love." Nevertheless,
Kondo accepts the ring Gale places on their finger, "his repetition of the
statement that we were married 'in the sight of man and God.'"⁹⁶ Their
first night together is for Kondo overwhelming and frightening: "I did so
want to do the right thing. I did love Gale so!"⁹⁷ Kondo cries out to
Pulcredo and attempts to reassert sovereignty by remembering their capacity to create selves and divinities: "I made you God. Help me! Me—the
Maker of God."⁹⁸ Their haunting suspicion of the white father's pseudo-
love persists as Gale seems to oscillate between coldness and warmth, but
Kondo insists, "I was happy."⁹⁹

Kondo and Gale move immediately from this fraught suturing of their
fragmented relationship into a highly conventional mode of domesticity,
engaging in an almost excessive performance of heteronormative bliss.
Gale purchases clothes for his wife, and they entertain together: "dinners
in large dining rooms, with Gale proud to exhibit me. I was always the
most chic woman in the room."¹⁰⁰ However, "as the months passed, Gale
became more distant .... God made Gale normal and Gale was only
decent. [...] I hated to kiss Gale and discover him in some little gesture of
disgust or boredom."¹⁰¹ The love of the white father proves to be unsatisfying and inadequate. The story draws to a very Decadent conclusion, as
Kondo, like Dorian, like Des Esseintes, finally finds the long pursued
transgression inadequate and must continue moving and searching for new
pleasures, new sensations. They decide finally to depart and to leave
behind an artifact that betrays the nature of their relation to one another:
"a photograph—the picture of a handsome American youth of sixteen or
seventeen—where he could see its inscription, where he could read, 'For
Yetsin (Gale), to keep my place while I'm away.' [...] I would hurt him—
hurt him for standing in my life like a stone and steel phallus hard and gray
against a happy sky."¹⁰² Kondo finally comes to feel anger about the

manner in which this longing for contact with their white kin has come to stand like a stone, like a god within their life. They cry out again to Pulcredo, "I would kill myself," but they follow almost immediately with the statement, "Always leave a dream unfinished. [...] Because if ever one should finish a dream, one would be dead."[103] Much like "Smoke, Lilies and Jade," which closes with Alex choosing to dwell in perpetual Paterian openness, with the words "to be continued," Kondo's story remains unfinished as they move from the dissatisfying home life they have constructed with Gale back into the city, back into the crowds, to continue, godlike, shifting and changing: "And with each step *a part of me dies*. Gods die. Even gods."[104] While the goal that propelled the entire narrative was attained, found dissatisfactory, and discarded, one is left with the sense that Kondo will continue their malleable existence, fashioning new selves to succeed in new cities with new loves.

In "Geisha Man," Nugent emphasizes the extent to which Kondo experiences multiraciality as a form of detachment. This detachment from kin offers a sense of pleasure, a sense of difference and distance across which Kondo's desire can travel so that they can experience their father as someone truly separate from and different from themselves. In Nugent's Decadent narrative, that sense of difference is eroticized. Incest fantasy operates here as a mode for figuring the desire for union with kin who do not feel like or look like kin. That sense of difference also enables Kondo's radical freedom as a chameleon of race and gender. Their dissimilarities from their mother, their father, and their mother's husband mean they can move from city to city across the globe, remaking themselves within each new context and passing across forms of racial and gender presentation. They can be a god, a maker of selves. The fact that Kondo's status as deity is perpetually threatened by the alternative god that is Gale, however, belies an aching sense of something missing. Detachment from kin engenders freedom as well as a sense of lack, a desire for union with absent kin. It is significant, however, that within Nugent's narrative, the absent relation is the white father, and reunion with that father proves to be fundamentally dissatisfying.

"Geisha Man" also negotiates the concept of mixed-race identity at the levels of style and form, and Nugent planned for this manuscript, once published, to embody on a material level Kondo's turn from whiteness. However, while the reader must wait until the story's conclusion for the pursuit of whiteness to be abandoned by its protagonist, Nugent's vision for the print version of "Geisha Man" would have allowed the text, from the moment the reader cracked its cover, to revel in the proliferation of color, in the juxtaposition of hues, in the manner in which contrast alters the manner one perceives pigments. Nugent imagined for the manuscript an intoxicating and vibrant future in which each page would be a different color printed in ink of a different hue: violet ink on canary paper, blue ink on heavy cream, crimson ink on white, white ink on black moiré paper, lemon yellow paper with sky blue ink, yellow rose paper with silver ink, mauve ink on pearl, bronze on green. This projected art book would mimic the riot of eroticized color present within the text at the level of content. Kondo announces that they see "life thru the parted iridescence of peacock feathers," and, though they are perpetually propelled forward by desire for their white father, the true pleasure in the text emerges from Kondo's eye for color, for the manner in which olive skin appears silver under a red light, for the "many tinted shadow of the stained glass window etched on the black of the floor."[105] Many of Nugent's works are similarly saturated in a Decadent profusion of wild, shifting, luxurious color. The queer dream sequence in "Smoke, Lilies and Jade," for example, finds its hero moving through "a field of blue smoke and black poppies and red calla lilies" as he finds his way first to Beauty's "strong white legs" and then Melva's "small feet olive-ivory."[106] Another unpublished manuscript at the Beinecke, "Half High," similarly concerned with divided mixed-race families finding their way back to one another, provides a key to the political valence of Nugent's deep investment in rich color. "America," Nugent notes in an introductory epistle to the story, "is White – and white is the absence of all color."[107] While many of Nugent's visual works mimic Beardsley's black and white aesthetic, his literary works insist on the presence and the significance of an infinite range of shifting colors brought into startling contact with one another.[108] The Decadent cataloging of shades, tints, and dyes, echoing *Dorian Gray*'s eleventh chapter awash in a profusion of brilliantly hued gems and textiles as well as the wild enumeration of artificial hues in *À Rebours*, allows Nugent to repopulate America with kaleidoscopic pigmentation and to insist, in a Decadent vein, on the superiority of ever-shifting color to whiteness. As Caroline Goeser has noted, Nugent's works often "satirized presumptions about mixed race identity in order to dismantle the fixity of racial identity," and, as J. Edgar Bauer argues, he conceived of race as an "inexhaustible continuum."[109] In stark contrast with the blacks and whites of his drawings of the 1920s, his literary works of this period, which often focus on mixed-race subjects, are drawn to intricate shading, peacock feathers, tints that shift in the light, insisting on color as infinite and overwhelming, almost incomprehensible in its complexity.[110]

This sense of color as infinitely complex is tied to the way Nugent conceptualizes mixed-race identity in his works of this period. Desire across difference appeals to Nugent, not as a mode of increasing amalgamation, of moving toward a future so hybrid that distinction disappears, but as a method for propagating variation. His is not a progressive scenario that looks toward a future in which racial difference is eliminated. His Decadent perspective centers the production of ever-more subtle hues that emerges from racially diverse kinship structures. *Gentleman Jigger*, a novel Nugent composed during this period, articulates this vision of ever-proliferating mixed-race identities, delineating complex family trees and the children that emerge from desire across difference, "artistically tinted," with "ecru" or "muddy" skin, auburn hair, "blond Negros," women with "light brown complexion" and "silky hair."[111] He is careful, in *Gentleman Jigger*, to acknowledge ideologies of colorism, holding up for ridicule the Nugentesque protagonist Stuartt, whose initial response to Raymond, a figure based upon Wallace Thurman, emerges from his "chauvinistic upbringing."[112] Upon meeting Raymond, Stuartt decides his new acquaintance is "too black," an assessment he almost immediately reconsiders as he experiences "revulsion at his own retrograde thinking" and returns to Raymond to "apologize for his thoughts."[113] Throughout the novel, Nugent skewers Stuartt's anti-Blackness, his desire to occupy the top of the "sepia-social ladder," subjecting his own interest in multiraciality to deep criticism. This extensive self-criticism, when integrated with his Decadent investment in kaleidoscopic color, allowed him to get somewhere new in his thinking about mixed-race identity, to move away from a progressive vision of increasingly tempered difference toward a privileging of distinctions, contrasts, and gradations. He departs from conventional multiracial discourse in his eager anticipation of ever-more colorful and complex futures, and "Geisha Man," once published, would have resembled this political horizon, a small textual resistance to the aversion to color Nugent associated with American white supremacy.

"Geisha Man" is made from Decadence, from Decadence's color and eroticism, from Salome's dances and Wildean Orientalism, from Paterian mobility and fin-de-siècle modes of sexual and gender dissidence. Nugent makes from these materials, however, something distinct and different, a brand of Harlem Decadence that repurposes these raw materials so they speak to racialization, mixed-race identity, and the rupture of Black familial structures in the United States. The arguments Nugent makes within "Geisha Man" only emerge clearly when the manuscript is placed within the web of Decadent visions and revisions Nugent wove in the

1920s and 1930s, and making sense of each of the points within this web of signification requires a broader engagement with Nugent's deep interest in Decadence during this period. Working with this material presents a set of challenges, requiring the disinterring of material from archives and conversation across national boundaries as well as boundaries of periodization. However, making "Geisha Man" meaningful in these ways illuminates the attractions Decadence might have held for queer writers of color in the early twentieth-century United States and the manner in which the Decadent representation of queer forms of kinship could perform crucial political functions for Black subjects in the early twentieth century. Reading the manuscript within this context allows us to see the long durée of Decadence as well as the work Decadence performed within the Harlem Renaissance, engendering new models for conceptualizing color, difference, and multiraciality.

CHAPTER 6

Hallowed Incest
Eric Gill, Indian Aesthetics, and Queer Catholicism

Figure 6.1   Eric Gill, *Madonna and Child*, 1912–13. William Andrews Clark Memorial
Library, University of California, Los Angeles.
Reproduced courtesy of the William Andrews Clark Memorial Library, University of California, Los
Angeles.

In June 1913, the Decadent poets Michael Field (Katharine Bradley [1846–1914] and Edith Cooper [1862–1913]) wrote to the modernist sculptor Eric Gill to thank him for a small statuette, *Madonna and Child* (1912–13), that had been sent to them after they admired a plaster cast from the same plasticine original in the home of their friend William Rothenstein (Figure 6.1). Though they acknowledge that "early French Madonnas have smiled freakishly as [his] creation," they state that the statuette seems to them "more of the East than of the Church," with a "Chinese forthrightness in dealing with a religious subject, a squareness of imagination that takes one Eastward, where belief is too calm to own to any vagueness of emotional appeal."[1] They note the warmth and corporeality in Gill's depiction of the Madonna and child: "Feeling is of the very essence of religion – that your figurine expresses solidly – with the sparseness of the fundamental art in the giver of food & the vivid joy & vivid love of the little mouth that has received the gift from the breast."[2] They seem to feel that Gill's work stresses Christ's body, his hunger, and Mary's emotions, her maternity, in a manner that is "solid" and "sparse" rather than ethereal. This is, in their eyes, a highly embodied form of Catholic worship that accentuates the fleshliness of both the Virgin and child, a mode of representation that, to them, speaks with an "Eastern" inflection.

While they note that they are strangers to Gill, they seem to believe that their shared status as artists and converts to Catholicism grants them the right to speak frankly and with a certain degree of intimacy about his art and their common faith. They "cannot write Dear Sir," they insist, so they open the letter with the salutation "Artist to artist," and they close by acknowledging that they have engaged in "frank speaking" around the topic of the figurine.[3] The letter is strikingly familiar. Bradley and Cooper congratulate Gill "that the best thing that can arrive to one by God's grace has been brought to [him] by that mysterious agency of godhead." They wish that he may "be as happy & sustained as [they] have been through the heaviest trial!" And they express the hope that Gill's art might "give to the Church what it so needs, reality of beauty in its images" and that the Church might "give to [his] art its own true unction!"[4] As fellow converts, fellow artists, they feel that they may converse freely and openly with Gill about the matter of faith as well as his artistic practice, as they are, though they have never met, deeply linked through their common religion.

I would like to use this strange letter and the figurine it describes as a starting point from which to initiate a reconsideration of Gill's aesthetic practice as well as his approach to kinship. Michael Field locates in Gill's work a devout Catholicism with an "Eastern" inflection, a highly embodied "freakishness" and "forthrightness" that they find immensely appealing. And they seem to feel that their shared status as artists and Catholic converts unites them and places them together within a community of dissident devotion. What they see in Gill is exactly what I wish to foreground. Michael Field's strange yet astute reading of this image of the *Madonna and Child* highlights Gill's sexual dissidence, his integration of "Eastern" and Catholic aesthetics, and his fleshly approach to the divine. Noting that his work appears to be "of the East," they gesture toward his relationship to the Indian and Egyptian sculptural traditions with which he was engaging at the time, a relationship at once Orientalist and cosmopolitan, emerging simultaneously from a fetishistic vision of "the East" as sensual and exotic and an authentic desire for knowledge of Indian and Egyptian art history. In addition, the manner in which this image circulated demonstrates Gill's connection to a Decadent and sexually dissident strain of Catholicism as well as the cosmopolitan aesthetic vision that Michael Field claims registers so clearly in the image itself. Copies of the original sculpture cast in bronze belonged to the Ceylonese art historian Ananda Coomaraswamy and to Wilde's literary executor and friend Robert Ross, who presented the work to the Johannesburg Art Gallery.[5] Plaster copies were sold to William Rothenstein (for himself and for Michael Field) and to the Meynells, a Catholic family with strong ties to the aestheticism of the 1890s, and plaster copies of a very similar sculpture from the same period, *Madonna and Child, Suckling* (1913), were bought by Marc-André Raffalovich and John Gray, two Catholic converts with connections to the Decadence of the fin de siècle.[6] While Gill is often thought of as a "distinctly heterosexual" figure with a circumscribed and highly localized vision, during the 1910s, he affiliated himself with a group of authors and artists whose nonnormative sexual identities were deeply intertwined with their Catholic religious identity, and he exhibited a tremendous thirst for information about global artistic practices, frequently writing to Ananda Coomaraswamy and engaging extensively with Indian art.[7] Though recent work on Gill has tended to represent him as a provincial paterfamilias, one who wished to withdraw from the world into a fantasy rural English pastoral, whose incestuous relationships with his family members amount to an amplification of patriarchal ideology with a stress on the ownership of women and the exaggeration of conventional masculinity, this figurine along with Michael Field's reading of it forces us to understand Gill and his kinship practices within a queer and transnational context.[8]

Reading Gill through Michael Field's eyes and alongside the work of their circle enriches our understanding of aesthetic history and queer history, allowing us to see the manner in which fin-de-siècle aesthetics remained present within the modernist moment and, in addition, providing insight into the manner in which the sexual dissidence of the 1890s informed highly disruptive forms of sexual radicalism in the twentieth century. In addition, just as seeing Michael Field's Eric Gill allows for insight into the afterlife of Decadence during the modernist period, examining the manner in which these aestheticist connections engendered transnational engagement for Gill allows us to perceive the role of transhistorical communication in the development of modernist forms of cosmopolitanism. Fin-de-siècle figures like William Rothenstein facilitated Gill's exposure to Indian art, Decadent writers like Michael Field admired and encouraged the evidence of this exposure in his artistic output, and his interest in Indian and Egyptian sculpture flourished while collaborating with Jacob Epstein on Wilde's tomb, a monument to the most significant figure associated with late-Victorian Decadence. Foregrounding this web of connections brings to light Gill's complex historical positioning as well as the manner in which his ties to Decadence opened into a cosmopolitan engagement with Indian and Egyptian aesthetic traditions.

Nevertheless, despite the fact that Gill's approach to kinship is informed by his openness to nonnormative sexual practices and wide-ranging aesthetic traditions, his practices are not, in the end, just nor fundamentally divorced from the power structures that inhere within the traditional patriarchal family. If anything, his experiments intensify the problems within that structure. Though I am working here to situate Gill's vision of desire and his aesthetic practices within a larger cosmopolitan and sexually dissident ethos, I am doing so in order to consider the potential for abuse and injustice when revising affiliation within this framework. Since the publication of Fiona MacCarthy's biography of Gill, which revealed that he had sex with his sisters and sexually abused his daughters and his dog, it is Gill's sexual practices that have attracted the most attention and caused the most discomfort in discussions of his work and career. While the UK's Survivors Trust, as well as the National Association for People Abused in Childhood, has called for the removal of Gill's sculptures from the façade of the BBC, his work remains on display there and at Westminster Cathedral and the League of Nations. As his work continues to be so public and prominent, his ideas about kinship and desire should be directly addressed, as they are central to his larger vision. In addition, reading his vision of divine eroticism within the Decadent context from which it emerged highlights the extent to which the dissident Decadent ethos, which we tend to associate with a more progressive sexual politics, could be repurposed and implemented within a program of abuse. This deserves to be considered, as engaging only with those elements of queer history that we find ethical results in a flattening of our understanding of the complex and divergent directions in which radical sexual practice moved in the late nineteenth and early twentieth centuries. Situating Gill's work and career within this context allows us to see how he transmuted the influences of Indian sculpture and a late-Victorian strain of sexually dissident faith into a startling, selfish, and highly disruptive approach to kinship. Highlighting the connections between Gill's vision of sexuality and the queer cosmopolitan networks from which it emerged forces us to acknowledge that the contestation of heteronormative social relations on the part of queer subjects working within a Decadent and cosmopolitan tradition did not always result in just or liberatory practices. It can, and it did in Gill's case, result in injustice and abuse. If I have worked in this book to consider the manner in which Decadent modernists made kinship new in the early twentieth century, I also want to be careful to acknowledge that new does not always mean better. Gill's approach to reformulating kinship is underwritten by an ethos from which we tend to expect positive results. Working from within a queer cosmopolitan framework, he nevertheless settled upon a set of practices that privileged his own pleasures and freedom above the wellbeing of the subjects with whom he lived in community. While looking closely at these practices inspires discomfort, I want to nevertheless insist that they require acknowledgment in a responsible history of the networks I am tracing within this project, as they speak to the broad range of outcomes that the Decadent undoing of conventional kinship might engender.

"Completely Enfolded in the Everlasting Arms": Eric Gill and Queer Catholicism

Critical treatments of Gill from the last forty years have often highlighted his preoccupation with sexuality. Malcolm Yorke's *Eric Gill: Man of Flesh and Spirit* (1981), for example, foregrounds Gill's attempts to fuse the erotic and the divine, and Anthony Hoyland's *Eric Gill: Nuptials of God* (1994) similarly stresses the eroticism of Gill's work, reading his art as a "hymn to the phallus."[9] MacCarthy's biography, with its scandalous revelations concerning Gill's discussions of incest and bestiality in his diaries, has had a tremendous impact on the field, forcing most critics who approach his work to at least acknowledge the forms of sexual experimentation and abuse in which he was engaged while producing his most well-known works. Previous biographers, such as Robert Speaight, had consulted the diaries, but they had chosen to suppress Gill's frank discussion of his affair with his sister Gladys, his abuse of his daughters Elizabeth and Petra, and his discovery "that a dog will join with a man."[10] MacCarthy speculates that previous biographers' decision to gloss over these events and behaviors had to do with their Catholicism and their wish to "present Gill as a Catholic artist and Catholic thinker whose way of work and worship held together with a kind of sweet reasonableness."[11] Her disclosures concerning Gill's sexual practices certainly disrupted this vision of Gill, leading to calls for the dismantling of his Stations of the Cross at Westminster Cathedral and his sculpture of Prospero and Ariel at the BBC Headquarters.[12]

As much as critics such as MacCarthy, Hoyland, and Yorke stress Gill's unconventional ideas about desire and the family, they nevertheless disregard evidence that might counter or complicate their representation of Gill as "heterosexist."[13] Yorke and Hoyland acknowledge Gill's intense interest in the male sexual organ, but they engage in complex critical negotiations in order to integrate this element of his work into a portrait of Gill as "distinctly heterosexual."[14] Hoyland argues that Gill treats the penis as an "object ... of vanity" and that his "cult of the phallus is the product of ... masculine narcissism."[15] Yorke similarly associates Gill's interest in the male form with "a certain vanity about his own physique" and insists that he "never became permissive, or even tolerant, by modern standards in his attitudes towards ... homosexuality."[16] Particularly striking is MacCarthy's decision to exclude from her biography evidence concerning Gill's sexual contact with men in the collection at the William Andrews Clark Memorial Library while calling previous authors to task for whitewashing Gill's biography. MacCarthy does cite the moment in Gill's diary in which he describes the "shape of the head of a man's erect penis" as "very excellent in the mouth."[17] However, she underplays Gill's interest in same-sex desire. On the whole, critics seem to accept Gill's later statement in the 1931 text *Clothes* that homosexuality is "the ultimate disrespect both to the human body and to human love" as a static and unchanging position on the concept of love between men.[18]

The criticism on Gill, then, seems to be operating in a complex and conflicted manner, advertising itself as honest and unabashed in its treatment of sexual content while suppressing or disregarding material that indicates that Gill was, at moments, erotically drawn to men. In 1913, inspired by his reading of Havelock Ellis, Gill composed a set of case studies concerning his own sexual development and asked his wife Ethel to do the same. Each wrote one narrative about their heterosexual experiences ("He & She") and another about their same-sex experiences ("He & He" and "She & She"). MacCarthy makes notes of "the sex-confessional manuscript *He and She*" in her biography, but she chooses not to mention Gill's "He & He," which is contained in the same bound notebook and discusses his sexual experiences with men explicitly and in detail.[19] In "He & He," Gill notes that when he was a child, he engaged in sexual contact, including fellatio, with other schoolboys. He states he often dreamt of himself naked before a group of sailors, performing various sexual acts with them, and fell in love with older boys at school. He recalls a cousin with whom he would practice mutual masturbation and remembers watching his brother orgasm with wonder. He notes that he found other boys' attraction to women and interest in pictures of nude women incomprehensible and states that his fantasies tend to dwell on visions of erect penises. He concludes the narrative by noting that these desires have persisted in his adult life, and he has engaged in affairs with men that have at times lasted for several years. He defends his practices as part of a healthy sexuality and his erotic friendships as beautiful. Gill does not cast his desire for men as a negligible phase within his sexual development. He instead describes his relationships with men as crucial to his wellbeing and central to his identity.[20] The sense of Gill's sexuality that emerges here is far more fluid than the aggressively heterosexual portraits painted by Yorke, Hoyland, and MacCarthy.

Gill's decision to create a document recording his sexual experiences with men two months after he converted to Catholicism seems noteworthy.[21] While MacCarthy's biography emphasizes the contradictions between Gill's Catholicism and "his urge to experiment with social conventions," the two are in fact linked and in accord with one another.[22] Gill's sexual practices need to be understood within a queer context, as motivated by a queer desire to undermine stable ideologies governing sexuality and affiliation and as occurring in conversation with the queer Catholicism of the turn of the century.[23] Catholicism's status as a dissident faith attracted Gill, and his initiation into the faith occurred in relationship to figures with ties to a particularly queer strain of Catholicism.[24] During this phase of his career when he was most actively engaged in sexual experimentation and theorizing, he was drawn to a religious practice that Marion Thain, drawing on the work of Ellis Hanson, has referred to as a "container" for sexual dissidence and a community whose sexual dissidence was articulated through their practice of that faith.[25]

Soon after his conversion and the composition of "He & He," Gill came to know two figures with strong ties to late-Victorian aestheticism and the queer Catholicism of the 1890s, Marc-André Raffalovich and his partner John Gray. Gray, who is often thought to have been the inspiration for Wilde's Dorian Gray, wrote Decadent poetry in the 1890s and had been ordained as a Catholic priest in 1901. Raffalovich, a French writer who had composed Decadent poetry as well as a defense of Uranian love in the 1890s, had converted to Catholicism and moved to Edinburgh to be with Gray as he served as the parish priest at St. Peter's Church. Gill first visited Raffalovich's home in 1914. Following this visit, Raffalovich wrote to express his pleasure at their developing friendship, setting the tone for an intimate and playful correspondence that continued for years: "It is a rare treat for me to find a roomy, spacious mind. I expect mine is more like a curio shop where one can pick up some bargains if one can stand the things one does not want."[26] He asked if he might drop "Mr." from his salutations and inquired about the possibility of Gill completing a series of commissions for him. Gill responded that Raffalovich should "treat [him] with the utmost familiarity" and that he would be "delighted to execute" the requested commissions.[27] Only a few days later, Gill wrote again to Raffalovich, explaining his dire economic circumstances, and asked if he might assist him financially.[28] Raffalovich replied in the affirmative and promised to keep their situation confidential: "Let all this be between us and do not tell people, only your wife. It is fairer both to you and to me and should be so."[29] He gave the sculptor £100 as a gift and requested that Gill complete another £200 worth of work for him, encouraging him to take his time. During the next six years, Gill executed a series of sculptures for Raffalovich, as well as a portrait and a bookplate. He became increasingly intimate with the pair and received frequent visits from Gray at his home in Ditchling. Gill was in fact staying at Gray's home on the night that Raffalovich died in 1934.

Gill's intimacy with Gray and Raffalovich in the years immediately following his conversion ensured that he was aware from the first of the rich possibilities Catholicism offered for the braiding together of eroticism and faith. As Frederick Roden notes in his discussion of sexuality and religious faith in Victorian England, Catholicism was understood as "culturally queer" during this period and attracted figures like Raffalovich and Gray who found in Catholic rhetoric concerning the longing for Christ a useful framework for the sublimated expression of same-sex desire.[30] Ellis Hanson argues, "Raffalovich and Gray both learned to master that slight and subtle shift of

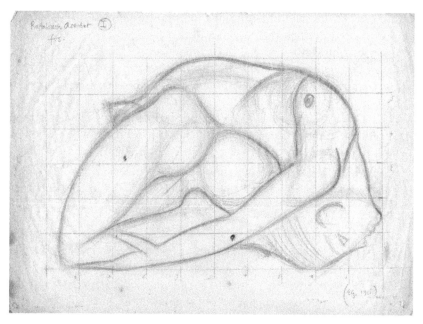

Figure 6.2   Eric Gill, *Sketch for Sculpture: Acrobat*, ca. 1915. William Andrews Clark
Memorial Library, University of California, Los Angeles.
Reproduced courtesy of the William Andrews Clark Memorial Library, University of California, Los
Angeles.

the lens by which sexual desire is re-envisioned as Christian or Platonic
agape."[31] In his *Uranisme et Unisexualité* (1896), Raffalovich "describes the
love of the virginal uranist for his 'young God, naked and bleeding, disfigured
and transfigured, wounded and wounding,'" and, in his translations of devo-
tional poetry, Gray "entertained a particular affection for the more homoerotic
and sensual of Catholic writers."[32] Gill's friendship with Raffalovich and Gray,
practitioners of what Raffalovich referred to as "sublime inversion," would have
exposed him to models for integrating Catholicism and sexual dissidence, and
his correspondence with and work for the pair reveals that he took great
pleasure in the erotic possibilities such an integration might offer.[33] The
sculptures he executed for Raffalovich revel in the beauty of the male form.
In 1915, he completed a sculpture of an *Acrobat* for Raffalovich. The location
of this sculpture is unknown, but the pencil sketches of the sculpture at the
Clark library depict a nude male figure resting on his back with his back arched
and his legs bent behind his back (Figure 6.2). In 1920, he completed a
similarly erotic treatment of the male form, a sculpture of Saint Sebastian with

Figure 6.3   Eric Gill, *Saint Sebastian*, 1920. Tate Britain, London.
Digital photograph © Tate.

his hands behind his head and a long lean torso (Figure 6.3). In a letter to
Raffalovich, Gill notes, "You will be amused to hear that the study from which
I did the carving was made from myself in a mirror."[34] This sculpture, like the
Madonna & Child, linked Gill to a community of sexually dissident Catholics,

and, in addition, placed his own physique on display, thereby entering his body into an erotic exchange with queer Catholic men, surrendering his own form to their gaze. At times, Gill's fusion of the carnal and the divine could even exceed his sexually dissident patrons' sense of propriety. Gray once asked Gill to carve a small statue of a man weeping for his sins. The resultant sculpture, which was deemed too "fleshly," was displayed on Gray's mantel "shrouded from head to foot."[35]

Through Raffalovich and Gray, Gill came to know another figure linked to Decadent strains of queer Catholicism, Father Vincent McNabb. McNabb, confessor to Michael Field, was a Dominican priest with ties to the doctrine of Distributism as articulated by G. K. Chesterton and Hilaire Belloc, a doctrine Gill, with his previous interest in socialism, found immensely appealing. While preserving the concept of private property, Distributism insisted that property ownership should be distributed as widely as possible so each family and individual might have access to the means of production. McNabb also argued that Catholics should return to the land and exist on self-sustaining farms. McNabb and his thinking played a central role in the development of the utopian community in the Sussex countryside of which Gill was the center. Eric Gill, Hilary Pepler, Desmond Chute, and Joseph Cribb became lay tertiaries of the Order of St Dominic and founded a guild of Catholic craftsmen, the Guild of St Joseph and St Dominic, at Ditchling in Sussex. The Guild was meant to be "a religious fraternity for those who make things with their hands," and the members labored in their own workshops but attended chapel together and participated enthusiastically in the activities of rural life, such as keeping bees, making beer, and haymaking.[36] McNabb was frequently present at Ditchling in the 1910s and 1920s, taking Gill's confession and spending long days talking with him about the Catholic faith and the future of the Guild. This was the period in Gill's life and career when he was most open to and interested in radically experimental forms of connection, desire, and cooperation, and his diary demonstrates that he spent hours during this period speaking with McNabb about the Guild, aesthetics and labor, and Irish nationalism.[37] Gill's ideas about community, politics, and art were heavily inflected by McNabb, and he should be understood as one of the most crucial influences in the development of Gill's vision of affiliation during early decades of the twentieth century.

McNabb's intense closeness with and reverence for Michael Field indicates that Gill would have found in McNabb a progressive confessor comfortable speaking frankly to bohemian artists about their sexuality.

McNabb first met Cooper and Bradley in 1908, and his treatment of Cooper during their initial meeting was seemingly quite open and kind. Cooper reported that there was "no shyness" between them.[38] When Cooper insisted that "he must know broadly the truth if he [was] to be of help to [her]" and spoke to him "of the ancient wrong, of the wild sinning & wild penances-in-vain," he responded, "You have known Christ's Redeeming Love" and spoke "of all the apostles – sinners, traitors to their Lord, chosen to reveal Him."[39] He seems to have operated as a patient and accepting spiritual advisor to the pair. As Marion Thain notes, the two struggled with how to integrate their previous pagan aesthetic with their new faith, and this struggle is reflected in a palimpsest version of their volume *Wild Honey from Various Thyme* in which they pasted new Catholic poems over the most pagan verses. This volume was presented to McNabb in 1911 and, according to a letter Bradley wrote to John Gray, elicited his approval: "Now the Church has welcomed the Honey-book. Fr. Vincent *amazes* me."[40] They composed a lyrical, mystical preface to a collection of McNabb's sermons, *The Orchard Floor* (1911), that attempts a similar integration of their pagan and Catholic passions, comparing the "Spirit of Revelation" that might pass through McNabb's sermon fragments to the wind passing through leaves to form an oracle.[41] McNabb seems to have accepted their peculiar integration of ancient and Christian forms of devotion as well as their passion for each other. In an introduction to a posthumous collection of Michael Field's poetry, *The Wattlefold* (1930), he speaks admiringly of the intimacy between Cooper and Bradley:

> I was given a priest's entry to their home life. To have that rare privilege was to witness a fellowship in life and love all too rare if not indeed unique in the history of letters. The full self-effacement of each in the life and life's work of the other was to my way of thinking the essential drama from which the drama of their pen was kept alight. ... These two poets who elected to be known as one had achieved a unity which if Plato is to be believed, is the divinest attribute of the ... Maker of the Universe.[42]

McNabb read their partnership as a model of sublime inversion. He remained close with the pair during their illness and until their deaths in 1913 and 1914. Cooper was diagnosed with cancer in 1911. When Bradley was diagnosed with cancer two years later, she told only McNabb and John Gray.[43] McNabb wrote to his brother Laurence after Cooper's death that it had been a "privilege to know this gifted woman."[44] After Cooper died, Bradley moved to Hawkesyard Priory to remain close to McNabb and, according to Mary Sturgeon, spent one of her final afternoons reading to him the poetry of her deceased beloved.[45] On the day Bradley died, McNabb immediately noted her absence from the chapel in the morning and "had a sudden certainty of the end."[46] He "ran down the grassy slopes to the house" to find her "stretched on the floor of her room, dead."[47] This does not seem to have been a detached or conventional relationship between priest and penitent but an extremely intimate friendship.

As Gill's friend, McNabb would have operated as another strong link to an aestheticist tradition of Catholic sexual dissidence, and, as his confessor, he would have represented a tolerant listener accustomed to the frank discussion of nonnormative sexual practices, including same-sex desire and incest. Gill first met McNabb in June 1914, a few months before Bradley's death, and he was, at the time, as his diary indicates, engaged in a sexual relationship with his sister Gladys. McNabb moved, then, very quickly from serving as the confessor to a set of writers involved in an incestuous relationship to operating as the confidante of another artist engaged in similar sexual practices.[48] The "unity" of Bradley and Cooper's incestuous "fellowship" would have been quite fresh in McNabb's mind. It seems likely that McNabb exhibited the same kinds of permissiveness and understanding in his treatment of this new penitent as he had when speaking to Cooper of her "wild sinning."[49]

Michael Field's relationship, as well as the manner in which their "fellowship" was reverenced by McNabb, may have operated as points of reference during the later phases of Eric and Gladys's relations with one another. In 1929, Gladys and Eric rekindled their sexual relationship. Glady's first husband had died, she had divorced her second, and she was living in a small cottage with her daughter where Gill would frequently come to visit.[50] The Wattlefold was published the following year, and Gill would have been well aware of McNabb's approving description of the love between these two "princesses of English song."[51] Gill's "working library" is housed at the Clark Library and includes his copy of The Wattlefold. Did Gill recognize in Bradley and Cooper fellow practitioners of a radical form of sexual dissidence? As Kate Thomas argues, the incestuous nature of Bradley and Cooper's relationship has been politely avoided in much recent criticism.[52] But was it something Gill and his sister actively discussed? Perhaps they found comfort in McNabb's endorsement of Bradley's and Cooper's "fellowship in life and love."[53] Perhaps they saw in the fellowship between these two rebels who nevertheless received Christ's redeeming love a model of sexual dissidence that remained in contact with the divine.

The Catholic community with which Gill engaged in the teens and twenties exposed him to new ways of conceiving of kinship and desire. Catholicism itself could be said to enable a queer approach to kinship. The rhetoric of Catholicism certainly does something queer with familial language, undoing the stability of our understanding of what maternity is, of the division between fathers and sons, facilitating a series of substitutions and sublimations that blur and redefine kinship roles and the primacy of blood ties. Within his new community of Catholic sexual dissidents, Gill was surrounded by figures who drew upon this element of Catholic rhetoric in rethinking and remaking their own bonds with others, resolving their own nonnormative kinship inclinations by integrating their approach to affiliation with their faith. The biographies of figures like John Gray and Vincent McNabb frequently stress the manner in which their frustrated familial desires were rerouted and satisfied through contact with the divine. Jerusha McCormack argues that Gray, whose father was not sympathetic to his son's artistic aspiration, pursued his religious vocation with a "new hunger for acceptance by another, more adequate father."[54] Ferdinand Valentine similarly argues that McNabb's "frustrated yearning for a loving father" was resolved by turning to God.[55] The familial rhetoric of Catholicism facilitates escape from the discipline of the father through a turn to a gentler, more forgiving parental figure. And it allows for the blurring of boundaries between biological and divine connections. Valentine notes, for example, that "Father Vincent's loving reverence for his mother was the natural foundation for his profound and characteristic devotion to Our Blessed Lady."[56] Maternal love and religious adoration can be intertwined and exchanged for one another. Gray, Gill, and Michael Field drew upon this model of substitution in renaming and redefining their connections with friends and mentors. As Chris White notes, Bradley and Cooper chose to exclude "the language of blood relatives" from the vocabulary concerning their union, turning instead to classical scholarship and then the language of Catholicism to rename their "Sacred Relation."[57] Marion Thain argues that Bradley and Cooper chose to figure their relationship with their dog Whym Chow as a Holy Trinity in order to deal with repressed incest anxiety. According to Thain, their identification with the Father and the Son within that Trinity "is a familial identification that neutralises and legitimises the intense erotic bond between aunt and niece."[58] Raffalovich referred to himself as Gray's "father & mother," and Gill referred to McNabb and Father John O'Connor, another Dominican priest with close ties to the community at Ditchling, as his "spiritual father and mother."[59] Incestuous ties could be renamed as divine, same-sex desire and friendship remade as familial. The Catholicism with which Gill was engaging in the 1910s offered numerous alternative models of affiliation and allowed for the conceptualization of all manners of nonnormative kinship and sexuality.

Gill's interest in testing out new ways of conceiving of kinship could be understood then as an offshoot from his engagement with queer Catholicism, and his interest in incest in particular is an outgrowth of his more general interest in undoing conventional conceptions of desire and affiliation. During the 1910s and 1920s, when Gill was most actively engaged in violating the norms that govern the conceptualization of home, community, and desire, he was drawn to the sexual practices that most violently unsettle and redefine these concepts. While scholarship on Gill has struggled with how to integrate Gill "the public intellectual," who composed strident critiques of industrialism and founded a utopian community to withdraw from the evils of capitalist modernity, with Gill "the private man," who obsessively recorded the details of his sexual abuse of his daughters, the two personae emerge from the same set of impulses.[60] Gill's public activities, his turn away from the city, his founding of the community at Ditchling, his reorganization of home and work, arise from a desire to radically rethink what it is to be human in much the same way that his private activities do. His violation of the incest taboo, a taboo that is understood as "foundational to human social organization," constitutes a radical attack on the core of culture and civilization.[61] As Gayle Rubin and Judith Butler have argued, the incest taboo plays a crucial role in the stabilizing of kinship systems and gender roles.[62] If the incest taboo operates as the centerpiece of the gender system and the stability of kinship structures, the practice of incest could be understood as one of the most extreme forms of sexual dissidence. Butler has raised questions about how the incest taboo demonstrates the persisting interest in recognizing certain social arrangements and not others as legitimate love. When we respond to the questioning of the incest taboo by exclaiming, "But it is the law," Butler asks, might we be "[resolving] by theological means the concrete dilemmas of human sexual arrangements that have no ultimate normative form?"[63] Gill's sexual experiments refuse the boundaries delineating legitimate and illegitimate love and call into question the most fundamental laws governing the expression of desire.

This is not to say that incest is necessarily destabilizing or oppositional. As Elizabeth Barnes notes in her introduction to *Incest and the Literary Imagination* (2002), while some critics have argued that incest transgresses normative kinship relations, others have argued that "incest is an *effect* of these sexual and familial norms, a patriarchal privilege of particular (read: white, middle class) nuclear family lives."[64] Fiona MacCarthy reads Gill's abuse of his daughters in this light, relating it to his "persona of domestic potentate, the notion of owning all the females in his household."[65] Gill's vision of gender was certainly retrograde. While the community at Ditchling was politically and economically radical, the division of labor was highly gendered, with the women functioning as domestic support staff, enabling the men's creative pursuits. Count Harry Kessler suggested Gill's carving *Votes for Women* (1910), which depicts a woman astride a man engaging in sexual intercourse, might be "an advertisement for the Anti-Votes for Women League," showing "how woman will sit upon man once she has the vote."[66] Gill frequently argued that women's proper role was the rearing of families, and his pamphlet *Birth Control* (1919) argues that contraception is a sin and that the "natural object and result of sexual intercourse is conception."[67] These conservative gender politics must be understood as inflecting his approach to sexual experimentation and his abuse of his daughters. Gill's extensive practice of incest, with his daughters Petra and Elizabeth and his sisters Gladys and Angela, might also be seen as further evidence of his provinciality, a refusal of exogamy and difference and the threat of miscegenation. However, it is necessary, if Gill's ideas about kinship and desire are to be properly understood, to view his interest in incest through the framework of his broader theories of desire and community. When read in light of his connections with queer Catholicism and the sexual experiments he conducted outside of his biological family, his interest in incest emerges as part of a larger attempt to abolish all boundaries and norms governing the expression of desire.

This tendency to radically contest the most fundamental norms governing sexual arrangements is similarly reflected in Gill's "experiments" with animals. If the incest taboo is, as Lévi-Strauss argues, "the fundamental step because of which, by which, but above all in which, the transition from nature to culture is accomplished," the taboo against bestiality might be understood as similarly foundational, "maintaining the ontological boundary between human and animals."[68] While rethinking affiliation between humans, Gill also grew curious about testing and reconsidering the division between human and nonhuman animals. At Ditchling, Gill seems to have become increasingly fascinated with the sexuality of nonhuman animals. In 1915, he recorded in his diary that he had watched a doe and buck rabbit copulate twice.[69] In a 1916 entry, he notes that he had examined his semen alongside a spaniel dog's under a microscope.[70] Gill brings to his investigation of nonhuman animals and their bodies a scientific curiosity as well as an apparent desire to set up equivalences as much as to establish difference. In a 1929 entry (that has been struck through), Gill records "experiments with dog in eve."[71] A few entries later, he states that he "continued experiment with dog after & discovered that a dog will join with a man."[72] Bestiality, like incest, violates the limits of conventional subject positions. While incest may contest the stability of kinship structures and the gender system, bestiality contests the structures that define what it is to be human. To transgress these boundaries is to call into question some of the most fundamental elements of our understanding of identity. Gill's sexual practices in the 1910s and 1920s are united by a desire to attack at their very core those concepts of identity that seem most inviolable and unquestionable. And again, these practices should be understood as of a piece with Gill's drive toward rethinking community and the concept of affiliation, his vision for the Guild, his economic thinking, and his ties to queer Catholicism. What is troubling and disappointing is the fact that, while a desire to reconceptualize basic human activities, such as love, work, desire, and home, unites his work and activities during this period, many of the experiments inspired by these desires result in abuse and the disregard of the involved subjects' capacity to consent. His violations of sexual norms indicate that as much as these norms might delimit and discipline, they can also provide forms of protection for disempowered or silenced subjects. Gill's radical impulses result at times in appealing experiments like the Guild, but his attempts at complete liberation and freedom just as often result in exploitation and disregard for the freedom of others.

As startling and strange as Gill's behavior during this period might seem, members of the queer Catholic community with which Gill was affiliated were engaged in similarly radical experiments concerning the process of affiliation. Michael Field's devotion to their dog Whym Chow called into question the distinction between human and nonhuman animals, placing the dog in a series of erotic and kinship positions and undoing the fixity of the boundary between species. Ruth Vanita argues that Whym Chow served as an erotic proxy for Bradley and Cooper.[73] Jill Ehnenn's reading of Michael Field's elegiac poetry stresses the poets' creation of an "eroticized narrative of their beloved dog as conduit for queer desire and interwoven subjectivity."[74] Frederick Roden asserts that their "devotion to their 'son,' a progeny who was not biologically procreated," allowed the two women to "come to God not as brides of Christ but as mothers and lovers of their dog."[75] Positing Whym Chow as proxy, conduit, son, and lover, Bradley and Cooper demonstrate their intense desire to cross species

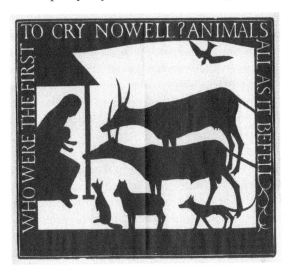

Figure 6.4   Eric Gill, *Animals All*, 1916. William Andrews Clark Memorial Library,
University of California.
Reproduced courtesy of the William Andrews Clark Memorial Library, University
of California, Los Angeles.

lines in the expression of intimacy. While readers have often struggled with how seriously to take their impassioned statements concerning their dog, their wish to be united with him can be linked conceptually to their interest in collaboration and their dissident approach to desire. Bradley and Cooper, like Gill, were drawn to ways of working and loving that necessitated a dramatic shift in the conception of identity and the boundary between self and other. Their queer approach to affiliation also seemed to facilitate a dissident understanding of the kinship between human and nonhuman animals. And, as Roden and Thain have noted, Michael Field's devotion to their dog is also bound up with their Catholicism. Catholicism's queer approach to kinship, its tendency to substitute and sublimate kinship positions and allow earthly contact to stand in for divine connection, also allowed them to translate their intimacy with their pet into a form of worship. In their poems about Whym Chow, the dog is compared to the Holy Spirit and to Christ. Loving Whym Chow became a way to love one another and a way to love God.

Gill's engraving *Animals All* (1916) similarly braids humans and animals together at the site of worship, representing animals adoring the Christ child (Figure 6.4). Depicting the familiar scene of the manger, Gill places a particular stress on the animals' attentiveness to Christ. They turn deliberately to look at him as he reaches his arms out to their outstretched faces. The animals are endowed here with sentience and the capacity to recognize divinity and participate in worship. During this particularly experimental phase in Gill's career, as he went "back to the land" and tried his hand at farming, raising pigs, and beekeeping, the presence of animals was crucial to the utopian scene he was working to establish. They were a central part of the holy community he established at Ditchling. With this belief in the essential divinity of the sexual act and his insistence that it allowed for the crossing of boundaries between subjects, it was perhaps unavoidable that his practices would take on a more sexual valence than Michael Field's.[76] However, in the case of Gill as well as in the case of Michael Field, the radical questioning of kinship structures engendered by queer Catholicism opened into the contestation of the fundamental otherness of nonhuman animals.

While at first glance the aesthetics of Eric Gill and Michael Field could not seem more different from one another, Bradley and Cooper's work, their thinking, and the members of their community provide an incredibly useful framework for understanding Gill's thinking about kinship and desire in the 1910s and 1920s. Gill expressed deep admiration for their writing. In a 1914 letter to William Rothenstein, Gill thanked Rothenstein for sending him Bradley's *Mystic Trees* (1913)[77] and noted that he had also acquired Cooper's *Poems of Adoration* (1912).[78] The poetry has, he states, "the extraordinary atmosphere of a shrine," and "to read ten or more of the poems one after the other is to feel that you are ... in a place where precious things are ritually preserved & worshipped."[79] The poetry has for him a physicality. It places you somewhere and makes you feel as if you are coming into contact with divine things. Nevertheless, he notes, they seem "withdrawn from the mess and dirt of this admirable world." However, while their extraordinary nature places them above the material world, that same nature places them on intimate terms with Christ. The two poets are, he insists, "completely enfolded in the everlasting arms."[80] Their mysticality and ethereality place them in a highly embodied embrace with Christ. They are in his arms.

This element of Michael Field's work must have held great appeal for Gill, as his work in the 1910s and 1920s expresses intense enthusiasm for the idea of entering into true intimacy with Christ. In a letter to Rayner Heppenstall from the early 1920s, he actually describes conversion as a form of intercourse: "Joining the Church is not like joining the I.L.P. or the 3rd International. It's like getting married and, speaking analogically, we are fucked by Christ."[81] His *Nuptials of God* (1922) from the same

Figure 6.5   Eric Gill, *Nuptials of God*, 1922.
Reproduced courtesy of the National Galleries of Scotland. Bequeathed by Sir David Young Cameron,
1945.

period places a similar emphasis on the erotic valence of the relationship
between Christ and the faithful, showing Christ in the embrace of his
bride, the Roman Catholic Church (Figure 6.5). And his countless
sketches of a nude Christ on the cross lavish great attention on the
contours of Christ's body and the details of his genitalia. Recalling the
work Gill completed for Raffalovich, Gill's representations of a nude
Christ integrate a queer appreciation for the beauty of the male form with
desire for true contact with the divine. In conversation with queer
Catholicism, Gill developed a vision of faith that was highly eroticized,
embodied, and sexually dissident.

"More of the East than of the Church"

Gill's interest in turning the representation of eroticized bodies to religious
ends must also be understood in relationship to his engagement with

Indian art, which was in part initiated by William Rothenstein. Rothenstein operated as a node of contact between Gill and an array of transhistorical and transnational aesthetic influences. As Rupert Arrowsmith notes, Rothenstein's "home generally served as an unofficial nexus point for various artists, poets, and scholars."[82] The longevity of Rothenstein's career as well as the breadth of his contacts meant his home was a site where one was just as likely to encounter either Max Beerbohm or Roger Fry. While he introduced Gill to modernist artists, including Jacob Epstein and Lucien Pissarro, he was, of course, also a link to the 1890s and to late-Victorian Decadence. Bradley and Cooper first encountered the *Madonna and Child* statuette that they so adored in Rothenstein's home, and he actively encouraged Gill to think of himself in relationship to Michael Field, writing to him about the pair's Catholicism during the period when Gill had begun toying with the idea of converting: "Your own hankerings and longings for [some kind of traditional discipline] & your expressed interest in Roman Catholicism made me think of my friends the Michael Fields & the comfort & guidance they have been able to get from submitting themselves to a tradition of ritual."[83] Rothenstein sat at the point of tension between the Victorian and modernist in Gill's career, carrying his eye back to the aestheticism of the fin de siècle while pointing him forward to the emergent avant-gardism of the 1910s. In addition, he broadened the geographical boundaries of Gill's aesthetic. Rothenstein participated in the founding of the India Society in 1910, an organization that aimed to promote Indian fine arts to the British public, and he transmitted his enthusiasm for Indian art to Gill. He wrote to Gill during a trip to India that he wished that Gill were there with him to see the carvings of "archaistic figures of naked Gods & Goddesses" on the cliff below Gwalior Fort in Rajasthan.[84] Gill in turn wrote to Rothenstein in India to indicate that he agreed with Rothenstein's "suggestion that the best route to Heaven is via Elephanta, Elura, & Ajanta."[85] By 1913, Rothenstein seems to have shared with Michael Field the opinion that Gill's work had begun to exhibit evidence of "Eastern" influences. Michael Field notes in a letter to Rothenstein following their receipt of the *Madonna and Child*, "I have had a letter from Eric Gill, wondering that we all find his work has an Eastern element in it."[86] If this element was present, it was due in large part to the influence of Rothenstein and the manner in which he also operated as a contact point between Gill and one of his most significant mentors, the Ceylonese art historian Ananda Coomaraswamy.

According to Gill, it was probably Rothenstein who first introduced him to Coomaraswamy, and Walter Shewring has asserted that this first encounter likely occurred in 1906.[87] While Coomaraswamy's educational background was in geology and mineralogy, he had by this time turned his attention to Ceylonese and Indian art history and begun collecting photographs of Indian sculpture and sharing them with artists in the West such as Gill and Epstein. As Rupert Arrowsmith notes, Coomaraswamy felt that European artistic techniques "had all but overwhelmed indigenous traditions of art production" during the nineteenth century, but he "wondered whether it might be possible to change the direction of this aesthetic tide so that Asian concepts of taste flowed westwards instead."[88] He hoped to do so by bringing information about the history of Indian art directly to European artists. Arrowsmith's discussion of the influence of Indian aesthetics on the work of Gill demonstrates that Coomaraswamy's writings and photographs had an enormous impact on his approach to artistic production. In his autobiography, Gill acknowledges how deeply influential and significant this relationship was, stating that he "dare not confess [himself Coomaraswamy's] disciple; that would only embarrass him."[89] He rhapsodizes about the brilliance of Coomaraswamy's work, arguing that "no other living writer has written the truth in matters of art and life and religion and piety with such wisdom and understanding."[90] Coomaraswamy remained a close friend and correspondent until the end of Gill's life, with Gill continuing to write to Coomaraswamy to express his excitement about and agreement with his theories when he moved to the United States.

While, as Arrowsmith reveals, contact with Indian traditions transformed Gill's technique, leading him to embrace the direct carving technique used by Indian sculptors, his engagement with Indian sculpture and his ongoing correspondence with Coomaraswamy also impacted his theories concerning faith and desire. It was in large part the significance of faith in Indian art that so attracted Gill. In an introduction to a 1914 collection of photographs of Indian sculpture selected by Coomaraswamy, Gill asserts that in "all Indian art there is a recognition of the fact that art is primarily prophecy – that it is a translation into material form of the inspiration man receives from God."[91] What seems to have so thrilled Gill about Indian religious sculpture was its successful integration of faith and sensuality, its equal interest in God and material form. As Sarah Victoria Turner has recently argued, Coomaraswamy's vision of the "vein of deep sex-mysticism" and the reconciliation of the sacred and the profane in Indian sculpture held intense appeal for Gill, "who was exploring the fusion of the sacred and the sexual in his own carvings."[92] In conversation with Coomaraswamy, Gill further developed his vision of a divine eroticism. As Richard Cork notes, Coomaraswamy's call for a "frank

recognition of the close analogy between amorous and religious ecstasy"
was enormously influential for Gill.[93] He found in the works that
Coomaraswamy showed him models of how the sculptor might integrate
eroticism with worship along with a demonstration, as Coomaraswamy
would later put it, of the extent to which spirituality and sensuality are
"inseparably linked," "merely the inner and outer aspects of one and the
same expanding life."[94] In his correspondence with Coomaraswamy, Gill
inquired about the possibility of integrating sex and worship. He wrote to
Coomaraswamy about his love of "bottoms," to which Coomaraswamy
replied:

> I would like to refer again to the matter of "bottoms" which you raised in a
> letter some time ago. Bottoms are amongst other goods certainly a good
> within the definition accepted by Thomas (that which all creatures desire).
> Now what is sin? 1) Thomas, "departure from the order to the end" and 2)
> Augustine, "to enjoy (i.e. merely enjoy) what one should use" (just as if in the
> work of art, the business of which is *docere, delectare, movere,* we take account
> only of the delectable and ignore what is taught and the direction in which
> we should be moved). Next, the world is a theophany. The nakedness of
> woman just as much as anything else is the handiwork and displays the glory.
> Moreover, everything is a trace (vestigium) of his foot and the symbol of the
> principle in which the thing shall exist a priori and "in a more excellent way"
> or as it is put more technically "eminently." I need not pursue the argument
> further. He is not going to deprive us of any good but will give us all good
> things "in a more excellent manner" – more excellent than they in them-
> selves, as temporalia, and corruptible as worldly "bottoms" are. We can,
> however, cut ourselves off from him and from the more excellent good by
> an attachment to the things as they are in themselves forgetting their
> implications: that becomes idolatry, whereas the understanding enjoyment,
> fruition, and delight we may take in anything, if we remember Him from
> whom it comes, is not idolatry but iconolatry – a different matter indeed,
> although the words grammatically are the same.... To put the matter
> another way, essence and nature are one in him.[95]

Coomaraswamy's thoughtful response grants Gill the right to see in the
naked body of a woman the glory of God. He is careful to distinguish
between the love of the body in itself as a form of idolatry and the love of
the body as a pathway to "Him from who it comes" as iconolatry.
However, practiced properly, Coomaraswamy insists, eroticism might
serve as a conduit to, rather than a distraction from, the divine. These
ideas about desire and spirituality played a central role in Gill's development of a vision of hallowed sensuality during the early years of his career
as a sculptor, and they continued to inform his thinking in later decades.

The impress of Coomaraswamy's loving treatment of the nude in his *Twenty-Eight Drawings* (1920), for example, registers clearly in Gill's *Twenty-Five Nudes* (1938), which appears to be a direct homage to his mentor. Coomaraswamy confirmed Gill's developing theories concerning the integration of faith and eroticism and directly impacted his approach to the representation of the body.

Rothenstein, then, linked Gill to Coomaraswamy and Indian art history as well as to Michael Field and the fin-de-siècle past, and, in addition, he "fostered the friendship" between Gill and Jacob Epstein, securing Gill's connections with both British modernism and the production of the Wilde memorial.[96] Gill's work with Epstein on Wilde's tomb, for which Gill designed the inscription and, according to Michael Pennington, carved the wings, enfolds his interest in sexual dissidence and his interest in global aesthetics.[97] It seems likely that Gill would have been eager to participate in the memorial project, as he was an admirer of Wilde's work. According to Rene Hague, he could not read *The Ballad of Reading Gaol* without weeping.[98] In his autobiography, he expresses enthusiastic agreement with Wilde's assertion that "all art is quite useless," stating that art, "in any human sense of the word, has nothing whatever to do with the monstrous filthiness of the man of business and his mechanized world."[99] Wilde's growing reputation as a martyr for the cause of sexual freedom probably held great appeal for Gill as well. His work on the construction of the tomb was a logical extension of his interest in queer Catholicism and the Decadence of the fin de siècle. In addition, his participation in the project provided an opportunity to integrate his interest in that tradition with his developing interest in "Eastern" art. Epstein received the commission to produce Wilde's tomb from Robert Ross in 1908, and his initial designs followed suggestions he received from "Wilde's admirers" to employ a Grecian aesthetic.[100] However, Gill and Epstein had begun to frequent the British Museum and the Victoria and Albert Museum in order to admire Indian, Assyrian, and Egyptian sculpture, and, due to the influence of Coomaraswamy, they became increasingly enthusiastic about the possibility of integrating these influences into their modernist sculptural practice. As a result, Epstein's vision for the monument transformed. As Arrowsmith notes, Epstein brought the Wilde tomb "from Classical Greece, through archaic Lykia, then Assyria, and finally Egypt."[101] The face of the winged sphinx that Epstein produced exhibits, Pennington argues, "a peculiar affinity to the face of the hieratic Egyptian pharaoh, Akhenaton (1300 B.C.)," and Arrowsmith's reading of the work highlights evidence of the influence of a fourteenth-century bust of Akhenaton that

Epstein would have encountered at the Louvre.[102] The time Gill and
Epstein spent admiring Indian and Egyptian sculpture in London
museums and in Coomaraswamy's photographs also informed their thinking about the frank representation of sex and the body. The new sensuality
of their shared aesthetic registers in Epstein's representation of the pronounced genitalia of the "flying demon angel," which caused such enormous scandal when the sculpture was placed in Père Lachaise in 1912.[103]
According to Pennington, "on the monument's arrival and during its
assembly ... the conservateur of Père Lachaise had considered that the
tomb was indecent because of the unusual size of the angel's testicles."[104]
Epstein arrived to discover that "the sex parts of the figure had been
swaddled in plaster."[105] After Epstein chipped away the plaster, a tarpaulin
was hung over the tomb and then a bronze plaque in the shape of a
butterfly was placed over the figure's genitalia. Aleister Crowley, who
unveiled the sculpture, seems to have finally removed the plaque,
approaching Epstein at the Café Royal with the bronze butterfly suspended from his neck. The memorial that Gill and Epstein produced
and the scandal it elicited honored the most famous sexual dissident with
an act of aesthetic dissidence that violated the norms governing the
representation of the male body as well as the prioritizing of European
artistic traditions, turning purposefully away from Europe and to India
and Egypt for inspiration.

Gill's collaboration with Epstein and his cosmopolitan engagement with
global art history also informed his treatment of kinship, resulting in one
of his best-known works, *They* (or *Ecstasy*, 1910–11), an attempt to hallow
incestuous desire and transform this sexual practice into an expression of
divine love (Figure 6.6). As Arrowsmith argues, Gill and Epstein's work of
this period suggests that Coomaraswamy probably showed them pictures
of the temple of the Hindu sun god Surya at Konark, which is decorated
with sculpture inspired by the Tantric belief that "formalized sexual acts"
might act as "an ecstatic shortcut to spiritual enlightenment."[106] Gill and
Epstein discussed plans to construct a temple of their own on the grounds
of a property named Asham House, a "twentieth-century Stonehenge," to
be decorated with carvings similar in both style and content to this type of
Indian temple sculpture.[107] The project, according to Pennington, was
meant to "celebrate the primal and the sexual on a grand scale."[108]
Epstein's Asham sketch *One of the Hundred Pillars of the Secret Temple*
(1910–11), which represents a man and woman engaged in sexual intercourse, registers clearly the influence of the sculptures at Konark, as does
Gill's contemporaneous *They*, which also represents a man and woman

Figure 6.6   Eric Gill, *They* (or *Ecstasy*), 1910–11. Tate Britain, London.
Digital photograph © Tate.

standing and engaged in sexual intercourse.[109] Judith Collins asserts that *They* was intended to stand in Gill and Epstein's "open-air temple dedicated to love."[110] Gill's sister Gladys and her husband Ernest Laughton were the models for *They*, and Gill's diary reveals that he was actively engaged in a sexual relationship with Gladys during this period. An entry in 1911, for example, notes that he slept with her at Epstein's home.[111] This work emerges directly from Gill's radical sexual experimentation and his attempts to rethink categories of kinship and the practice of affiliation. Representing his own sister engaging in sexual intercourse, making material evidence of his own longing for her in the style of temple sculpture that links sex acts with worship operates here as a method for sanctifying incestuous desire. Gill titled a drawing for the work, "Christ and the Church."[112] Gill so believed in the divinity of his sexual practices, he thought he might use his own incestuous desire as the source material for a representation of Christ's relationship with his followers. Roger Fry's response to the sculpture highlighted these elements of Gill's thinking. On first seeing a photograph of the work, Fry wrote to say, "This is real religious art."[113] A few days later, he wrote to request additional photographs of the work, stating, "I want to send one to Ed Carpenter who will welcome it immensely."[114] Fry comprehended immediately that Gill wished to fuse the erotic and the divine and, in addition, that Gill's work would be of interest to Edward Carpenter, one of the most well-known proponents of sexual dissidence. *They* can be understood then as an integration of the multiple strands of influence and experimentation under discussion here. A representation of incestuous desire informed by Gill's contact with queer Catholic communities and stylistically inflected by his engagement with Hindu temple sculpture, *They* reflects Gill's belief in the holiness of sexual acts and the divinity of erotic union and provides clear insight into how he made sense to himself of the incestuous practices that were so central to his own approach to familial affiliation. The same vision that hallowed his love for Gladys could be extended to the abuse to which he subjected his daughters.

Engaging with the work of Catholics with ties to late-Victorian aestheticism and Indian temple sculptors allowed Gill to believe that he was, in his desire to integrate his sexual practices with religious faith, part of a larger community of erotic artists and iconoclasts. During the 1910s and 1920s, when Gill seemed so determined to extricate himself from every ideology that might inhibit his desires, to abolish all norms and customs governing sexual practice, queer Catholicism, along with his engagement with Coomaraswamy's reading of Indian sculpture, inflected his thinking and enabled his extreme contestations of conventional sexual ideologies. As he so purposefully undid all norms governing affiliation and community, forging transhistorical and transnational bonds with representatives of Indian aesthetics and the queer Catholicism of the fin de siècle facilitated his radical reconfiguration of kinship and desire and provided him with a means to consecrate incestuous desire. He built from a foundation of liberatory influences a method for understanding his abuses as divine.

In 1928, G. K. Chesterton, whose Distributist theories were so influential for Gill and his community at Ditchling, published an essay in the *Red Book Magazine* entitled "Why Abolish the Family?" He notes that, of late, the "most fundamental human creation called the Household or the Home" is under attack.[115] He traces the problem in part to Ibsen, but he notes that this discourse seems to be part of a more widely held sense of irritation with the torments of home life. Across the novels and newspapers of the epoch, he sees insistent assertions that "all souls must be free" alongside critiques of "the absurdity of authority or the degradation of obedience" and calls for a broader reorganization of child-rearing that would allow the state to play a "parental function."[116] These arguments, in Chesterton's eyes, are fundamentally absurd, necessitating compensated labor on the part of state-appointed surrogate parents, when a "normal person" is "urged by a natural force" to do this labor for free within the confines of the family.[117] These calls to "destroy the family" are, he argues, "mere talk and tomfoolery," for the "social structure of mankind," according to which "a commonwealth is made up of a number of small kingdoms of which a man and a woman become the king and queen and in which they exercise a reasonable authority," is "far older" than all of humanity's records "and more universal than any of its religions."[118] The domestic division of human society may not be, Chesterton admits, perfect, but it allows individuals the freedom to shape and control their personal lives. The home, he argues, is the only remaining place "for individuality and liberty," in which individual pleasures can be pursued without scrutiny and discipline can be allotted by parents with a sympathy and humor that the state would be unable to approximate.[119] Chesterton does note that greater equality in the distribution of private property would vastly improve private lives by allowing family units to enter into more "festive intercourse" with each other, but it is vital, he insists, that families preserve their separation from one another so as to remain sites in which individual difference might thrive.[120] He concludes that the recent "anti-domestic drift" is fundamentally "unintelligent" and that the preservation of the family will ultimately enable the greatest liberty and happiness for all.[121]

If any one family might be held up as a counterargument to Chesterton's claims, it would have to be his friend Eric Gill's. Like Chesterton, Gill was drawn to a broader reimagining of the economic organization of society, and he seemed capable of extricating himself from all sorts of cultural prejudices concerning sexual desire, but he remained invested in the concept of the family as a social unit, an enclave in which he reigned as king and within which he was able to pursue pleasures and enact dominance and abuse. Gill's family was, as Chesterton envisions, a site in which he could pursue unmitigated liberty and individuality, but this came at the expense of the liberty and individuality of his subjects. To choose to end this book with a focus on his approach to kinship might appear to be a dark choice, but I have done so because of the larger questions his practices raise about the kinds of power and domination that inhere within the family structure. Gill understood himself to be radically re-envisioning connection, desire, and love, but in the end, he did not get far from the kinds of oppression and control that inspired the very calls for family abolition to which Chesterton is responding. I am interested in, and troubled by, the persistent allure of the family and the fact that so many attempts to revise domestic life retained the tendency to domination and exploitation that inspired the desire on the part of queer subjects to retool kinship structures.

The strands of family abolition discourse critiqued by Chesterton in the 1920s are taken up later in the century by feminist thinkers. In *The Dialectic of Sex* (1970), for example, Shulamith Firestone echoes the 1920s chorus to which Chesterton was responding in arguing that "the biological family is an inherently unequal power distribution."[122] She reaches the conclusion that, in order for the "tyranny of the biological family" to be broken, reproductive labor on the part of women should be replaced with artificial reproduction.[123] This is, of course, a very Wildean conclusion, mimicking Wilde's turn to machines as the way out of the persistent problem of unpleasant forms of work in "The Soul of Man Under Socialism." Contemporary critics writing about Firestone, such as Caroline Bassett, have in fact linked the two thinkers together, referencing Wilde's assertion in "The Soul of Man" that "a map of the world that does not include Utopia is not worth even glancing at" when discussing the utopian dimensions of second-wave feminisms.[124] Firestone's radical re-envisioning of social organization, which seeks to eschew the "oppressive power structures set up by Nature" by liberating women from reproductive work and all subjects from the "power psychology created by the family," like Wilde's technophilic vision of a future in which robots sweep so poets might write, necessitates a utopian razing of those structures that Chesterton insisted are universal and fundamental.[125]

The authors and artists I have discussed here are heavily indebted to Wilde, but they do not get to a point on the map that Wilde might have labeled Utopia. As much as they work to rethink the family, to make kinship do new things and accommodate different desires and sexual practices, they do not wish to sweep the family away, to replace kinship with machines or the protections of the state. They are perpetually drawn back to the concepts of parental love, sibling affection, and marriage. This is not surprising. As Sophie Lewis has recently noted, "If it is easier to imagine the end of the world than the end of capitalism, it is still perhaps easier to imagine the end of capitalism than the end of the family."[126] As I hope to have shown, these twentieth-century Decadent attempts to loosen the boundaries of the concept of kinship so it could accommodate new formations – textual connections with the father, domestic units built around sibling love, open marriages – did often produce novel networks of support for queer subjects. However, this renovation work operated to preserve a structure that some critics insist relies so heavily on insularity, power differences, and ownership that it ought instead to be done away with entirely. In *Tendencies* (1993), Eve Kosofsky Sedgwick raised the question, "Can the family be redeemed?" and acknowledged the possibility of a "more elastic, inclusive definition of 'family'" that might "do justice to the depth and sometimes durability of nonmarital and/or nonprocreative bonds, same-sex bonds, nondyadic bonds, bonds not defined by genitality, 'step'-bonds, adult sibling bonds, nonbiological bonds across generations, etc."[127] In the end, however, she concludes that "too much, too important ground is given up in letting the problematic of 'family' define these intimate and political structurations – 'family' even in the most denaturalized and denaturalizing, the most utopian possible uses of the term."[128] I close with Gill in part to acknowledge that line of thinking. The call to abolish the family along with the critique of pronatalism articulated by thinkers like Firestone and Lee Edelman have, of course, come under critique as a operating with a white bias, neglecting the manner in which processes of enslavement and colonization denied subjects of color access to particular kinship formations as well as the fact that "some subjects (rich and/or white) are more incentivized to reproduce than other (poor and/or black)."[129] This is why I have placed my consideration of Gill right beside my reading of Nugent's investment in reconnection with displaced kin. Some subjects have been denied the right to kinship, so the allure of the family, the desire for that rootedness and connection, should not be a complete mystery.

What I have endeavored to stress throughout this book is that the renovation work familial structures underwent so as to create new spaces that might accommodate queer affiliation involved both preservation and harm. That element of harm perhaps emerges most clearly in my chapter on Gill. By attending to the manner in which cosmopolitan expansion and appropriation informed Decadent experiments with kinship, however, I have also tried, across these chapters, to attend to the forms of curiosity as well as violence that underwrote these experiments. Decadent modernists used travel, translation, and transnational collaboration to open up their sense of what kinship might be, but they also relied on pleasure and ideas extracted from bodies that were Orientalized, colonized, and instrumentalized. The map I have drawn here does not include Utopia. It includes a whole host of efforts informed by lofty aspirations and constrained by deep limitations. This map is meant to reveal the pressures that operated upon individuals working extremely hard to make families freer and more fulfilling, individuals who thought by thinking expansively, both backward and forward in time and outside of national boundaries, they could make family mean something different and be something different. It is meant to point to the moments when these individuals experienced something like success as well as the plunder and exploitation that engendered those achievements. Laurence Housman's imaginative moves toward the struggle for Indian independence have to be marked on this map as clearly as the Mackenzies' sex tourism on Capri. Though this map might have a tremendous gap in the place Utopia ought to be, I hope it might still be worth examining and that it might indicate how challenging it is to theorize and enact truly new and truly ethical modes of connection.

Notes

Introduction

1 *Extraordinary Women*, photo album, undated, Box 58, Norman Douglas
Collection, Beinecke Rare Book and Manuscript Library, New Haven, CT.
The album in the Beinecke is undated, but it is a photographic reproduction
of an original album housed at the Centro Caprense Ignazio Cerio Library
that is dated 1918. Thanks to Rachel Hope Cleves for drawing my attention
to this album.
For further discussion of Capri's reputation as a refuge for sexual dissidents,
see Eugenio Zito, "'Amori et Dolori Sacrum': Canons, Differences, and
Figures of Gender Identity in the Cultural Panorama of Travellers in Capri
between the Nineteenth and Twentieth Centuries," in *Homosexuality in
Italian Literature, Society, and Culture, 1789–1919*, eds. Lorenzo Benadusi,
Paolo L. Bernardini, Elisa Bianco, and Paola Guazzo (Newcastle upon Tyne:
Cambridge Scholars, 2017), 129–54.
2 James Money, *Capri: Island of Pleasure* (London: Hamish Hamilton,
1986), 149.
3 Ibid., 150.
4 See Marianne Hirsch, "Introduction" to *The Familial Gaze*, ed. Marianne
Hirsch (Hanover: University Press of New England, 1999), xi–xxv.
5 Jamie James, *Pagan Light: Dreams of Freedom and Beauty in Capri* (New York:
Farrar, Straus, and Giroux, 2019), 195.
6 Elizabeth Freeman, "Queer Belongings: Kinship Theory and Queer Theory,"
in *A Companion to Lesbian, Gay, Bisexual, and Transgender Studies*, eds.
George Haggerty and Molly McGarry (Hoboken, NJ: Blackwell Press,
2007), 307.
7 Ibid., 307.
8 Compton Mackenzie, *Extraordinary Women: Theme and Variations* (New
York: Macy-Masius, 1928), 5.
9 Paul Fussell, *Abroad: British Literary Traveling between the Wars* (New York:
Oxford University Press, 1980), 20.
10 Rachel Hope Cleves, *Unspeakable: A Life beyond Sexual Morality* (Chicago:
University of Chicago Press, 2020), 3, 13, 12.

11 Susan McCabe, "Bryher's Archive: Modernism and the Melancholy of Money," in *English Now: Selected Papers from the 20th IAUPE Conference*, ed. Marianne Thormählen (Lund, Sweden: Lund University Press, 2008), 119.

12 It is not clear when exactly the *Extraordinary Women* album came to be a part of the Norman Douglas collection. Due to the fact that the novel for which it is named was dedicated to Douglas, it would make sense that someone might have presented this bound reproduction to him as a gift. However, in *Capri: Island of Pleasure*, James Money notes that Maurice Yates, a gay set designer who lived on Capri in later years and amused himself by identifying the characters and homes described in Compton Mackenzie's Capri novels, "scored a success by finding in Naples an album, which must have belonged to one of the 'extraordinary women,' with contemporary snapshots of Mackenzie himself and the main characters in his book" (Money, *Capri: Island of Pleasure*, 258). According to Money, Yates and Macpherson toyed with the idea of republishing Mackenzie's Capri novels with reproductions of these photographs. Perhaps Yates presented a reproduction of the album he "scored" in Naples to Macpherson.

13 I have chosen throughout the manuscript to capitalize the words "Decadent" and "Decadence." I am very sympathetic with recent moves to enlarge our understanding of the concept of decadence and expand the confines of decadence beyond the fin de siècle and outside of Britain, which the choice to not capitalize the term is meant to enable. However, here I am discussing a set of individuals turning very purposefully back to the British Decadence of the 1890s, to Decadence with a capital *D*, to Oscar Wilde, Aubrey Beardsley, Vernon Lee, and Michael Field, so I felt it made sense to preserve the capitalization of the term.

14 A series of significant works tracing lines of continuity between the nineteenth and twentieth centuries and revealing the sustained conversations taking place across the century's turn have appeared during the last two decades. See, for example, Jessica R. Feldman, *Victorian Modernism: Pragmatism and the Varieties of Aesthetic Experience* (New York: Cambridge University Press, 2002); Ruth Livesey, *Socialism, Sex, and the Culture of Aestheticism in Britain, 1880–1914* (New York: Oxford University Press, 2007); Anne Elizabeth Jamison, *Poetics en Passant: Redefining the Relationship between Victorian and Modern Poetry* (New York: Palgrave Macmillan, 2009); and Rachel Teukolsky, *The Literate Eye: Victorian Art Writing and Modernist Aesthetics* (New York: Oxford University Press, 2009). Scholars of late-Victorian Decadence in particular have worked to call the Victorian/modern divide into question. Recent work by, for example, Alex Murray, Kate Hext, and Vincent Sherry has built on previous scholarship, such as David Weir's *Decadence and the Making of Modernism* (Amherst: University of Massachusetts Press, 1996), to call further attention to the persistence of Decadent aesthetics during the early twentieth century. See, for example, Alex Murray, "Decadence Revisited: Evelyn Waugh and the Afterlife of the

1890s," *Modernism/modernity* 22.3 (2015), 593–607; Vincent Sherry, *Modernism and the Reinvention of Decadence* (New York: Cambridge University Press, 2015); and Kate Hext and Alex Murray, eds., *Decadence in the Age of Modernism* (Baltimore: Johns Hopkins University Press, 2019). And Robert Stilling's *Beginning at the End: Decadence, Modernism, and Postcolonial Poetry* (Cambridge: Harvard University Press, 2018) carries the afterlife of Decadence even further into the twentieth century by examining the uses to which the aesthetic is put by postcolonial artists and writers.

15 Elizabeth Freeman, *Time Binds: Queer Temporalities, Queer Histories* (Durham, NC: Duke University Press, 2010), 8.

16 Ibid., 19.

17 Christopher Reed, *Bloomsbury Rooms: Modernism, Subculture, and Domesticity* (New Haven, CT: Yale University Press, 2004), 8.

18 Freeman, *Time Binds*, 62.

19 Freeman, "Queer Belongings," 295.

20 Lee Edelman, *No Future: Queer Theory and the Death Drive* (Durham, NC: Duke University Press, 2004), 16.

21 For discussion of the manner in which "the modern gay male identity often traced to the late Victorian constructions of 'invert' and 'homosexual' occupies not the periphery of the nation but rather a cosmopolitan locus instrumental to projects of war, colonialism, and neoliberalism," see Hiram Pérez, *A Taste for Brown Bodies: Gay Modernity and Cosmopolitan Desire* (New York: New York University Press, 2015), 3.

22 Kadji Amin, *Disturbing Attachments: Genet, Modern Pederasty, and Queer History* (Durham, NC: Duke University Press, 2017), 10.

23 Ibid., 11.

24 Ibid., 13, 17–18.

25 Cleves, *Unspeakable*, 1.

26 See Elaine Showalter, *Sexual Anarchy: Gender and Culture at the Fin de Siècle* (New York: Viking, 1990).

27 Holly Furneaux, *Queer Dickens: Erotics, Families, Masculinities* (New York: Oxford University Press, 2009), 9.

28 This is what distinguishes the networks I describe here from the queer experiments in affiliation being performed at the heart of the British establishment by families like the Bensons as described by Simon Goldhill in *A Very Queer Family Indeed: Sex, Religion, and the Bensons in Victorian Britain* (Chicago: University of Chicago Press, 2016). Goldhill notes that the story he tells of the Benson family is "not the self-consciously shocking, modernizing, self-dramatizing life of a Carpenter, a Whitman, or a Strachey: it takes place at Eton, Windsor Castle, in the church" (15). In contrast, the figures under discussion in *Queer Kinship after Wilde* self-consciously separate and distinguish themselves from the British establishment, and they do so in a manner that is informed by their indebtedness to the purposefully shocking and taunting Decadent aesthetic.

29 Alex Murray, "Introduction" to *Decadence: A Literary History*, ed. Alex Murray (New York: Cambridge University Press, 2020), 7.

30 Holbrook Jackson, *The Eighteen-Nineties: A Review of Art and Ideas at the Close of the Nineteenth Century* (London: Grant Richards, 1913), 19–20.

31 Kate Hext and Alex Murray, "Introduction" to *Decadence in the Age of Modernism* (Baltimore: Johns Hopkins University Press, 2019), 10.

32 Diana Maltz, "Ardent Service: Female Eroticism and New Life Ethics in Gertrude Dix's *The Image Breakers* (1900)," *Journal of Victorian Culture* 17, no. 2 (2012): 151.

33 Hext and Murray, "Introduction," 12.

34 Oscar Wilde, "The Soul of Man under Socialism," *Fortnightly Review* 49, no. 340 (February 1891): 300.

35 Ibid.

36 Oscar Wilde, *Intentions* (Leipzig: Heinemann & Balestier, 1891), 140.

37 Oscar Wilde, "The Portrait of Mr. W. H.," *Blackwood's Edinburgh Magazine* 146, no. 885 (July 1889): 4, 6.

38 Ibid., 3.

39 Ibid., 6. For discussion of the sources upon which Wilde drew in representing this theory, see Joseph Bristow and Rebecca N. Mitchell, "Forging Literary History: 'The Portrait of Mr. W. H.,'" in *Oscar Wilde's Chatterton: Literary History, Romanticism, and the Art of Forgery*, eds. Joseph Bristow and Rebecca N. Mitchell (New Haven, CT: Yale University Press, 2015).

40 Ibid., 12–13.

41 Ibid., 13.

42 Ibid.

43 James Campbell, *Oscar Wilde, Wilfred Owen, and Male Desire: Begotten, Not Made* (New York: Palgrave Macmillan, 2015), 28.

44 Wilde, "The Portrait of Mr. W. H.," 14.

45 Oscar Wilde, *The Portrait of Mr. W. H.* (New York: Mitchell Kennerley, 1921), 42–3.

46 Ibid., 44.

47 Ibid.

48 Ibid.

49 For further discussion of Mitchell Kennerley's edition of the "The Portrait of Mr. W. H.," see Greg Mackie, *Beautiful Untrue Things: Forging Oscar Wilde's Extraordinary Afterlife* (Toronto: University of Toronto Press, 2019), 205–12. As Mackie notes, after publishing his expanded edition of the story based on a recently recovered "lost manuscript," Kennerley sold the manuscript to Dr. A. S. W. Rosenbach. Ian Small, however, has established that there are "significant discrepancies between the Rosenbach manuscript and the Kennerley edition," leading him to conclude that Kennerly was also working with additional material marked for insertion that is now missing. Despite these inconsistencies, I have chosen to cite this edition because it was in circulation during the early twentieth century and therefore was available to the figures under discussion in this project.

50 Freeman, "Queer Belongings," 299.

51 Lawrence Danson, "Oscar Wilde, W. H., and the Unspoken Name of Love," in *Oscar Wilde: A Collection of Critical Essays*, ed. Jonathan Freedman (Upper Saddle River, NJ: Prentice Hall, 1998), 91.

52 Campbell, *Oscar Wilde, Wilfred Owen, and Male Desire*, 29.

53 Freeman, "Queer Belongings," 299.

54 Wilde, "The Portrait of Mr. W. H.," 21.

55 Richard Ellmann, *Oscar Wilde* (New York: Vintage Books, 1988), 463. This version of the speech is drawn from Christopher Sclater Millard's account of the trials, *Oscar Wilde: Three Times Tried* (London: Ferrestone Press, 1912), which, as Leslie J. Moran has demonstrated, is longer than and contains significant differences from an earlier version that appeared in a 1906 account of the trials. The 1906 version of the speech does, however, also include a reference to the sonnets of Shakespeare. See Leslie J. Moran, "Transcripts and Truth: Writing the Trials of Oscar Wilde," in *Oscar Wilde and Modern Culture: The Making of a Legend*, ed. Joseph Bristow (Athens: Ohio University Press, 2008), 243–5.

56 Moran, "Transcripts and Truth," 243.

57 Amin, *Disturbing Attachments*, 118–19. For further discussion of age-differentiated eroticism and queer kinship see the introduction to Patrick Califia, *Doing It for Daddy* (Boston: Alyson Publications, 1994); and a chapter devoted to "Age" in Alan Sinfield, *On Sexuality and Power* (New York: Columbia University Press, 2004).

58 Ellis Hanson, "Must We Arrest Oscar Wilde Again?" (paper presented at the "Curiosity and Desire in Fin-de-Siècle Art and Literature" conference at the William Andrews Clark Memorial Library, UCLA, May 11–12, 2018).

59 Richard Kaye, "Oscar Wilde and the Politics of Posthumous Sainthood: Hofmannsthal, Mirbeau, Proust," in *Oscar Wilde and Modern Culture: The Making of a Legend*, ed. Joseph Bristow (Athens: Ohio University Press, 2008), 117.

60 Matthew Potolsky, *The Decadent Republic of Letters: Taste, Politics, and Cosmopolitan Community from Baudelaire to Beardsley* (Philadelphia: University of Pennsylvania Press, 2013), 1–2.

61 Quoted in Michèle Mendelssohn, "Reading Aestheticism, Decadence, and Cosmopolitanism," in *Late Victorian into Modern*, eds. Laura Marcus, Michèle Mendelssohn, and Kirsten E. Shepherd-Barr (New York: Oxford University Press, 2016), 483.

62 Ellmann, *Oscar Wilde*, 178–9.

63 Oscar Wilde, "The English Renaissance in Art," in *Essays and Lectures*, ed. Robert Ross (Methuen: London, 1908), 144.

64 Stefano Evangelista, "Oscar Wilde: European in Sympathy," in *The Reception of Oscar Wilde in Europe*, ed. Stefano Evangelista (New York: Continuum, 2010), 1, 3. Wilde characterized himself this way in a letter to Edmond de Goncourt written in 1891.

65 Ibid., 3.

66 Amanda Anderson, *The Powers of Distance: Cosmopolitanism and the Cultivation of Detachment* (Princeton: Princeton University Press, 2001), 153.

67 Jessica Berman, *Modernist Fiction, Cosmopolitanism and the Politics of Community* (New York: Cambridge University Press, 2001), 47.

68 Margaret S. Kennedy, "Wilde's Cosmopolitanism," in *Wilde's Wiles: Studies of the Influences on Oscar Wilde and His Enduring Influences in the Twenty-First Century*, ed. Annette M. Magid (Newcastle upon Tyne: Cambridge Scholars Publishing, 2013), 111.

69 Elleke Boehmer, *Indian Arrivals, 1870–1915: Networks of British Empire* (New York: Oxford University Press, 2015), 141.

70 Katharina Herold, "Cosmopolitan Conglomeration and Orientalist Appropriation in Oscar Wilde's 'The Sphinx'" (paper presented at the Cosmopolis and Beyond: Literary Cosmopolitanism after the Republic of Letters conference, Trinity College, University of Oxford, March 18–19, 2016).

71 Grace Lavery, *Quaint, Exquisite: Victorian Aesthetics and the Idea of Japan* (Princeton: Princeton University Press, 2019), 57, 71, 73.

72 Michèle Mendelssohn, *Making Oscar Wilde* (New York: Oxford University Press, 2018), 119, 192.

73 Imani Perry, *Vexy Thing: On Gender and Liberation* (Durham, NC: Duke University Press, 2018), 75.

74 Laurence Housman, unpublished manuscript entitled "What I Believe," n.d., Box 13, Folders 8–10, Laurence Housman Papers, Bryn Mawr College Library, Bryn Mawr, PA.

75 Laurence Housman to Reginald Reynolds, December 12, 1943, Bromsgrove Public Library, Bromsgrove, UK.

76 Willy, *The Third Sex*, ed. Lawrence R. Schehr (Urbana: University of Illinois Press, 2007), 25.

77 Hortense Spillers, "'The Permanent Obliquity of an In(pha)llibly Straight': In the Time of the Daughters and the Fathers," in *Black, White, and in Color: Essays on American Literature and Culture* (Chicago: University of Chicago Press, 2003), 249.

78 Ibid., 99.

Chapter 1

1 Vyvyan Holland, *Son of Oscar Wilde* (New York: Carroll & Graf, 1999), 91.

2 Constance Wilde to Vyvyan Holland, September 27, 1896, Eccles Bequest, Vol. CIX, Correspondence of Constance Wilde and Vyvyan Holland, 1891–8, Add. MS. 81727, British Library, London.

3 Holland, *Son of Oscar Wilde*, 76.

4 Vyvyan Holland to Christopher Millard, March 3, 1921, Oscar Wilde and his Literary Circle Collection: Correspondence, MS. Wilde, William Andrews Clark Memorial Library, University of California, Los Angeles.

5 A. B. Dulau and Co., *A Collection of Original Manuscripts Letters and Books of Oscar Wilde* (London: Dulau, 1928).

6 Holland, *Son of Oscar Wilde*, 63.

7 Ibid., 137.

8 Ibid.

9 Ibid., 164.

10 Ibid., 184.

11 Ibid., 185.

12 Ibid., 187.

13 Ibid., 186.

14 Joshua J. Weiner, and Damon Young, "Introduction: Queer Bonds," *GLQ: A Journal of Lesbian and Gay Studies* 17, no. 2–3 (2011): 236.

15 Robert Ross to Vyvyan Holland, August 1, 1907, Eccles Bequest, Vol. CI, Correspondence of Robert Baldwin Ross and Vyvyan Holland; 1907–18, Add. MS. 81719, British Library, London.

16 Holland, *Son of Oscar Wilde*, 186.

17 Robert Ross to Vyvyan Holland, August 1, 1907, Eccles Bequest, Vol. CI, Correspondence of Robert Baldwin Ross and Vyvyan Holland; 1907–18, Add. MS. 81719, British Library, London.

18 Holland, *Son of Oscar Wilde*, 188.

19 Vyvyan Beresford Holland, *Time Remembered after Père Lachaise* (London: Gollancz, 1966), 35.

20 Jonathan Fryer, *Robbie Ross: Oscar Wilde's Devoted Friend* (New York: Carroll & Graf, 2002), 238.

21 Holland, *Time Remembered*, 102; Maureen Borland, *Wilde's Devoted Friend: A Life of Robert Ross 1869–1918* (Oxford: Lennard, 1990), 286.

22 Holland, *Son of Oscar Wilde*, 195.

23 Borland, *Wilde's Devoted Friend*, 85.

24 Ibid.

25 Holland, *Son of Oscar Wilde*, 195.

26 Ellen Crowell, "'We Are Odd!': Ye Archive of Ye Sette of Odd Volumes," *The Center & Clark Newsletter: UCLA Center for 17th- and 18th-Century Studies* 54 (2011): 9.

27 Oscar Wilde, "The Critic as Artist," in *The Complete Works of Oscar Wilde, Vol. IV*, ed. Josephine Guy (New York: Oxford University Press, 2007), 174.

28 Vyvyan Holland to Ada Leverson, July 28, 1914, Oscar Wilde and his Literary Circle Collection: Correspondence.

29 Oscar Wilde, "*Olivia* at the Lyceum," *Dramatic Review* 1, no. 18 (May 30, 1885): 278; Oscar Wilde, "The Decay of Lying," in Wilde, *The Complete Works of Oscar Wilde: Vol. IV*, 85. See Vyvyan Holland, *A Few Odd Reflections on Idleness* (London: Curwen, 1927).

30 Holland, *Time Remembered*, 134.

31 Laura Marcus, *Dreams of Modernity* (New York: Cambridge University Press, 2014), 143.

32 Vyvyan Holland to Reggie Turner, August 14, 1935, Oscar Wilde and his Literary Circle Collection: Correspondence.

33 Marcus, *Dreams of Modernity*, 143.

34 Holland, *Son of Oscar Wilde*, 7.

35 Ibid., 165.

36 Weiner and Young, "Queer Bonds," 231.

37 As Elizabeth Adams recent work indicates, while Millard is frequently referred to as Wilde's first bibliographer, he was highly indebted in his work to the Wilde collector Walter Ledger, with whom he had planned to collaborate on a bibliography of Wilde's works and who shared many discoveries with Millard. See Elizabeth Adams, "Walter Edwin Ledger, Christopher Sclater Millard, and the Bibliography of Oscar Wilde," *Studies in Walter Pater and Aestheticism* 5 (2020): 105–17.

38 Vyvyan Holland to Christopher Millard, August 5, 1921, Oscar Wilde and his Literary Circle Collection: Correspondence.

39 Vyvyan Holland to Christopher Millard, October 30, 1920 and October 26, 1920, Oscar Wilde and his Literary Circle Collection: Correspondence.

40 See Daniel A. Novak, "Picturing Wilde: Christopher Millard's 'Iconography of Oscar Wilde,'" *Nineteenth-Century Contexts* 32, no. 4 (2010): 305–35.

41 Vyvyan Holland to Christopher Millard, October 3, 1920, Oscar Wilde and his Literary Circle Collection: Correspondence.

42 Oscar Wilde to Robert Ross [October 1, 1897], in *The Complete Letters of Oscar Wilde*, eds. Merlin Holland and Rupert Hart-Davis (New York: Henry Holt, 2000), 950. For edited letter, see Oscar Wilde, *After Berneval: Letters of Oscar Wilde to Robert Ross* (Westminster: Beaumont Press, 1922), 11.

43 Vyvyan Holland to Christopher Millard, October 30, 1920, Oscar Wilde and his Literary Circle Collection: Correspondence.

44 Ibid.

45 Oscar Wilde to Robert Ross, [?October 3, 1897], in *Complete Letters of Oscar Wilde*, 955. For edited letter, see Wilde, *After Berneval*, 14.

46 Novak, "Picturing Wilde," 306.

47 Ibid., 328.

48 Ibid.

49 For a discussion of Holland's friendship and correspondence with Scott Moncrieff, see Jean Findlay, *Chasing Lost Time: The Life of C. K. Scott Moncrieff: Soldier, Spy, and Translator* (London: Chatto & Windus, 2014).

50 Quoted in Gregory Mackie, "Forging Oscar Wilde: Mrs. Chan-Toon and for Love of the King," *English Literature in Transition, 1880–1920* 54, no. 3 (2011): 272.

51 Vyvyan Holland to Osbert Burdett, November 26, 1926, RP 8947, Western Manuscripts, British Library, London.

52 Vyvyan Holland to Christopher Millard, March 3, 1921, Oscar Wilde and his Literary Circle Collection: Correspondence.

53 See Roxana Verona, "A Cosmopolitan Orientalism: Paul Morand Goes East," *Sites* 5, no. 1 (2001): 157–69.

54 See Dayton Kohler, "Julian Green: Modern Gothic," *The Sewanee Review* 40, no. 2 (1932): 139–48. Green was christened "Julian," but his publishers altered the spelling to "Julien." See I. W. Brock, "Julien Green: A Biographical and Literary Sketch," *The French Review* 23, no. 5 (1950): 347.

55 George Orwell, "Review of *Landfall* by Nevil Shute; *Nailcruncher* by Albert Cohen, translated from the French by Vyvyan Holland; and *A Dark Side Also* by Peter Conway," *New Statesman and Nation* 20, no. 511 (December 7, 1940): 574.

56 Holland, *Son of Oscar Wilde*, 61.

57 Ibid.

58 Ibid., 63.

59 Ibid., 81.

60 Ibid., 146.

61 Ibid., 166.

62 Ibid., 201.

63 Ibid.

64 Holland, *Time Remembered*, 15.

65 Holland, *Son of Oscar Wilde*, 87.

66 Vyvyan Holland, "Once upon a Time: A Critical Note on Oscar Wilde's Fairy Stories," *Adelphi* 30, no. 3 (1954): 249.

67 Holland, *Son of Oscar Wilde*, 198.

68 Ibid., 205.

69 Vyvyan Holland, *Oscar Wilde: A Pictorial Biography* (London: Thames & Hudson, 1960), 5.

70 Ibid.

71 Ibid., 70.

72 Ibid., 86–7.

73 For a discussion of cosmopolitanism as a process of cultural translation, see Gerard Delanty, *The Cosmopolitan Imagination: The Renewal of Critical Social Theory* (New York: Cambridge University Press, 2009), 193–8.

74 Esperança Bielsa, "Cosmopolitanism as Translation," *Cultural Sociology* 8, no. 4 (2014): 395.

75 Lawrence Venuti, *The Translator's Invisibility: A History of Translation* (New York: Routledge, 2008), 14; Bielsa, "Cosmopolitanism as Translation," 403.

76 Holland, *Time Remembered*, 125.

77 Julian Jackson, *Living in Arcadia: Homosexuality, Politics, and Morality in France from the Liberation to AIDS* (Chicago: University of Chicago Press, 2009), 76; Kathryn Eberle Wildgen, *Julien Green: The Great Themes* (Birmingham, AL: Summa Publications, 1993), 19.

78 Wildgen, *Julien Green*, 28.

79 See Julian Green, *The Dark Journey* (New York: Harper & Brothers, 1929), 59.

80 Julian Green, *The Strange River* (New York: Harper & Brothers, 1932), 82.

81 Glenn S. Burne, *Julian Green* (New York: Twayne, 1972), 84.

82 Julian Green, *The Dreamer* (New York: Harper & Brothers, 1934), 262, 264.
83 See Wildgen, *Julien Green*, 21.
84 Burne, *Julian Green*, 98.
85 Wildgen, *Julien Green*, 36.
86 See Ibid., 22.
87 Julien Green, *Midnight* (New York: Harper & Brothers, 1936), 72.
88 Ibid., 331.
89 Ibid., 344.
90 Holland, *Son of Oscar Wilde*, 76, 95.
91 Green, *The Dreamer*, 303–4.
92 Julien Green, *Le Visionnaire* (Paris: Plon, 1934), 222; Green, *The Dreamer*, 304.
93 As Colm Tóibín notes, while Holland stressed the accuracy of this edition, "there were . . . considerable differences between the manuscript and the typed copy [used by Holland for this edition]. Some of these were caused by errors in the typing and dictating; others were caused by Ross, who, for example, removed more than a thousand words, almost all of them fiercely critical of Douglas and his father." See Colm Tóibín's notes in Oscar Wilde, *De Profundis and Other Prison Writings* (London: Penguin, 2013).
94 Vyvyan Holland, Introduction to *De Profundis*, by Oscar Wilde (London: Methuen & Co., 1949), 12.
95 Vyvyan Holland, Foreword to *Salomé*, by Oscar Wilde (London: Folio Society, 1957), 8.

Chapter 2

1 The "What I Believe" essay was a popular subgenre in the 1920s and 1930s, with examples by Bertrand Russell and E. M. Forster, and extended back into the nineteenth century with, for example, Tolstoy's *What I Believe* (or *My Religion*) (1884).
2 Laurence Housman, unpublished manuscript entitled "What I Believe," n.d., Box 13, Folders 8–10, Laurence Housman Papers, Bryn Mawr College Library, Bryn Mawr, PA.
3 Ibid.
4 Housman's formulation of expansive love here echoes the Stoics' expression of the ideal interplay between local and global identifications, described by Martha Nussbaum in the following manner:

> They suggest that we think of ourselves not as devoid of local affiliations, but as surrounded by a series of concentric circles. The first one encircles the self, the next takes up the immediate family, then follows the extended family, then, in order, neighbors or local groups, fellow city-dwellers, and fellow countrymen. . . . Outside all these circles is the largest one, humanity as a whole. Our task as citizens of the world will be to 'draw the circles somehow toward the center' (Stoic philosopher Hierocles, 1st-2nd CE), making all human beings like our fellow city dwellers. (Martha Nussbaum, "Patriotism and Cosmopolitanism," in *For Love of Country?*, ed. Joshua Cohen [Boston: Beacon Press, 2002], 9.)

5 Laurence Housman to Sarah Clark, 1912, quoted in Jill Liddington, *Vanishing for the Vote: Suffrage, Citizenship and the Battle for the Census* (Manchester: Manchester University Press, 2014), 41.

6 Lorraine Janzen Kooistra, *The Artist as Critic: Bitextuality in Fin-de-Siècle Illustrated Books* (Hants: Scholar Press, 1995), 219.

7 Lesley A. Hall, "'Disinterested Enthusiasm for Sexual Misconduct': The British Society for the Study of Sex Psychology, 1913–47," *Journal of Contemporary History* 30, no. 4 (1995): 665.

8 Laurence Housman, "A. E. Housman's 'De Amicitia,'" *Encounter* 29 (1967): 36–7.

9 Rodney K. Engen, *Laurence Housman* (Stroud: Catalpa, 1983), 30.

10 Leonore Davidoff, *Thicker Than Water: Siblings and Their Relations, 1780–1920* (New York: Oxford University Press, 2011), 29, 31.

11 Valerie Sanders, "'Lifelong Soulmates?': The Sibling Bond in Nineteenth-Century Fiction," *Victorian Review* 39, no. 2 (2013): 54.

12 Valerie Sanders, *The Brother-Sister Culture in Nineteenth-Century Literature: From Austen to Woolf* (New York: Palgrave Macmillan, 2002), 6; Leila Silvana May, *Disorderly Sisters: Sibling Relations and Sororal Resistance in Nineteenth-Century British Literature* (Lewisburg, PA: Bucknell University Press, 2001), 19; Sanders, *Brother-Sister Culture*, 5.

13 Laurence Houmsan, *The Relation of Fellow-Feeling to Sex* (London: Battley Bros., [n.d.]), 11. The pamphlet, part of a series published for the British Society for the Study of Sex Psychology, is not signed or dated. However, it was attributed to Housman in the next volume in the series, Havelock Ellis's *The Erotic Rights of Women, and the Objects of Marriage*, which was published in 1918, and Laurence Housman acknowledges authorship in his correspondence with the BSSSP (later called the British Sexological Society), which is housed at the Harry Ransom Center in Austin, Texas. The preceding pamphlet, *Sexual Variety and Variability among Women and Their Bearing upon Social Reconstruction* by Stella Browne, was published in 1917 (London: C. W. Beaumont), and *The Relation of Fellow-Feeling to Sex* was probably printed in 1917.

14 Ibid., 3.

15 Ibid.

16 Ibid., 5.

17 Ibid., 7.

18 Ibid., 7–10.

19 Ibid., 15.

20 Laurence Housman to Edward Carpenter, September 2, 1897, Sheffield Archives: Carpenter/Mss/386/75, Edward Carpenter Collection, Sheffield City Archives, Sheffield, UK.

21 Ibid.

22 Ibid.

23 Ibid.

24 Ibid.

25 Ibid.
26 Audrey Doussot, "Laurence Housman (1865–1959): Fairy Tale Teller, Illustrator and Aesthete," *Cahiers Victoriens & Édouardiens* 73 (Printemps 2011): 142–3.
27 Lorraine Janzen Kooistra, "Wilde's Legacy: Fairy Tales, Laurence Housman, and the Expression of 'Beautiful Untrue Things,'" in *Oscar Wilde and the Cultures of Childhood*, ed. Joseph Bristow (New York: Palgrave, 2017), 90.
28 Ibid., 98, 105.
29 See Kooistra, *The Artist as Critic*, 219.
30 Laurence Housman, *Echo de Paris: A Study from Life* (London: Jonathan Cape, 1923), 14.
31 Ibid., v; Laurence Housman, unpublished manuscript entitled "Outrageous Fortune," 36, 1933, Box 13, Folder 7, Laurence Housman Papers. In the manuscript of "Outrageous Fortune," Housman describes his friendship with a man twelve years younger than him that became the "great devotion of [his] life," though this younger man's "inclinations" were not the same as Housman's (32, 37). He states that the young man spent time abroad in India and died of "black-water fever" in Nigeria. This would suggest that the friend Housman is describing is Shadwell Boulderson, who was born in 1877, contributed "An Indian Road-Tale" (1903) to the *Venture: An Annual of Art and Literature*, the periodical edited by Housman and W. Somerset Maugham (London: The Pear Tree Press), and is listed in the *Blue-Book: Colony & Protectorate of Nigeria* in 1923.
32 Laurence Housman, *All-Fellows: Seven Legends of Lower Redemption with Insets in Verse* (London: Kegan, Paul, Trench, Trübner, & Co., 1896), 2.
33 Lorraine Janzen Kooistra, "The Artist as Critic: Bi-Textuality in Fin-de-Siècle Illustrated Books," PhD dissertation (McMaster University, 1992), 288.
34 Housman, *All-Fellows*, 21.
35 Ibid., 22.
36 Ibid., 25.
37 Ibid., 28.
38 Ibid., 29–30.
39 Laurence Housman, *The Cloak of Friendship* (London: J. Murray, 1905),139.
40 Laurence Housman, unpublished manuscript entitled "Outrageous Fortune," 36, 1933, Box 13, Folder 7, Laurence Housman Papers, 1.
41 Ibid.
42 Laurence Housman to Clemence Housman, n.d., Housman Papers, Alfred Gillett Trust, Street, UK.
43 While the photogravure process was used to reproduce the illustrations for *All-Fellows*, the majority of the fairy tale collections include engravings of Laurence's illustrations completed by Clemence.
44 James Guthrie, "The Wood Engravings of Clemence Housman," *The Print Collector's Quarterly* 11 (1924): 192.
45 Laurence Housman, unpublished manuscript entitled "The Family Remains," 2, Box 12, Folder 6, Laurence Housman Papers.

46 Laurence Housman, *The Unexpected Years* (London: Jonathan Cape, 1937), 104–5.

47 Laurence Housman to "Frank," n.d., Box 5, Folder 7, Laurence Housman Papers; Laurence Housman to Clemence Housman, n.d., Housman Papers, Alfred Gillett Trust, Street, UK.

48 Elizabeth Oakley, *Inseparable Siblings* (Studley: Brewin Books, 2009), 94.

49 Ibid.

50 Ibid., 46.

51 Kooistra, "Wilde's Legacy," 103.

52 Clemence Housman, *The Were-Wolf* (London: John Lane at the Bodley Head, 1896), 23.

53 Ibid., 106.

54 There has been some disagreement concerning the text's gender politics. Elizabeth Oakley argues that "White Fell seems to embody the neurotic fear of the New Woman and her depraved sexual appetites" (Oakley, *Inseparable Siblings*, 53). Lorraine Kooistra argues that, while White Fell seems to "emblematize" the "nineties' fear of aggressive women," the text "implies a critique of patriarchal culture" in its favorable representation of the "feminized man" (Kooistra, "The Artist as Critic: Bi-Textuality in Fin-de-Siècle Illustrated Books," 250–1). Rechelle Christie similarly acknowledges that the story could be read as "a conservative, Christian allegory with a moralizing message about the wages of sin ... and the penalty of wayward femininity" while insisting that Clemence's representation of Christian, "the self sacrificing and androgynous hero," indicates that the work should rather be understood as "an attempt to critique and deconstruct prescribed gender roles" (Rechelle Christie, "The Politics of Representation and Illustration in Clemence Housman's *The Were-Wolf*," *Housman Society Journal* 33 [2007]: 66.). More recently, Kooistra has returned to the story to argue that, with its emphasis on transformation and its querying of the "fixing of identities," *The Were-Wolf* asks to be read "from the fluidity of trans theory" (Lorraine Janzen Kooistra, "Clemence Housman's *The Were-Wolf*: Querying Transgression, Seeking Trans/Formation," *Victorian Review* 44, no. 1 [2018]: 64, 66).

55 Clemence Housman, *The Were-Wolf*, 122.

56 Oakley, *Inseparable Siblings*, 50.

57 Clemence Housman, *The Unknown Sea* (London: Duckworth & Co., 1898), 154.

58 Ibid., 258–9.

59 Ibid., 280.

60 Ibid., 315.

61 Lorraine Kooistra's reading of the text as a "cross-dressing confession of the writer's sexual desire" emphasizes the manner in which the composition of the novel allowed Laurence to obliquely engage in an act of sexual confession. See Lorraine Janzen Kooistra, "Cross-Dressing Confessions: Men Confessing as Women," in *Confessional Politics: Women's Sexual Self-Representations in Life Writing and Popular Media*, ed. Irene Gammel (Carbondale and Edwardsville: Southern Illinois University Press, 1999), 174.

62 Laurence Housman, *An Englishwoman's Love Letters* (New York: Doubleday, Page & Co., 1900), 14.
63 Ethel Hill, "Mr. Laurence Housman: An Impression," *The Vote*, December 2, 1909, 64.
64 Ibid.
65 Laurence Housman, *The Unexpected Years*, 63.
66 Ibid., 64.
67 Ibid., 65.
68 Ibid.
69 Ibid.
70 Elizabeth Oakley relies on Arnold Bax's discussion of a visit to the Housmans' home, which was decorated with suffrage slogans, in his *Farewell My Youth* (1943) to date the Housmans' turn to suffrage to around 1908. See Oakley, *Inseparable Siblings*, 70–1.
71 Laurence Housman, *The Unexpected Years*, 264.
72 Ibid.
73 Ibid., 274.
74 Stephen Housman, "The Housman Banners," *Housman Society Journal* 18 (1992): 39. Housman also discusses the exhibition history of the banner.
75 Laurence Housman, postcard, printed inscription front: "IN THIS SIGN CONQUER. TO OPEN THE EYES OF THE BLIND & TO BRING THE PRISONER OUT OF CAPTIVITY," from a design for a banner, The Women's Library, London School of Economics, London, UK.
76 Laurence Housman, suffrage banner, carried by the Hampstead Church League for Women's Suffrage, Museum of London, London, UK.
77 Tara Morton, "Changing Spaces: Art, Politics, and Identity in the Home Studios of the Suffrage Atelier," *Women's History Review* 21, no. 4 (2012): 627.
78 For a discussion of the suffragettes' evasion of the 1911 census, see Jill Liddington and Elizabeth Crawford, "'Women Do Not Count, Neither Shall They be Counted': Suffrage, Citizenship and the Battle for the 1911 Census," *History Workshop Journal* 71, no. 1 (2011): 98–127.
79 Oakley, *Inseparable Siblings*, 78.
80 Ibid..
81 Engen, *Laurence Housman*, 106.
82 Laurence Housman, *Sex-War and Women's Suffrage* (London: Women's Freedom League, 1912), 11–12.
83 Ibid., 52.
84 Ibid., 53.
85 Housman, *The Unexpected Years*, 297.
86 Ibid., 297.
87 Ibid., 298.
88 Ibid.
89 Ibid., 297.
90 Laurence Housman, "The True Realism," *Peace News*, August 22, 1941, 2.

91 Laurence Housman, *The Unexpected Years*, 304–6.
92 Ibid., 334.
93 Laurence Housman, "Retaliation," *Peace News*, October 25, 1940, 1.
94 Laurence Housman, unpublished manuscript entitled "What I Believe," n. d., Box 13, Folders 8–10, Laurence Housman Papers.
95 Ibid.
96 Ibid.
97 Ibid.
98 Ibid.
99 Laurence Housman, "The Makings of the War Mind – Its Cause and the Cure," *Peace News*, June 19, 1937, 6.
100 Laurence Housman, "Why Man Has Failed," *Peace News*, September 10, 1938, 7.
101 Laurence Housman, "Mankind Is Growing Up," *Peace News*, May 5, 1939, 9.
102 Laurence Housman, "The Corruption of Power," *Peace News*, September 5, 1941, 2.
103 Ibid.
104 Laurence Housman, unpublished manuscript entitled "What I Believe," n.d., Box 13, Folders 8–10, Laurence Housman Papers.
105 Laurence had come to know Reynolds in 1926 through Roger and Sarah Clark, members of the shoe manufacturing family, whom Laurence met through his work on the suffrage campaign. Reynolds was Roger Clark's cousin.
106 L. C. Webb, "Indian Portraits II," *Press*, December 5, 1931, 13.
107 Laurence Housman, preface to *The Truth about India: Can We Get It*, ed. Verrier Elwin (London: G. Allen & Unwin, 1932), 7–8.
108 Laurence Housman, "Gandhi and the Future of Pacifism," in *Mahatma Gandhi: Essays and Reflections on His Life and Work*, ed. Sarvepalli Radhakrishnan (London: George Allen & Unwin, 1949), 123–4.
109 Laurence Housman, unpublished manuscript entitled "What I Believe," n.d., Box 13, Folders 8–10, Laurence Housman Papers.
110 Laurence Housman to Clemence Housman, May 4, 1936, Box 6, Folder 7, Laurence Housman Papers.
111 Laurence Housman to Reginald Reynolds, December 12, 1943, Bromsgrove Public Library, Bromsgrove, UK.
112 Housman, *The Unexpected Years*, 18, 90–1.
113 Laurence Housman, *A. E. H.: Some Poems, Some Letters, and a Personal Memoir* (London: Jonathan Cape, 1937), 62.
114 Richard Perceval Graves, *A. E. Housman: The Scholar-Poet* (London: Routledge & Kegan Paul, 1979), 132.
115 Grant Richards, *Housman: 1897–1936* (Oxford: Oxford University Press, 1942), 104.
116 A. E. Housman to Laurence Housman, April 27, 1911, quoted in Archie Burnett, ed. *The Letters of A. E. Housman*, vol. 1 (Oxford: Oxford University Press, 2007), 266.

117 Housman, *The Unexpected Years*, 162.

118 A. E. Housman to Laurence Housman, March 31, 1895, quoted in Burnett, *The Letters of A. E. Housman*, 82.

119 Ibid., 83.

120 A. E. Housman to Laurence Housman, December 14, 1894, quoted in Burnett, *The Letters of A. E. Housman*, 81.

121 Quoted in Housman, *The Unexpected Years*, 163.

122 A. E. Housman to Laurence Housman, June 27, 1908, quoted in Burnett, *The Letters of A. E. Housman*, 222.

123 Quoted in Housman, *The Unexpected Years*, 360.

124 Housman, *The Unexpected Years*, 364.

125 Jeffrey Weeks, "Movements of Affirmation: Sexual Meanings and Homosexual Identities," in *Passion and Power: Sexuality in History*, eds. Kathy Peiss and Christina Simmons (Philadelphia: Temple University Press, 1989), 82.

126 Laurence Housman, unpublished manuscript entitled "Outrageous Fortune," 6, 1933, Box 13, Folder 7, Laurence Housman Papers.

127 Housman, *A. E. H.: Some Poems, Some Letters, and a Personal Memoir*, 13, 11.

128 Ibid., 11.

129 Ibid., 43.

130 Ibid., 61.

131 Ibid., 62.

132 Ibid., 283.

133 Ibid.

134 Ibid.

135 Veronica Alfano, "A. E. Housman's Ballad Economies," in *Economies of Desire at the Victorian Fin de Siècle: Libidinal Lives*, eds. Jane Ford, Kim Edwards Keates, and Patricia Pulham (New York: Routledge, 2016), 45–6.

136 Christopher Ricks, "A. E. Housman and 'the Colour of His Hair,'" *Essays in Criticism* 47, no. 3 (1997): 244.

137 Housman, *A. E. H.: Some Poems, Some Letters, and a Personal Memoir*, 105.

138 Ibid.

139 Ibid.

140 Ibid.

141 Housman, "A. E. Housman's 'De Amicitia,'" 36.

142 Ibid.

143 Ibid., 37.

144 Ibid.

145 Ibid.

146 Ibid.

147 Ibid., 39.

148 Laurence Housman to Houston Martin, June 4, 1939, Box 4, Folder 5, Laurence Housman Papers.

149 Laurence Housman to Houston Martin, June 29, 1939, Box 4, Folder 5, Laurence Housman Papers.
150 Housman, "A. E. Housman's 'De Amicitia,'" 39.
151 Ibid.
152 Ibid., 39–40.
153 Ibid., 34.
154 Housman, *The Unexpected Years*, 19.
155 Laurence Housman, unpublished manuscript entitled "Outrageous Fortune," 36, 1933, Box 13, Folder 7, Laurence Housman Papers.

Chapter 3

1 "Willy" is the pseudonym of Colette's first husband, Henry Gauthier-Villars. As Lawrence Schehr notes in his translator's introduction to *The Third Sex*, Gauthier-Villars often assigned his pseudonym to texts he did not, in fact, write, and he is probably not the true author of *The Third Sex*.
2 Willy, *The Third Sex*, 25.
3 Ibid., 25.
4 Ibid., 25–6.
5 Ibid., 26.
6 See Harford Montgomery Hyde, *Lord Alfred Douglas: A Biography* (London: Methuen, 1984), 93, 115. Wilde also noted that, as the tomb was not truly Tiberius's, he would place the flowers with more emotion.
7 Talia Schaffer, *Romance's Rival: Familiar Marriage in Victorian Fiction* (New York: Oxford University Press, 2016), 15.
8 Other Italian locations fostered similarly innovative and sexually dissident communities during the nineteenth and early twentieth centuries. The American actress Charlotte Cushman's circle of "jolly female bachelors" in Rome in the 1850s and 1860s, for example, offers an additional example of expatriates turning to Italy with an idea that this location offered freedoms and sexual possibilities unavailable elsewhere. (For further discussion of this community and its development of a lesbian cultural space in Rome, see Lisa Merrill, "'Old Maids, Sister-Artists, and Aesthetes': Charlotte Cushman and Her Circle of 'Jolly Bachelors' Construct an Expatriate Women's Community in Rome," *Women's Writing* 10, no. 2 [2003]: 367–83.) However, Capri's islandness seemed to compound the liberatory possibilities of Italy's mainland in the minds of the post-Victorian Decadents who arrived there in the late nineteenth and early twentieth centuries, providing an additional buffer or disconnect from moral oversight and the disciplining of sexuality. This might be compared to the reputation of Taormina in Sicily, where sexually dissident artists from abroad, such as the German photographer Wilhelm von Gloeden and the English artist Robert Hawthorn Kitson, settled at the end of the nineteenth century and the beginning of the twentieth. Taormina's remoteness offered the promise of concealment and sexual freedom in the decades

preceding the rise of fascism in Italy. (For further discussion of Wilhelm von Gloeden's time on Taormina, see Mario Bolagnori, "Taormina and the Strange Case of Baron von Gloeden," in *Homosexuality in Italian Literature, Society, and Culture, 1789–1919*, eds. Lorenzo Benadusi, Paolo L. Bernardini, Elisa Bianco, and Paola Guazzo [Newcastle-upon-Tyne: Cambridge Scholars, 2017], 155–83.)

9 Whitney Chadwick, *Amazons in the Drawing Room: The Art of Romaine Brooks* (Berkeley: University of California Press, 2000), 14.

10 Gillian Beer, "Island Bounds," in *Islands in History and Representation*, ed. Rod Edmond (London: Routledge, 2003), 39.

11 Marc Shell, *Islandology: Geography, Rhetoric* (Stanford: Stanford University Press, 2014), 18.

12 In his work on sexuality and the Mediterranean, Robert Aldrich has highlighted the role "the South" played in the sexual self-realization of travelers from northern Europe. See Robert Aldrich, *The Seduction of the Mediterranean: Writing, Art and Homosexual Fantasy* (New York: Routledge, 2002). R. C. Bleys's discussion of "homosexual exile" similarly stresses the manner in which tourism engendered resistance to heteronormativity, becoming linked within the queer imagination with "an aspiration to a sociality that is amorphous, temporary, orgiastic and atomic" (Rudi Bleys, "Homosexual Exile: The Textuality of the Imaginary Paradise, 1800–1980," *Journal of Homosexuality* 25, no. 1–2 [1993]: 167).

13 See Gordon Waitt and Kevin Markwell, *Gay Tourism: Culture and Context* (Binghamton, NY: Haworth Press, 2006).

14 Richard Francis Burton makes these claims in the "Terminal Essay" in *The Book of the Thousand Nights and a Night*, 12 vols. (London: H. S. Nichols & Co.).

15 Herzfeld states that he offers the term "Mediterraneanism" on the model of Said's "Orientalism" and that "both terms suggest the reification of a zone of cultural difference through the ideologically motivated representation of otherness" (Michael Herzfeld, *Anthropology Through the Looking-Glass: Critical Ethnography in the Margins of Europe* [New York: Cambridge University Press, 1989], 64).

16 In attending to the complex political implications of queer cosmopolitanism, I am following the lead of Joseph Boone and Rudi Bleys. In his discussion of the homoerotics of Orientalism, Joseph Boone acknowledges that, for voyagers to the East, "the geopolitical realities of the Arabic Orient became a psychic screen on which to project fantasies of illicit sexuality and unbridled excess – including as, Malek Alloula has observed, visions of '*generalized perversion*' and, as Edward Said puts it, 'sexual experience unobtainable in Europe'" (Joseph Allen Boone, "Vacation Cruises; or, the Homoerotics of Orientalism," *PMLA* 110, no. 1 [1995]: 89). Nevertheless, Boone endeavors to consider erotic "collisions" between East and West as encounters "that generate ambiguity and contradiction rather than reassert an unproblematic intellectual domination over a mythic East as an object of desire" (Boone,

"Vacation Cruises," 91). Similarly, Rudi Bleys, in considering the practice of "homosexual exile," has emphasized that, though colonial ideology and history often underwrote erotic travel, exile provided opportunities to "live a sexuality outside the discursive patterns of the West" (Bleys, "Homosexual Exile," 177).

17 Compton Mackenzie, *My Life and Times*, vol. 2 (London: Chatto & Windus, 1963), 255.

18 Ibid.

19 Ibid., 255.

20 Ibid., 256.

21 Ibid., 257.

22 Ibid., 268.

23 Compton Mackenzie, *My Life and Times*, vol. 3 (London: Chatto & Windus, 1964), 226.

24 Compton Mackenzie, *My Life and Times*, 2:268.

25 Ibid., 257.

26 Harry Pirie-Gordon collaborated with Corvo in the writing of *The Weird of the Wanderer* (1912) and *Hubert's Arthur* (1935).

27 Andro Linklater, *Compton Mackenzie: A Life* (London: Chatto & Windus, 1987), 66.

28 Compton Mackenzie, *My Life and Times*, 3:186.

29 Ibid., 119; quoted in Linklater, *Compton Mackenzie*, 61.

30 Compton Mackenzie, *My Life and Times*, 3:155, 56.

31 See Diana Maltz, "The Good Aesthetic Child and Deferred Aesthetic Education," in *Oscar Wilde and the Culture of Childhood*, ed. Joseph Bristow (New York: Palgrave, 2017), 69–88.

32 Compton Mackenzie, *Sinister Street* (London: Martin Secker, 1913), 4, 84.

33 Theodore Erlandson, "A Critical Study of Some Early Novels (1911–1920) of Sir Compton Mackenzie," PhD dissertation (University of Southern California, 1965), 44.

34 S. N. Behrman, *Portrait of Max* (New York: Random House, 1960), 288; Edmund Wilson, *The Shores of Light: A Literary Chronicle of the Twenties and Thirties* (New York: Farrar, Straus and Young, 1952), 28.

35 Faith Compton Mackenzie, *As Much as I Dare* (London: Collins, 1938), 175.

36 Ibid., 188.

37 Ibid., 197–8.

38 Compton Mackenzie, *My Life and Times*, vol. 4 (London: Chatto & Windus, 1965), 38.

39 Faith Compton Mackenzie, *As Much as I Dare*, 208.

40 Compton Mackenzie, *My Life and Times*, 3:254.

41 Faith Compton Mackenzie, *As Much as I Dare*, 217; quoted in Linklater, *Compton Mackenzie*, 107.

42 Compton Mackenzie, *My Life and Times*, 4:132.

43 Ibid., 182.

44 Faith Compton Mackenzie, *As Much as I Dare*, 230.

45 Compton Mackenzie, *My Life and Times*, 4:182.
46 Ibid., 182.
47 Faith Compton Mackenzie, *As Much as I Dare*, 277–8.
48 Ibid., 231.
49 Aldrich, *The Seduction of the Mediterranean*, 129.
50 Faith Compton Mackenzie, *Always Afternoon* (London: Collins, 1943), 97; Faith Compton Mackenzie, *As Much as I Dare*, 231.
51 Money, *Capri: Island of Pleasure*, 88.
52 Will H. L. Ogrinc, "Frère Jacques: A Shrine to Love and Sorrow: Jacques D'adelswärd Fersen (1880–1923)," 2006, http://semgai.free.fr/doc_et_pdf/Fersen-engels.pdf. This is a revised and updated version of an article that first appeared in *Paidika: The Journal of Paedophilia* 3, no. 2 (1994): 30–58.
53 Compton Mackenzie, *My Life and Times*, 4:184.
54 Ibid.
55 Faith Compton Mackenzie, *As Much as I Dare*, 232.
56 Ibid., 231.
57 Jeremy Reed, introduction to Jacques Fersen, *Lord Lyllian: Black Masses* (North Pomfret, VT: Elysium, 2005), iii.
58 Jacques Fersen, *Lord Lyllian: Black Masses* (North Pomfret, VT: Elysium, 2005), 27, 35.
59 Ibid., 37.
60 Ibid., 70–1.
61 Compton Mackenzie, *My Life and Times*, 4:233; James Money states that, while living in Germany, Brooks

> had a brief love affair with the young Maugham, who after a short public-school education at the King's School, Canterbury, was sent at the age of sixteen to complete his education in Germany. Brooks, then twenty-four, was in the vanguard of the aesthetic movement and well-read in the authors of the fin de siècle, to whose books he introduced the impressionable young Maugham. (Money, *Capri: Island of Pleasure*, 54)

62 Faith Compton Mackenzie, *Always Afternoon*, 90.
63 Ibid., 91.
64 Linklater, *Compton Mackenzie*, 124.
65 Neil Pearson, *Obelisk: A History of Jack Kahane and the Obelisk Press* (Liverpool: Liverpool University Press, 2007), 54; Faith Compton Mackenzie, unpublished manuscript entitled "Douglasiana," n.d., Compton Mackenzie Collection, Harry Ransom Center, Austin, TX.
66 George Woodcock, "Norman Douglas: The Willing Exile," *Ariel* 13, no. 4 (1982): 89–90.
67 Faith Compton Mackenzie, unpublished manuscript entitled "Douglasiana," n.d., Compton Mackenzie Collection.
68 Norman Douglas to Faith Compton Mackenzie, February 10, 1927, in Arthur S. Wensinger and Michael Allan, eds. *Respectful Ribaldry: A Selection of Letters from Norman Douglas to Faith Compton Mackenzie* (Graz/Feldkirch: W. Neugebauer Verlag, 2008), 41; Norman Douglas to Faith Compton

Mackenzie, November 7, 1939, in *Respectful Ribaldry*, 115; Norman Douglas to Faith Compton Mackenzie, April 13, 1932, in *Respectful Ribaldry*, 84.

69 Diary of Faith Compton Mackenzie, January 19, 1922, Compton Mackenzie Collection.

70 Ibid.

71 Aldrich, *The Seduction of the Mediterranean*, 131.

72 Norman Douglas, *South Wind* (London: Martin Secker, 1917), 9, 17.

73 In his *Pinorman*, Aldington recounts a debate with his friend "J. S.," who convinces him finally that Douglas borrowed heavily from Wilde in *South Wind*. See Richard Aldington, *Pinorman: Personal Recollections of Norman Douglas, Pino Orioli and Charles Prentice* (London: William Heinemann, 1954), 129–46. The rhetoric concerning the pursuit of pleasure in *South Wind* echoes and mimics Pater's discussion of "multiplied consciousness" in the Conclusion to *Studies in the History of the Renaissance* as well as Wilde's representation of Dorian Gray's endless quest for new "sensations ... at once new and delightful" (Walter Pater, *Studies in the History of the Renaissance* [London: Macmillan, 1873], 213; Oscar Wilde, *The Picture of Dorian Gray* [London: Ward, Lock, Co., 1891], 196). However, while for Pater it is "poetic passion" and the "love of art" that quickens consciousness, and Dorian is altered by his contact with a "yellow book," Douglas's characters are undone by the island of Nepenthe. Heard, for example, is described as "open[ing] out" on the island: "Here he expanded. New interests, new sensations, seemed to lie in wait for him. Never had he felt so alert, so responsive to spiritual impressions, so appreciative of natural beauty" (Douglas, *South Wind*, 218).

74 Norman Douglas, *Alone* (New York: Robert M. McBride & Co., 1922), 168.

75 Douglas, *South Wind*, 244, 271.

76 Ibid., 448.

77 Ibid., 159.

78 Ibid., 159, 171–2.

79 Ibid., 226.

80 Ibid., 225.

81 See Money, *Capri: Island of Pleasure*, 135.

82 Compton Mackenzie, *My Life and Times*, vol. 5 (London: Chatto & Windus, 1966), 122.

83 Ibid., 131.

84 Money, *Capri: Island of Pleasure*, 146; Diary of Faith Compton Mackenzie, July 2, 1917, Compton Mackenzie Collection.

85 Linklater, *Compton Mackenzie*, 184.

86 Diary of Faith Compton Mackenzie, November 29, 1917, Compton Mackenzie Collection.

87 Diary of Faith Compton Mackenzie, December 30, 1917, Compton Mackenzie Collection; Diary of Faith Compton Mackenzie, December 21, 1917, Compton Mackenzie Collection.

88 Diary of Faith Compton Mackenzie, May 17, 1918, Compton Mackenzie Collection; Diary of Faith Compton Mackenzie, June 9, 1918, Compton Mackenzie Collection; Diary of Faith Compton Mackenzie, June 16, 1918, Compton Mackenzie Collection.

89 Faith Compton Mackenzie, *More Than I Should* (London: Collins, 1940), 112; Maria Di Rienzo, "Renata Borgatti," in *Who's Who in Gay and Lesbian History: From Antiquity to World War II*, eds. Robert Aldrich and Garry Wotherspoon (New York: Routledge, 2002), 70.

90 Faith Compton Mackenzie, *More Than I Should*, 112. As Alison Oram and Annmarie Turnbull note, "In the interwar years, tailor-made suits with simple lines were part of a highly fashionable, 'modernist' style for women" (Alison Oram and Annmarie Turnbull, *The Lesbian History Sourcebook: Love and Sex between Women in Britain from 1780–1970* [New York: Routledge, 2001], 15). Faith made frequent note in her diaries of the modernist fashion worn by the women who began arriving on Capri after the war.

91 Faith Compton Mackenzie, *More Than I Should*, 16.

92 Diary of Faith Compton Mackenzie, June 21, 1918, Compton Mackenzie Collection.

93 Faith Compton Mackenzie, *More Than I Should*, 112.

94 Ibid., 19.

95 Ibid., 15.

96 Terry Castle, *The Apparitional Lesbian: Female Homosexuality and Modern Culture* (New York: Columbia University Press, 1995), 202. For a discussion of the exoticization of the Italian opera singer in nineteenth-century discourse, see chapter 6, "Opera and Exoticism in Bulwer Lytton and Vernon Lee" in Piya Pal-Lapinski, *The Exotic Woman in Nineteenth-Century British Fiction and Culture: A Reconsideration* (Durham: University of New Hampshire Press, 2005).

97 Diary of Faith Compton Mackenzie, October 25, 1918, Compton Mackenzie Collection; Diary of Faith Compton Mackenzie, March 15, 1919, Compton Mackenzie Collection.

98 Diary of Faith Compton Mackenzie, March 16, 1919, Compton Mackenzie Collection.

99 Diary of Faith Compton Mackenzie, March 17, 1919, Compton Mackenzie Collection.

100 Diary of Faith Compton Mackenzie, April 2, 1919, Compton Mackenzie Collection.

101 Compton Mackenzie, *My Life and Times*, 5:153.

102 Ibid.

103 See ibid., 185.

104 Compton Mackenzie, *Unconsidered Trifles* (London: Martin Secker, 1932), 61.

105 D. J. Dooley, *Compton Mackenzie* (New York: Twayne Publishers, 1974), 76.

106 Howard J. Booth, "Experience and Homosexuality in the Writing of Compton Mackenzie," *English Studies* 88, no. 3 (2007): 324; Dominic Janes, *Visions of Queer Martyrdom from John Henry Newman to Derek Jarman* (Chicago: University of Chicago Press, 2015), 104.

107 Compton Mackenzie, *Vestal Fire* (London: Cassell, 1927), 3, 148.

108 Ibid., 31.

109 Ibid., 5.

110 Ibid., 34.

111 Ibid., 36.

112 Ibid., 71–4, 136.

113 D. H. Lawrence complained in 1920 that he had become sick of the "stew-pot of semi-literary cats" on Capri and wanted to flee "Cat Cranford" (quoted in Mark Kinkead-Weekes, *The Cambridge Biography of D. H. Lawrence*, vol. 2 [New York: Cambridge University Press, 2011], 556).

114 Compton Mackenzie, *Vestal Fire*, 89–90.

115 Ibid., 182, 184–5.

116 Ibid., 184.

117 Ibid., 185.

118 Ibid., 187.

119 Ibid., 419.

120 Dooley, *Compton Mackenzie*, 77.

121 Compton Mackenzie, *Vestal Fire*, vii.

122 Compton Mackenzie, *My Life and Times*, vol. 6 (London: Chatto & Windus, 1967), 94.

123 Florence Tamagne, *A History of Homosexuality in Europe: Berlin, London, Paris; 1919–1939*, vol. 1 (New York: Algora Publishing, 2006), 247.

124 Rachel Annand Taylor, "Fiction: Deeps and Shallows," *Spectator* 139 (1927): 681.

125 Ibid.

126 Edwin Muir, "Fiction," *The Nation & Athenaeum* 42, no. 3 (1927): 122.

127 Faith Compton Mackenzie's copy of Compton Mackenzie, *Vestal Fire*, Harry Ransom Center Book Collection, Austin, TX.

128 Ibid.

129 Max Beerbohm referred to his copies of books in which he had pasted in images and drawn caricatures of authors as "improved" books. Compton Mackenzie encountered an example of Beerbohm's "improving" work while visiting him in Rapallo in 1913. Beerbohm had "improved" an issue of the *Bookman* devoted to George Bernard Shaw, altering photographs of Shaw to make him look more absurd. He had then cut the photographs from the issue, had them re-photographed and printed with a faded appearance, and asked friends to send them to Shaw with a request for Shaw to autograph and return the enclosed pictures. He had also gone through a copy of Herbert Trench's *Apollo and the Seaman* with a penknife and cut the letter "h" from the beginnings of words and inserted an apostrophe to make it appear that the seaman "[dropped] his aitches." See Compton Mackenzie, *My Life and Times*, 4:204–6.

130 Deborah Cohler argues that, in *Extraordinary Women*, Mackenzie "pokes fun at England's postwar obsessions with sex while also maintaining British masculinity as the normative standard against which his lampoon is grounded" (Deborah Cohler, *Citizen, Invert, Queer: Lesbianism and War in Early Twentieth-Century Britain* [Minneapolis: University of Minnesota Press, 2010], 153).

131 Cyril Connolly "The Vulgarity of Lesbianism," *New Statesman* (August 25, 1928): 614.

132 Compton Mackenzie, *Extraordinary Women*, 111.

133 Booth, "Experience and Homosexuality in the Writing of Compton Mackenzie," 326.

134 Faith Compton Mackenzie, *More Than I Should*, 158, 168.

135 Ibid., 203.

136 Bashir Abu-Manneh, *Fiction of the New Statesman, 1913–1939* (Newark: University of Delaware Press, 2011), 125.

137 Faith Compton Mackenzie, *Mandolinata* (London: Cope & Fenwick, 1931), 23.

138 Ibid., 37.

139 Ibid., 49.

140 Faith Compton Mackenzie, *The Sibyl of the North: The Tale of Christina, Queen of Sweden* (New York: Houghton Mifflin Company, 1931), 13.

141 Ibid., 27, 37.

142 Ibid., 42, 115–16.

143 Ibid., 152.

144 See Marcia Landy and Amy Villarejo, "Queen Christina," in *British Film Institute Film Classics*, vol. 1, eds. Rob White and Edward Buscombe (New York: Fitzroy Dearborn, 2003), 229.

145 Laura Horak, *Girls Will Be Boys: Cross-Dressed Women, Lesbians, and American Cinema* (New Brunswick, NJ: Rutgers University Press, 2016), 208. Compton, too, was responsible for a text that inspired a film about cross-dressing. His *The Early Life and Adventures of Sylvia Scarlett* (1918) was made into a 1935 film starring Katharine Hepburn, *Sylvia Scarlett*. As Horak states, while the film "includes many innuendoes around accidental same-sex desire," it was "nonetheless a fairly typical 'temporary transvestite' comedy" (220).

146 D. H. Lawrence, "The Man Who Loved Islands," *Dial* 83 (1927): 1, 22. For a discussion of the story in relationship to Mackenzie, see Viktor Link, "D. H. Lawrence's 'The Man Who Loved Islands' in Light of Compton Mackenzie's Memoirs," *D. H. Lawrence Review* 15, no. 1–2 (1982): 77–86.

147 Faith Compton Mackenzie, *More Than I Should*, 34.

148 D. H. Lawrence, "Two Blue Birds," *Dial* 82 (1927): 287.

149 Ibid.

150 Ibid.

151 Ibid., 294–5.

152 Linklater, *Compton Mackenzie*, 208.

153 Faith wrote to Compton from Capri:

> I sent you a 35 lire wire to try to stop A coming to Guernsey in case you really contemplated such a step. And now that I've seen M it is more imperative still. He says he will divorce her if she does! And he may turn nasty any time & his story is that he hasn't condoned anything & hasn't believed there was anything to condone all the time. . . . It will be a *fatal* step if she is allowed to go to Guernsey. You will be most horribly compromised. (Faith Compton Mackenzie to Compton Mackenzie, December 25, 1920, Compton Mackenzie Collection)

154 Faith Compton Mackenzie, Notes for *This Is Your Life* program, Compton Mackenzie Collection. Faith is quoting from the section "On Marriage" in Gibran's *The Prophet*.

Chapter 4

1 Harold Acton, *Memoirs of an Aesthete* (London: Methuen & Co., 1948), 1.

2 Ibid., 213; Peter Quennell, "The Undergraduate," in *Oxford, China, and Italy: Writings in Honor of Sir Harold Acton on His Eightieth Birthday*, eds. Edward Chaney and Neil Ritchie (New York: Thames & Hudson, 1984), 57.

3 Jim Knapp-Fisher, quoted in Marie-Jacqueline Lancaster, ed., *Brian Howard: Portrait of a Failure* (London: Anthony Blond, 1968), 122; Acton, *Memoirs of an Aesthete*, 111.

4 Acton, *Memoirs of an Aesthete*, 2.

5 Pater argues that, if we are all condemned to die, we must make the most of and expand that "interval" that remains, and the "love of art" is one of the true passions that allows us to do so. Pater, *Studies in the History of the Renaissance*, 212–13; Acton, *Memoirs of an Aesthete*, 2.

6 Acton, *Memoirs of an Aesthete*, 2.

7 Ibid., 404. I have throughout the chapter provided the names of the individuals with whom Acton interacted as well as the characters in his fiction in pinyin romanization, but I also often include a reference to the Wade-Giles romanization used by Acton. For further discussion of Kang Tongbi's feminism, see Zhongping Chen, "Kang Tongbi's Pioneering Feminism and the First Transnational Organization of Chinese Feminist Politics, 1903–1905," *Twentieth Century China* 44, no. 1 (2019): 3–32.

8 Acton, *Memoirs of an Aesthete*, 404.

9 Ibid.; D. E. Mungello translates the inscription in the following manner: "To a man learned in both East and West, / the world calls you a venerable poet. . . . A follower of both Jesus and the Buddha, / you harmonize their different teachings in yourself" (D. E. Mungello, *Western Queers in China: Flight to the Land of Oz* [New York: Rowman & Littlefield, 2012], 97).

10 Acton, *Memoirs of an Aesthete*, 404. While James Lord insists that Acton "made a serious study of Buddhism" without repudiating "the Roman theology of his upbringing," it is hard to see much evidence in Acton's published writings of a sustained investment in either Christianity or Buddhism (James Lord, *Some Remarkable Men: Further Memoirs* [New York: Farrar, Straus &

Giroux, 1996], 16–17). The two faiths stand in here, it seems, for Acton's European and Asian cultural investments. The harmony for which he strives is not necessarily an integration of religious practices but a cosmopolitan braiding together of Chinese aesthetic traditions with his Anglo-Italian heritage.

11 Acton expressed a deep admiration for Chinese culture, but his work is nevertheless marked by anxiety concerning his own slippage into patterns of Orientalism. In my discussion of the textures and nuances of Acton's Orientalism, I am indebted to Ross Forman's work, which emphasizes the fact, that for British writers engaging with China, Orientalism was "an evolving, unstable, and sometimes ideologically inconsistent means to grapple with their changing position in Asia and beyond" (Ross Forman, *China and the Victorian Imagination: Empires Entwined* [New York: Cambridge University Press, 2013], 7).

12 For a discussion of the politics of transnational adoption of children from Asia in a contemporary context, see David L. Eng, *The Feeling of Kinship: Queer Liberalism and the Racialization of Intimacy* (Durham, NC: Duke University Press, 2010). Eng's discussion of transnational adoption, like Acton's, draws attention to the manner in which theorizing the practice can allow for the consideration of troubling modes of consuming alterity. Eng raises questions about how adoptive parents "utilize discourses of both multiculturalism and colorblindness to absorb racial difference into the intimate space of the family" (110).

13 Quoted in Anthony B. Chan, *Perpetually Cool: The Many Lives of Anna May Wong (1905–1961)* (Oxford: Scarecrow Press, 2003), 97.

14 Acton, *Memoirs of an Aesthete*, 7.

15 Ibid., 40.

16 Ibid., 24.

17 Ibid., 65.

18 Ibid., 55, 66.

19 On March 14, 1958, Waugh wrote to the Earl Baldwin, "There is an aesthetic bugger who sometimes turns up in my novels under various names – that was 2/3 Brian and 1/3 Harold Acton. People think it was all Harold, who is a much sweeter and saner man" (*The Letters of Evelyn Waugh*, ed. Mark Amory [London: Weidenfeld & Nicolson, 1980], 506).

20 [Brian Howard], Dedication, *The Eton Candle* 1 (March 1922): n.p.

21 Acton, *Memoirs of an Aesthete*, 97.

22 Harold Acton, "Hansom Cab No. 213 bis," *The Eton Candle* 1 (March 1922): 93; Sir Shane Leslie to Brian Howard, quoted in *Brian Howard: Portrait of a Failure*, 87; Humphrey Carpenter, *The Brideshead Generation: Evelyn Waugh and His Friends* (London: Weidenfeld & Nicolson, 1989), 28.

23 Martin Green, *Children of the Sun: A Narrative of "Decadence" in England after 1918* (New York: Basic Books, 1976), 157.

24 A. L. Rowe, "The Good-Natured Man," in *Oxford, China, and Italy: Writings in Honor of Sir Harold Acton on His Eightieth Birthday*, eds. Edward Chaney and Neil Ritchie (New York: Thames & Hudson, 1984), 64.

25 Acton, *Memoirs of an Aesthete*, 111.

26 Ibid., 118.

27 Ibid., 173.

28 Ibid., 173–4.

29 Harold Acton, Review of *The Beardsley Period* by Osbert Burdett, *The Cherwell* 13, no. 4 (February 14, 1925): 142.

30 Harold Acton, Review of *The Golden Keys* by Vernon Lee, *The Cherwell* 14, no. 5 (May 30, 1925): 133.

31 Ibid.

32 Ibid.

33 Ibid.

34 Ibid.

35 Ibid.

36 Ibid.

37 Ibid.

38 Ibid.

39 Acton, *Memoirs of an Aesthete*, 1.

40 Ibid., 2.

41 Harold Acton, "Vernon Lee: Rediscovery," translated by Shirley Hazzard, *Belles Lettres* 12, no. 1 (1986): 12. This is a translation from the proceedings of the Inghilterra e Italia nel '900 Bagni de Lucca conference, published in 1973.

42 Harold Acton, "Vernon Lee," in *Inghilterra e Italia nel '900* (Florence: La Nuova Italia, 1973), 3. Translation courtesy of Alice Fischetti. (This portion of the lecture was not included in Hazzard's published translation.)

43 Acton, "Vernon Lee," transl. by Hazzard, 12.

44 Ibid.

45 Ibid.

46 Ibid. This quotation appears in Irene Cooper Willis's preface to an edition of Lee's letters: "From my friends' matrimonial adventures I avert my eyes and say: There goes something primaeval!" (Irene Cooper Willis, Preface to *Vernon Lee's Letters*, ed. Irene Cooper Willis [London: Privately Printed, 1937], xiii).

47 Acton, "Vernon Lee," transl. by Hazzard, 12.

48 Ibid.

49 Ibid. This quotation also appears in Willis's preface to Lee's letters: "I *cannot* like, or love, at the expense of having my skin rubbed off. I can do without people" (Willis, Preface, x).

50 Acton, "Vernon Lee," transl. by Hazzard, 12.

51 Ibid.

52 For further discussion of cosmopolitan bachelordom and transnational contact, see Christopher Reed, *Bachelor Japanists: Japanese Aesthetics and Western Masculinities* (New York: Columbia University Press, 2017). For further discussion of the manner in which the figure of the bachelor highlights the limits of conventional masculinity, see Katherine V. Snyder, *Bachelors, Manhood, and the Novel, 1850–1925* (New York: Cambridge University Press, 1999).

53 Naim Attalah, *Singular Encounters* (New York: Quartet Books, 1990), 13.

54 Dialta Alliata-Lensi Orlandi, *My Mother, My Father and His Wife Hortense: Provenance – Villa La Pietra* (North Charleston, SC: CreateSpace Independent Publishing Platform, 2013), 62–3.
55 Green, *Children of the Sun*, xix.
56 Ibid., 10.
57 Acton, *Memoirs of an Aesthete*, 167.
58 See Harold Acton, *Humdrum* (London: Chatto & Windus, 1928).
59 Acton, *Memoirs of an Aesthete*, 227.
60 Ibid., 243.
61 Ibid., 275.
62 Ibid., 296.
63 Ibid.
64 Pater, *Studies in the History of the Renaissance*, 210.
65 Acton, *Memoirs of an Aesthete*, 323.
66 Ibid., 327.
67 For further discussion of the manner in which British subjects understood the seeing of China and Chinese cultural objects as having the potential to change British eyes, see Elizabeth Hope Chang, *Britain's Chinese Eye: Literature, Empire, and Aesthetics in Nineteenth-Century Britain* (Stanford, CA: Stanford University Press, 2010).
68 Acton, *Memoirs of an Aesthete*, 351.
69 See Patricia Ondek Laurence, *Lily Briscoe's Chinese Eyes: Bloomsbury, Modernism, and China* (Columbia: University of South Carolina Press, 2003).
70 Acton, *Memoirs of an Aesthete*, 340.
71 Ibid., 330.
72 Harold Acton to Roy Harrod, December 14, 1935, Harrod Papers, Vol. I, Special Correspondence, Western Manuscripts Add MS 71181, British Library.
73 Acton, *Memoirs of an Aesthete*, 335.
74 Dominic Cheung, "The Parting of Ways: Anthologies of Early Modern Chinese Poetry in English Translation," in *Translating Chinese Literature*, eds. Eugene Eoyang and Lin Yao-fu (Bloomington: Indiana University Press, 1995), 208.
75 Ibid., 209.
76 Harold Acton, Introduction to *Modern Chinese Poetry*, eds. Harold Acton and Ch'en Shih-hsiang (London: Duckworth, 1936), 13, 15–16.
77 Ibid., 20–1.
78 Cyril Birch, "Harold Acton as a Translator from the Chinese," in *Oxford, China, and Italy: Writings in Honor of Sir Harold Acton on His Eightieth Birthday*, eds. Edward Chaney and Neil Ritchie (New York: Thames & Hudson, 1984), 43.
79 Acton, *Memoirs of an Aesthete*, 335.
80 Ibid.
81 Chen Shixiang to Harold Acton, February 22, 1940, Box 3, Folder 196, Harold Acton Papers, General Collection, Beinecke Rare Book and Manuscript Library, Yale University.

82 Harold Acton to Bernard Berenson, February 24, 1946, Box 24, Bernard and Mary Berenson Papers, Biblioteca Berenson, I Tatti – The Harvard University Center for Italian Renaissance Studies, Courtesy of the President and Fellows of Harvard College.

83 Harold Acton to Bernard Berenson, June 4, 1948, Box 24, Bernard and Mary Berenson Papers.

84 Harold Acton to Bernard Berenson, July 11, 1948, Box 24, Bernard and Mary Berenson Papers.

85 Harold Acton, Preface to *The Peach Blossom Fan* by K'ung Shang-jen, trans. Chen Shih-Hsiang, Harold Acton, and Cyril Birch (New York: New York Review Books, 2015), xvii.

86 Mungello, *Western Queers in China*, 56.

87 Acton, *Memoirs of an Aesthete*, 380.

88 Lord, *Some Remarkable Men*, 13.

89 Harold Acton to Roy Harrod, December 14, 1935, Harrod Papers, Vol. I, Special Correspondence, Western Manuscripts Add MS 71181, British Library.

90 Mungello, *Western Queers in China*, 56.

91 Harold Acton, *More Memoirs of an Aesthete* (London: Methuen: 1970), xiii.

92 Ibid.

93 Ibid., xiv.

94 Ibid., 223.

95 See Nancy Cunard, ed., *Negro: An Anthology* (London: Wishart, 1934).

96 Acton, *More Memoirs of an Aesthete*, 224.

97 Ibid.

98 Ibid.

99 Laura Winkiel, "Nancy Cunard's *Negro* and the Transnational Politics of Race," *Modernism/modernity* 13, no. 3 (September 2006): 510.

100 Nancy Cunard, "Black Man and White Ladyship," in *Nancy Cunard: Brave Poet, Indomitable Rebel*, ed. Hugh Ford (New York: Chilton Book Company, 1968), 103.

101 Nancy Cunard, *Black Man and White Ladyship: An Anniversary* (London: Utopia Press, 1931).

102 Jane Marcus, *Hearts of Darkness: White Women Write Race* (New Brunswick: Rutgers University Press, 2004), 132.

103 Harold Acton to Nancy Cunard, April 14, 1931, Box 11, Folder 6, Nancy Cunard Collection, Harry Ransom Center, The University of Texas at Austin.

104 Marcus, *Hearts of Darkness*, 129.

105 Harold Acton to Nancy Cunard, n.d., Box 11, Folder 6, Nancy Cunard Collection.

106 Harold Acton, "From Tiresias," in *Henry-Music* by Henry Crowder, ed. Nancy Cunard (Paris: Hours Press, 1930), n.p.

107 Anne Chisholm, *Nancy Cunard: A Biography* (New York: Knopf, 1979), 192.

108 Nancy Cunard, "Equatorial Way," in *Henry-Music* by Henry Crowder, ed. Nancy Cunard (Paris: Hours Press, 1930), n.p.
109 Marcus, *Hearts of Darkness*, 133.
110 Maureen Moynagh, "Cunard's Lines: Political Tourism and Its Texts," *New Formations* 34 (1998): 71.
111 Chisholm, *Nancy Cunard*, 134.
112 Anne-Marie Brady, "Adventurers, Aesthetes and Tourists: Foreign Homosexuals in Republican China," in *Foreigners and Foreign Institutions in Republican China*, eds. Anne-Marie Brady and Douglas Brown (New York: Routledge, 2013), 153–4.
113 Karl E. Meyer and Shareen Blair Brysac, *The China Collectors: America's Century-Long Hunt for Asian Art Treasures* (New York: Palgrave Macmillan, 2015), 113.
114 Kun Xi, "Picturing an Aesthetic and Homoerotic Space: Harold Acton's Travel Writing of China in the 1930s," *Interactions* 28, no. 1–2 (2019): 89.
115 Ibid., 89, 90.
116 Harold Acton, *Peonies and Ponies* (London: Chatto & Windus, 1941), 1.
117 Ibid., 1–2.
118 Ibid.
119 Ibid.
120 Ibid., 12.
121 Ibid., 72–3.
122 Ibid., 78.
123 Ibid.
124 Ibid., 79.
125 Ibid., 84.
126 Acton, *More Memoirs of an Aesthete*, 2. For discussion of the association of *dan* actors with sex work and shifting ideas about desire between men in China in the early twentieth century, see chapter 5, "Actors and Patrons," in Wenqing Kang, *Obsession: Male Same-Sex Relations in China, 1900–1950* (Hong Kong: Hong Kong University Press, 2009).
127 L. C. Arlington and Harold Acton, eds., *Famous Chinese Plays* (Peiping [Beijing]: Henri Vetch, 1937), xviii, 403.
128 Acton, *Peonies and Ponies*, 96.
129 Ibid., 98–9.
130 Ibid., 102.
131 Ibid., 106.
132 Ibid., 162.
133 Ibid., 194
134 Ibid., 257.
135 Ibid.
136 Ibid., 273–4.
137 Ibid., 309.
138 Ibid., 309–10.
139 Ibid., 310.

140 Ibid.
141 Ibid., 79.
142 Shirley Lim, *Anna May Wong: Performing the Modern* (Philadelphia: Temple University Press, 2019), 27.
143 Anna May Wong, "Anna May Wong Tells of Voyage on 1st Trip to China," *New York Herald Tribune* (May 17, 1936), 1.
144 Carolyn Anspacher, "Star Goes 'Home,'" *San Francisco Chronicle* (January 24, 1936), 17.
145 Graham Russell Gao Hodges, *Anna May Wong: From Laundryman's Daughter to Hollywood Legend* (New York: Palgrave Macmillan, 2004), 159.
146 Anna May Wong, "Anna May Wong Recalls Shanghai's Enthusiastic Reception," *New York Herald Tribune* (May 31, 1936), 6.
147 Quoted in Lim, *Anna May Wong*, 161.
148 Hodges, *Anna May Wong*, 168.
149 Quoted in Lim, *Anna May Wong*, 169.
169 Ibid.
150 Xi, "Picturing an Aesthetic and Homoerotic Space," 90.
151 Quoted in Chan, *Perpetually Cool*, 119.
152 Lim, *Anna May Wong*, 3.
153 Acton, *Peonies and Ponies*, 307.

Chapter 5

1 Wallace Thurman, *Infants of the Spring* (Boston: Northeastern University Press, 1992), 282–3.
2 Ibid., 283.
3 Ibid.
4 Ibid., 283–4.
5 Ibid., 282.
6 The Bruce Nugent collection includes two stenographic "Geisha Man" notebooks along with a twelve-page holograph manuscript entitled "Kandy," which is an alternate version of the story. The Beinecke dates both of these manuscripts ca. 1927.
7 See, for example, Fiona I. B. Ngô, *Imperial Blues: Geographies of Race and Sex in Jazz Age New York* (Durham, NC: Duke University Press, 2014), 110–19; Tyler Schmidt, "'In the Glad Flesh of My Fear': Corporeal Inscriptions in Richard Bruce Nugent's 'Geisha Man,'" *African American Review* 40, no. 1 (2006): 161–73; and A. B. Christa Schwarz, *Gay Voices of the Harlem Renaissance* (Bloomington: Indiana University Press, 2003), 131–41.
8 Ngô, *Imperial Blues*, 29.
9 Schwarz, *Gay Voices of the Harlem Renaissance*, 5.
10 Michèle Mendelssohn, "A Decadent Dream Deferred: Bruce Nugent and the Harlem Renaissance's Queer Modernity," in *Decadence in the Age of Modernism*, eds. Kate Hext and Alex Murray (Baltimore: Johns Hopkins University Press, 2019), 253.

11 Elisa Glick, "Harlem's Queer Dandy: African-American Modernism and the Artifice of Blackness," *Modern Fiction Studies* 49, no. 3 (2001): 415.

12 Ngô, *Imperial Blues*, 29.

13 Richard Bruce [Nugent], "Smoke, Lilies and Jade," *Fire!! Devoted to Younger Negro Artists* 1, no. 1 (1926): 33.

14 Ibid.

15 Ibid.

16 Joseph Allen Boone, *Libidinal Currents: Sexuality and the Shaping of Modernism* (Chicago: University of Chicago Press, 1998), 225–6.

17 [Nugent], "Smoke, Lilies and Jade," 34 (ellipses in original; ellipses in brackets added).

18 Ibid. (ellipses in original).

19 Ibid. (ellipses in original; ellipses in brackets added).

20 Boone, *Libidinal Currents*, 226.

21 Ibid.

22 Ibid.

23 [Nugent], "Smoke, Lilies and Jade," 34.

24 Ibid., 35 (ellipses in original).

25 Ibid., 36.

26 Ibid.

27 Ibid., 37.

28 Ibid. (ellipses in original).

29 Ibid. (ellipses in original).

30 Ibid., 39 (ellipses in original).

31 Ibid. (ellipses in original; ellipses in brackets added).

32 Nugent used this term in a January 24, 1929 letter to Alain Locke. Quoted in Schwarz, *Gay Voices of the Harlem Renaissance*, 123.

33 Pater, *Studies in the History of the Renaissance*, 211.

34 Aida Overton Walker's 1908 and 1912 Salome performances allowed her to pursue recognition as a modern choreographer during the Salome craze, a period in which dances inspired by the biblical story were in vogue. See David Krasner, "Black *Salome*: Exoticism, Dance, and Racial Myth," in *African American Performance and Theater History: A Critical Reader*, eds. Harry J. Elam and David Krasner (New York: Oxford University Press, 2001, 192–211). Poueymirou argues that the Ethiopian Art Players' 1923 staging of *Salome* "emerged as a symbol and signature of [the group's] modernity and seriousness, and of the ambitious potentials of black drama in America in the early 1920s" (Margaux Poueymirou, "The Race to Perform: *Salome* and the Wilde Harlem Renaissance," in *Refiguring Oscar Wilde's Salome*, eds. Michael Y. Bennett [New York: Rodopi, 2011], 205). Hemsley Winfield's performance as Salome in the New Negro Art Theater's production in the late 1920s foregrounded the utility of Decadence to the practice of self-fashioning within the realms of both race and gender. In a 1982 interview, Nugent discussed Winfield's turn as Salome: "And, well, it sounds like a laugh, but it wasn't a laugh, because he just was Salome. There was nothing camp about it."

He just was Salome" (James V. Hatch, "An Interview with Bruce Nugent," in *Artists and Influences*, eds. Camille Billops and James V. Hatch [New York: Hatch-Billops Collection, 1982], 99).

35 Richard Bruce Nugent, Tape 12 of 15, Side 1 of 2, Interviews with Thomas Wirth, June–September 1983, Box 95, Bruce Nugent Papers, James Weldon Johnson Collection in the Yale Collection of American Literature, Beinecke Rare Book and Manuscript Library, New Haven, CT.

36 Yeeyon Im, Oscar Wilde's *Salomé*: Disorienting Orientalism," *Comparative Drama* 4, no. 4 (2011): 368.

37 See Amy Koritz, "Dancing the Orient for England: Maud Allan's 'The Vision of Salome,'" *Theatre Journal* 46, no. 1 (1994): 63–78.

38 As many critics have remarked, incest, as one of the most taboo of sexual practices, figured prominently within Decadent art and literature. Ian Fletcher notes that incest was a "widespread [theme] during the Decadence," pointing, for example, to the androgynous figures who could be siblings in the paintings of Moreau and Simeon Solomon and Huysmans's discussion of "the androgynous Saint Quintin implicated in incest" in his study of the *Virgin and Saints* (Ian Fletcher, *Romantic Mythologies* [London: Routledge & K. Paul, 1967], 53).

39 Oscar Wilde, *Salome* (London: Elkin Mathews & John Lane, 1894), 26. Herodias was the daughter of one of Herod's half-brothers, Aristobulus.

40 Wirth states that the Bible stories were "written in the late twenties and early thirties" (Richard Bruce Nugent, *Gay Rebel of the Harlem Renaissance*, ed. Thomas H. Wirth [Durham, NC: Duke University Press, 2002], 113).

41 Christopher Vitale, "The Untimely Richard Bruce Nugent," PhD dissertation (New York University, 2007), 406–7.

42 Ibid., 416–17.

43 Schwarz, *Gay Voices of the Harlem Renaissance*, 126.

44 Nugent, *Gay Rebel of the Harlem Renaissance*, 130.

45 Ibid.

46 Ibid., 131.

47 Ibid., 134.

48 Ibid., 136.

49 Ibid., 137–8.

50 Richard Bruce Nugent, Tape 12 of 15, Side 1 of 2, Interviews with Thomas Wirth, June–September 1983, Box 95, Bruce Nugent Papers.

51 Ngô, *Imperial Blues*, 116.

52 Nina Miller asserts that the face of Nugent's "Negrotesque" Salome, "though marked as racially African, has more the look of an African mask than an African American person, suggesting that even on the point of racial identification, Nugent weighs in as more a international modernist than a citizen of Harlem" (Nina Miller, *Making Love Modern: The Intimate Public Worlds of New York's Literary Woman* [New York: Oxford University Press, 1999], 175). Miller stresses the "tawdriness" of Nugent's "Negrotesque" Salome, which transforms the dance of the seven veils into a "striptease," but

I would suggest that, in this image, Nugent seems to feel into the experience of being placed on display and subjected to an exoticizing gaze (175).

53 Nugent, *Gay Rebel of the Harlem Renaissance*, 131.

54 Ibid.

55 Hortense Spillers, "Mama's Baby, Papa's Maybe," *Diacritics* 17, no. 2 (1987): 74.

56 Nugent, *Gay Rebel of the Harlem Renaissance*, 132.

57 Ibid., 133.

58 Ibid., 138.

59 Ibid., 139.

60 While Kondo does state in the opening pages of the text, "I was the son of Yetsin Matzuika," as Tyler Schmidt argues, Kondo's gender identity is "not assuredly fixed, but fluid and destabilized" (Schmidt, "'In the Glad Flesh of My Fear,'" 168). I have therefore chosen to use they/them pronouns to refer to Kondo throughout the chapter.

61 Nugent, "Geisha Man" notebooks, ca. 1927, 13–14, Series II, Box 18, Bruce Nugent Papers.

62 Schmidt, "'In the Glad Flesh of My Fear,'" 162. Spillers argues that the representation of incestuous desire in African American literature "speaks for [the] losses, confusions," and the "dispersal of the historic African American domestic unit" (Spillers, "'The Permanent Obliquity of an In(pha)llibly Straight,'" 249).

63 Schmidt, "'In the Glad Flesh of My Fear,'" 171.

64 Ibid.

65 Cedric Essi, "Mama's Baby, Papa's, Too – Toward Critical Mixed Race Studies," *Zeitschrift für Anglistik und Amerikanistik* 65, no. 2 (2017): 162.

66 See Hortense Spillers, "Mama's Baby, Papa's, Too," *Trans-Scripts* 1 (2011): 1–4; Brigitte Fielder, *Relative Races: Genealogies of Interracial Kinship in Nineteenth-Century America* (Durham, NC: Duke University Press, 2020), 203.

67 Tavia N'yongo, *The Amalgamation Waltz: Race, Performance, and the Ruses of Memory* (Minneapolis: University of Minnesota Press, 2009), 5.

68 Nugent, "Geisha Man" notebooks, 1–2. While Thomas Wirth regularized the punctuation in the published excerpts of "Geisha Man" included in *Gay Rebel of the Harlem Renaissance*, I have chosen to preserve Nugent's use of dashes when citing the original manuscript in the Beinecke. Nugent moves between using multiple en dashes and a single em dash to connect portions of text, and I have tried to preserve these stylistic choices in my transcription as well. Throughout my citations from this manuscript, dashes appear in the orginal while ellipses are added to indicate omissions.

69 Ibid., 3.

70 Ibid., 5.

71 Ibid., 6.

72 Ibid., 9–10.

73 Ibid., 11.

74 Ibid.

75 Ibid., 12.
76 Nugent narrates an encounter like this between two brothers, Stuartt, a member of the New Negro movement, and Aeon, who is passing as white, from Stuartt's perspective in his novel *Gentleman Jigger* (Philadelphia: Da Capo, 2008) and from Aeon's in the unpublished manuscript "Half High." Aeon describes the encounter in the following manner: "I meet Stuartt. Who is my brother, a son of my parents, and who seems to know it not. ... He knows me not nor shall I know him. But I find myself likewise snared by his eyes and throat.... Perhaps through him I can glimpse that for which I long" ("Half High" [Novella], 44, Box 19, Folder 1, Bruce Nugent Papers).
77 Nugent, "Geisha Man" notebooks, 13–14.
78 Ibid., 14.
79 Ibid., 18.
80 Ibid., 19.
81 Ibid., 19–21.
82 Ibid., 31.
83 Ibid., 44. This name seems to be derived from the Spanish term "*pulcro*," or beautiful. Wirth transcribes the god's name as "Pulcreado" in the published portion of the manuscript.
84 Ibid., 49.
85 Ibid., 90.
86 Ibid., 65–6.
87 Ibid., 67.
88 Ibid., 66, 89
89 Nugent, *Gay Rebel of the Harlem Renaissance*, 94. I quote here and whenever possible from the published portion of the manuscript in Wirth's edition, as this is the version of the text that will be accessible to most readers. I have preserved Wirth's punctuation when citing from his transcription of the text. Ellipses are present in the original in citations from Wirth's edition unless enclosed in brackets.
90 Ibid., 100.
91 Ibid. (ellipses in brackets added).
92 Ibid., 101–2 (ellipses in brackets added).
93 Ibid., 102 (ellipses in original).
94 Ibid.
95 Ibid., 103.
96 Ibid., 104.
97 Ibid., 105.
98 Ibid., 106.
99 Ibid., 108.
100 Ibid., 109.
101 Ibid. (ellipses in original; ellipses in brackets added).
102 Ibid., 110 (ellipses in brackets added).
103 Ibid. (ellipses in brackets added).

104 Ibid., 111. Schwarz argues that the story ends with "Kondo's suicide" (Schwarz, *Gay Voices of the Harlem Renaissance*, 131). Ngô reads the conclusion as "an ambiguous form of suicide" (Ngô, *Imperial Blues*, 114). The portion of the manuscript that Wirth included in *Gay Rebel of the Harlem Renaissance* concludes with the words "Life or death or life and death or life or . . ." (111). However, the manuscript continues for three more pages, with Kondo moving through Union Square and stating, "My silver evening gown was attracting attention" (Nugent, "Geisha Man" notebooks, 177). We are left at the manuscript's end with Kondo still alive, still moving through the city.

105 Nugent, "Geisha Man" notebooks, 23, 44.

106 [Nugent], "Smoke, Lilies and Jade," 37.

107 Nugent, "Half High – Epistle," December 17, 1928, Series II, Box 103, Bruce Nugent Papers.

108 Glick notes that "Nugent's debt to Aubrey Beardsley is apparent in his striking composition and mannered formalism" (Glick, "Harlem's Queer Dandy," 427).

109 Caroline Goeser, "The Case of Ebony and Topaz: Racial and Sexual Hybridity in Harlem Renaissance Illustrations," *American Periodicals: A Journal of History & Criticism* 15, no. 1 (2005): 109; J. Edgar Bauer, "On the Transgressiveness of Ambiguity: Richard Bruce Nugent and the Flow of Sexuality and Race," *Journal of Homosexuality* 62, no. 8 (2015): 1039.

110 As Wirth notes, with his colorful Salome series of the 1930s and into the 1940s, Nugent began to augment "his exquisite pen and ink drawings with the transparent Japanese dyes that were used at the time to tint photographs" (Thomas H. Wirth, Introduction to *Gay Rebel of the Harlem Renaissance*, ed. Thomas H. Wirth [Durham, NC: Duke University Press, 2002], 61).

111 Nugent, *Gentleman Jigger*, 4, 7, 15.

112 Ibid., 20.

113 Ibid., 20–21. This scenario is modeled upon Nugent's first meeting with Thurman, which he discusses in a taped interview at the Beinecke, noting that he had thought Thurman's work brilliant, but upon meeting him had been startled by his Blackness. He, like Stuartt, felt such shame about his own prejudice that he apologized to Thurman.

Chapter 6

1 Michael Field to Eric Gill, June 3, 1913, Collection on Eric Gill, MS. Gill, William Andrews Clark Memorial Library, University of California, Los Angeles.

2 Ibid.

3 Ibid.

4 Ibid.

5 Judith Collins, *Eric Gill: The Sculpture* (New York: Overlook Press, 1998), 79.

6 Ibid., 80, 87–8.
7 Anthony Hoyland, *Eric Gill: Nuptials of God* (Kent: Crescent Moon, 1994), 63.
8 Fiona MacCarthy, for example, stresses Gill's "sexually possessive attitude to his own daughters" and his tendency to "retreat," evident in the move to Ditchling and Capel-y-Finn. See Fiona MacCarthy, *Eric Gill: A Lover's Quest for Art and God* (New York: E. P. Dutton, 1989), xi, 84, 187. She also refers often to the "Englishness" of his work and his character. See ibid., 22, 272. Rupert Arrowsmith's recent work on global aesthetics and the British avant-garde troubles this vision of Gill as provincial and removed from the international scene. See Rupert Arrowsmith, *Modernism and the Museum: Asian, African, and Pacific Art and the London Avant-Garde* (New York: Oxford University Press, 2011).
9 Hoyland, *Nuptials*, 67.
10 Quoted in MacCarthy, *Eric Gill*, 239.
11 Ibid., viii.
12 In 1998, Margaret Kennedy of Ministers and Clergy Sexual Abuse Survivors, called for the Stations of the Cross at Westminster Cathedral to be dismantled: "Survivors couldn't pray at the Stations of the Cross. They were done by a paedophile. The very hands that carved the stations were the hands that abused." See Finlo Rohrer, "Can the Art of a Paedophile Be Celebrated?" *BBC News* (September 5, 2007), http://news.bbc.co.uk/2/hi/uk_news/magazine/6979731.stm. In 2013, Fay Maxted, chief executive of the Survivors Trust, which represents organizations that support survivors of rape, sexual violence, and childhood sexual abuse, made a similar claim concerning Gill's carvings at the BBC, asserting, "It's an insult to allow a work like this to remain in such a public place. It is almost mocking survivors, it is intolerable." Peter Saunders, chief executive of the National Association for People Abused in Childhood, added, "There's a strong argument that this (the statue) should be removed." See News.com.au, "BBC Told to Remove Work by Pedophile Sculptor Eric Gill" (April 23, 2013), www.news.com.au/world/bbc-told-to-remove-work-by-pedophile-sculptor-eric-gill/story-fndir2ev-1226626709154.
13 Hoyland, *Nuptials*, 57.
14 Ibid., 63.
15 Ibid., 53.
16 Michael Yorke, *Eric Gill: Man of Flesh and Spirit* (New York: Universe Books, 1981), 102, 105.
17 MacCarthy, *Eric Gill*, 191.
18 Eric Gill, *Clothes: An Essay upon the Nature and Significance of the Natural and Artificial Integuments Worn by Men and Women* (London: Jonathan Cape, 1931).
19 MacCarthy, *Eric Gill*, 30.
20 See Eric Gill, "He & He," in bound collection of various manuscript items, 1910–14, Collection on Eric Gill.

21 Gill converted to Catholicism in February of 1913. The "He & He" and "He & She" entries in the bound notebook at the Clark are dated April 1913.
22 MacCarthy, *Eric Gill*, xi.
23 I borrow the term "queer Catholicism" from Patrick O'Malley's investigation of the manner in which "the formulation and articulation of Catholic subjectivity in Britain comes to be particularly related to that of nonnormative sexual subjectivities" (Patrick O'Malley, "Epistemology of the Cloister: Victorian England's Queer Catholicism," *GLQ: A Journal of Gay and Lesbian Studies* 15, no. 4 [2009]: 541).
24 In his autobiography, Gill implies that Catholicism enables dissident or transgressive behavior: "They say there are more Roman Catholics in gaol than any other kind of person; but in a manner of speaking, they can afford to be. Other people can't afford to take risks and if you've got no 'rock of ages' to hang on to when shipwrecked, you'd better take care to keep off the rocks" (Eric Gill, *Autobiography* [New York: Devin-Adair, 1941], 168).
25 Marion Thain, *"Michael Field": Poetry, Aestheticism, and the Fin de Siècle* (New York: Cambridge University Press, 2007), 169.
26 Marc-André Raffalovich to Eric Gill, July 1, 1914, Collection on Eric Gill.
27 Eric Gill, *Letters of Eric Gill*, ed. Walter Shewring (New York: Devin-Adair, 1948), 55.
28 See Eric Gill to Marc-André Raffalovich, July 8, 1914, Manuscript Collections, National Library of Scotland, Edinburgh, UK.
29 Marc-André Raffalovich to Eric Gill, July 11, 1914, Collection on Eric Gill.
30 Frederick Roden, *Same-Sex Desire in Victorian Religious Culture* (New York: Palgrave Macmillan, 2002), 2.
31 Ellis Hanson, *Decadence and Catholicism* (Cambridge, MA: Harvard University Press, 1997), 323.
32 Ibid., 323, 325.
33 As Hanson notes, Raffalovich used the term "sublime invert" in his discussion of "the capacity for intense religious feeling among inverts" (Hanson, *Decadence*, 323).
34 Gill, *Letters*, 138.
35 Jerusha McCormack, *The Man Who Was Dorian Gray* (New York: St. Martin's Press, 2000), 258.
36 Gill described the Guild this way in an article published in the *Game* in 1921. Quoted in Robert Speaight, *The Life of Eric Gill* (London: Methuen & Co.), 110.
37 See, for example, Diary of Eric Gill, October 5, 1917, Collection on Eric Gill; Diary of Eric Gill, October 8, 1917, Collection on Eric Gill; and Diary of Eric Gill, July 18, 1922, Collection on Eric Gill.
38 Marion Thain and Ana Vadillo, eds., *Michael Field, The Poet* (Buffalo, NY: Broadview, 2009), 283.
39 Ibid., 285–6.
40 Quoted in Thain, *"Michael Field,"* 172. While Thain does not state explicitly that the book was presented to McNabb, she does note that it is inscribed "To

the Very Revd, the Prior of Holy Cross" (Ibid., 171). McNabb was Prior of the Holy Cross Priory from 1908 to 1914. See Ferdinand Valentine, *Father Vincent McNabb, O.P.: The Portrait of a Great Dominican* (London: Burns & Oates, 1955), 237.

41 Michael Field, Preface to *The Orchard Floor: Selected Passages from Sermons by the Very Rev. Vincent McNabb, Compiled by Miss E.C. Fortey* (London: R. & T. Washbourne, 1912), vii.

42 Michael Field, *The Wattlefold* (Oxford: Basil Blackwell, 1930), v–vi.

43 See Roden, *Same-Sex Desire*, 198.

44 Valentine, *McNabb*, 384.

45 Mary Sturgeon, *Michael Field* (London: George G. Harrap, 1922), 57.

46 Ibid., 61.

47 Ibid.

48 While Gill does not state explicitly in his diaries that he informed McNabb about his incestuous relationships, he does make note of McNabb taking his confession, and in a 1921 entry he records that he made a confession to Fr. O'Connell concerning Elizabeth and his affairs, presumably referencing his sexual abuse of his daughter Elizabeth (See Diary of Eric Gill, July 25, 1921, Collection on Eric Gill). This would seem to indicate that he spoke to his Catholic confessors about his incestuous sexual practices.

49 McNabb and Gill did eventually fall out with one another. In 1935, Gill published an article in the *Sun Bathing Review* that McNabb found objectionable, and McNabb wrote to Gill to ask him to inform those who coupled their names that they were no longer united. See Vincent McNabb to Eric Gill, January 20, 1935, Collection on Eric Gill.

50 MacCarthy notes that Gill recorded in his diary on November 1, 1929, "Bath and slept with Gladys" (MacCarthy, *Eric Gill*, 239).

51 Vincent McNabb, Introduction to *The Wattlefold*, by Michael Field (Oxford: Basil Blackwell, 1930), vi.

52 Kate Thomas, "'What Time We Kiss': Michael Field's Queer Temporalities," *GLQ: A Journal of Lesbian and Gay Studies* 13, no. 2–3 (2007): 329. A recent notable exception to this tendency is Carolyn Tate's "Lesbian Incest as Queer Kinship: Michael Field and the Erotic Middle-Class Victorian Family," *Victorian Review* 39, no. 2 (2013): 181–99.

53 McNabb, Introduction, v.

54 Jerusha McCormack, *John Gray: Poet, Dandy, and Priest* (Waltham, MA: Brandeis University Press, 1991), 97.

55 Valentine, *McNabb*, 33.

56 Ibid., 34.

57 Chris White, "Poets and Lovers Ever More: The Poetry and Journals of Michael Field," in *Sexual Sameness: Textual Difference in Gay and Lesbian Writing*, ed. Joseph Bristow (New York: Routledge, 1992), 34. The relationship is referred to as a "Sacred Relation" in their journals. See Ivor Treby, *Uncertain Rain: Sundry Spells of Michael Field* (Bury St. Edmunds: De Blackland, 2002), 27.

256 *Notes to pages 199–206*

58 Thain, *"Michael Field,"* 192.
59 Hanson, *Decadence*, 318; Gill, *Autobiography*, 219.
60 Dennis P. Doordan, "Trousers as an Industrial Product: The Case of Eric Gill," Paper Presented at the Design History Society Annual Conference 2011, Barcelona, Spain, September 7–10, 2011, 3, www.historiadeldisseny .org/congres/pdf/27%20Doordan,%20Dennis%20TROUSERS%20AS% 20AN%20INDUSTRIAL%20PRODUCT%20THE%20CASE%20OF% 20ERIC%20GILL.pdf.
61 Joseph E. Davis, "Incest," in *Encyclopedia of Social Problems*, ed. Vincent Parillo (Thousand Oaks, CA: Sage Publications, 2008), 485.
62 See Gayle Rubin, "The Traffic in Women: Notes on the Political Economy of Sex," in *Toward an Anthropology of Women*, ed. Rayna R. Reiter (New York: Monthly Review Press, 1975), 157–210; Judith Butler, *Antigone's Claim* (New York: Columbia University Press, 2002).
63 Butler, *Antigone's Claim*, 21.
64 Elizabeth Barnes, Introduction to *Incest and the Literary Imagination*, ed. Elizabeth Barnes (Gainesville: University Press of Florida, 2002), 9–10.
65 MacCarthy, *Eric Gill*, 156.
66 Count Harry Kessler to Eric Gill, October 26, 1910, Collection on Eric Gill.
67 Eric Gill, *Birth Control* (Ditchling: St. Dominic's Press, 1919), 6.
68 Claude Levi-Strauss, *The Elementary Structures of Kinship* (Boston: Beacon Press, 1969), 24; Kathy Rudy, "LGBTQ…Z?" *Hypatia* 27, no. 3 (2012): 607.
69 See Diary of Eric Gill, April 12, 1915, Collection on Eric Gill.
70 See Diary of Eric Gill, October 25, 1916, Collection on Eric Gill.
71 Quoted in MacCarthy, *Eric Gill*, 239.
72 Ibid.
73 See Ruth Vanita, *Sappho and the Virgin Mary: Same Sex Love and the English Literary Imagination* (New York: Columbia University Press, 1996).
74 Jill R. Ehnenn, "'Drag(ging) at Memory's Fetter': Michael Field's Personal Elegies, Victorian Mourning, and the Problem of Whym Chow," *The Michaelian* 1 (2009), www.thelatchkey.org/Field/MF1/ehnennarticle.htm.
75 Roden, *Same-Sex Desire*, 194.
76 For further discussion of Gill's belief that "the erotic and the spiritual are not opposites or separable" and that "human love is a participation in Divine Love," see Yorke, *Eric Gill*, 120–2.
77 See Michael Field, *Mystic Trees* (London: Eveleigh Nash, 1913).
78 See Michael Field, *Poems of Adoration* (London: Sands & Co., 1912).
79 Gill, *Letters*, 58.
80 Ibid.
81 Quoted in MacCarthy, *Eric Gill*, 162.
82 Arrowsmith, *Modernism and the Museum*, 53–4.
83 William Rothenstein to Eric Gill, November 30, 1911, Collection on Eric Gill.

84 William Rothenstein to Eric Gill, November 26, 1910, quoted in Arrowsmith, *Modernism and the Museum*, 79.

85 Gill, *Letters*, 37.

86 Quoted in William Rothenstein, *Men and Memories* (New York: Coward-McCann, 1932), 280.

87 See Walter Shewring, "Ananda Coomaraswamy and Eric Gill," in *Ananda Coomaraswamy: Remembering and Remembering Again and Again*, ed. S. Durai Raja Singam (Kuala Lumpur: S. D. Raja Singam, 1974), 189.

88 Arrowsmith, *Modernism and the Museum*, 51.

89 Gill, *Autobiography*, 179.

90 Ibid., 179–80.

91 Eric Gill, Introduction to *Viśvakarmā: Examples of Indian Architecture, Sculpture, Painting, Handicraft, Chosen by Ananda Coomaraswamy, First Series: One Hundred Examples of Indian Sculpture* (London: Messrs. Luzac, 1914), 6.

92 Sarah Victoria Turner, "The 'Essential Quality of Things': E. B. Havell, Ananda Coomaraswamy, Indian Art and Sculpture in Britain, c. 1910–14," *Visual Culture in Britain* 11, no. 2 (2010): 255.

93 Richard Cork, *Wild Thing: Epstein, Gaudier-Brzeska, Gill* (London: Royal Academy of Arts, 2009), 37.

94 Ananda Coomaraswamy, typescript of lecture, "Understanding the Art of India," 1935, Collection on Eric Gill.

95 Ananda Coomaraswamy to Eric Gill, n.d., Collection on Eric Gill.

96 Speaight, *The Life of Eric Gill*, 48. Gill had contact with Epstein and his work prior to Rothenstein's "fostering" of the friendship. He had defended Epstein's controversial frieze for the British Medical Association building in the Strand. However, according to Rothenstein's memoirs, it was Rothenstein who "sent Gill down to Epstein, thinking he might work with him for a time, and the two became friends" (Rothenstein, *Men and Memories*, 195).

97 According to Pennington, "The wings, with their machine-like accuracy of line, form and repetition, owe more to the expert carving techniques of Gill than the expressiveness of Epstein. Recent evidence has come to light in a letter from A. Mola to J. Stern (in the possession of Richard Buckle), which confirms that Gill was seen working on the wings in Epstein's studio" (Michael Pennington, *An Angel for a Martyr: Jacob Epstein's Tomb for Oscar Wilde* [Reading: Whiteknights Press, 1987], 42).

98 See Douglas Cleverdon, Portrait of Eric Gill, compiled by Douglas Cleverdon and Guy Brenton, for BBC program, typed manuscript, May–July 1961, Eric Gill Collection, Harry Ransom Center, University of Texas, 9.

99 Gill, *Autobiography*, 140.

100 According to H. Montgomery Hyde, "Wilde's more enthusiastic admirers would have liked a Greek youth standing by a broken column, or some scene from his work, such as *The Young King*, which was suggested many times" (*Oscar Wilde: A Biography* [London: Methuen, 1975], 382).

101 Arrowsmith, *Modernism and the Museum*, 95.

102 Pennington, *An Angel for a Martyr*, 42; Arrowsmith, *Modernism and the Museum*, 94.
103 Jacob Epstein, *Epstein: An Autobiography* (New York: E. P. Dutton, 1955), 51.
104 Pennington, *An Angel for a Martyr*, 49.
105 Ibid.
106 Arrowsmith, *Modernism and the Museum*, 80.
107 Gill, *Letters*, 32–3.
108 Pennington, *An Angel for a Martyr*, 27.
109 See Arrowsmith, *Modernism and the Museum*, 80–1.
110 Collins, *Sculpture*, 72.
111 See Diary of Eric Gill, January 12, 1911, Collection on Eric Gill.
112 "Catalogue Entry: *Ecstasy* (1910–11), Eric Gill," tate.org.uk, accessed June 9, 2014, www.tate.org.uk/art/artworks/gill-ecstasy-t03477/text-catalogue-entry.
113 Roger Fry to Eric Gill, February 15, 1911; quoted in "Catalogue Entry: *Ecstasy* (1910–11), Eric Gill," tate.org.uk, accessed June 9, 2014, www.tate.org.uk/art/artworks/gill-ecstasy-t03477/text-catalogue-entry.
114 Roger Fry to Eric Gill, February 18, 1911; www.tate.org.uk/art/artworks/gill-ecstasy-t03477/text-catalogue-entry.
115 G. K. Chesterton, "Why Abolish the Family?" *Red Book Magazine* 50, no. 2 (1928): 50.
116 Ibid., 51.
117 Ibid.
118 Ibid., 51, 102.
119 Ibid., 102.
120 Ibid., 104.
121 Ibid., 102.
122 Shulamith Firestone, *The Dialectic of Sex* (New York: William Morrow and Company, 1970), 8.
123 Ibid., 12.
124 Wilde, "The Soul of Man under Socialism," 303. See Caroline Bassett, "Impossible, Admirable, *Androgyne*," in *Further Adventures of* The Dialectic of Sex: *Critical Essays on Shulamith Firestone*, eds. Mandy Merck and Stella Sandford (New York: Palgrave Macmillan, 2010), 85–110.
125 Firestone, *The Dialectic of Sex*, 16, 62.
126 Sophie Lewis, *Full Surrogacy Now: Feminism Against Family* (Brooklyn: Verso, 2019), 119.
127 Eve Kosofsky Sedgwick, *Tendencies* (Durham, NC: Duke University Press, 1993), 71.
128 Ibid.
129 Lisa Downing, "Antisocial Feminism? Shulamith Firestone, Monique Wittig, and Proto-Queer Theory," *Paragraph* 41, no. 3 (2018): 376.

References

Primary Sources

Archives Consulted

Bernard and Mary Berenson Papers, Biblioteca Berenson, I Tatti – The Harvard University Center for Italian Renaissance Studies, Florence, Italy.

Bromsgrove Public Library, Bromsgrove, UK.

Bruce Nugent Papers, James Weldon Johnson Collection in the Yale Collection of American Literature, Beinecke Rare Book and Manuscript Library, Yale University, New Haven, CT.

Collection on Eric Gill, William Andrews Clark Memorial Library, University of California, Los Angeles.

Compton Mackenzie Papers, Harry Ransom Center, The University of Texas at Austin.

Edward Carpenter Collection, Sheffield City Archives, Sheffield, UK.

Eric Gill Collection, Harry Ransom Center, The University of Texas at Austin.

Harold Acton Papers, General Collection, Beinecke Rare Book and Manuscript Library, Yale University, New Haven, CT.

Harrod Papers, British Library, London, UK.

Housman Papers, Alfred Gillett Trust, Street, UK.

Lady Eccles Oscar Wilde Collection, British Library, London, UK.

Laurence Housman Papers, Bryn Mawr College Library, Bryn Mawr, PA.

Manuscript Collections, National Library of Scotland, Edinburgh, UK.

Museum of London, London, UK.

Nancy Cunard Collection, Harry Ransom Center, The University of Texas at Austin.

Norman Douglas Collection, Beinecke Rare Book and Manuscript Library, Yale University, New Haven, CT.

Oscar Wilde and His Literary Circle Collection, William Andrews Clark Memorial Library, University of California, Los Angeles.

Western Manuscripts, British Library, London, UK.

The Women's Library, London School of Economics, London, UK.

Printed Sources

Acton, Harold. "Hansom Cab No. 213 bis." *The Eton Candle* 1 (March 1922): 92–100.

——. *Humdrum*. London: Chatto & Windus, 1928.

——. Introduction to *Modern Chinese Poetry*, edited by Harold Acton and Ch'en Shih-Hsiang, 13–31. London: Duckworth, 1936.

——. *Memoirs of an Aesthete*. London: Methuen, 1948.

——. *More Memoirs of an Aesthete*. London: Methuen, 1970.

——. *Peonies and Ponies*. London: Chatto & Windus, 1941.

——. Preface to *The Peach Blossom Fan*, by K'ung Shang-jen, translated by Chen Shih-Hsiang, Harold Acton, and Cyril Birch, xvii–xxii. New York: New York Review Books, 2015.

——. "Review of *The Beardsley Period* by Osbert Burdett." *The Cherwell* 13, no. 4 (February 14, 1925): 142–3.

——. "Review of *The Golden Keys* by Vernon Lee." *The Cherwell* 14, no. 5 (May 30, 1925): 133.

——. "From Tiresias." In *Henry-Music* by Henry Crowder, edited by Nancy Cunard, n.p. Paris: Hours Press, 1930.

——. "Vernon Lee." In *Inghilterra e Italia nel '900*, 3–8. Florence: La Nuova Italia, 1973.

——. "Vernon Lee: Rediscovery." Translated by Shirley Hazzard. *Belles Lettres* 2, no. 1 (1986): 12.

Anspacher, Carolyn. "Star Goes 'Home.'" *San Francisco Chronicle* (January 24, 1936): 17.

Arlington, L. C. and Harold Acton, eds. *Famous Chinese Plays*. Peiping [Beijing]: Henri Vetch, 1937.

Boulderson, Shadwell. "An Indian Road-Tale." In *The Venture: An Annual of Art and Literature*, edited by Laurence Housman and W. Somerset Maugham, 133–5. London: The Pear Tree Press, 1903.

Burton, Richard Francis. *The Book of the Thousand Nights and a Night*. 12 vols. London: H. S. Nichols & Co., 1894–7.

Chesterton, G. K. "Why Abolish the Family?" *Red Book Magazine* 50, no. 6 (1928): 50–51, 102, 104.

Connolly, Cyril. "The Vulgarity of Lesbianism." *New Statesman* (August 25, 1928): 614.

Cunard, Nancy. "Black Man and White Ladyship." In *Nancy Cunard: Brave Poet, Indomitable Rebel*, edited by Hugh Ford, 103–9. New York: Chilton Book Company, 1968.

——. *Black Man and White Ladyship: An Anniversary*. London: Utopia Press, 1931.

——. "Equatorial Way." In *Henry-Music* by Henry Crowder, edited by Nancy Cunard, n.p. Paris: Hours Press, 1930.

——. ed. *Negro: An Anthology*. London: Wishart, 1934.

Douglas, Norman. *Alone*. New York: Robert M. McBride, 1922.

Respectful Ribaldry: A Selection of Letters from Norman Douglas to Faith Compton Mackenzie. Edited by Arthur S. Wensinger and Michael Allan. Graz/Feldkirch: W. Neugebauer Verlag, 2008.

South Wind. London: Martin Secker, 1917.

Dulau, A. B. & Co. *A Collection of Original Manuscripts Letters and Books of Oscar Wilde.* London: Dulau, 1928.

Ellis, Havelock. *The Erotic Rights of Women, and the Objects of Marriage.* Battersea: Battley Bros., 1918.

Epstein, Jacob. *Epstein: An Autobiography.* New York: E. P. Dutton, 1955.

Fersen, Jacques. *Lord Lyllian: Black Masses.* North Pomfret, VT: Elysium, 2005.

Field, Michael. *Mystic Trees.* London: Eveleigh Nash, 1913.

Poems of Adoration. London: Sands & Co., 1912.

Preface to *The Orchard Floor: Selected Passages from Sermons by the Very Rev. Vincent McNabb, Compiled by Miss E.C. Fortey*, v–viii. London: R. & T. Washbourne, 1912.

The Wattlefold. Oxford: Basil Blackwell, 1930.

Firestone, Shulamith. *The Dialectic of Sex.* New York: William Morrow and Company, 1970.

Gibran, Kahlil. *The Prophet.* New York: Alfred A. Knopf, 1923.

Gill, Eric. *Autobiography.* New York: Devin-Adair, 1941.

Birth Control. Ditchling: St. Dominic's Press, 1919.

Clothes: An Essay upon the Nature and Significance of the Natural and Artificial Integuments Worn by Men and Women. London: Jonathan Cape, 1931.

Introduction to *Viśvakarmā: Examples of Indian Architecture, Sculpture, Painting, Handicraft, Chosen by Ananda Coomaraswamy, First Series: One Hundred Examples of Indian Sculpture*, 1–7. London: Messrs. Luzac, 1914.

Letters of Eric Gill. Edited by Walter Shewring. New York: Devin-Adair, 1948.

Green, Julian. *The Dark Journey.* New York: Harper & Brothers, 1929.

The Dreamer. New York: Harper & Brothers, 1934.

Midnight. New York: Harper & Brothers, 1936.

The Strange River. New York: Harper & Brothers, 1932.

Le Visionnaire. Paris: Plon, 1934.

Hill, Ethel. "Mr. Laurence Housman: An Impression." *The Vote* (December 2, 1909), 64.

Holland, Vyvyan. *A Few Odd Reflections on Idleness.* London: Curwen, 1927.

Foreword to *Salomé*, by Oscar Wilde, 5–8. London: Folio Society, 1957.

Introduction to *De Profundis*, by Oscar Wilde, 7–12. London: Methuen, 1949.

"Once Upon a Time: A Critical Note on Oscar Wilde's Fairy Stories." *Adelphi* 30, no. 3 (1954): 241–51.

Oscar Wilde: A Pictorial Biography. London: Thames & Hudson, 1960.

Son of Oscar Wilde. New York: Carroll & Graf, 1999.

Time Remembered after Père Lachaise. London: Gollancz, 1966.

Housman, A. E. *The Letters of A. E. Housman*, vol. 1. Edited by Archie Burnett. Oxford: Oxford University Press, 2007.

Housman, Clemence. *The Unknown Sea.* London: Duckworth, 1898.

The Were-Wolf. London: John Lane at the Bodley Head, 1896.

Housman, Laurence. "A. E. Housman's 'De Amicitia.'" *Encounter* 29 (1967): 33–41.

A. E. H.: Some Poems, Some Letters, and a Personal Memoir. London: Jonathan Cape, 1937.

All-Fellows: Seven Legends of Lower Redemption with Insets in Verse. London: Kegan, Paul, Trench, Trübner, & Co., 1896.

The Cloak of Friendship. London: J. Murray, 1905.

"The Corruption of Power." *Peace News* (September 5, 1941), 2.

An Englishwoman's Love Letters. New York: Doubleday, Page & Co., 1900.

Echo de Paris: A Study from Life. London: Jonathan Cape, 1923.

"Gandhi and the Future of Pacifism." In *Mahatma Gandhi: Essays and Reflections on His Life and Work*, edited by Sarvepalli Radhakrishnan, 123–34. London: George Allen & Unwin, 1949.

"The Makings of the War Mind – Its Cause and the Cure." *Peace News* (June 19, 1937), 6.

"Mankind Is Growing Up," *Peace News* (May 5, 1939), 9.

Preface to *The Truth about India: Can We Get It*, edited by Verrier Elwin, 7–8. London: G. Allen & Unwin, 1932.

The Relation of Fellow-Feeling to Sex. London: Battley Bros., [n.d.].

"Retaliation." *Peace News* (October 25, 1940), 1.

Sex-War and Women's Suffrage. London: Women's Freedom League, 1912.

"The True Realism." *Peace News* (August 22, 1941), 2.

The Unexpected Years. London: Jonathan Cape, 1937.

"Why Man Has Failed." *Peace News* (September 10, 1938), 7.

[Howard, Brian.] Dedication. *The Eton Candle* 1 (March 1922): n.p.

Lawrence, D. H. "The Man Who Loved Islands." *Dial* 83 (1927): 1–23.

"Two Blue Birds." *Dial* 82 (1927): 287–301.

Mackenzie, Compton. *Extraordinary Women: Theme and Variations.* New York: Macy-Masius, 1928.

My Life and Times. 10 vols. London: Chatto & Windus, 1963–71.

Sinister Street. London: Martin Secker, 1913.

Unconsidered Trifles. London: Martin Secker, 1932.

Vestal Fire. London: Cassell, 1927.

Mackenzie, Faith Compton. *Always Afternoon.* London: Collins, 1943.

As Much as I Dare. London: Collins, 1938.

Mandolinata. London: Cope & Fenwick, 1931.

More Than I Should. London: Collins, 1940.

The Sibyl of the North: The Tale of Christina, Queen of Sweden. New York: Houghton Mifflin Company, 1931.

McNabb, Vincent. Introduction to *The Wattlefold*, by Michael Field, v–vi. Oxford: Basil Blackwell, 1930.

[Millard, Christopher]. *Oscar Wilde: Three Times Tried.* London: Ferrestone Press, 1912.

Muir, Edwin. "Fiction." *The Nation & Athenaeum* 42, no. 3 (1927): 120–22.

Nugent, Richard Bruce. *Gay Rebel of the Harlem Renaissance*. Edited by Thomas H. Wirth. Durham, NC: Duke University Press, 2002.

Gentleman Jigger. Philadelphia: Da Capo, 2008.

"Smoke, Lilies and Jade." *Fire!! Devoted to Younger Negro Artists* 1, no. 1 (1926): 33–9.

Orwell, George. "Review of *Landfall* by Nevil Shute; *Nailcruncher* by Albert Cohen, translated from the French by Vyvyan Holland; and *A Dark Side Also* by Peter Conway." *New Statesman and Nation* 20, no. 511 (December 7, 1940): 574.

Pater, Walter. *Studies in the History of the Renaissance*. London: Macmillan, 1873.

Rothenstein, William. *Men and Memories*. New York: Coward-McCann, 1932.

Sturgeon, Mary. *Michael Field*. London: George G. Harrap, 1922.

Taylor, Rachel Annand. "Fiction: Deeps and Shallows." *Spectator* 139 (1927): 678–81.

Thurman, Wallace. *Infants of the Spring*. Boston: Northeastern University Press, 1992.

Waugh, Evelyn. *The Letters of Evelyn Waugh*. Edited by Mark Amory. London: Weidenfeld & Nicolson, 1980.

Webb, L. C. "Indian Portraits II." *Press* (December 5, 1931), 13.

Wilde, Oscar. *After Berneval: Letters of Oscar Wilde to Robert Ross*. Westminster: Beaumont Press, 1922.

The Complete Letters of Oscar Wilde. Edited by Merlin Holland and Rupert Hart-Davis. New York: Henry Holt, 2000.

"The Critic as Artist." In *The Complete Works of Oscar Wilde*, edited by Josephine Guy, vol. 4, 124–206. New York: Oxford University Press, 2007.

"The Decay of Lying." In *The Complete Works of Oscar Wilde*, edited by Josephine Guy, vol. 4, 73–103. New York: Oxford University Press, 2007.

"The English Renaissance in Art." In *Essays and Lectures*, edited by Robert Ross, 109–56. London: Methuen, 1908.

Intentions. Leipzig: Heinemann & Balestier, 1891.

"Olivia at the Lyceum." *Dramatic Review* 1, no. 18 (1885): 278.

The Picture of Dorian Gray. London: Ward, Lock, Co., 1891.

"The Portrait of Mr. W. H." *Blackwood's Edinburgh Magazine* 146, no. 885 (1889): 4, 6.

The Portrait of Mr. W. H. New York: Mitchell Kennerley, 1921.

Salome. London: Elkin Mathews & John Lane, 1894.

"The Soul of Man under Socialism." *The Fortnightly Review* XLIX (1891): 292–319.

Willis, Irene Cooper. Preface to *Vernon Lee's Letters*, edited by Irene Cooper Willis, i–xiv. London: Privately Printed, 1937.

Willy. *The Third Sex*. Edited by Lawrence R. Schehr. Urbana: University of Illinois Press, 2007.

Wong, Anna May. "Anna May Wong Recalls Shanghai's Enthusiastic Reception." *New York Herald Tribune* (May 31, 1936), 6.

Wong, Anna May. "Anna May Wong Tells of Voyage on 1st Trip to China." *New York Herald Tribune* (May 17, 1936), 1.

Secondary Sources

Abu-Manneh, Bashir. *Fiction of the New Statesman, 1913–1939.* Newark: University of Delaware Press, 2011.

Adams, Elizabeth. "Walter Edwin Ledger, Christopher Sclater Millard, and the Bibliography of Oscar Wilde." *Studies in Walter Pater and Aestheticism* 5 (2020): 105–17.

Aldington, Richard. *Pinorman: Personal Recollections of Norman Douglas, Pino Orioli and Charles Prentice.* London: William Heinemann, 1954.

Aldrich, Robert. *The Seduction of the Mediterranean: Writing, Art and Homosexual Fantasy.* New York: Routledge, 2002.

Alfano, Veronica. "A. E. Housman's Ballad Economies." In *Economies of Desire At the Victorian Fin de Siècle: Libidinal Lives*, edited by Jane Ford, Kim Edwards Keates, and Patricia Pulham, 35–61. New York: Routledge, 2016.

Amin, Kadji. *Disturbing Attachments: Genet, Modern Pederasty, and Queer History.* Durham, NC: Duke University Press, 2017.

Anderson, Amanda. *The Powers of Distance: Cosmopolitanism and the Cultivation of Detachment.* Princeton, NJ: Princeton University Press, 2001.

Arrowsmith, Rupert. *Modernism and the Museum: Asian, African, and Pacific Art and the London Avant-Garde.* New York: Oxford University Press, 2011.

Attalah, Naim. *Singular Encounters.* London: Quartet Books, 1990.

Barnes, Elizabeth. Introduction to *Incest and the Literary Imagination*, edited by Elizabeth Barnes, 1–13. Gainesville: University Press of Florida, 2002.

Bassett, Caroline. "Impossible, Admirable, *Androgyne*: Firestone, Technology, and Utopia." In *Further Adventures of The Dialectic of Sex: Critical Essays on Shulamith Firestone*, edited by Mandy Merck and Stella Sandford, 85–110. New York: Palgrave Macmillan, 2010.

Bauer, J. Edgar. "On the Transgressiveness of Ambiguity: Richard Bruce Nugent and the Flow of Sexuality and Race." *Journal of Homosexuality* 62, no. 8 (2015): 1021–57.

Beer, Gillian. "Island Bounds." In *Islands in History and Representation*, edited by Rod Edmond, 32–42. London: Routledge, 2003.

Behrman, S. N. *Portrait of Max.* New York: Random House, 1960.

Berman, Jessica. *Modernist Fiction, Cosmopolitanism and the Politics of Community.* New York: Cambridge University Press, 2001.

Bielsa, Esperança. "Cosmopolitanism as Translation." *Cultural Sociology* 8, no. 4 (2014): 392–406.

Birch, Cyril. "Harold Acton as a Translator from the Chinese." In *Oxford, China, and Italy: Writings in Honor of Sir Harold Acton on His Eightieth Birthday*, edited by Edward Chaney and Neil Ritchie, 37–44. New York: Thames & Hudson, 1984.

Bleys, Rudi. "Homosexual Exile: The Textuality of the Imaginary Paradise, 1800–1980." *Journal of Homosexuality* 25, no. 1–2 (1993): 165–82.

Boehmer, Elleke. *Indian Arrivals, 1870–1915: Networks of British Empire.* New York: Oxford University Press, 2015.

Bolagnori, Mario. "Taormina and the Strange Case of Baron von Gloeden." In *Homosexuality in Italian Literature, Society, and Culture, 1789–1919*, edited by Lorenzo Benadusi, Paolo L. Bernardini, Elisa Bianco, and Paola Guazzo, 155–83. Newcastle-upon-Tyne: Cambridge Scholars, 2017.

Boone, Joseph Allen. *Libidinal Currents: Sexuality and the Shaping of Modernism.* Chicago: University of Chicago Press, 1998.

"Vacation Cruises; or, the Homoerotics of Orientalism." *PMLA* 110, no. 1 (1995): 89–107.

Booth, Howard J. "Experience and Homosexuality in the Writing of Compton Mackenzie." *English Studies* 88, no. 3 (2007): 320–31.

Borland, Maureen. *Wilde's Devoted Friend: A Life of Robert Ross 1869–1918.* Oxford: Lennard, 1990.

Brady, Anne-Marie. "Adventurers, Aesthetes and Tourists: Foreign Homosexuals in Republican China." In *Foreigners and Foreign Institutions in Republican China*, edited by Anne-Marie Brady and Douglas Brown, 146–68. New York: Routledge, 2013.

Bristow, Joseph, and Rebecca N. Mitchell. "Forging Literary History: 'The Portrait of Mr. W. H.'" In *Oscar Wilde's Chatterton: Literary History, Romanticism, and the Art of Forgery*, edited by Joseph Bristow and Rebecca N. Mitchell, 245–92. New Haven, CT: Yale University Press, 2015.

Brock, I. W. "Julien Green: A Biographical and Literary Sketch." *The French Review* 23, no. 5 (1950): 347–59.

Browne, Stella. *Sexual Variety & Variability among Women and Their Bearing upon Social Reconstruction.* London: C. W. Beaumont, [1917].

Burne, Glenn S. *Julian Green.* New York: Twayne, 1972.

Butler, Judith. *Antigone's Claim.* New York: Columbia University Press, 2002.

Califia, Patrick. *Doing It for Daddy.* Boston: Alyson Publications, 1994.

Campbell, James. *Oscar Wilde, Wilfred Owen, and Male Desire: Begotten, Not Made.* New York: Palgrave Macmillan, 2015.

Carpenter, Humphrey. *The Brideshead Generation: Evelyn Waugh and His Friends.* London: Weidenfeld & Nicolson, 1989.

Castle, Terry. *The Apparitional Lesbian: Female Homosexuality and Modern Culture.* New York: Columbia University Press, 1995.

"Catalogue Entry: *Ecstasy* (1910–11), Eric Gill." tate.org.uk, 2014, accessed June 9, 2014, www.tate.org.uk/art/artworks/gill-ecstasy-t03477/text-catalogue-entry.

Chadwick, Whitney. *Amazons in the Drawing Room: The Art of Romaine Brooks.* Berkeley: University of California Press, 2000.

Chan, Anthony B. *Perpetually Cool: The Many Lives of Anna May Wong (1905–1961).* Oxford: Scarecrow Press, 2003.

Chang, Elizabeth Hope. *Britain's Chinese Eye: Literature, Empire, and Aesthetics in Nineteenth-Century Britain.* Stanford, CA: Stanford University Press, 2010.

Chen, Zhongping. "Kang Tongbi's Pioneering Feminism and the First Transnational Organization of Chinese Feminist Politics, 1903–1905." *Twentieth Century China* 44, no. 1 (2019): 3–32.

Cheung, Dominic. "The Parting of Ways: Anthologies of Early Modern Chinese Poetry in English Translation." In *Translating Chinese Literature*, edited by Eugene Eoyang and Lin Yao-fu, 207–20. Bloomington: Indiana University Press, 1995.

Chisholm, Anne. *Nancy Cunard: A Biography*. New York: Knopf, 1979.

Christie, Rechelle. "The Politics of Representation and Illustration in Clemence Housman's *The Were-Wolf*." *Housman Society Journal* 33 (2007): 54–67.

Cleves, Rachel Hope. *Unspeakable: A Life beyond Sexual Morality*. Chicago: University of Chicago Press, 2020.

Cohler, Deborah. *Citizen, Invert, Queer: Lesbianism and War in Early Twentieth-Century Britain*. Minneapolis: University of Minnesota Press, 2010.

Collins, Judith. *Eric Gill: The Sculpture*. New York: Overlook Press, 1998.

Cork, Richard. *Wild Thing: Epstein, Gaudier-Brzeska, Gill*. London: Royal Academy of Arts, 2009.

Crowell, Ellen. "'We Are Odd!': Ye Archive of Ye Sette of Odd Volumes." *The Center & Clark Newsletter: UCLA Center for 17th- and 18th-Century Studies* 54 (2011): 9–10.

Danson, Lawrence. "Oscar Wilde, W. H., and the Unspoken Name of Love." In *Oscar Wilde: A Collection of Critical Essays*, edited by Jonathan Freedman, 81–98. Upper Saddle River, NJ: Prentice Hall, 1998.

Davidoff, Leonore. *Thicker Than Water: Siblings and Their Relations, 1780–1920*. New York: Oxford University Press, 2011.

Davis, Joseph E. "Incest." In *Encyclopedia of Social Problems*, edited by Vincent Parillo, 484–6. Thousand Oaks, CA: Sage Publications, 2008.

Delanty, Gerard. *The Cosmopolitan Imagination: The Renewal of Critical Social Theory*. New York: Cambridge University Press, 2009.

Di Rienzo, Maria. "Renata Borgatti." In *Who's Who in Gay and Lesbian History: From Antiquity to World War II*, edited by Robert Aldrich and Garry Wotherspoon, 70–71. New York: Routledge, 2002.

Dooley, D. J. *Compton Mackenzie*. New York: Twayne Publishers, 1974.

Doordan, Dennis P. "Trousers as an Industrial Product: The Case of Eric Gill." Paper presented at the Design History Society Annual Conference 2011, Barcelona, Spain (September 7–10, 2011), 1–9. www.historiadeldisseny.org/congres/pdf/27%20Doordan,%20Dennis%20TROUSERS%20AS%20AN%20INDUSTRIAL%20PRODUCT%20THE%20CASE%20OF%20ERIC%20GILL.pdf.

Doussot, Audrey. "Laurence Housman (1865–1959): Fairy Tale Teller, Illustrator and Aesthete." *Cahiers Victoriens & Édouardiens* 73 (Printemps 2011): 131–45.

Downing, Lisa. "Antisocial Feminism? Shulamith Firestone, Monique Wittig, and Proto-Queer Theory." *Paragraph* 41, no. 3 (2018): 364–79.

Edelman, Lee. *No Future: Queer Theory and the Death Drive*. Durham, NC: Duke University Press, 2004.

Ehnenn, Jill R. "'Drag(ging) at memory's fetter': Michael Field's Personal Elegies, Victorian Mourning, and the Problem of Whym Chow." *The Michaelian* 1

(2009): n.p. www.thelatchkey.org/Field/MF1/ehnennarticle.htm (accessed June 9, 2014).

Ellmann, Richard. *Oscar Wilde*. New York: Vintage Books, 1988.

Eng, David L. *The Feeling of Kinship: Queer Liberalism and the Racialization of Intimacy*. Durham, NC: Duke University Press, 2010.

Engen, Rodney K. *Laurence Housman*. Stroud, UK: Catalpa, 1983.

Erlandson, Theodore. "A Critical Study of Some Early Novels (1911–1920) of Sir Compton Mackenzie." PhD dissertation. University of Southern California, 1965.

Essi, Cedric. "Mama's Baby, Papa's, Too – Toward Critical Mixed Race Studies." *Zeitschrift für Anglistik und Amerikanistik* 65, no. 2 (2017): 161–72.

Evangelista, Stefano. "Oscar Wilde: European by Sympathy." In *The Reception of Oscar Wilde in Europe*, edited by Stefano Evangelista, 1–19. New York: Continuum, 2010.

Feldman, Jessica R. *Victorian Modernism: Pragmatism and the Varieties of Aesthetic Experience*. New York: Cambridge University Press, 2002.

Fielder, Brigitte. *Relative Races: Genealogies of Interracial Kinship in Nineteenth-Century America*. Durham, NC: Duke University Press, 2020.

Findlay, Jean. *Chasing Lost Time: The Life of C. K. Scott Moncrieff: Soldier, Spy, and Translator*. London: Chatto & Windus, 2014.

Fletcher, Ian. *Romantic Mythologies*. London: Routledge & K. Paul, 1967.

Forman, Ross. *China and the Victorian Imagination: Empires Entwined*. New York: Cambridge University Press, 2013.

Freeman, Elizabeth. "Queer Belongings: Kinship Theory and Queer Theory." In *A Companion to Lesbian, Gay, Bisexual, and Transgender Studies*, edited by George Haggerty and Molly McGarry, 295–314. Hoboken, NJ: Blackwell Press, 2007.

   Time Binds: Queer Temporalities, Queer Histories. Durham, NC: Duke University Press, 2010.

Fryer, Jonathan. *Robbie Ross: Oscar Wilde's Devoted Friend*. New York: Carroll & Graf, 2002.

Furneaux, Holly. *Queer Dickens: Erotics, Families, Masculinities*. New York: Oxford University Press, 2009.

Fussell, Paul. *Abroad: British Literary Traveling between the Wars*. New York: Oxford University Press, 1980.

Glick, Elisa. "Harlem's Queer Dandy: African-American Modernism and the Artifice of Blackness." *Modern Fiction Studies* 49, no. 3 (2001): 414–42.

Goeser, Caroline. "The Case of Ebony and Topaz: Racial and Sexual Hybridity in Harlem Renaissance Illustrations." *American Periodicals: A Journal of History & Criticism* 15, no. 1 (2005): 86–111.

Goldhill, Simon. *A Very Queer Family Indeed: Sex, Religion, and the Bensons in Victorian Britain*. Chicago: University of Chicago Press, 2016.

Graves, Richard Perceval. *A. E. Housman: The Scholar-Poet*. London: Routledge & Kegan Paul, 1979.

Green, Martin. *Children of the Sun: A Narrative of "Decadence" in England after 1918*. New York: Basic Books, 1976.

Guthrie, James. "The Wood Engravings of Clemence Housman." *The Print Collector's Quarterly* 11 (1924): 190–204.

Hall, Lesley A. "'Disinterested Enthusiasm for Sexual Misconduct': The British Society for the Study of Sex Psychology, 1913–47." *Journal of Contemporary History* 30, no. 4 (1995): 665–86.

Hanson, Ellis. *Decadence and Catholicism*. Cambridge, MA: Harvard University Press, 1997.

"Must We Arrest Oscar Wilde Again?" Paper presented at the Curiosity and Desire in Fin-de-Siècle Art and Literature, William Andrews Clark Memorial Library, UCLA, May 11–12, 2018.

Hatch, James V. "An Interview with Bruce Nugent." In *Artists and Influences*, edited by Camille Billops and James V. Hatch, 81–104. New York: Hatch-Billops Collection, 1982.

Herold, Katharina, 2016. "Cosmopolitan Conglomeration and Orientalist Appropriation in Oscar Wilde's 'The Sphinx.'" Paper presented at the Cosmopolis and Beyond: Literary Cosmopolitanism after the Republic of Letters Conference, Trinity College, University of Oxford, March 18–19, 2016.

Herzfeld, Michael. *Anthropology through the Looking-Glass: Critical Ethnography in the Margins of Europe*. New York: Cambridge University Press, 1989.

Hext, Kate and Alex Murray, eds. *Decadence in the Age of Modernism*. Baltimore: Johns Hopkins University Press, 2019.

Hext, Kate, and Alex Murray. Introduction to *Decadence in the Age of Modernism*, edited by Kate Hext and Alex Murray, 1–26. Baltimore: Johns Hopkins University Press, 2019.

Hirsch, Marianne. Introduction to *The Familial Gaze*, edited by Marianne Hirsch, xi–xxv. Hanover: University Press of New England, 1999.

Hodges, Graham Russell Gao. *Anna May Wong: From Laundryman's Daughter to Hollywood Legend*. New York: Palgrave Macmillan, 2004.

Horak, Laura. *Girls Will Be Boys: Cross-Dressed Women, Lesbians, and American Cinema*. New Brunswick, NJ: Rutgers University Press, 2016.

Housman, Stephen. "The Housman Banners." *Housman Society Journal* 18 (1992): 39–47.

Hoyland, Anthony. *Eric Gill: Nuptials of God*. Kent, UK: Crescent Moon, 1994.

Hyde, Harford Montgomery. *Lord Alfred Douglas: A Biography*. London: Methuen, 1984.

Oscar Wilde: A Biography. London: Methuen, 1975.

Im, Yeeyon. "Oscar Wilde's *Salomé*: Disorienting Orientalism." *Comparative Drama* 4, no. 4 (2011): 361–80.

Jackson, Holbrook. *The Eighteen-Nineties: A Review of Art and Ideas at the Close of the Nineteenth Century*. London: Grant Richards, 1913.

Jackson, Julian. *Living in Arcadia: Homosexuality, Politics, and Morality in France From the Liberation to AIDS*. Chicago: University of Chicago Press, 2009.

James, Jamie. *Pagan Light: Dreams of Freedom and Beauty in Capri.* New York: Farrar, Straus, & Giroux, 2019.

Jamison, Anne Elizabeth. *Poetics en Passant: Redefining the Relationship Between Victorian and Modern Poetry.* New York: Palgrave Macmillan, 2009.

Janes, Dominic. *Visions of Queer Martyrdom from John Henry Newman to Derek Jarman.* Chicago: University of Chicago Press, 2015.

Kang, Wenqing. *Obsession: Male Same-Sex Relations in China, 1900–1950.* Hong Kong: Hong Kong University Press, 2009.

Kaye, Richard. "Oscar Wilde and the Politics of Posthumous Sainthood: Hofmannsthal, Mirbeau, Proust." In *Oscar Wilde and Modern Culture: The Making of a Legend,* edited by Joseph Bristow, 110–32. Athens: Ohio University Press, 2008.

Kennedy, Margaret S. "Wilde's Cosmopolitanism." In *Wilde's Wiles: Studies of the Influences on Oscar Wilde and His Enduring Influences in the Twenty-First Century,* edited by Annette M. Magid, 90–113. Newcastle upon Tyne: Cambridge Scholars Publishing, 2013.

Kinkead-Weekes, Mark. *The Cambridge Biography of D.H. Lawrence.* Vol. 2. New York: Cambridge University Press, 2011.

Kohler, Dayton. "Julian Green: Modern Gothic." *The Sewanee Review* 40, no. 2 (1932): 139–48.

Kooistra, Lorraine Janzen. "The Artist as Critic: Bi-Textuality in Fin-de-Siècle Illustrated Books." PhD dissertation. McMaster University, 1992.

The Artist as Critic: Bitextuality in Fin-de-Siècle Illustrated Books. Hants: Scholar Press, 1995.

"Clemence Housman's *The Were-Wolf:* Querying Transgression, Seeking Trans/Formation." *Victorian Review* 44, no. 1 (2018): 55–67.

"Cross-Dressing Confessions: Men Confessing as Women." In *Confessional Politics: Women's Sexual Self-Representations in Life Writing and Popular Media,* edited by Irene Gammel, 167–84. Carbondale and Edwardsville: Southern Illinois University Press, 1999.

"Wilde's Legacy: Fairy Tales, Laurence Housman, and the Expression of 'Beautiful Untrue Things.'" In *Oscar Wilde and the Cultures of Childhood,* edited by Joseph Bristow, 89–118. New York: Palgrave, 2017.

Koritz, Amy. "Dancing the Orient for England: Maud Allan's 'The Vision of Salome.'" *Theatre Journal* 46, no. 1 (1994): 63–78.

Krasner, David. "Black *Salome*: Exoticism, Dance, and Racial Myth." In *African American Performance and Theater History: A Critical Reader,* edited by Harry J. Elam and David Krasner, 192–211. New York: Oxford University Press, 2001.

Lancaster, Marie-Jacqueline, ed. *Brian Howard: Portrait of a Failure.* London: Anthony Blond, 1968.

Landy, Marcia, and Amy Villarejo. "Queen Christina." In *British Film Institute Film Classics,* edited by Rob White and Edward Buscombe, vol. 1, 221–48. New York: Fitzroy Dearborn, 2003.

Laurence, Patricia Ondek. *Lily Briscoe's Chinese Eyes: Bloomsbury, Modernism, and China*. Columbia: University of South Carolina Press, 2003.

Lavery, Grace. *Quaint, Exquisite: Victorian Aesthetics and the Idea of Japan*. Princeton, NJ: Princeton University Press, 2019.

Lévi-Strauss, Claude. *The Elementary Structures of Kinship*. Boston: Beacon Press, 1969.

Lewis, Sophie. *Full Surrogacy Now: Feminism against Family*. Brooklyn: Verso, 2019.

Liddington, Jill. *Vanishing for the Vote: Suffrage, Citizenship and the Battle for the Census*. Manchester: Manchester University Press, 2014.

Liddington, Jill, and Elizabeth Crawford. "'Women Do Not Count, Neither Shall They Be Counted': Suffrage, Citizenship and the Battle for the 1911 Census." *History Workshop Journal* 71, no. 1 (2011): 98–127.

Lim, Shirley. *Anna May Wong: Performing the Modern*. Philadelphia: Temple University Press, 2019.

Link, Viktor. "D. H. Lawrence's 'The Man Who Loved Islands' in the Light of Compton Mackenzie's Memoirs." *D. H. Lawrence Review* 15, no. 1–2 (1982): 77–86.

Linklater, Andro. *Compton Mackenzie: A Life*. London: Chatto & Windus, 1987.

Livesey, Ruth. *Socialism, Sex, and the Culture of Aestheticism in Britain, 1880–1914*. New York: Oxford University Press, 2007.

Lord, James. *Some Remarkable Men: Further Memoirs*. New York: Farrar, Straus & Giroux, 1996.

MacCarthy, Fiona. *Eric Gill: A Lover's Quest for Art and God*. New York: E. P. Dutton, 1989.

Mackie, Gregory. *Beautiful Untrue Things: Forging Oscar Wilde's Extraordinary Afterlife*. Toronto: University of Toronto Press, 2019.

"Forging Oscar Wilde: Mrs. Chan-Toon and for Love of the King." *English Literature in Transition, 1880–1920* 54, no. 3 (2011): 267–88.

Mahoney, Kristin. *Literature and the Politics of Post-Victorian Decadence*. New York: Cambridge University Press, 2015.

Maltz, Diana. "Ardent Service: Female Eroticism and New Life Ethics in Gertrude Dix's The Image Breakers (1900)." *Journal of Victorian Culture* 17, no. 2 (2012): 147–63.

"The Good Aesthetic Child and Deferred Aesthetic Education." In *Oscar Wilde and the Cultures of Childhood*, edited by Joseph Bristow, 69–88. New York: Palgrave, 2017.

Marcus, Laura. *Dreams of Modernity*. New York: Cambridge University Press, 2014.

Hearts of Darkness: White Women Write Race. New Brunswick: Rutgers University Press, 2004.

May, Leila Silvana. *Disorderly Sisters: Sibling Relations and Sororal Resistance in Nineteenth-Century British Literature*. Lewisburg, PA: Bucknell University Press, 2001.

McCabe, Susan. "Bryher's Archive: Modernism and the Melancholy of Money." In *English Now: Selected Papers from the 20th IAUPE Conference*, edited by Marianne Thormählen, 118–25. Lund: Lund University Press, 2008.

McCormack, Jerusha. *John Gray: Poet, Dandy, and Priest*. Waltham, MA: Brandeis University Press, 1991.

The Man Who Was Dorian Gray. New York: St. Martin's Press, 2000.

Mendelssohn, Michèle. "A Decadent Dream Deferred: Bruce Nugent and the Harlem Renaissance's Queer Modernity." In *Decadence in the Age of Modernism*, edited by Kate Hext and Alex Murray, 251–75. Baltimore: Johns Hopkins University Press, 2019.

Making Oscar Wilde. New York: Oxford University Press, 2018.

"Reading Aestheticism, Decadence, and Cosmopolitanism." In *Late Victorian into Modern*, edited by Laura Marcus, Michèle Mendelssohn, and Kirsten E. Shepherd-Barr, 481–96. New York: Oxford University Press, 2016.

Merrill, Lisa. "'Old Maids, Sister-Artists and Aesthetes': Charlotte Cushman and Her Circle of 'Jolly Bachelors' Construct an Expatriate Women's Community in Rome." *Women's Writing* 10, no. 2 (2003): 367–83.

Meyer, Karl E., and Shareen Blair Brysac. *The China Collectors: America's Century-Long Hunt for Asian Art Treasures*. New York: Palgrave Macmillan, 2015.

Miller, Nina. *Making Love Modern: The Intimate Public Worlds of New York's Literary Woman*. New York: Oxford University Press, 1999.

Money, James. *Capri: Island of Pleasure*. London: Hamish Hamilton, 1986.

Moran, Leslie J. "Transcripts and Truth: Writing the Trials of Oscar Wilde." In *Oscar Wilde and Modern Culture: The Making of a Legend*, edited by Joseph Bristow, 234–58. Athens: Ohio University Press, 2008.

Morton, Tara. "Changing Spaces: Art, Politics, and Identity in the Home Studios of the Suffrage Atelier." *Women's History Review* 21, no. 4 (2012): 623–37.

Moynagh, Maureen. "Cunard's Lines: Political Tourism and Its Texts." *New Formations* 34 (1998): 70–90.

Mungello, D. E. *Western Queers in China: Flight to the Land of Oz*. New York: Rowman & Littlefield, 2012.

Murray, Alex. "Decadence Revisited: Evelyn Waugh and the Afterlife of the 1890s." *Modernism/modernity* 22, no. 3 (2015): 593–607.

Introduction to *Decadence: A Literary History*, edited by Alex Murray, 1–17. New York: Cambridge University Press, 2020.

News.com.au. "BBC Told to Remove Work by Pedophile Sculptor Eric Gill" (April 23, 2013), www.news.com.au/world/bbc-told-to-remove-work-by-pedophile-sculptor-eric-gill/story-fndir2ev-1226626709154 (accessed June 9, 2014).

Ngô, Fiona I. B. *Imperial Blues: Geographies of Race and Sex in Jazz Age New York*. Durham, NC: Duke University Press, 2014.

Novak, Daniel A. "Picturing Wilde: Christopher Millard's 'Iconography of Oscar Wilde.'" *Nineteenth-Century Contexts* 32, no. 4 (2010): 305–35.

Nussbaum, Martha. "Patriotism and Cosmopolitanism." In *For Love of Country?*, edited by Joshua Cohen, 3–17. Boston: Beacon Press, 2002.

N'yongo, Tavia. *The Amalgamation Waltz: Race, Performance, and the Ruses of Memory*. Minneapolis: University of Minnesota Press, 2009.

Oakley, Elizabeth. *Inseparable Siblings*. Studley: Brewin Books, 2009.

Ogrinc, Will H. L. "Frère Jacques: A Shrine to Love and Sorrow: Jacques D'adelswärd Fersen (1880–1923)" (2006), http://semgai.free.fr/doc_et_pdf/Fersen-engels.pdf (accessed March 27, 2016).

"A Shrine to Love and Sorrow: Jacques D'adelswärd Fersen (1880–1923)." *Paidika: The Journal of Paedophilia* 3, no. 2 (1994): 30–58.

O'Malley, Patrick. "Epistemology of the Cloister: Victorian England's Queer Catholicism." *GLQ: A Journal of Gay and Lesbian Studies* 15, no. 4 (2009): 535–64.

Oram, Alison, and Annmarie Turnbull. *The Lesbian History Sourcebook: Love and Sex between Women in Britain from 1780–1970*. New York: Routledge, 2001.

Orlandi, Dialta Alliata-Lensi. *My Mother, My Father and His Wife Hortense: Provenance – Villa La Pietra*. North Charleston, SC: CreateSpace Independent Publishing Platform, 2013.

Pal-Lapinski, Piya. *The Exotic Woman in Nineteenth-Century British Fiction and Culture: A Reconsideration*. Durham: University of New Hampshire Press, 2005.

Pearson, Neil. *Obelisk: A History of Jack Kahane and the Obelisk Press*. Liverpool: Liverpool University Press, 2007.

Pennington, Michael. *An Angel for a Martyr: Jacob Epstein's Tomb for Oscar Wilde*. Reading: Whiteknights Press, 1987.

Pérez, Hiram. *A Taste for Brown Bodies: Gay Modernity and Cosmopolitan Desire*. New York: New York University Press, 2015.

Perry, Imani. *Vexy Thing: On Gender and Liberation*. Durham, NC: Duke University Press, 2018.

Potolsky, Matthew. *The Decadent Republic of Letters: Taste, Politics, and Cosmopolitan Community from Baudelaire to Beardsley*. Philadelphia: University of Pennsylvania Press, 2013.

Poueymirou, Margaux. "The Race to Perform: *Salome* and the Wilde Harlem Renaissance." In *Refiguring Oscar Wilde's Salome*, edited by Michael Y. Bennett, 201–19. New York: Rodopi, 2011.

Quennell, Peter. "The Undergraduate." In *Oxford, China, and Italy: Writings in Honor of Sir Harold Acton on His Eightieth Birthday*, edited by Edward Chaney and Neil Ritchie, 57–9. New York: Thames & Hudson, 1984.

Reed, Christopher. *Bachelor Japanists: Japanese Aesthetics and Western Masculinities*. New York: Columbia University Press, 2017.

Bloomsbury Rooms: Modernism, Subculture, and Domesticity. New Haven, CT: Yale University Press, 2004.

Reed, Jeremy. Introduction to *Lord Lyllian: Black Masses*, by Jacques Fersen, i–vii. North Pomfret, VT: Elysium, 2005.

Richards, Grant. *Housman: 1897–1936*. Oxford: Oxford University Press, 1942.

Ricks, Christopher. "A.E. Housman and 'the Colour of His Hair.'" *Essays in Criticism* 47, no. 3 (1997): 240–56.

Roden, Frederick. *Same-Sex Desire in Victorian Religious Culture.* New York: Palgrave Macmillan, 2002.

Rohrer, Finlo. "Can the Art of a Paedophile Be Celebrated?" *BBC News* (September 5, 2007), http://news.bbc.co.uk/2/hi/uk_news/magazine/6979731.stm (accessed June 9, 2014).

Rowe, A. L. "The Good-Natured Man." In *Oxford, China, and Italy: Writings in Honor of Sir Harold Acton on His Eightieth Birthday*, edited by Edward Chaney and Neil Ritchie, 63–5, New York: Thames & Hudson, 1984.

Rubin, Gayle. "The Traffic in Women: Notes on the Political Economy of Sex." In *Toward an Anthropology of Women*, edited by Rayna R. Reiter, 157–210. New York: Monthly Review Press, 1975.

Rudy, Kathy. "LGBTQ...Z?" *Hypatia* 27, no. 3 (2012): 601–15.

Sanders, Valerie. *The Brother-Sister Culture in Nineteenth-Century Literature: From Austen to Woolf.* New York: Palgrave Macmillan, 2002.

"'Lifelong Soulmates?': The Sibling Bond in Nineteenth-Century Fiction." *Victorian Review* 39, no. 2 (2013): 54–7.

Schaffer, Talia. *Romance's Rival: Familiar Marriage in Victorian Fiction.* New York: Oxford University Press, 2016.

Schmidt, Tyler. "'In the Glad Flesh of My Fear': Corporeal Inscriptions in Richard Bruce Nugent's 'Geisha Man.'" *African American Review* 40, no. 1 (2006): 161–73.

Schwarz, Christa. *Gay Voices of the Harlem Renaissance.* Bloomington: Indiana University Press, 2003.

Sedgwick, Eve Kosofsky. *Tendencies.* Durham, NC: Duke University Press, 1993.

Shell, Marc. *Islandology: Geography, Rhetoric.* Stanford, CA: Stanford University Press, 2014.

Sherry, Vincent. *Modernism and the Reinvention of Decadence.* New York: Cambridge University Press, 2015.

Shewring, Walter. "Ananda Coomaraswamy and Eric Gill." In *Ananda Coomaraswamy: Remembering and Remembering Again and Again*, edited by S. Durai Raja Singam, 189–90. Kuala Lumpur: S. D. Raja Singam,1974.

Showalter, Elaine. *Sexual Anarchy: Gender and Culture at the Fin de Siècle.* New York: Viking, 1990.

Sinfield, Alan. *On Sexuality and Power.* New York: Columbia University Press, 2004.

Snyder, Katherine V. *Bachelors, Manhood, and the Novel, 1850–1925.* New York: Cambridge University Press, 1999.

Speaight, Robert. *The Life of Eric Gill.* London: Methuen, 1966.

Spillers, Hortense. "Mama's Baby, Papa's Maybe." *Diacritics* 17, no. 2 (1987): 64–81.

"Mama's Baby, Papa's, Too." *Trans-Scripts* 1 (2011): 1–4.

"'The Permanent Obliquity of an In(pha)llibly Straight': In the Time of the Daughters and the Fathers." In *Black, White, and in Color: Essays on American Literature and Culture*, 230–50. Chicago: University of Chicago Press, 2003.

Stilling, Robert. *Beginning at the End: Decadence, Modernism, and Postcolonial Poetry* (Cambridge, MA: Harvard University Press, 2018).

Tamagne, Florence. *A History of Homosexuality in Europe: Berlin, London, Paris; 1919–1939*, vol. 1. New York: Algora Publishing, 2006.

Tate, Carolyn. "Lesbian Incest as Queer Kinship: Michael Field and the Erotic Middle-Class Victorian Family." *Victorian Review* 39, no. 2 (2013): 181–99.

Teukolsky, Rachel. *The Literate Eye: Victorian Art Writing and Modernist Aesthetics*. New York: Oxford University Press, 2009.

Thain, Marion. *"Michael Field": Poetry, Aestheticism, and the Fin de Siècle*. New York: Cambridge University Press, 2007.

Thain, Marion, and Ana Vadillo, eds. *Michael Field, The Poet*. Buffalo, NY: Broadview, 2009.

Thomas, Kate. "'What Time We Kiss': Michael Field's Queer Temporalities." *GLQ: A Journal of Lesbian and Gay Studies* 13, no. 2–3 (2007): 327–51.

Tóibín, Colm. Introduction to *De Profundis and Other Prison Writings*, by Oscar Wilde, xi–xxxii. London: Penguin, 2013.

Treby, Ivor. *Uncertain Rain: Sundry Spells of Michael Field*. Bury St. Edmunds: De Blackland, 2002.

Turner, Sarah Victoria. "The 'Essential Quality of Things': E. B. Havell, Ananda Coomaraswamy, Indian Art and Sculpture in Britain, c. 1910–14." *Visual Culture in Britain* 11, no. 2 (2010): 239–64.

Valentine, Ferdinand. *Father Vincent McNabb, O.P.: The Portrait of a Great Dominican*. London: Burns & Oates, 1955.

Vanita, Ruth. *Sappho and the Virgin Mary: Same Sex Love and the English Literary Imagination*. New York: Columbia University Press, 1996.

Venuti, Lawrence. *The Translator's Invisibility: A History of Translation*. New York: Routledge, 2008.

Verona, Roxana. "A Cosmopolitan Orientalism: Paul Morand Goes East." *Sites* 5, no. 1 (2001): 157–69.

Vitale, Christopher. "The Untimely Richard Bruce Nugent." PhD dissertation. New York University, 2007.

Waitt, Gordon, and Kevin Markwell. *Gay Tourism: Culture and Context*. Binghamton, NY: Haworth Press, 2006.

Weeks, Jeffrey. "Movements of Affirmation: Sexual Meanings and Homosexual Identities." In *Passion and Power: Sexuality in History*, edited by Kathy Peiss and Christina Simmons, 70–86. Philadelphia: Temple University Press, 1989.

Weiner, Joshua J., and Damon Young, "Introduction: Queer Bonds." *GLQ: A Journal of Lesbian and Gay Studies* 17, no. 2–3 (2011): 223–41.

Weir, David. *Decadence and the Making of Modernism*. Amherst: University of Massachusetts Press, 1996.

White, Chris. "Poets and Lovers Ever More: The Poetry and Journals of Michael Field." In *Sexual Sameness: Textual Difference in Gay and Lesbian Writing*, edited by Joseph Bristow, 26–43. New York: Routledge, 1992.

Wildgen, Kathryn Eberle. *Julien Green: The Great Themes.* Birmingham, AL: Summa Publications, 1993.

Wilson, Edmund. *The Shores of Light: A Literary Chronicle of the Twenties and Thirties.* New York: Farrar, Straus & Young, 1952.

Winkiel, Laura. "Nancy Cunard's *Negro* and the Transnational Politics of Race." *Modernism/modernity* 13, no. 3 (September 2006): 507–30.

Wirth, Thomas. Introduction to *Gay Rebel of the Harlem Renaissance*, edited by Thomas H. Wirth, 3–64. Durham, NC: Duke University Press, 2002.

Woodcock, George. "Norman Douglas: The Willing Exile." *Ariel* 13, no. 4 (1982): 87–101.

Xi, Kun. "Picturing an Aesthetic and Homoerotic Space: Harold Acton's Travel Writing of China in the 1930s." *Interactions* 28, no. 1–2 (2019): 87–93.

Yorke, Michael. *Eric Gill: Man of Flesh and Spirit.* New York: Universe Books, 1981.

Zito, Eugenio. "'Amori et Dolori Sacrum': Canons, Differences, and Figures of Gender Identity in the Cultural Panorama of Travellers in Capri between the Nineteenth and Twentieth Centuries." In *Homosexuality in Italian Literature, Society, and Culture, 1789–1919*, edited by Lorenzo Benadusi, Paolo L. Bernardini, Elisa Bianco, and Paola Guazzo, 129–54. Newcastle upon Tyne: Cambridge Scholars, 2017.

Index

Abu-Manneh, Bashir, 121
abuse, 12, 29, 191, 201–2, 213, *See also* Eric Gill;
    incest; sexuality
  familial, 51–4
  sexual, 29, 189–90, 200–2
activism, 58–9, 89, *See also* feminism
  animal rights, 80
  anti-colonial and anti-imperial, 25–6, 77,
    80–2, 130
  antiracist, 77, 81, 130, 145
  anti-war and pacifist, 25, 57–8, 60–1, 65, 68,
    77–82, 91
  for queer rights and sex reform, 14, 25–6, 68,
    81, 90–2
  for suffrage, women's rights, and feminism,
    57–61, 74–9, 85, 91
  labor politics, 80
  sex reform, 58–61, 64, 86, 89
Acton, Harold, 10–11, 27, 126–56
  Anna May Wong and, 153, 155
  Aquarium, 132
  at Oxford, 131–4
  Chen Shixiang and, 141–5
  childhood, 131
  cosmopolitanism and, 127–9, 137, 141,
    145–6, 148–53
  Decadence and, 126–34, 137–8
  Famous Chinese Plays, 150
  feminism and, 127, 130, 136
  "Hansom Cab No. 213 bis," 132
  Humdrum, 138
  in China, 138–45, 148–53
  life writing and memoirs, 126–33, 136, 138,
    143–5, 149–50, 152
  Memoirs of an Aesthete, 126–7, 131
  Modern Chinese Poetry, 141
  More Memoirs of an Aesthete, 144
  Nancy Cunard and, 145–7
  Peonies and Ponies, 127–9, 148–54,
    156
  poetry, 145, 147

  This Chaos, 145
  Vernon Lee and, 130, 134–8
Adey, More, 37
adoption, 12, 27, 129, 148–54, *See also* Harold
    Acton
affect, 2, 6, *See also* affiliation; desire; eroticism;
    family
  difference and, 23–4
  queerness and, 10
affiliation, 8–11, 14, 16, 29, 37, 79, *See also*
    amativeness; cosmopolitanism; queerness
  affective labor involved in, 67
  alternative forms of, 13, 26, 36, 67–9, 79,
    82–3, 130, 149, 162, 164–5, 202
  Catholicism and, 200
  conventional forms of, 130, 192
  friendship and, 46
  heteronormativity and, 14, 162
  incest and, 211
  national, 21
  political activism and, 79, 81
  queerness and, 8–9, 14–15, 29, 61, 67, 97,
    202–3
  textually based, 38, 46
Aldington, Richard, 108
Aldrich, Robert, 98, 104, 108
Alfano, Veronica, 88
alienation, 12, 54, 176
Allan, Maud, 167
amativeness, 61–7, 69, 76, 80–1, 91, *See also*
    fellow-feeling; Laurence Housman
Amin, Kadji, 13, 20–1, *See also* deidealization
Anderson, Amanda, 22
androgyny, 53, 70, 112, 122
anti-colonialism. *See* activism; colonialism
appropriation, 12, 23, 27, 127–30, 146–7, 149,
    151
Aragorn, Louis, 145
archives, 8
Arrowsmith, Rupert, 206–12
Art Nouveau, 105

Attallah, Naim, 137
autobiography. *See* life writing

banners, 9, 58, 75–6
Banting, John, 127
Baoquin, Yang (Yang Pao-ch'in), 150
Barbusse, Henri
    Staline: Un monde nouveau vu à travers un homme, 47
Barnes, Elizabeth, 200
Bassett, Caroline, 214
Baudelaire, Charles, 21, 142
Bauer, Edgar, 183
Beardsley, Aubrey, 14, 23, 60, 62, 114, 126, 131–2, 183, *See also* illustrations
Beaton, Cecil, 127
beauty, 17–19, 23, 69, 102–3, 126, 129, 131, 135, 156, 162–5
    Chinese culture and, 148–50
    Japanese objects and, 23
    male form and, 194, 205
Beckett, Samuel, 145
Beer, Gillian, 97
Beerbohm, Max, 37, 101–2, 131–3, 137, 206
Beinecke Library (Yale University), 1, 5, 8, 143, 160, 170, 183
    Norman Douglas Collection, 7–8
Bell, Julian, 139
Belloc, Hilaire, 196
belonging, 3–7, 19, 21, *See also* community; connection
Benson, E. F., 106
Berenson, Bernard, 143
Berman, Jessica, 22
bestiality, 62, 201–2, *See also* Eric Gill
Bielsa, Esperança, 50
Birch, Cyril, 142–4
Birkenruth, Adolf, 100
bisexuality, 53, 160, 162, *See also* queerness; sexuality
Blackwood's Magazine, 17
BLAST (periodical), 132
Bleys, R. C., 98
Bloomsbury Group, 10, 139
Bodley Head, 18
Boehmer, Elleke, 23
book collecting, 39–41, 43, *See also* First Editions Club; Vyvyan (Vivian) Holland; Sette of Odd Volumes
Boone, Joseph Allen, 162–4
Booth, Howard J., 114, 120
Borgatti, Renata, 109–13, 120
Borland, Maureen, 39
Boulderson, Shadwell, 64
Bradley, Katharine. *See* Michael Field

Brady, Anne-Marie, 148
British Museum, 89, 91, 209
British Society for the Study of Sex Psychology, 59, 61, 86
Brittain, Vera, 80
Brooks, John Ellingham, 106, 110, 112, 117
Brooks, Romaine, 110, 124
Bryher (Annie Winifred Ellerman), 7
Brysac, Shareen Blair, 148
Buddhism, 127, 138, 152
Burdett, Osbert, 46, 134
    Beardsley Period, The, 134
Burne, Glenn S., 52
Burton, Richard, 98
Butler, Judith, 200

Califia, Patrick, 20
camp, 6, 9, 114, 132, 152
Campbell, James, 17
capitalism, 49, 80, 200, 215
Capri (Italy), 1, 12, 26, 95–9, 103–7, 113–14
    cosmopolitan progressiveness of, 103
    Decadence and, 95–6, 106
    exoticism of, 98, 103
    prewar society of, 116
    queer community of, 26, 95, 97–9, 104–21, 124
Caracciolo, Nini, 109–10
care, 7–8, 13, 19, 26, 60, 65, 68
Carew, Helen, 36
Carpenter, Edward, 63, 82, 212
    Homogenic Love and Its Place in a Free Society, 63
Carpenter, Humphrey, 132
Carter, John, 90
Castle, Terry, 111
Catholicism, 10, 28–9, 47, 187, 192
    bestiality and, 202
    Decadence and, 10–11, 28, 187–9, 193–8
    desire and eroticism in, 190, 193, 198
    doctrine of Distributism, 196, 213
    incest and, 199
    kinship and, 198–200, 202–5
    queerness and, 10, 28, 187–205, 209–13
Centro Caprense Ignazio Cerio Library, 5
Chan, Anthony B., 154
Charoensuk, Manop, 8
Cherwell (periodical), 133–5
Chesterton, G. K., 196
    "Why Abolish the Family?," 213
Cheung, Dominic, 141
childhood and children, 17–18, 51, 54, 61, 68, 73–4, 131
China, 11, 27, 129–30, 138–45, 148–56, *See also* Harold Acton; Anna May Wong

China (cont.)
  Chinese theater, 150–1, 153
  Decadence and, 138, 142
  modernism and, 139–42
  translation and, 141
Chisholm, Anne, 147
Christianity. *See also* Catholicism; faith
  cultivation of the self, 16
  queerness and, 12
  racial domination and, 81
Christina, Queen of Sweden, 121–2
Church League for Women's Suffrage, 76
Chute, Desmond, 196
Clark, Sarah, 58
Clark, William Andrews, 45
Cleves, Rachel Hope, 7, 13
closet, 45–6, *See also* queerness; sexuality
Cohen, Albert
  Mangeclous (Nailcruncher), 47
collaboration, 11, 18, 25–6, 33–5, 42–3, 46,
    57–8, 60, 67–9, 75–7, 79–80, 83, 85,
    89–92, 97, 99, 101, 113, 122, 132, 141–4,
    189, 196, 203, 210, 215, *See also* ethics
Collins, Judith, 211
colonialism, 13, 22, 24, 26, 58, 77, 80–2, 129,
    175, *See also* imperialism
color, 182–5, *See also* Richard Bruce Nugent,
    "Geisha Man"
colorism. *See* race, racialization, and racism
Commonwealth of India League, 81
community, 4, 15–17, 37, 59, 96–8, 196,
    200–1, *See also* affiliation; cosmopolitanism
  cosmopolitanism and, 8, 12, 24, 26, 95–6
  expatriatism and, 26, 104, 111, 114, 136,
    138–45, 149, 152–3
  failures of, 190
  faith and, 14, 29, 187, 192–6, 198–200,
    202–4, 212
  feminism and, 76–7
  kinship and, 26, 57, 68, 79, 82, 204, 212
  longing for, 176
  negotiating, 65–7
  nonhuman animals and, 67
  ostracism and, 36–8
  political activism and, 81
  queer forms of, 1, 14–17, 25–6, 35, 37–8, 46,
    58–60, 63, 67, 84, 91, 95–100, 104,
    109–22, 124, 136, 176, 188, 195,
    198–203, 212
  textually based, 34, 44
connection, 5, 9, *See also* affiliation; belonging;
    community; cosmopolitanism; desire;
    family; fellow-feeling; queerness
  alternative forms of, 7–14, 16–17, 27, 34–9,
    61, 97–8, 162, 166, 196, 199, 214

cosmopolitanism and, 21, 131, 146, 150
  desire and, 3, 52, 61–7, 176, 178–80
  family and, 33–5, 39–41, 168, 174, 178–80,
    215
  queerness and, 8, 19, 21, 27, 34, 41
  textually based, 34, 39, 47
Coomaraswamy, Ananda, 11, 28–9, 187–9, 206,
    210
  Twenty-Eight Drawings, 209
Cooper, Edith. *See* Michael Field
cooperation. *See* collaboration
Cork, Richard, 207
Corvo, Baron. *See* Frederick Rolfe
cosmopolitanism, 3, 7–9, 13, 21–5, 27, 29,
    47–52, 60, 78, 80, 82, 103–4, 127–9, 139,
    153–6, 187–90, 210, *See also* community;
    connection; detachment; translation
  aestheticism and, 21, 24, 35, 104, 129, 133–6
  detachment and, 21–3, 35, 48, 129
  difference and, 22, 99, 111, 148–53
  intimacy and, 129
  limits and failures of, 135, 148, 153, 190
  Orientalism and, 23–4
  pleasure and, 21
  queerness and, 25, 54, 95–6, 98, 104, 109,
    111, 114–17, 124, 136, 190
Crescent Moon Group, 139
Cribb, Joseph, 196
cross-dressing, 122
Crowder, Henry, 146–7
Crowell, Ellen, 39
Crowley, Aleister, 210
Cullen, Countee, 163
Cunard, Nancy, 27, 130, 145–7
  appropriation of Black culture, 147
  *Black Man and White Ladyship: An
    Anniversary*, 146
  Negro: An Anthology, 145, 147
  Parallax, 145

Danson, Lawrence, 18
Davidoff, Leonore, 60
Decadence, 7–16, 24–7, 39–42, 60–1, 96, 131,
    163, 165, 189, *See also* Catholicism;
    modernism; Orientalism; Oscar Wilde
  aestheticism and, 10, 14, 21, 24, 26, 39, 47,
    100–1, 126–31
  art for art's sake, 14
  as alternative to masculinist modernism, 133
  at Oxford, 131–4
  color in, 182–5
  detachment and, 15, 149
  difference and, 23–4, 148–53
  failures and limits of, 70, 105, 124, 190
  fairy tales and, 64

family and, 14, 24, 162–6
  in France, 35, 50, 55, 96, 104–7, 193
  influence on modern Chinese poetry, 142
  Japan and, 23
  maturation and, 163
  pleasure and, 15
  queerness and, 1, 14–15, 29, 97–9, 114
  racial politics of, 23–4
  radicalism of, 15
  satirical representations of, 117, 129
  sexual politics of, 190
deidealization, 13, 21, 24
democracy, 60, 81
desire, 61–4, *See also* amativeness; Catholicism;
    connection; difference; fellow-feeling;
    queerness
  conventions of, 72–3, 162
  failures and limits of, 52, 62
  incest and, 62, 175–6, 178–82
  queer forms of, 9, 20, 42, 47–8, 52–3, 55, 59,
    63–4, 67, 100, 111, 117, 160, 191, 193,
    198, 200
  sexual, 70, 162, 168
  sociability and, 37, 97
detachment. *See* cosmopolitanism; Decadence;
    kinship; race, racialization, and racism
Dickens, Charles, 14
difference, 23, 166–70, *See also* cosmopolitanism;
    Decadence; Orientalism
  consumption of, 25, 151–3, 167, 170
  desire and, 151–2, 168–70, 174, 182–5
  encounters with, 24
  race and, 166–7, 176–7, 184
Distributism. *See* Catholicism
Dolley, D. J., 114
domesticity, 9–11, 16, 26–7, 58, 68, 110, 129,
    138, 181, *See also* family; heteronormativity
  revolt against, 213–14
Dooley, D. J., 116
Doolittle, Hilda. *See* H. D.
Douglas, Lord Alfred, 20, 24, 34, 38, 44–5, 96,
    100, 106
  City of the Soul, The, 100
  "Two Loves," 20
Douglas, Norman, 7–8, 13, 103–4, 107–9, 119,
    121, 125, 133, 138, 145
  Siren Land, 103
  South Wind, 107–9, 114–15, 117
  trials for indecent behavior, 107
Doussot, Audrey, 63, 67
Dowson, Ernest, 39

Ebony and Topaz (magazine), 160
Edelman, Lee, 12
Ehnenn, Jill, 202

Eliot, T. S., 10, 141
  Waste Land, The, 132
Ellerman, Annie Winifred. *See* Bryher
Ellerman, John, 8
Ellis, Havelock, 80, 192
Ellmann, Richard, 22
Elwin, Verrier, 81
  Truth About India, The, 81
Elysium Press, 8
empathy, 63, 68, 75–6, 79, 83
Engen, Rodney, 60, 77
engraving, 9, 25, 58, 68, 72
enslavement, 167, 171–6, *See also* Richard
    Bruce Nugent; race, racialization, and
    racism
Epstein, Jacob, 189, 206, 209–12
  One of the Hundred Pillars of the Secret Temple,
    210
equality, 58, 64, 69, 83, *See also* gender
Erlandson, Theodore, 102
eroticism, 20, 27, 47, 51–5, 98, 168, 170, 175,
    182, *See also* bestiality; Catholicism; desire;
    difference; kinship; Orientalism
  affinity and, 61–3
  divinity and, 29, 189–90, 193–5, 199–200,
    203–13
  power and, 13, 21, 167
  threat of, 70–2
  unconventional forms of, 53, 161
  vilifying, 70
Essi, Cedric, 176
ethics, 11–15, 24, 26, 29, 58, 65, 68–9, *See also*
    activism; care; collaboration; difference;
    equality
Ethiopian Art Players, 166
Eton Candle (periodical), 132
Evangelista, Stefano, 22
Evening Standard (newspaper), 84
exile, 7, 25, 33, 36, 41, 47–8, 50, 95–6, 98–9,
    104–8, 153, 164, *See also* community;
    expatriatism; sexuality, criminalization of
exoticism, 12, 23–4, 98–9, 103, 130, 148, 151,
    167, 169–72, 179, *See also* desire; fetishism;
    Orientalism
expatriatism, 26, 111, 114, 136, 138–42, 149,
    152–3, *See also* Harold Acton; Capri (Italy);
    China; exile; Compton and Faith
    Mackenzie; sexuality, criminalization of
Extraordinary Women (album), 1, *See also*
    Beinecke Library (Yale University);
    Compton Mackenzie, *Extraordinary*
    Women

fairy tales, 58, 63–7, *See also* Laurence Housman
faith. *See also* Catholicism; community; Eric Gill

faith. (cont.)
  militarism and, 80
  queerness and, 14, 190, 192–5, 198–200, 212
  sexuality and, 188, 193–5, 198–9
family, 2, *See also* connection; Decadence; incest;
    kinship; queerness
  abolition of, 16, 213–14
  alternative forms of, 6, 10–11, 13, 25, 28, 35,
    45, 51, 65, 150, 215–16
  as a source of trauma, 51–3
  biological basis of, 10–11, 33, 36–7, 47, 52,
    59, 70, 130, 162–6, 214
  burdens and obligation of, 65, 136–8, 162,
    164
  Catholicism and rhetoric of, 198–200
  conventional forms of, 11–12, 27, 60, 96, 129,
    162, 189, 213–14
  cosmopolitanism and, 57, 68, 76, 79, 82, 129
  detachment from, 138, 146, 164–6, 176–80
  disorder and fragmentation of, 25, 28, 41,
    162, 167–8, 171–6
  parenting and, 17–18
  queer forms of, 17, 45, 59–61, 69
  siblings and, 57, 59–61, 67–72, 79, 83, 91
feeling. *See* affect; desire; eroticism; fellow-feeling
fellow-feeling, 57–9, 61–7, 75, *See also*
    community; cosmopolitanism; kinship
  affective labor of, 64–7, 73
  desire and, 61–3
  failures of, 74
  political activism and, 76, 79–81
  promiscuity of, 82, 92
  racial boundaries of, 67
Fellowship of the New Life, 15
feminism, 26, 58, 60, 69, 74, 76–8, 91, 122,
    127, 130, 214, *See also* activism; gender
Fersen, Jacques d'Adelswärd-, 96, 104–6, 114,
    119, 125
  Messes Noires: Lord Lyllian, 105
fetishism, 111, 129, 134, 146–8, 153, 159, 167,
    170, 174, 179, 188, *See also* exoticism;
    Mediterraneanism; Orientalism
Field, Michael, 10, 28, 189–215
  death of Edith Cooper, 197
  death of Katharine Bradley, 197
  Mystic Trees (Bradley), 204
  Poems of Adoration (Cooper), 204
  Wattlefold, The, 197–8
  Wild Honey from Various Thyme, 197
Fielder, Brigitte, 176
Firbank, Ronald, 10, 133
Fire!! (periodical), 160, 162
Firestone, Shulamith
  Dialectic of Sex, The, 214
First Edition Club, 40, *See also* A. J. A. Symons

Fitzgerald, C. P., 148
flânerie, 21, 164–5
Ford, Ford Madox, 133
France, Anatole, 135
Franchetti, Mimi, 2–7, 110–13, 119–21, 124
Freeman, Elizabeth, 4–7, 10–11, 18
Friends of India Society, 81
friendship, 2, 18, *See also* community
  cosmopolitanism and, 22, 145
  marriage and, 26, 97
  queerness and, 45–6, 136, 200
  textually based, 39–41
Fry, Roger, 206, 212
Furneaux, Holly, 14
Fussell, Paul, 7

Gandhi, Mahatma (M. K.), 80–2
Gauthier-Villars, Henry
  Third Sex, The, 95
Gautier, Théophile, 100
gender, 35, 51, 134, 177, 200, 202, *See also*
    feminism; queerness
  conventional forms of, 11, 14, 130, 134, 177,
    201
  cosmopolitanism and, 57–8
  dissident forms of, 43, 47, 52, 70, 107, 114,
    121–2, 135, 151, 160, 166, 182, 184
  equality, 69
  identification across, 60, 68–70, 75, 124
Gibran, Kahlil, 124
Gide, André, 24
  Oscar Wilde: A Study, 43
Gill, Eric, 10–11, 25, 28–9, 80, 215, *See also*
    bestiality; Catholicism; incest
  abuse and, 28–9, 189–90, 198, 200–2,
    210–13
  Acrobat, 194
  Ananda Coomaraswamy and, 206–12
  Animals All, 203
  Birth Control, 201
  Catholicism and, 187–215
  Clothes, 191
  community and, 196, 202
  conservative gender politics, 201
  Decadence and, 189, 193, 196, 209, 212
  Father Vincent McNabb and, 196–200
  interest in Egyptian and Indian art, 187–90,
    205–13
  kinship and, 189–90, 200–1, 204, 210–13
  life writing and diaries, 191, 196, 198, 201,
    207, 209, 211
  Madonna and Child, 189–215
  Madonna and Child, Suckling, 188
  Marc-André Raffalovich, John Gray, and,
    193–5

Michael Field and, 189–215
Nuptials of God, 204
Oscar Wilde's memorial tomb, 209–11
sculpture, 187–90, 193–5, 201, 203, 207–12
sexuality and, 189–205, 207–13
socialism and, 196, 200
They (Ecstasy, 1910–11), 28, 210–12
Twenty-Five Nudes, 209
Votes for Women, 201
William Rothenstein and, 205–7, 209
Glick, Elisa, 161
Goeser, Caroline, 183
Gray, John, 10, 14, 188, 193–200
Green, Julien (Julian), 25, 35, 47, 50–5, *See also*
Vyvyan (Vivian) Holland
Dark Journey, The (Léviathan), 52
Dreamer, The (Le Visionnaire), 47, 52–4
Midnight (Minuit), 47, 52–4
Moïra, 53
Strange River, The (Épaves), 52
Green, Martin, 132, 137
Guild of St Joseph and St Dominic, 196
Guthrie, James, 68
Gyles, Althea, 102

H. D. (Hilda Doolittle), 8
Hague, Rene, 209
Hall, Radclyffe, 86
Handforth, Thomas, 127
Hanson, Ellis, 20, 192–5
Harlem Renaissance, 11, 27, 159–61, 180, *See
also* Richard Bruce Nugent
Harrod, Roy, 141, 144
Harry Ransom Center, 26
Compton Mackenzie Collection, 99, 117
Hegel, Georg Wilhelm Friedrich, 60
Heiskell, Ann, 110, 123–4
Hemingway, Ernest, 10, 133
Heppenstall, Rayner, 204
Herold, Katharina, 23
Heron-Allen, Edward, 39
Herzfeld, Michael, 99
heteronormativity, 11, 14, 16, 27, 34–5, 59–61,
69–70, 129–31, 134, 138, 162, 165, 181,
190, *See also* family; marriage; queerness
Hewlett, Dick, 100
Hext, Kate, 15
Hill, Ethel, 74
Hinduism, 28, 206–9, *See also* Ananda
Coomaraswamy; Eric Gill; India
Hirsch, Marianne, 2
history, 5, 8–9, 11–14, 18–19, 21, 29, 136, 161,
187–90, 207, 209–10
Hodges, Graham Russell Gao, 154
Holland, Cyril, 33, 36, 39, 45, 48

Holland, Vyvyan (Vivian), 10–11, 25, 33–56,
See also Henri Barbusse; Albert Cohen;
Julien (Julian) Green; Paul Morand
A. J. A. Symons and, 40
book collecting and, 39
childhood, 36, 54
Few Odd Reflections on Idleness, A, 40
Irishness, 49
life writing, 48–50
Oscar Wilde and, 33–5, 39, 42–6, 49, 55
Oscar Wilde: A Pictorial Biography, 49
Robert Ross and, 37–40
Son of Oscar Wilde, The, 34, 36–7, 41, 54–5
Time Remembered: After Père Lachaise, 34, 51
translations, 35, 47–56
home. *See* domesticity; family; kinship
homelessness. *See* cosmopolitanism; exile
Hope, Adrian, 39
Horak, Laura, 122
Hours Press, 145, 147
Housman, A. E. (Alfred Edward), 26, 58–9,
83–92, *See also* Laurence Housman
diary, 89–91
homosexuality, 83
Laurence Housman and, 84–6
Moses Jackson and, 87–9
Oscar Wilde and, 87–8
poetry, 86, 88–9
Shropshire Lad, A, 84, 88
Housman, Clemence, 25, 57–92, *See also*
activism, for women's rights and feminism;
banners; A. E. (Alfred Edward) Housman;
Laurence Housman
A. E. Housman and, 84, 91
banners, 58, 75–6
engravings, 58, 68, 72–3
feminist activism, 76–7, 84
"From Prison to Citizenship," 75
Unknown Sea, The, 72–3
Were-Wolf, The, 58, 69–72, 76
writing, 69–73
Housman, Laurence, 11, 25, 57–92, *See also*
activism; cosmopolitanism; fellow-feeling;
fairy tales; A. E. (Alfred Edward) Housman;
Clemence Housman
*A. E. H.: Some Poems, Some Letters and a
Personal Memoir by His Brother*, 86–9
A. E. Housman and, 58, 83–92
"A. E. Housman's 'De Amicitia,'" 89–91
*All-Fellows: Seven Legends of Lower Redemption
with Insets in Verse*, 58, 64–7
banners, 58, 75–6
"Brutality Under British Rule," 80
"Cause of Indian Freedom," 81
Cloak of Friendship, The, 66

Housman, Laurence (cont.)
  Echo de Paris: A Study from Life, 64, 86
  Englishwoman's Love Letters, An, 74–5
  fairy tales, 58, 63–7, 69–70, 81
  fellow-feeling and, 61–2
  "From Prison to Citizenship," 75
  "Glorious Liberty of the Children of God,
    The," 76
  Green Arras, 67, 85
  illustrations, 58, 70, 73
  "In This Sign Conquer: To Open the Eyes of
    the Blind & To Bring the Prisoner Out of
    Captivity," 76
  Indian independence movement and, 81–3
  "Luck of Roses, The," 69
  Mahatma (M. K.) Gandhi and, 81–2
  "Makings of the War Mind, The," 80
  Oscar Wilde and, 64
  "Outrageous Fortune: The Story of a
    Concealed Life, 1862–1933," 64, 67, 86, 91
  Pains and Penalties, 85
  political activism, 74–86, 89–91
  Preparation of Peace, The, 78
  Relation of Fellow-Feeling to Sex, The,
    59, 61–3
  Sex-War and Woman's Suffrage, 77
  "Troubling of the Waters, The," 66, 79
  "Truce of God, The," 64, 79–80
  Unexpected Years, The, 74, 91
  "We Must Give Up the Colonies," 80
  "What I Believe," 57, 61, 79
  "Who Bears the Burden of Empire?," 80
  "Why Man Has Failed," 80
Howard, Brian, 126, 131, 137, 145
Hoyland, Anthony, 190–2
Hughes, Langston, 145, 163
Hurston, Zora Neale, 145
Huxley, Alduous, 133
Huysmans, Joris-Karl, 160
  À Rebours, 183
  Against Nature, 105
hybridity, 51, 127–31, 150, 153, 155, 177, 184,
  See also race

identification. *See* gender
identity. *See* gender; queerness; race
idleness, 40
illustrations, 25, 58, 63, 65, 68, 70, 73, 114, 127,
  160, 171, 183, *See also* Aubrey Beardsley;
  Laurence Housman; Richard Bruce Nugent
Im, Yeeyon, 167
imperialism, 13, 25, 80–2, 97, *See also*
  colonialism
incest, 25, 27–9, 62, 160–2, 167, 169, 174–85,
  188–90, 198–201, 210–12, *See also* desire;

  Eric Gill; kinship; Richard Bruce Nugent,
  "Geisha Man"
  race and, 175–7
  social organization and, 200–1
India, 80, *See also* activism; colonialism;
  imperialism
  art and art history of, 11, 28–9, 187–9,
    205–10
  faith and, 207, 210
  independence movement, 11, 26, 58, 81–2
India Society, 206, *See also* William Rothenstein
internationalism, 58–9, 68, 77–80, 95, 97, *See
  also* community; cosmopolitanism; fellow-
  feeling
interpretation, 18–20
intersectionality, 78
intimacy, 2–3, 6, 10, 16, 23, 37, 43, 46, 68, 84,
    187, 203, *See also* affiliation; collaboration;
    community; desire; eroticism; family;
    friendship; queerness
  cosmopolitanism and, 129, 142, 145, 149–51
  textually based, 38, 42, 44, 90
islands and islandness, 27, 97–9, 103, 124, *See
  also* Capri (Italy)
Ives, George, 58

Jackson, Holbrook, 15, 134
Jackson, Julian, 51
Jackson, Moses, 26, 59, 83–4, 86–8, *See also* A.
  E. (Alfred Edward) Housman
James, Henry, 22, 102
James, Jamie, 3
Janes, Dominic, 114
Japan and Japonisme, 23–4, *See also* exoticism;
  Orientalism
Jerome, Jerome K., 40
Johannesburg Art Gallery, 188
Johnson, Lionel, 39
Johnson, Samuel, 40
Joyce, James, 10

Kates, George N., 148
Kennedy, Margaret S., 22
Kennerley, Mitchell, 18
Ker-Seymer, Barbara, 147
Kessler, Harry, 201
kinship, 68, 130, 201–4, 210, *See also* adoption;
  affiliation; community; cosmopolitanism;
  enslavement; family; queerness
  alternative forms of, 10, 13, 15–18, 24, 36, 39,
    41–2, 46, 54, 65, 130
  burdens and limits of, 52, 64–5, 124, 137,
    162–6, 174
  Catholicism and, 202–4
  cosmopolitanism and, 11, 27, 129

desire for, 178–80
detachment from, 146, 162–6, 174–6, 178, 182
disorder and fragmentation of, 162, 166–8, 171–6
eroticism and, 20, 25, 27, 202
incest and, 161, 175, 178, 200–2, 210–13
political activism and, 11, 25–6, 57–61, 75–6, 79, 84, 91
queer forms of, 3–14, 19–20, 34–5, 37, 52, 59–61, 67–70, 79, 91, 129, 150, 198, 202–4
race and, 11, 28, 161–2, 166, 168, 171–4, 176
sibling bonds and, 60, 73, 91
textually based, 34–6, 38–43, 50, 54
Kooistra, Lorraine Janzen, 58, 63–4, 67, 69
Krasner, David, 166

labor politics. *See* activism
Lane, John, 40, 70
Langfang, Mei, 150
Laughton, Ernest, 28
Laughton, Gladys, 28
Laurence, Patricia Ondek, 139
Lavery, Grace, 23
Lawrence, D. H., 113, 115
   "Man Who Loved Islands, The," 122
   "Two Blue Birds," 123
League of Nations, 78, 189
Lee, Vernon, 10, 27, 130, 133–8, *See also* Harold Acton
   gender identity of, 134–5
   Golden Keys, The, 134
   queer cosmopolitanism of, 134–7
Leslie, Shane, 132
Leverson, Ada, 40
Lévi-Strauss, Claude, 201
Lewis, Sophie, 215
Lewis, Wyndham, 132, 145
life writing, 9, 26, 28, 33–5, 41, 48–50, 52, 54, 64, 67, 75, 78, 84–92, 100, 103–4, 106, 123, 126–8, 144
Lim, Shirley Jennifer, 153–6
Link, Viktor, 122
Linklater, Andro, 107, 109–10, 123
Lloyd, Francesca "Checca," 2, 5, 110, 113
Locke, Alain, 145
Lord, James, 144
Love, Heather, 10
Lyons, Algernon Islay de Courcy, 8

MacCarthy, Fiona, 189–92, 201
Mackenzie, Compton, 1, 26–7, 95–125, *See also* Norman Douglas; *Extraordinary Women* (album); Faith Mackenzie

affairs, 109–10, 124
after Capri, 113–14, 122–4
chronic pain, 103
Decadence and, 100–2, 117
Extraordinary Women, 3–14, 112–14, 119, 121
life writing, 100–1, 103, 112, 123
marriage with Faith Mackenzie, 102–3, 109–10
My Life and Times, 100–1, 113
on *This Is Your Life*, 124
queer community on Capri and, 109–13
Sinister Street, 101
"Undergraduate's Garden, The," 101
Vestal Fire, 104, 113–18
Mackenzie, Faith, 1, 26–7, 95–125, *See also* Norman Douglas; *Extraordinary Women* (album); Compton Mackenzie
affairs, 96–7, 109–10
after Capri, 113, 117–24
Always Afternoon, 106
attraction to Italian women, 111
gender dissidence, 121
life writing and diaries, 106, 110–13, 123
Mandolinata, 121
marriage with Compton Mackenzie, 102–3, 109–10
miscarriage, 102
Norman Douglas and, 107–9
on *This Is Your Life*, 124
queer community on Capri and, 110–13
Sibyl of the North, The, 121
writing, 121
Macpherson, Kenneth, 8
Mallarmé, Stéphane, 142
Maltz, Diana, 101
Marcus, Jane, 147
Marcus, Laura, 40
Markwell, Kevin, 98
marriage, 8, 17–18, *See also* family; kinship; reproduction
abolition of, 16
alternative forms of, 9, 12–14, 17–18, 24, 60, 95, 102, 124
companionate versus familiar forms of, 96
heteronormative boundaries of, 9–11, 59–61, 130
open, 6, 12, 15, 26–7, 47, 96–7, 109–10, 124
sibling bonds and, 25, 58, 68
Martin, Houston, 89
Mason, Stuart. *See* Christopher Sclater Millard
maturation, 14, 59, 70, 73, 102, 138, *See also* heteronormativity
rejection of, 136, 162–4

Maude, Chrissie, 103, 123
Maugham, William Somerset, 106
May, Leila Silvana, 60
McCabe, Susan, 8
McCormack, Jerusha, 199
McNabb, Father Vincent, 196–200
  Orchard Floor, The, 197
Mediterraneanism, 27, 99, 103–6, 108–11,
  113–15, 120, 125, *See also* Capri (Italy);
  exoticism; fetishism; Orientalism
memoir. *See* life writing
Mendelssohn, Michèle, 21, 24, 160
mentorship, 20–1
Meyer, Karl E., 148
Millard, Christopher Sclater, 33–5, 42–7
  Oscar Wilde: Art and Morality, 43
miscegenation. *See* race, racialization, and racism
Mitchell, Guy, 138
modernism, 9–11, *See also* Bloomsbury Group;
  China
  Decadent past and, 9–12, 16, 25, 27, 114,
    126, 131–4, 137, 160–2, 189–90, 206
  fascism and, 47
  global forms of, 25, 40–50, 139–42, 189
  masculinism of, 10, 133–4
  national boundaries of, 13
  queerness and, 7–11, 26
  race and, 166
Moncrieff, C.K. Scott, 45
Money, James, 2, 109
Moran, Leslie J., 20
Morand, Paul, 51
  Lewis et Irène (*Lewis and Irene*), 47
  Ouvert la nuit (*Open All Night*), 47
Morlière, Jacques-Rochette de La
  Angola, histoire Indienne, 48
Morton, Tara, 76
Moruo, Guo (Kuo Mo-jo), 142
Moynagh, Maureen, 147
Muddiman, Bernard, 134
Muir, Edwin, 117
Mungello, D. E., 142–5
Munthe, Axel, 96, 109, 122, 124
Murray, Alex, 15–16
Museum of London, 76

Nadegin (Nadezhin), Nikolai, 110, 112–13, 121,
  124
nandan. *See* China, Chinese theater
Nation & Athenaeum (periodical), 117
nation and nationalism, 27, 80, 134–6, *See also*
  cosmopolitanism; internationalism
  crossing the borders of, 13, 22–3, 130, 136,
    142, 145, 185, 216
  histories of, 13

National Association for People Abused in
  Childhood, 189
network. *See* affiliation; cosmopolitanism;
  kinship; queerness
New Statesman (periodical), 119–21
Ngô, Fiona I. B., 161
Nordau, Max, 15
Novak, Dan, 45
novel, 3–7, 9, 42, 47–8, 50–5, 72–5, 101, 105,
  108–9, 113–21, 148–53, 159–60, 174–85,
  213, *See also* individual novels by author
  and title
Nugent, Richard Bruce, 11, 25, 27, 159–85
  Decadence and, 160–85
  drawings and illustrations, 170–2, 183
  fascination with Oscar Wilde's Salome figure,
    166–75
  "Geisha Man," 27, 160–2, 164,
    174–85
  Gentleman Jigger, 175, 184
  "Half High," 175, 183
  Harlem Renaissance and, 180
  Harlem: A Forum of Negro Life, 171
  multiraciality and, 27, 160–2, 174–85
  Orientalism and, 170
  plans for publication and use of color, 177,
    182–5
  queer identity of, 160
  "Saffron and Calamous," 168
  Salome before Herod, 170–2
  Salome: Negrotesque I, 171
  "Slender Length of Beauty," 167–75
  "Smoke, Lilies and Jade," 160, 162–6, 174,
    182–3
Nyong'o, Tavia, 177

O'Connor, Father John, 199
Oakley, Elizabeth, 68–9, 72, 76–7
Ogrinc, Will H. L., 105
Opportunity (periodical), 160
Order of Chaeronea, 58, 86
Orientalism, 11–14, 24, 26–8, 48, 98–9, 115,
  124, 127–30, 146, 148–50, 153, 160–2,
  166–7, 169–75, 188, *See also*
  cosmopolitanism; exoticism;
  Mediterraneanism
  Decadence and, 23–4, 105, 159, 161, 179
  sex tourism and, 12
orphans, 19, 51–4, *See also* childhood; Julien
  (Julian) Green
Orwell, George, 47
otherness, 12, 22, 63, 67, 69, 98, 204, *See also*
  cosmopolitanism; eroticism; ethics;
  Orientalism
Oxford Point of View (periodical), 101

pacifism. *See* activism, anti-war
Pai Hua movement, 139
Pater, Walter, 14–15, 101–2, 126, 130, 137–40, 149, 151–2, 165
   Studies in the History of the Renaissance, 21
patriarchalism, 12, 60, 74, 77, 173, 187–90, 201, *See also* family; heteronormativity; marriage; reproduction
peace movement. *See* activism, anti-war
Peace News (periodical), 78, 80–1
Peace Pledge Union, 78
pedagogy, 20–1
pederasty, 7, 13, 20, *See also* queerness; sexuality, dissident forms of; Uranianism
Pélissier, Harry, 103
Pennington, Michael, 209–12
Pepler, Hilary, 196
Père Lachaise, 36
Perry, Imani, 24
photography, 1, 117–18, 141, 150–3, 155, 206–12, *See also Extraordinary Women* (album)
   family albums, 7
   group, 4–7
   transmission of, 7
Pirie-Gordon, Harry, 101
Pissarro, Lucien, 206
Plato, 20
pleasure. *See* cosmopolitanism
poetry, 59, 84–6, 88–90, 100, 132, 139–42, 145, 147, 193–8, 202, 204, *See also* Harold Acton, *Modern Chinese Poetry*; Michael Field; A. E. Housman; translation
Poetry (periodical), 141
Potolsky, Matthew, 21
Poueymirou, Margaux, 166
Pound, Ezra, 10, 47, 133, 145
Pre-Raphaelite Brotherhood, 14
promiscuity. *See* cosmopolitanism; fellow-feeling
property, 8, *See also* Catholicism, and doctrine of Distributism
   kinship and, 171–4
   private forms of, 16, 196, 213
Proust, Marcel, 45, 105
psychoanalysis, 60
public sphere, 7

Quakerism, 81
Queen Christina (dir. Mamoulian), 122
queerness, 8–9, 14, 18, 21, 59, 67, 96, *See also* activism; affiliation; Catholicism; community; cosmopolitanism; Decadence; desire; expatriatism; family; heteronormativity; intimacy; kinship; sexuality; Oscar Wilde

affect and, 10
alternative forms of kinship and, 7–11, 14–15, 17–20, 28, 34–6, 41, 52, 54, 59–61, 69–70, 73, 79, 91, 98, 192–205, 209–13
deidealizing, 13
desire and, 20, 63
failures and limits of, 98, 190
group photography and, 7
race and, 160–1
repudiating, 69
translation and, 51
Quennell, Peter, 126

race, racialization, and racism, 13, 24, 27–8, 67, 161, 167–72, 177, 184, *See also* Decadence; difference; exoticism; hybridity; incest; kinship
   antiracism and, 77–8, 81, 130, 145–8
   Blackness and, 24, 147, 160–1, 166, 170–2, 174, 176, 184
   cultural extraction and, 175
   detachment and, 182
   kinship and, 28, 174–7
   miscegenation and, 168, 175
   multiraciality and, 28, 160–2, 174–85
   white supremacy and, 77, 81, 176, 184
Raffalovich, Marc-André, 188, 193–5, 199
   Uranisme et Unisexualité, 194
Red Book Magazine, 213
Reed, Christopher, 10
Reed, Jeremy, 105
reform. *See* activism
relationality. *See* affiliation; community; kinship
religion. *See* Catholicism; Christianity; faith
reproduction, 69, *See also* domesticity; heteronormativity; family; kinship
   alternatives to, 17–18, 60
   empathy and, 63
   heteronormativity and, 10, 60, 69, 130, 138
   intergenerational transmission and, 19
Reynolds, Reginald, 81, 83–4
Richards, Grant, 85
Ricketts, Charles, 37, 60
Ricks, Christopher, 88
Roden, Frederick, 202
Rolfe, Frederick (Baron Corvo), 40, 101
Ross, Robert, 10, 34, 37–9, 43–5, 55, 100–1, 188, 209
   as executor of Oscar Wilde's literary estate, 38–9
Rothenstein, William, 37, 187–9, 204–6
Rowse, A. L., 132
Rubin, Gayle, 200

sadomasochism. *See* desire
Sanders, Valerie, 60
Sassoon, Siegfried, 80
Schaffer, Talia, 96
Schmidt, Tyler, 175–6
Schwarz, A. B. Christa, 160, 168
sculpture, 9–10, 63, 187–8, 193–5, 205–13, *See also* engravings; Eric Gill
Sedgwick, Eve Kosofsky, 215
Sergeant, Philip, 100
Sette of Odd Volumes, 39–41
Sexual Offences Act (1967), 90
sexuality. *See also* community; cosmopolitanism; Decadence; faith; gender; incest; queerness
  abuse and, 12, 24, 191, 200
  closet and, 45
  criminalization of, 7, 14, 25, 35, 41, 43, 64, 86–7, 89–90, 97
  dissident forms of, 1, 7–8, 10–17, 19, 22, 25, 28–9, 35, 47–8, 54, 60–1, 89, 97–100, 107, 111, 114, 134, 136–7, 160, 187–216
  self-determination and, 16
  social conventions of, 192
Shakespeare, William, 17–20
Shannon, Charles, 37
Shell, Marc, 97
Shewring, Walter, 206
Shixiang, Chen (Ch'ên Shih-Hsiang), 139–45
Showalter, Elaine, 14
siblings. *See* family
Sinfield, Alan, 20
Sitwell, Edith, Osbert, and Sacheverell, 10, 132–3
  Wheels (anthology), 132
socialism, 15–17, 81, 196, 200, 214
Soldatenkov, Helène, 2
Sotadic Zone, 98, *See also* Richard Burton; Orientalism; tourism
Speaight, Robert, 191
Spectator (periodical), 117
Spillers, Hortense, 28, 173, 175–6
Spirit Lamp (periodical), 100–1
Stalin, Joseph, 47
statue. *See* sculpture
Stein, Gertrude, 134
Stevenson, Robert Louis, 40
Stone, Lawrence, 96
Sturgeon, Mary, 197
Suffrage Atelier, 75–6
suffrage movement. *See* activism, for suffrage, women's rights, and feminism
suicide, 19, 88, 159
Survivors Trust (UK), 189
Swinburne, Algernon Charles (A. C.), 14, 132
Symbolism, 142

Symons, A. J. A. (Alphonse James Albert)
  biography of Wilde, 40
  Quest for Corvo, The, 40
Symons, Arthur, 39, 142
Symons, Jerry, 69
sympathy. *See* fellow-feeling

taboo. *See* bestiality; incest; sexuality
Tamagne, Florence, 117
Taylor, Rachel Annand, 117
Thain, Marion, 192, 197, 199, 203
This Is Your Life (TV show), 124
Thomas, Kate, 198
Thurman, Wallace, 159–61
  Infants of the Spring, 159
Tongbi, Kang (K'ang T'ung-pi), 127
Toomer, Jean, 163
tourism, 149, *See also* exoticism; Orientalism; sexuality
  exile and, 98
  queerness and, 98
  sex and, 12, 24, 109
translation, 9, 11–12, 25, 35, 47–56, 139–42, *See also* Harold Acton; Vyvyan (Vivian) Holland
transnationalism, 8, 11, 23–5, 27, 35, 47–8, 129–31, 139–42, 148, 189, *See also* adoption; connection; cosmopolitanism; Decadence
trauma, 51–3, *See also* abuse; family; race, racialization, and racism
  family and, 33, 36
  racial, 13
  sexual legislation and, 35
travel and travel writing, 7, 12, 22, 47, 107, 134, *See also* cosmopolitanism; exile; transnationalism
Turner, Reginald (Reggie), 10, 36–8, 100–1, 131
Tzara, Tristan, 145

Uranianism, 42–6, 54, 58–9, 193–5
utopianism, 13, 64, 91, 98, 196, 200, 204, 214, *See also* deidealization

Valentine, Ferdinand, 199
Van Vechten, Carl, 10, 127, 163
Vanita, Ruth, 202
vegetarianism. *See* activism, animal rights
Venuti, Lawrence, 51
Verona, Roxana, 47
Victor, Pierre, Baron de Beseval, 47
Victoria and Albert Museum, 209
Victorian Era, 9, 11
  conventions of, 16, 49, 60, 68, 96

gender ideologies of, 14
national boundaries of, 13
queerness and, 14
sexual legislation during, 25, 41, 64
Vitale, Christopher, 168

Waitt, Gordon, 98
Walker, Aida Overton, 166
War Resisters' International, 78
Waugh, Evelyn
    Brideshead Revisited, 132
Webb, L. C., 81
Weeks, Jeffrey, 86
Weiner, Joshua, 37, 41
Westminster Cathedral, 189, 191
white supremacy. *See* race, racialization, and
    racism
Wilde, Constance, 33, 36, 41, 44–5
Wilde, Oscar, 15, 58, 60, 86, 107, 130, 133,
    137, 151, 160, 162, *See also* Decadence;
    Vyvyan (Vivian) Holland
    After Berneval, 43–5
    After Reading, 43–5
    American tour, 22, 24
    anti-Black racism, 24
    Ballad of Reading Gaol, 131, 209
    class differences and, 21
    *Collection of Original Manuscripts Letters and
        Books of Oscar Wilde, A*, 34
    cosmopolitanism and, 21–3, 49, 54–6
    "Critic as Artist, The," 16
    De Profundis, 34, 55, 101, 106
    "Devoted Friend, The," 49
    fairy tales, 64
    family and, 35, 44–5
    forgeries, 46
    House of Pomegranates, 131
    iconography of, 20, 45
    Importance of Being Earnest, The, 49
    imprisonment, 33–4, 36, 96
    Intentions, 131
    kinship and, 16–18, 25, 37, 60, 100

Lady Windermere's Fan, 49
    letters, 33–5, 42–4, 54–6
    memorial tomb, 189, 209–11
    national identity of, 22–4
    Orientalism and, 23
    pederasty and, 20, 59
    Picture of Dorian Gray, The, 43, 50, 105, 114,
        131, 134, 183, 193
    "Portrait of Mr. W. H., The," 17–20
    reputation and appeal, 10, 16, 49–50, 55
    Salomé, 23, 27, 50, 55, 114, 162, 167–9, 175
    sex tourism in Algeria, 24
    "Soul of Man Under Socialism, The,"
        16, 214
    "Sphinx, The," 23
    transnationalism, 35
    trial, 8, 10, 14, 20, 25, 33, 41, 48, 64, 68, 87,
        126
Wildgen, Kathryn Eberle, 51–4
William Andrews Clark Memorial Library, 28,
    191, 194, 198
Wilson, Edmund, 102
Winfield, Hemsley, 166
Winkiel, Laura, 146
Wirth, Thomas, 160
Wolcott-Perry, Kate and Saidee, 104–5, 114,
    125
Women's Library (London School of
    Economics), 75
Women's Social and Political Union, 75
Wong, Anna May, 27, 130, 153–6, *See also*
    Harold Acton; China
Woodcock, George, 107
World War I, 7, 75, 78, 109
World War II, 7, 68, 79–80, 144

xenophobia, 47
Xi, Kun, 148, 155

Yellow Book (periodical), 10, 40, 126, 131–3
Yorke, Malcolm, 190–2
Young, Damon, 37, 41